Global Battlefields

MEMOIR OF A LEGENDARY PUBLIC INTELLECTUAL FROM THE GLOBAL SOUTH

Walden Bello

Clarity Press, Inc.

ISBN: 978-1-963892-10-9
EBOOK ISBN: 978-1-963892-11-6

In-house editor: Diana G. Collier
Book design: Becky Luening

Library of Congress Control Number: 2024950082

Clarity Press, Inc.
2625 Piedmont Rd. NE, Ste. 56
Atlanta, GA 30324, USA https://
www.claritypress.com
businessmanager@clarlitypress.com

For...

Princess and Dodong Nemenzo, who've never given up on the dream,
The late Jose Maria Sison, a towering figure despite our differences,
The late Hugo Chavez, an unforgettable class act against empire,
The Lost Generation, who made a difference.

Contents

1. The Lost Generation 1
2. From Princeton to Santiago de Chile. 6
3. Cadre 22
4. "Behind Enemy Lines". 45
5. EDSA, or The Revolution Derailed. 60
6. The Movement Disarmed. 70
7. Becoming an International Activist. 80
8. The Neoliberal Challenge. 98
9. Global Battlefields 109
10. Alternative Futures 137
11. Jousting with Empire 151
12. From "Counterrevolutionary" to Congressman 182
13. Fighting the New Slave Trade 201
14. Forays in Foreign Policy 214
15. Memorable and "Memorable" Moments at the
    House of Representives. 223
16. Love, Death, and Love in Bangkok 237
17. Reign of Darkness . . . and Light. 248
18. A Luta Continua. 269
19. A Reckoning. 283

Acknowledgments. 295

Endnotes 300

Index 311

1. The Lost Generation

"... [M]en will not understand us—for the generation that grew up before us, though it has passed these years with us, already had a home and a calling ... and the generation that that has grown up after us will be strange to us and push us aside. We will be superfluous even to ourselves, we will grow older, a few will adapt themselves, some others will merely submit, and most will be bewildered. ..."

ERICH MARIA REMARQUE, *All Quiet on the Western Front*

"The older and wiser heads have always described revolution and love to us as the most foolish and loathsome of human activities. ... Revolution and love are, in fact, the best, most pleasurable things in the world, and we realize it is precisely because they are so good that the older and wiser heads have spitefully fobbed off on us their sour grapes of a lie. This I want to believe implicitly: Man was born for love and revolution."

KAZUKO, IN OSAMU DAZAI, *The Setting Sun*

FOR SOME, Kyoto is probably not the best place to start a writing project. The sheer beauty of that city, which escaped the apocalypse visited on other Japanese urban centers by the American bomber command during the Second World War, can be very distracting, making one simply a passive absorber of its seductive sights and disarming delicacies. Kyoto's magic, however, had the opposite of a calming effect on an inveterate jogger like me. While I was running along the Takano, a lovely, meandering trickle of a river, amidst falling cherry blossoms during the month of April 2023, the mind-body connection unleashed a torrent of writing that ceased only when I crossed the last "T" and dotted the last "I" six months later in Bangkok.

My dear friend Carol Hau, the distinguished professor of Southeast Asian Studies at Kyoto University, proposed that I write my memoir when I began my fellowship at the Center for Southeast Asian Studies. My response was to demur since I doubted whether my life was sufficiently significant.

This was not the first time someone had asked me to write about my life and times, nor was this the first time I reacted this way.

A few years earlier, my good friend, the eminent sociologist Erik Ohlin Wright, invited me and my late wife, Suranuch ("Ko) Thongsila, to the A.E. Havens Center at the University of Wisconsin in 2015, so I could write something on my experience as a "public intellectual" from the Global South. Those months in Wisconsin were productive. But I wrote about things I considered important, and my life, while maybe interesting, was not among them.

Then there was another prod, this time coming from my good friend and mentor Richard Falk, the former UN Special Rapporteur for the Occupied Palestinian Territory. I gave the same response, which he respected but disagreed with in his usual engaging way.

I was wrestling with what I have come to call the "Pramoedya Problem." Pramoedya Ananta Toer was one of the celebrated intellectuals of the Indonesian Left in the years leading up to the Suharto counterrevolution in 1965–66, when about one million people, most from or allied with the Left, were massacred and tens of thousands were arrested and imprisoned. While in prison for 14 years on the hardscrabble island of Buru, he narrated, then later put into paper, the four novels known collectively as the "Buru Quartet," the great epic on the birth of the Indonesian nation. But what puzzled many was that after his release from incarceration in 1979, the great novelist never followed up his prison novels with any other writing of value, either fictional or non-fictional.

Pramoedya often blamed "writer's block" as the reason why he stopped writing. His translator, Max Lane, theorizes that this writer's block was actually a symptom of something much bigger: the failure of the Indonesian Left to interrogate itself about what happened in 1965, what led up to it, and what happened afterwards. "This was ... the origin of Pramoedya's writer's block. Such a failure is a double failure: because Indonesia as we know it today was, in many ways, a product of the failure of the Left. Without understanding that history, contemporary Indonesia will remain mostly a mystery, beyond anybody's effort to change it."[1]

Lane certainly is right. There can be no understanding of the past without an effort to come to terms with it, analytically and politically. But one can also understand why Pramoedya advised younger people that "they should write their elders off as unable to make any new contributions." I would not even dare compare myself to this giant of Indonesian literature, but I was dealing with a psychological condition that was similar. As I wrote to Carol Hau by way of explaining my reluctance:

The truth is that more than feeling my life is not significant, I feel like a failure. And the reason is that I was fully involved in two movements that failed.

The first of these was the progressive movement in the Philippines. If the Left was a central force driving politics in the Philippines in the 1960s and 1970s, today, as you very well know, it is a shadow of its former self, one that is marginalized from politics. The drift to political irrelevance of this movement stemmed mainly from its being an onlooker rather than a player in the events of 1986, the so-called EDSA Uprising. The failure to be a decisive player in that landmark political event led to a vicious split that, along with disenchantment with progressive ideologies in the larger society and repression, consigned it to the sidelines of Philippine politics during the next three decades.

The other movement I have been and still am part of is the international movement for socialism, the collapse of which was symbolized by the unravelling of the Soviet Union and the Eastern European socialist regimes in 1989–1992 and the turn to state-led capitalism in China in the late 1980s. True, socialism is not coterminous with the Soviet and Chinese experiences, but their failures had a negative impact on related social and political movements, like social democracy, and the post-1989 anti-globalization movement in which I played a leading role internationally, as well as the Occupy Movement, and the climate justice movement. The fact that neoliberal capitalism has had its share of crises over the last two decades has not translated into a rejuvenation of the vision of socialism in mass consciousness, whether in the Global North or the Global South.

In other words, however "successful" one may be in professional terms as an individual, if that dimension of one's life that one sees as providing one's central identity, one's "anchor," has failed, then one feels rather uneasy being regarded as a "success" who has merited a memoir or autobiography. In my case, that central identity was being an activist, a partisan of collective movements for social transformation, that, to be brutally honest, crashed. We failed, so I failed, and it is a failure I live with every day as traditional elite politics reigns supreme and unchallenged in our country and capitalism lurches on drunkenly but similarly unchallenged globally.

We're called the boomer generation. I could also call us Generation R, the revolutionary generation, the generation that crashed.

This does not mean that one has abjured one's being a progressive or a partisan of economic democracy or whatever term one uses as a euphemism for socialism these days. Unlike turncoats, be they ideological or opportunistic, I remain committed to a truly just and democratic Philippine society and to the vision of a post-capitalist global order—and indeed, these may still become realities in the future. I have no regrets for my progressive choices and will continue to defend them passionately as offering the best hopes for humanity and the planet. But I am also no cheery optimist, Carol, one willing to overlook the dismal present to bask in the dream of a distant future. In this connection, If I may be allowed to define my current vantage point, it is that of a "progressive realist."

Why dispense advice to the young when your generation lost the struggle? To ensure successor generations don't make the same mistakes is certainly a noble motive but one that is hardly compelling for those who now see themselves as losers. In most cases, it is the victors that not only are empowered to write their versions of history but also are motivated to do so. As the saying goes, success has a thousand fathers, but failure is an orphan. And the last thing I wanted was to be remembered as having come out with a memoir that came across as rationalizing or justifying failure.

But, unlike Pramoedya, I did take up the pen, albeit reluctantly, perhaps initially not to disappoint Carol, but soon because I had no more excuse not to write.

As I wrote, I began to realize that I was probably too negative in assessing the outcomes of my political commitments. Yes, the National Democratic Revolution failed, and the socialist states did collapse, but wasn't I part of the anti-globalization movement that stopped the World Trade Organization from becoming an effective engine of trade liberalization? Wasn't I part of the intellectual struggle that discredited neoliberalism? Wasn't I part of the global resistance to the U.S. empire that resulted in its defeat in the Middle East?

Perhaps a more fundamental consideration is that, given how they turned out, maybe we should regard the outcomes of the 1917 Revolution and the National Democratic Revolution not so much as failures but as initial setbacks in a longer-term enterprise, with flaws that need to be addressed and corrected to bring about the goal of genuine social liberation.

But this reassessment of the balance of my political history was just one consideration that overcame my reluctance to write. Why does one write in the first place? I asked. Does the answer, because one has "something to say," really serve as the primordial basis for writing? I became increasingly convinced that that answer had the wrong premise—that one writes because one is seen as having something of value to say. I began to realize that the reason for writing a memoir was no different from writing in any other genre, like writing poetry or a novel, and the block that prevented me from taking up the pen was asking myself the wrong question—that is, whether I had something significant to communicate, whether my life was successful enough to warrant a memoir. Upon reflecting on Carol's request from the vantage point of my experience as a writer and not as the object of writing, I came to the realization that one writes, be it a novel, a political essay, or a memoir, simply because one needs to write, to articulate an experience, a vision, an idea, both for oneself and for others.

Moreover, the value of what one writes is not a given, there from the very beginning with one just having to unravel it. It emerges in the process of writing. It remains to be discovered, and writing and communicating with one's readers is the process of discovery.

Thus, writing about oneself, about one's life, about one's engagement with one's era involves a huge gamble. Ultimately, the jury on the significance of one's memoir will be one's readers. They may find treasures in the modest recollections of a bystander as history unfolded while dismissing as hollow and self-serving the recitation of grand events by a participant with a famous name. And different audiences many react differently. One generation may love a memoir that the next generation throws to the trash heap. As with all writing, you take a great risk of being rejected, ridiculed, or dismissed—or worse, ignored.

I asked myself if I was willing to take that risk, and I thought, shoot, why not?

I wrote non-stop for the next six months on this memoir of my 78 years, pausing only for a few hours of sleep and fortified by the improbable combination of jogging and single malt whisky.

2. From Princeton to Santiago de Chile

WHEN I ARRIVED in Princeton in September 1969, the campus had on the surface that languid atmosphere that F. Scott Fitzgerald memorialized in *This Side of Paradise*, but below it, the place was convulsed by struggles over racism, women's rights, capitalism, and above all Vietnam, as was the rest of the United States.

I was, of course, not unfamiliar with the ongoing conflict less than 900 miles from the Philippines, where two giant U.S. military bases, Clark Air Force Base and Subic Naval Base, were playing a critical role supporting the massive American intervention in Vietnam. And, of course, the war was in the Manila papers, especially during the Tet Offensive of 1968. But personally, Vietnam was rather distant. When I left the Philippines to do a PhD in sociology, my politics was still in its anti-clerical, anti-religious phase. I had exchanged Catholicism for the existentialism of Albert Camus, but I still had to graduate to a truly political consciousness.

Aerial view of Cielito Lindo island. "Never mind if it's shaped like a toothbrush," the *Philippine Panorama* writes, "it's the Bellos' own special island."

PHILIPPINE PANORAMA 13 APRIL 1980 ISSUE; COURTESY OF MANILA BULLETIN

The Bellos at their first bamboo house. Walden, the family's
"island baby," is being carried by his father, Jesse.

PHILIPPINE PANORAMA 13 APRIL 1980 ISSUE; COURTESY OF *MANILA BULLETIN*

Before Princeton...

My 23 years of existence till then had its own significant and interesting events. I was born on an island in the middle of the country's largest
lake, Laguna de Bay. My father was reading Thoreau when I was born on
November 11, 1945—thus the name "Walden." Both my parents were of a
decidedly artistic temperament, and they fell for each other while singers
on the radio in the 1930s. They went on to become a popular duet in the
entertainment circles of pre–World War II Philippines.

During the war, my father, Jesse, was picked up by the Japanese as
a suspected resistance courier and tortured and imprisoned at the infamous

Fort Santiago. His older brother, Buenaventura, was hailed as a war hero for refusing a Japanese officer's command to haul down the American flag at the school where he was the principal and being bayoneted for his obstinacy. Brought to the hospital just in time, he survived. News of his cheating death did not, however, get around in occupied wartime Philippines, much less reach the United States, and in the 1945 propaganda film *Back to Bataan* starring John Wayne, Hollywood, in typical Hollywood fashion, "killed" him, not with the bayonet but by hanging him, draped with the Stars and Stripes, on the school's flagpole.

After the war and the country's formal independence from the U.S., Jesse went on to become an impresario, promoting, among other things, Hollywood films. My mother, Luz, became a celebrated writer in her regional language, Ilocano, composed songs, and painted on any surface—wood, glass, or canvass. Their relationship was rendered stormy by my father's relationships with other women, but they loved each other nonetheless and wrote poems to each other. As for me and the other children—my older brothers, Dennis and Melvyn, and my younger sister Gwethalyn—while we were loved, we were mere satellites orbiting around two individuals that were permanently infatuated with each other.

My lasting lesson from childhood is that it is not easy to be the child of artists, for they live above the material world in a place where the laws of gravity are suspended, unlike the rest of us humans who must contend with toiling to earn our bread and cannot rely on good fortune to come our way. In the case of Luz and Jesse, good fortune somehow always came through in the clutch in the form of caring relatives and children who were willing to forget their childlike irresponsibility because they were gifted.

I did my primary, secondary, and tertiary schooling at the Jesuit university Ateneo de Manila. It was there that I discovered that I was not bad at writing, though it was always a bloody process. Upon graduating from college in 1966, I journeyed to the far south of the Philippines, to the fabled city of Jolo in the Muslim province of Sulu, to escape Manila and in search of adventure. I got more than I bargained for. I had two scrapes with death and was stripped of my first two jobs, as a college professor and associate editor of the provincial newspaper, for offending two religious establishments—the Christian and the Muslim—with my writing. But from Jolo, I brought back a wife, Madge, with whom I eloped in a Cessna private plane in 1969.

At the time of the fabled "First Quarter Storm" of 1970, which marked the radicalization of student politics in the Philippines, I had been out of college for four years and had just begun graduate school at Princeton.

Becoming an Activist

An important person in my radicalization stateside was Paul Wheatley, a professor in the Sociology Department, who was rumored to have had the worst disciplinary record as a West Point undergraduate after that of General George Armstrong Custer of Little Big Horn notoriety. I attended an undergraduate lecture by him because I was told it would be brilliant. Indeed, it was, connecting as it did the system of monopoly capitalism with the imperial venture in Vietnam. Wheatley's lecture and the graduate course I took under him inspired me to tailor my reading not only to Vietnam but to Marx and capitalism. Wheatley disappeared from Princeton and, indeed, from sociology, but for me, he was the spark that led to Marx, Lenin, Louis Althusser, Nicos Poulantzas, Perry Anderson, and other luminaries of what came to be known as "Western Marxism" to distinguish it from "Orthodox Marxism."

Even as I was immersing myself in radical writings in addition to the courses in methodology, sociological theory, and other required courses, I was being slowly drawn into activism. An important step forward was my accompanying my ex-Peace Corps friend Ed Fischer and his partner Vanessa to the November 15 anti-war march in Washington, DC, which was said to be the largest anti-war demonstration in American history. I remember my excitement at being part of a huge collective outpouring against a bloody, unjust war being fought in my part of the world. I also remember how cold it was that day, but how warm the demonstrators' feelings were toward one another.

Participating in demonstrations and rallies, as I did during those first few months in the U.S., was important in priming me to be an activist. But professional concerns were still uppermost. I was training to be a sociologist, though under the impact of readings, my orientation was turning into being a radical sociologist within the academy, a critical sociologist like Alvin Gouldner, the author of *The Coming Crisis in Western Sociology*, with its passionate denunciation of "value-free sociology" and its call for intellectual and ethical engagement for progressive change.[2]

My transition from intellectual to activist took place unexpectedly. This happened in April 1970, when President Richard Nixon and his secretary of state, Henry Kissinger, said they were going to end the war in Vietnam by expanding it to Cambodia. I was rushing en route to class along Prospect Road—where Princeton's "eating clubs" or fraternities were located—when I was attracted to a commotion at a building housing the Institute of Defense Analysis (IDA). There was a crowd of about 100 surrounding some 15 people who were sitting down with linked arms, blocking the entrance to the Institute, which was known to be doing contract work for the Pentagon. I crossed the street to see more, out of curiosity rather than anything else. Then a phalanx of policemen arrived and shoved people aside to clear a path to arrest those who were seated on the ground with arms linked.

When the police started to brutally cut the human chain and pull people into the paddy wagon, something in me snapped and I leaped into the empty space opened up by an arrest and found myself linking up with two people whom I later learned were Arno Mayer, a distinguished professor of diplomatic history, and Stanley Stein, an equally prominent professor of Latin American history. All I was conscious of as I joined them was the thought that there goes my PhD, since at that time, foreign students who were arrested in political events could expect deportation, according to Immigration and Naturalization Service rules. In a split second, I had given up my future as a sociologist.

As we were processed after arrest at the Princeton Police Headquarters, I called Madge, my wife, and told her what had happened but left unmentioned the likelihood that we would be deported. I had made the leap, and, surprisingly, I had no regrets. In fact, I felt I had found my place: being an activist, an organizer for social change. Like the other participants in the IDA rally, I was judged guilty of trespassing and given the punishment of community service, that is, cleaning the streets on weekends for a whole month. I waited for the deportation order. And waited. After a month of waiting, I began to realize what was happening. The local government in Princeton was not coordinating its work with the Immigration and Naturalization Service, as I had been led to expect.

My professional future as a sociologist was given a new lease on life. But I was no longer the same. My act of leaping into that chain of protesters engaged in civil disobedience was spontaneous, made at the spur of the moment. Yet, the ground had been prepared by my earlier participation in protests, both on campus and in Washington, DC, against the Vietnam War as well as my exposure to Marxist and other progressive writings during that memorable fall and winter of 1969 and spring of 1970. Still, I could not ignore the fact that there had been an act of will, a "leap" that left behind calculations of likely consequences. There have been intellectuals that have been progressive in their outlook but never crossed the line to activism. That leap "into the unknown" transformed me from an engaged intellectual into an activist.

In early 1970, young people who had participated in the fabled First Quarter Storm of resistance to the increasingly arbitrary and repressive President Ferdinand Marcos or were inspired by it began arriving in the U.S. from the Philippines. I had missed out on the student protests that took place after I finished college, so I listened eagerly to accounts of the movement, its leaders, and its overriding ideology, "national democracy." Madge and I travelled to New York on weekends, and there we participated in discussion groups led by newly minted activists like Cynthia Maglaya, Becky Maglaya, and Marilen Abesamis. In the summer of that year, Filipino graduate and undergraduate students in Cornell University in Ithaca, New York, hosted a landmark conference attended by people from all over the United States, though mainly from the East Coast. If my memory serves me right, among those in attendance were people who were later to play major roles in progressive activism and scholarship both in the Philippines and the U.S., such as Rey Ileto, Joel Rocamora, Sonny San Juan, Delia Aguilar, Ben Lim, and Roxy Lim.

Theory and Practice

But my focus at that point was still on acquainting myself with classical Marxism, on the latest Marxist thinking coming out of Europe and on organizing against the Vietnam War. I struggled through Volume I of *Capital* but was fascinated by Marx's deconstruction of the "commodity" and inspired by his passionate analysis and denunciation of "primitive accumulation" in the 16th and 17th centuries that had involved the subjugation of non-western societies via colonialism. The *Communist Manifesto* swept me off my feet, as it did millions of people before me, and the *Theses on Feuerbach* fascinated me, especially Thesis 11: "The philosophers have only interpreted the world, in various ways; the point is to change it."

Among the thinkers identified with the neo-Marxism coming out of Europe and the U.S., the ones that made the deepest impression on me were Perry Anderson, Barrington Moore, Louis Althusser, and Nicos Poulantzas. Anderson's *Passages from Antiquity to Feudalism* and *Lineages of the Absolutist State* provided an impressive theoretical synthesis of much of the best work on the transition from pre-capitalist modes of production to capitalism.[3] One could find no better deployment of sophisticated Marxian analysis than what Barrington Moore accomplished in his classic *The Social Origins of Dictatorship and Democracy: Lord and Peasant in the Modern World*, a comparative study of political change amidst capitalist transformation in China, India, Japan, France, the U.S., and Britain.[4] Moore's deft juggling of multiple variables to deliver eminently credible explanations for different outcomes in different societies provided a model both for theoretical analysis and elegant writing.

Louis Althusser made an influential theoretical breakthrough with his concept of "determination in the last instance," that is, while relations of production play the decisive role in the structure and dynamics of a society, politics and culture also have an active role and are not limited to being passive forces responding to changes in the "economic base."[5] This allowed theoretical space for the "relatively autonomous" play of political and cultural factors that did not exist in the orthodox Marxist paradigm. Following Althusser, Nicos Poulantzas introduced the concept of "social formation" as the dynamic articulation of different modes of production, so that a concrete society would have features associated with pre-capitalist modes on which the dominant mode, capitalism, had both "dissolving" and "conserving" effects.[6] This insight was especially useful for understanding societies in the Global South reeling under the impact of western capital.

These breakthroughs, which took place in the midst of the discrediting of the McCarthyist hold on American intellectual life by a generation in revolt, reinvigorated Marxism as both a method of analysis and a guide for social change. My one regret after my Princeton sojourn was that I missed the post-modern, post-structural, and post-colonial schools that swept through social science departments in the U.S. in the late seventies and eighties, after I was done with graduate school and had plunged fully into activist work. It was only when I began teaching at the University of the Philippines in the mid-nineties that I got the chance to read thinkers like Michel Foucault and Edward Said and realized what I had missed. But even as I was fascinated by the rich insights of Marxists and other path-breaking thinkers, both during and after graduate school, I never forgot that theory was, as the 11th thesis on Feuerbach admonished us, in the service of practice.

Taking over Woodrow Wilson School

The overriding aim of practice in my Princeton years was to stop the war in Vietnam, and when I was not deep into reading Marx and the school of thought he had spawned, much of my work was leading or participating in discussion groups on how to organize more and more students into a critical mass against the war on campus.

By the time that Nixon and Kissinger invaded Laos early in 1971 to destroy the traffic on the Ho Chi Minh Trail, I had become part of the informal leadership of the anti-war movement on campus. We called for a boycott of classes, but the *coup de main* was taking over and shutting down what was then called the Woodrow Wilson School, Princeton's school of public administration that served as a recruiting ground for the Central Intelligence Agency and trained bureaucrats of foreign governments allied with the U.S. I led the successful occupation of the School by hundreds of students, but at the price of my incurring the perpetual enmity of one of its professors, the theorist of modernization Marion Levy, who tried his best in the next few years to worm his way into my dissertation panel with the sole aim of torpedoing the person he regarded as sullying his beloved Woodrow Wilson School.

In my first years at Princeton, I was not unaffected by the "sunshine creeping across the long, green swards, dancing on the leaded windowpanes, and swimming around the tops of spires and towers and battlemented walls" that had seduced Amory Blaine in F. Scott Fitzgerald's *This Side of Paradise*. But what the university primarily gave me, for which I was grateful, were the intellectual space and resources that enabled me to graduate from anti-clericalism to Marxism and become immersed in a vibrant student political culture that transformed me from being a political bystander into an activist.

Thus, when I got the news that Salvador Allende had been elected president of Chile in September 1970 and had announced a program to move his country along the "peaceful, constitutional road to socialism," I began to follow events there closely. By the fall of 1971, I was determined to gain first-hand experience of how to build socialism using democratic and legal means. My passport to doing this was to formulate a PhD proposal that would enable me to be in Chile to immerse myself in politics at the same time I was doing an academic study. My proposal, which was quickly approved, was to study the dynamics of the mobilization of shantytowns by political parties, which I would do largely by participant observation, supplemented by interviews and documentary research.

Off to Allende's Chile

I rushed off to take a crash course in Spanish in Cuernavaca in the Mexican state of Morelos, the birthplace of the legendary peasant leader, Emiliano Zapata, whose life had been made into a movie starring Marlon Brando that I had seen and liked as a teenager. After three weeks in May 1972, I felt that the course had substantially improved the rudimentary Spanish I had from high school and flew from Mexico City to Santiago.[i]

When Allende's Unidad Popular came to power after its triumph in the presidential elections of September 1970, it saw its mission as leading the country on the "peaceful, constitutional road to Socialism." The key forces

---

i Though probably a majority of Filipinos have Spanish surnames owing to the country's colonization and over 350-year occupation by Spain, Spanish was replaced by English as the language of administration and commerce during the 46-year occupation by the United States that succeeded Spanish rule. Today, *Tagalog* or *Pilipino* is officially the national language but English is used along with it as a *lingua franca*.

in the UP were the Communist Party, the Socialist Party and the Radical Party. Its main goals were to raise the living standards of the lower classes, nationalize the foreign-owned Kennecott and Anaconda copper mines, bring key industrial firms under state control using existing legal mechanisms, and complete land reform.

Over the next three years, national politics became polarized between the UP, whose base was the working class and peasantry, and a counterrevolutionary alliance between the landed elite, the big bourgeoisie and the middle classes. Parliament was initially the main arena of struggle, but as the government and Parliament (which was controlled by an alliance between Christian Democrats and the National Party) deadlocked, the struggle shifted to the streets of the capital, Santiago, where the Right and Left battled for control through large demonstrations, riots, strikes and food blockades.

I arrived in the capital in the midst of the Chilean winter, greeted by tear gas and skirmishes of opposing political groups in the aftermath of a demonstration. Hauling two suitcases, I made my way with great difficulty from the bus depot to the historic Hotel Claridge.

Two expectations were immediately dashed when I arrived in Santiago. The first was that I could get by with my "Mexican-Filipino Spanish." This could only be remedied through daily conversations with Chileans, and I soon learned how to swallow consonants at the end of a word, as in *mao o meno* instead of *mas o menos.*

The second was that the topic for my dissertation, leftist organizing in the *callampas*, or shantytowns, was worth pursuing. A few weeks in Santiago disabused me of the impression of the existence of a revolutionary momentum that I had gathered through reading about events in Chile in left-wing publications in the U.S. People on the left were constantly being mobilized for marches and rallies in the center of Santiago, but increasingly, the reason for this was to counter the demonstrations mounted by the right. My friends brought me to these events, where there were an increasing number of skirmishes with right-wing thugs.

The Revolution on the Defensive

I noticed a certain defensiveness among participants in these mobilizations and a reluctance to be caught alone when leaving them, for fear of being harassed or worse by roaming bands of rightists. The revolution, it dawned on me, was on the defensive, and the right was beginning to take command of the streets. Twice I was nearly beaten up because I made the stupid mistake of observing right-wing demonstrations with *El Siglo*, the Communist Party newspaper, tucked prominently under my arm. Stopped by some Christian

Democratic youth partisans, I said I was a Princeton University graduate student doing research on Chilean politics. They sneered and told me I was one of Allende's "thugs" imported from Cuba. I could understand why they thought that I was a provocateur, with *El Siglo* tucked under my arm. Thankfully, the sudden arrival of a Mexican friend saved me from a beating. On the other occasion, my fleet feet did the job.

When I looked at the faces of the predominantly white right-wing crowds, many of them blond-haired, I imagined the same enraged faces at the fascist and Nazi demonstrations that took control of the streets in Italy and Germany. These were people who looked with disdain at what they called the *rotos*, or "broken ones," that filled the left-wing demonstrations, people who were darker, many of them clearly of indigenous extraction.

I had wanted to do a thesis that would make some contribution to activist organizing in revolutionary times. This had been overtaken by events, and I made the painful decision to do, instead, a thesis aimed at gaining an understanding of the rise of a counterrevolution, something that would be of greater relevance for progressive analysts and organizers—but also something that would be difficult owing to the rightists' suspicion of what an Asian interviewer, allegedly from an American Ivy League university, was up to.

As I took in the political scene, it quickly became clear to me that the middle class was a central actor. Chile's middle class, at 30–35 percent of the population, was Latin America's second biggest after Argentina. Both left and right knew that the middle class was the force on which the future of the revolution would pivot. As in other countries, there was only a rough correlation between party allegiance and social class. The Christian Democratic Party accounted for some 34 percent of the vote, and this came largely from the middle class. At the same time, a not-insignificant part of the 19 percent who voted for the right-wing National Party and the 43 percent who voted for the left-wing Popular Unity parties were also from the middle class. The right wing sought to convince the middle class that socialism would mean a redistribution of poverty, their descent into the working class, and the collectivization of small farms.

The strategy of the *Unidad Popular* (*UP*), in contrast, was to try to convince the middle-class base of the Christian Democrats that their interests were best served in a united front with the popular classes, the expression of which would be an informal UP–Christian Democratic political alliance. Moreover, whether or not the interests of the middle strata and the working class actually coincided, to the UP political strategists, there was an inescapable defensive rationale for placating the former.

Over the next few months, I interviewed both people on the right and partisans of the left. Some respondents on the right saw Allende and the *UP* as a "minority government" out to impose itself on the majority through "questionable" constitutional measures. Others saw the "constitutional road to socialism" as simply a cover for a plot to impose a "Stalinist dictatorship." Still others saw the appeal to the middle class as "pure demagoguery" meant to lull the middle class into complacency as the left set about to "destroy democracy." Most of the right-wingers I interviewed were Christian Democrats, who saw former Christian Democrats who had joined the *UP* and even such true-blue Christian Democrats as Radomiro Tomic, Allende's rival in the 1970 elections, as "people who had been fooled by the Communists." Practically all had become entrenched in their attitude of great suspicion, disdain, or hostility to the left.

Interviews with people on the left brought up a uniform response: that the middle class was being misled and manipulated by the right wing to believe that their class interest was to side with the rich rather than with the working class. Most believed in the *Unidad Popular's* formula for revolution, that a broad alliance among the working class, middle class, and constitutionally oriented sectors of the upper class would be the social engine of revolutionary transformation. There was a discounting of the independent dynamic of the middle sectors, a view of them as a passive mass that would eventually respond to their "real" class interests, which lay in an alliance with the working class.

Reality Check in Valdivia

The myopia of this view was underlined by a confrontation with a small farmer, or *pequeño agricultor*, in southern Chile. I went to Valdivia with an American friend, Bill Blum, to look up a Christian Democratic farmer who had been recommended by a fellow graduate student at the Princeton sociology department. After a couple of weeks of intensive interviewing and documentary research in Santiago, I thought I would relax a bit and enjoy the famed Chilean hospitality. We were warmly received by the farmer and his family, which included a son and two teenage daughters. A goat was slaughtered for us, and we sat down to a hearty dinner on our first night. Then our host started cursing Allende, calling him simply a tool for the Communist Party to "impose its dictatorship on Chile." The Socialist Party of Allende was no better than the Communists, and the *Izquierda Cristiana*, composed of former Christian Democrats that had joined the *Unidad Popular*, were "traitors." Bill and I kept our politics to ourselves and tried to guide the discussion to more innocuous topics. I wanted to interview him on his views, I said, but we could do that after dinner. He said fine, but after a few minutes, the farmer again began his anti-leftist tirade.

The next day at breakfast, lunch, and dinner was more of the same hospitality punctuated by lengthy invective against "communists who will take away my property and give them to the *rotos*." Finally, at dinner on our second day, I could no longer tolerate his litany of "crimes of the left" and said I actually thought Allende was fighting for social justice and the land reform he was trying to push would actually benefit medium farmers like him and would negatively impact only the big landholders.

Chileans, I had been told, could be really friendly and hospitable until they smelled your politics, after which you either became a really close friend or you became an outcast. Bill and I became outcasts, and our not being asked to breakfast the next day was a clear sign that we had overstayed our welcome. This was unfortunate, not least owing to the fact that one of the farmer's daughters and I were already on very friendly terms.

This experience brought home to me how ghettoized Chile's classes were, how class formed such gulfs between the elite, the middle class, and workers. Chile's roughly equal electoral division between the National Party, the Christian Democratic Party, and the *Unidad Popular* reflected class solidarities that were difficult to bridge. My experience in Valdivia confirmed my worst fear, that is, that the *Unidad Popular* had lost the middle classes and that this did not stem so much from what its policies actually were than from deep-seated fears that the gains of workers and the lower classes would only come at their expense.

The social security measure and wage increases of the UP in the three years it was in power had been carefully calibrated to win over the urban middle class. By the end of the first year of the government, small businesspeople had been integrated into the social security system and tax rates were lowered for small industries. And despite the risk of triggering inflation, middle-class salaried workers received bigger increases in their pay than was originally planned by the UP government, with the result that they raised their portion of the total national income from 53.7 percent in 1970 to 58.6 percent in 1971.

Indeed, the UP government's best year in terms of its social security and income policies toward the middle class and its management of the economy, combining high economic growth and relatively low inflation, was 1971. Yet by the end of the year, a counterrevolutionary movement based on the middle class erupted into the political scene, with the famous march of thousands of women banging pots and pans that became an icon of counterrevolutionary mobilization, complete with *grupos de choque* or paramilitary groups similar to the fascist *squadristi* in Italy that beat up and provoked violent clashes with UP supporters and construction workers.

The danger of an inflamed middle class that saw its status and interests threatened from below, pushing it to a counterrevolutionary position that was abetted but not manipulated by the elite, was confirmed as I read up on the events leading up to Mussolini's taking of power in Italy and Hitler's ascent to power during the Weimer Republic in Germany.

This brings up the question of what to expect from the middle class in conditions of severe class conflict. Among both liberals and progressives at that time, it was common to portray the middle class as an ally of the working class and the lower classes generally and to consider that it was by and large a force for democratization. But Chile showed that, contrary to this assumption, the middle classes were not necessarily forces for democratization in developing countries. In fact, when the poorer classes were being mobilized with a revolutionary agenda, the middle classes could become a mass base for counterrevolution, as in Germany and Italy in the 1920s, when the middle class provided the foot soldiers of the fascist movements.

It was a phenomenon that I was again to encounter forty years later, when I had a front row seat at middle-class mobilizations against the elected government of Yingluck Shinawatra in Thailand. Yingluck was a stand-in for her brother Thaksin, who had revolutionized Thai politics by mobilizing the rural poor. Supported by the middle class and the Thai elite, the military seized power in Thailand in 2014, ushering in nearly a decade of military rule.

Seymour Martin Lipset famously argued that the middle class was a force for democratization in the developing world. After observing counterrevolutionary movements against the lower classes in Chile and Thailand, I see instead a Janus-faced class: a force for democracy when it is fighting elites defending their power and privileges, but alternatively a force for reaction when confronted with lower classes seeking a revolutionary transformation of society.

The roles of the Central Intelligence Agency, the Chilean elites, the Chicago Boys, and the Chilean military in the coup that overthrew Allende and the neoliberal transformation of Chile under Pinochet have been well-documented and widely studied. There have, however, been few studies apart from my thesis, on the role of the middle class, which served as the mass base of the counterrevolution. Yet this angry middle-class mob was one of the central features of the Chilean political scene leading up to the coup.

Explaining Sept 11, 1973

The lack of theoretical and political appreciation of the independent class dynamics of the middle class led to myopic interpretations of the coup of September 11, 1973. After the coup, progressive analysis of the tragedy and the steps leading up to it focused on the role of the United States, which was seen as directing or working intimately with Pinochet and the leadership of the National and Christian Democratic parties. That a counterrevolutionary mass base had been central in the overthrow tended to be omitted, or if it wasn't, the tendency was to regard it as largely a force manipulated by the CIA and the elites.

The reality, however, was that, contrary to the prevailing explanations of the coup, which attributed Pinochet's success to U.S. intervention and the CIA, the counterrevolution was already there prior to the U.S. destabilization efforts; that it was largely determined by internal class dynamics; and that the Chilean elites were able to connect with middle-class sectors terrified by the prospect of poor sectors rising up with their agenda of justice and equality.

In short, the U.S. intervention was successful because it was inserted into an ongoing counterrevolutionary process that had its base in the middle class. CIA destabilization efforts were just one of the factors that contributed to the victory of the right, and not the decisive one. This was not something that progressives wanted to hear then, since many wanted a simple black-and-white picture, that is, that the overthrow of Allende was orchestrated from the outside by the United States. Being of the left, I could understand why politics and indeed, personal psyches, demanded such a portrayal of events. Being a sociologist, I realized that the situation was much more nuanced.

Analysis and Activism: A Tense Relationship

These considerations made me realize that I was both an intellectual and an activist, and that there would always be tensions between these two roles, between the demands of truth-telling and the demands of action. When I talk about this contradiction, I mean the contradiction between what is actually occurring and what political or organizing strategy is being pursued. In the Chilean case, the truth was that the middle class had become the base of counterrevolution but the policies of the *Unidad Popular* continued to treat it as an ally of the revolution. *In this case, yes, there was action, but it was the wrong kind that contradicted the real movement of the class struggle revealed by theoretically informed political analysis.* It was a disconnect that led to disaster. Had the left not been in denial that the middle class had irretrievably moved to the right, another strategy could have been adopted, even if this was one of retreat. As it was, the left was frozen into pushing even more stubbornly an approach that was backfiring.

Departure

By the time I left Chile around March of 1973, I had witnessed two milestones in middle-class radicalization toward the right: the strike of small-truck owners and the marches of middle-class women banging pots and pans. The right by then controlled the streets, mounting demonstration after demonstration and subjecting people identified with the *Unidad Popular* to harassment and beatings. The left still mounted demonstrations, and the streets still resounded with the happy chant, "*El que no salta es momio*" ("He who does not jump is a reactionary"), but the mood of defensiveness had deepened.

I sensed it was only a matter of time before the united right would act against the *Unidad Popular* government. How they would do so and if they would be successful were questions I could not answer then. Still, I was surprised at how brutal, thorough, and long the counterrevolution was once it gained the upper hand with Gen Augusto Pinochet's military coup.

The report of the government commission that investigated human rights violations under the Pinochet regime placed the number of people killed or disappeared at 3,065 and those tortured and imprisoned at 40,018. For a country of four million people, these figures were relatively high. The terror was probably more severe in the countryside.

The "*matanza masiva*," or indiscriminate massacre, was designed not only to decapitate the left but to wipe it out completely. The left in Chile had not only come close to power; it had actually seized a part of the state, the executive. To the right, the situation necessitated a root-and-branch response that was so completely out of line with the country's tradition of political moderation that it shocked many Chileans who had initially supported the coup.

Postscript

I successfully defended my dissertation in 1975, and thanks to the department chairman, Marvin Bressler, my bête noire, Marion Levy, was not able to get into my committee to derail me. One surprising development was that one of the people in my committee, Paul Sigmund, who had the reputation of being with the CIA, spoke highly of my thesis in spite of its Marxist orientation and urged me to publish it.[7] But I was not in the mood to work on it for publication immediately after having lived with it for four years.

Besides, my engagement in full-time work for the revolutionary struggle in the Philippines was long overdue. I never did publish the dissertation.

In the next few years, I was involved in doing solidarity work with Chilean exiles in the United States even as I worked to dislodge Marcos in the Philippines. I never could get Chile out of my mind, not least because I was haunted by what might have happened to my friends on the left. I was able to get in touch with only a few when I returned to Chile around 1993—20 years later—to speak on what lessons the newly developing countries of Asia had to offer Chile. It was the period of decompression, under the so-called *Concertacion* government that succeeded the Pinochet regime. Despite the looser political climate, there was still a great deal of reluctance on the part of the centrist government and, indeed, of the broad left to rehabilitate Allende, the man who had clung to the peaceful *Via Chilena*, the Chilean Road to Socialism, till the end. He may have been naïve, but he was brave and principled, traits underlined by the act of taking his life rather giving up the presidency.

Allende was a romantic revolutionary in the tradition of another martyred Marxist, Che Guevara, whose memorable words must have been in Allende's mind as he gazed at the Chilean Air Force planes swooping in to bomb La Moneda, the early 19th century neoclassical presidential palace in the center of Santiago: "Whenever death may surprise us, let it be welcome if our battle cry has reached even one receptive ear and another hand reaches out to take up our arms."

I will never forget that day sometime in November 1972, outside La Moneda, when my hand reached out for Allende's as his open-air motorcade rolled by, and he shook it.

3. Cadre

WHEN Madge and I left Chile around March 1973, we flew to Lima, and from there to Cuzco, where we took a bus that wound its way up to Machu Picchu, the city high up in the Peruvian Andes that was one of the architectural jewels of Inca civilization. That lost city in the clouds, with its lonely, unearthly beauty, with llamas frolicking among the ruins, was the perfect site for the honeymoon that Madge and I had never had. Looking back, those three days were the summit of our relationship, a wonderful time that would never be recaptured.

We returned to a campus that was no longer riled by war, to a place that had lapsed back to the languid Princeton of *This Side of Paradise*. The Paris Peace Accords that silenced the guns in Vietnam to allow the extrication of U.S. forces that had been defeated in a war that Washington had inherited from the French nearly three decades earlier had also ended the anti-war movement. But that the Accords simply provided a hiatus to allow Nixon and Kissinger to withdraw "with honor" became clear as the South Vietnamese regime underwent an unraveling that ended with the National Liberation Front's capture of Saigon as helicopters loaded with panic-stricken people departed from the roof of the U.S. Embassy in the spring of 1975.

With Vietnam liberated, was the Philippines next? My conviction was that it was.

On September 21, 1972, Ferdinand Marcos declared martial law in the Philippines, ending the regime of elite liberal democracy that had reigned since the country was granted formal independence by the United States in 1946. Over the next 14 years, thousands were imprisoned, tortured, or extra-judicially executed under a dictatorship that can best be described as a predatory, kleptocratic state. During those 14 years, bringing down that regime became my raison d'etre.

In the three tumultuous years before the imposition of martial law, the student movement had exploded, producing a generation of activists mobilized against Marcos' increasingly authoritarian rule, an oppressive class system dominated by landlords, and the country's subordination to the United States, which maintained military bases throughout the country.

Those student activists became the main recruits to the National Democratic Front (NDF) led by the Communist Party of the Philippines (CPP), which ultimately became the spearhead of the opposition to the regime.

Upon my return to Princeton from Chile, I traveled almost every weekend to New York, which had become the Mecca, along with San Francisco, of former activists coming from the Philippines. Having missed the famous "First Quarter Storm" of student opposition to Marcos in January 1970 and the declaration of martial law, I was eager to learn from these young exiles and related to them as a neophyte to seasoned veterans.

In New York, I reconnected with activists led by Rene and Aimee Cruz, former leaders of the *Samahan ng Demokratikong Kabataan,* or Association of Democratic Youth (SDK). I also took the train down to Washington, DC, where I met with Severina Rivera-Drew, an energetic, single-minded activist who had begun a lobby operation to influence the U.S. Congress to cut off aid to Marcos. Severina's being located in Washington was especially important since the U.S. capital had become the center of the Movement for a Free Philippines (MFP), which was founded by former Senator Raul Manglapus, who had escaped from the Philippines. Severina and I saw eye to eye in our assessment that the MFP represented a rival "bourgeois" center to the progressive groups in the U.S. that had come together under the temporary umbrella of the National Committee for the Restoration of Civil Liberties in the Philippines (NCRCLP). The Ateneo de Manila-educated Manglapus was widely regarded as an "Amboy," or "American Boy," whose aim from the very start was to get Washington to intervene and oust Marcos, in contrast to the progressive line, which was to cut off U.S. aid and all other forms of U.S. intervention so as to give the Filipino people the space to follow their own destiny. A Christian Democrat and anti-communist, Manglapus returned the hostility. He was a good orator, in the Ciceronian style favored by the Jesuits, who is now best remembered, unfortunately, for a terrible misogynistic remark he made as foreign secretary when invading Iraqi troops were reportedly raping Filipina overseas workers in Kuwait in 1990: "If you're going to get raped anyway, you might as well relax and enjoy it."

Washington, DC, circa 1973

A skilled lobbyist and networker, Severina, who was married to James Drew, a prominent progressive lawyer affiliated with the Communist Party USA, built the Congress Education Project, lodged at the historic Methodist Building at 110 Maryland Avenue Northeast, into an effective professional operation that outclassed both the MFP and the Philippine Embassy. For a few years, I worked closely with Rivera, providing some of the data and analysis that she wielded as she trudged the halls of the House of Representatives and the Senate to convince legislators to cut the flow of aid on which the Marcos regime was dependent for its survival.

One of the first fruits of this cooperation was the publication in 1977 of our book, *The Logistics of Repression*, which was the first effort to comprehensively detail the military and economic aid being received by Marcos from the United States.[8] Severina appreciated the research and analysis that went into the work, but she was highly critical of its cover, which depicted a soldier superimposed on a concentration camp full of people, with a generous helping of bloody red blots, on the ground that it would look hysterical to the congressional aides she was lobbying.

DC in those years was a huge, dusty construction zone, with traffic constantly tied up in strategic places like Dupont Circle, as the metropolitan subway was being built. The center of the city was the federal district, which housed Congress, the White House, the national government agencies, and the grand marble monuments. That was the DC of federal office workers and tourists. After 5 pm, white politicians, workers, and tourists would retire either to the white enclave of Northwest DC or flee across the Potomac to Northern Virginia. Black workers would go to their ghettoes in Southwest, Southeast, or Northeast DC. Geographically, DC, like every other big American city, was essentially racially segregated, though there were border areas like Mount Pleasant in Northwest DC, where I stayed whenever I visited the city, that were racially mixed, with growing numbers of Latinos and Asians living alongside blacks and whites.

DC was also a "war zone," especially in the evenings, and holdups were not uncommon. When I first got there, there was a crime wave, where the victims were not only robbed but shot. One evening, after we feasted on crabs at Severina and Jim's house in Mount Pleasant, I was hit by an allergy, and I went out, itching and scratching, in search of a drug store at midnight. Before I knew it, there was a gun on my back and another on my chest, and a voice that said, "Gimme your wallet." I immediately threw my wallet to the ground and waited for the expected shot. As with my encounters with people with guns in Jolo years earlier, my luck held out. The gunmen picked up my wallet and ran, leaving me unscathed. But the shock was so great that my allergy magically disappeared! I was so relieved at the disappearance of the intense itching that it was only after a minute that I realized that, hey, I could have been killed, for devouring crabs, for Christ's sake! I abstained from crabs, lobsters, and shrimps for a long time after that memorable evening.

Building the Anti-Dictatorship Movement

The years 1973 to 1976 saw the founding of three organizations that supplanted the NCRCLP as the progressive opposition to the anti-Marcos alliance: the Friends of the Filipino People (FFP), *Katipunan ng mga Demokratikong Pilipino,* or Union of Democratic Filipinos (KDP), and the Anti-Martial Law Coalition (AMLC).

The FFP was an organization of non-Filipinos and Filipinos whose main personages were Rivera and Daniel Boone Schirmer, a radical historian who had written *Republic or Empire,* an enlightening study of the Anti-Imperialist League that had opposed the U.S. annexation of the Philippines at the turn of the twentieth Century.[9] The AMLC—later renamed the Coalition against the Marcos Dictatorship (CAMD)—was the anti-dictatorship "united front" that was mainly rooted in Filipino communities in New York, Philadelphia, Washington, DC, the San Francisco Bay Area, Los Angeles, Seattle, and Honolulu. Closely linked to the AMLC and its driving force was the KDP, an organization of Filipinos and Filipino Americans that politically and organizationally evolved along Marxist-Leninist lines and became, for a few years, the main representative of the left wing "National Democratic Front" in the U.S.

I worked with all three organizations, but they were relationships that had their share of tensions and conflicts. In hindsight, this was not surprising since exile movements, be they right, center, or left in orientation, have always been wracked by conflicts of a personal, political, or ideological kind.

The KDP Years

I had my first taste of how sharp and deep political conflicts could become even among broadly like-minded people in my first years with the now legendary KDP. When activists from throughout the U.S. came together in a camp near San Francisco to found KDP in 1973, they came with different expectations about the organizational form of the new formation. Some expected a loose network, others something of a tighter formation along the lines of "democratic centralism." In the struggle between these two organizational visions, the latter won out, and key leaders of the former expelled.

Being mainly in Washington, DC, and working with Rivera's Congress Education Project in lobbying Congress, I was not in the thick of the fight between these two tendencies, which took place among activists located in the San Francisco Bay Area. Thus, I was surprised that when activists reassembled in 1975, two years after the founding of the Congress, there was a "Speak Bitterness" session denouncing the two expelled leaders, "Comrade

Pepe" and "Comrade Deks." This session, I learned later, was patterned after criticism-self-criticism sessions (CSC) of the Communist Party of the Philippines, which in turn were copied from Mao's famous method of isolating "deviationists." But what did I know? I was a neophyte and respected the practice of those more experienced than me. Still, while my head said it was only right that "opportunists" should be treated this way, my instincts told me that Pepe and Deks were probably not as scheming as they were painted. This was not the last time my instincts would rebel against my mind. And, indeed, when I was a member of the Philippine House of Representatives decades later, I got to work with Pepe and found him a consistent and determined advocate of the interests of the Philippines and the Filipino community in the United States.

That community numbered over 500,000 in the mid-1970s. Filipinos had first come to the U.S. in significant numbers in the first decades of the 20th century to serve as farm workers in Hawaii and as farm and cannery workers on the West Coast and Alaska. Harsh anti-miscegenation laws and immigration restrictions slowed the expansion of the Filipino population until the mid-sixties, when the 1965 Immigration Act liberalized entry into the U.S., mitigating but not eliminating its bias against Asians and other non-white people. With liberalization, the community became more diverse, with female nurses becoming a significant component of the Filipino working class and medical doctors of the middle class.

The KDP brought activists influenced by the ongoing armed revolution in the Philippines together with second generation Filipino-American youth that were politicized in housing struggles for elderly Filipinos in San Francisco, participation in the historic fight to unionize Chicano and Filipino workers in the United Farm Workers in the Central Valley in California, and efforts to organize cannery workers in Seattle. These young progressives saw themselves as heirs to the radical tradition of Filipino working class organizing of the 1930s and 1940s epitomized by Carlos Bulosan, the gifted novelist whose *America is in the Heart* remains one of most heart-rending accounts of struggle against both class exploitation and racism in American labor literature.[10] Other heroes of this earlier generation included Chris Mensalvas and Ernesto Mangaoang of Local 37, Seattle's legendary union of cannery workers. Mensalvas and Mangaoang were among those that the U.S. sought to deport owing to alleged links with the Communist Party USA. This pantheon of labor fighters was joined in the 1960s by Larry Itliong and Philip Vera Cruz, who gained fame as the farm workers who triggered the strike that ultimately led to the victory of the United Farm Workers (UFW) of the fabled Mexican American union leader, Cesar Chavez.

KDP paralleled the radical organizing among racial and ethnic minorities in the late 1960s and 1970s—by the Black Panther Party among Blacks, the Young Lords among Puerto Ricans, I Wor Kuen among Chinese Americans, and La Raza among Mexican Americans. It was a product of the ferment of the 1960–1980 period, where the center of gravity of American society moved briefly to the left, triggered by the civil rights movement in the U.S. and the opposition to the war in Vietnam.

From 1975 to the mid-eighties, KDP established itself as a disciplined Leninist force in Filipino communities in a number of cities, including the San Francisco Bay Area, Los Angeles, New York, Chicago, Seattle, and Washington, DC, as well as in Toronto and Vancouver in Canada. Aside from mobilizing to counter the pro-Marcos activities of Philippine consulates and popularizing the revolutionary alternative, National Democracy, KDP activists moved to organize Filipino students, cannery workers, and nurses, combining political organizing with militant cultural performances that introduced the revolutionary culture of the Philippine movement to the Filipino community.[11]

The organization became an important institution transmitting radical politics to Fil-Am youth growing up in the seventies and eighties. Perhaps its best-known struggle was winning back control of the International Longshore and Warehouse Union (ILWU Local 37) from a corrupt union leadership and sending to jail a pro-Marcos union president who had ordered the brutal assassination of two KDP union activists, Silme Domingo and Gene Viernes, at the union's office in Seattle in 1981.

In the beginning, KDP had a dual program of mobilizing support for the Philippines revolution and organizing the Filipino community in the U.S. "from a socialist perspective." By the early 1980s, however, organizing for a socialist revolution in the United States had become the dominant focus, and the KDP leadership, notably a brilliant pair, Bruce Occena and Melinda Paras, engaged in what came to be known as "pre-party formation" that would hopefully lead to the reestablishment of a new, revolutionary Communist Party in the United States to replace the old Communist Party, the CPUSA, that was regarded by the New Left generation as having been marginalized and rendered irrelevant by a combination of McCarthyite repression during the Cold War and "reformism."

There were then a number of candidates for the honor of becoming the new Communist Party "along Marxist-Leninist lines" that were jostling for position during that period, including the Revolutionary Communist Party and the League of Revolutionary Struggle. One of the key leaders of KDP became one of the central figures in the formation of "Line of March," which brought together like-minded progressives from other activist groups. He was, by all accounts, an inspiring figure, one who was not only a skilled political operator but also a sharp theoretical polemicist. But just when Line of March was showing promise of eventually becoming the U.S.'s Marxist-Leninist center, he became severely physically and psychologically incapacitated owing to drug use. Given his prominent intellectual and political role, his collapse left a leadership vacuum. It was a stunning, unexpected blow that was a key factor that led to the disbanding of both Line of March and KDP by the early 1990s.

Everyone, and I certainly, was profoundly shocked at how drugs could destroy a very promising mind at its prime. But this activist handled his situation with honor and grace. At a conference on the future of the Philippine progressive movement in Berkeley in 1993, he bravely publicly declared, "I am a recovering drug user."

Although I was a member of KDP, my being for the most part in Washington, DC, led to my being insulated from the political and theoretical debates that were taking place mainly in the San Francisco Bay Area, especially on the issue of whether KDP ought to prioritize support for the National Democratic Revolution in the Philippines or for the struggle for socialism in the U.S. While I appreciated theoretically the turn of the KDP leadership to prioritize the struggle for socialism in the U.S., there was never any doubt in my mind that my priority was the overthrow of Marcos and advancing the Philippine revolution. It was a priority that the KDP leadership recognized and respected, owing to its maintaining a close relationship with the revolutionary center in the Philippines, even as its prime focus shifted to organizing for socialist change in the U.S. But this was not the only reason for my remaining distant from socialist organizing; though my radical theoretical perspective led me to a declaration of faith in a socialist future for the U.S., the actual experience of living there and witnessing the tremendous hold of capitalist consumption culture on ordinary Americans engendered a deep skepticism as to the possibility of radical, much less revolutionary change. Curiously, I maintained this detachment from the politics of the United States, even as I was academically engaged with its dynamics as a "late capitalist society," being strongly influenced by C. Wright Mills' *The Power Elite* and Paul Baran and Paul Sweezy's *Monopoly Capital*.[12]

In any case, I saw myself as an exile, one that was caught abroad by the declaration of martial law but had every intention of returning to the Philippines once the dictatorship was overthrown. I finished my dissertation and immediately became a full-time activist from 1975 on, not returning to academic life, except for taking on part-time teaching jobs to keep body and soul together, until the mid-1990s. Having missed being politicized by the First Quarter Storm and the wave of student activism in the Philippines during the late sixties and early seventies, it was during my sojourn in Washington, DC, in the late seventies and early eighties, that I gained full appreciation of the movement that was unfolding 10,000 miles away.

Joining the Underground Elite

I had become a Marxist and activist while in graduate school and a socialist while I was in Chile, but I had not been part of a disciplined Leninist organization. But shortly after I joined KDP, I was also recruited into the Communist Party of the Philippines (CPP), which existed as a parallel underground organization within KDP. When I recited my oath of allegiance to the CPP while walking with my recruiter around a block in Chicago one cold December night in 1974, I was a star-struck novice becoming part of an underground organization with a powerful revolutionary mystique.

Over the next 15 years, I was a disciplined member of this organization, forsaking a steady job, sleeping on the couches of comrades' homes, crisscrossing the U.S. on cheap "red-eye" flights from which I would emerge totally exhausted, subsisting on Doritos and burritos and cigarettes, wearing for the longest time just one tweed coat donated by a friend for all occasions—all in the service of a revolution I thoroughly believed in and felt was inevitable since history was on the side of the party. Commitment to the CPP was also the priority that inevitably led to crises in my personal life, unmade relationships and friendships and owing to my frequent absences on missions, contributed to the erosion of my marriage to Madge. It also brought me into confrontations with the hard fist of the state.

Different Takes on Joma Sison

The CPP and the revolutionary movement in the Philippines were inseparable from the figure of Jose Maria Sison. Although I was to break with Sison and the Communist Party of the Philippines CPP in the early 1990s, I never abandoned my appreciation of his historical significance. At the time of his death in December 2022, I posted this obituary:

> Many of us had differences with Sison, and on important issues. However, this is not the time to dwell on these. Sison was a giant of the Philippine Left. He played a key role, if not the most decisive one, in the rebirth of the Philippine Left in the mid-1960s. He was a Marxist who sought to translate theory into

practice, to apply Marxism to the Philippine context, as a method not only for understanding it but changing it.

His was a great mind, but even the greatest of minds are not infallible. Revolutionary theory must evolve to meet new realities, and it was in grappling with these realities that different sections of the movement he was central in founding went in divergent ways. Despite their differences, however, there was always that deeper unity in bringing about a revolutionary transformation of Philippine society.

History's judgment on Sison will only become clearer many years from now. But of one thing we in *Laban ng Masa* [People's Struggle] are certain: he was from beginning to end a true revolutionary.[13]

Testifying to the sharp disagreements about Sison's historical role, this drew the following riposte from a prominent student of the Philippine left:

I don't as a general principle respond to mass emails, but in this instance I feel compelled to do so.

I respectfully but strongly disagree with this assessment of Sison.

I wrote a preliminary obituary . . . "Founder and lifelong leader of the Stalinist Communist Party of the Philippines, Jose Maria Sison, died on December 16 at the age of 83. No figure in the past half-century was more instrumental in the betrayal of the Filipino working class and oppressed masses than Joma Sison."

I take no pleasure in my assessment, but more important than the injunction not to speak ill of the dead, is the injunction to always speak the truth.

Sincerely,
Joseph Scalice[14]

The debate over Sison's place in history will not be settled any time soon, but while I would later be involved in both theoretical and political conflicts with him, I saw him in the late seventies and early eighties as a larger-than-life personality who helped create a student movement in the early 1960s, then transformed it into a revolutionary movement that sped through the country from the late sixties to the mid-eighties. It may be hard to imagine today, with the left in disarray and marginalized that, personally and ideologically inspired by the charismatic Sison, what came to be known as the National

Democratic Revolution was once the wave of the future that swept a whole generation off its feet.

To fully appreciate the place of Sison and the CPP in Philippine history, one must begin with the collapse of the once formidable *Partido Komunista ng Pilipinas* (PKP) in the early 1950s. Founded in 1930 by the printer, Crisanto Evangelista, and other working-class leaders, the PKP emerged as a major force in Philippine politics during World War II, when it forged a peasant guerrilla army, the Hukbalahap, or Huks, that led the anti-Japanese struggle in Central Luzon. In a climate of severe class conflict between peasants and a landlord-dominated government in the late 1940s, the leadership decided to risk all on launching an uprising that was meant to bring the left to power within two years. But, with the help of the U.S., the Philippine government turned the tide in 1951 with a cunning strategy that combined the promise of free land and land reform, counter-guerrilla military operations, "clean elections," and the successful projection of elite politician Ramon Magsaysay as a reformist, populist president. Washington worked through Edward Lansdale, a CIA agent working under a U.S. Air Force cover, who pioneered the deployment of unorthodox tactics.

The PKP's defeat inaugurated a period of demoralization of the left and of McCarthyism in the larger society. It also produced Young Turks within the party like Francisco Nemenzo and Jose Maria Sison, who refused to place the blame principally on external causes but rather on what they considered to be strategic and ideological errors. Both formed breakaway groups, and both played key roles in creating a nationalist student movement in the early sixties. But while Nemenzo chose mainly to use the University of the Philippines as his base for politically educating young Filipinos, Sison took the route of forming an organization to displace the PKP as a revolutionary center.

It is not my intention to write a history of the CPP. Others have done that.[15] I am writing a memoir, and what I am trying to convey is a narrative of revolutionary theory and practice that was so compelling to me personally that it became my paradigm for interpreting past and concurrent developments in the Philippines during the 15 years I was a card-carrying member of the CPP. In a nutshell, what Sison's writings provided to me and my generation was a theoretical framework to interpret the Philippines' history as a country politically and economically subjugated by the United States and ruled by a subservient elite, along with a convincing political formula for liberating it. Probably only those of my generation can understand how heady that intellectual encounter was, and why we were ready to stake our lives and future in the revolution.

Fortunately, while doing research for this memoir, I came upon a long piece that I wrote for the *Third World Quarterly* shortly after the assassination of Marcos' main political rival Benigno Aquino in 1983, an event of tremendous significance that is the focus of Chapter 5.[16] Part paean to Sison and the CPP, part political analysis from a Marxist perspective, and certainly with no pretense of being "value free," the article was titled "From the Ashes: The Rebirth of the Philippine Left." I am reproducing a large part of it here to enable the reader to capture my state of mind at the height of the influence of the CPP, in the early 1980s. So here goes.

From the Ashes: The Rebirth of the Philippine Left

. . . To understand the revitalization of the left and its current position of strength, one must start with Jose Maria Sison. . . . The interaction of personality and history continues to be a major topic of academic debate, but there is no doubt that Sison played a decisive role as a [midwife] of the current Philippine revolution.

Amado Guerrero [Sison's nom de guerre] is, by most accounts, a remarkable individual. . . . Guerrero, however, is no mere revolutionary optimist. He is also a superb theoretician, a skillful and sharp polemicist, a master of organization, and a very determined leader. All these qualities were evident in the internal party report, "Rectify Errors and Rebuild the Party," a relentless and comprehensive criticism of the ideological, political, organizational, and military practice of the PKP which served as the founding document of the CPP.

Unlike "Rectify Errors and Rebuild the Party," Guerrero's *Philippine Society and Revolution* was intended to be a document for public debate and popular education.[17] It is not a work which academics will find congenial, for its perspective is not that of a detached observer or an academic Marxist. It shifts easily from profound analysis to sharp polemic to passionate prescription. Nonetheless, as a theoretical enterprise, *PSR*, as the book came to be called, is remarkable—a work against which all previous and subsequent Marxist works on the Philippines have to be measured.

Guerrero was attempting what Mao had done in China and what Mariategui has accomplished in Peru: that is, drawing out the "laws of motion" of Philippine society through an application of the concepts of class, class conflict, mode of production, and imperialism to Philippine history. The Philippine social formation which emerges from this analysis is a semi-colonial, semi-feudal society. Colonization by Spain and later imperial control by the United States disrupted the internal evolution of Philippine class society. The contradiction between the Filipino people and imperialism and the social classes which constituted imperialism's "domestic social base" consequently became the engine of historical motion.

The Philippine "bourgeois-democratic revolution" still has to be completed, asserts Guerrero. The Revolution of 1896, directed both at ending Spanish control and preventing the Philippines from passing into American hands, was aborted, not only by superior U.S. military force but also by the desertion to the American authorities of the rising Filipino liberal bourgeoisie (*ilustrados*) who provided the class leadership for the struggle. Since then, except for a brief interregnum of Japanese control during World War II, the country has served as a military base for the projection of U.S. power to mainland Asia and as a profitable investment area for U.S. corporations. Loaded down with all sorts of unequal treaties like the infamous Parity Amendment to the Philippine Constitution, which gave Americans rights equal to those of Filipinos to exploit the natural resources of the country, the Philippines, despite its formal independence, can be most accurately described as a semi-colony. When the U.S. has not been intervening directly, its influence has been exercised through a domestic coalition of comprador bourgeoisie, "bureaucrat capitalists," and landlords.

Indeed, it was to create a reliable agent of social and political control that the U.S. forged the different regional landlord elites into a national ruling class. This explains capitalist America's refusal to carry out capitalist land reform in the Philippines: the quid pro quo of this social pact was the maintenance of the archaic and oppressive landlord-tenant system of agricultural production. Thus Guerrero's characterization of the dominant mode of production in the Philippines as "semi-feudal."

The influence of Mao's "On Social Classes" and "On New Democracy" is obvious, and it is a legacy that Guerrero gladly acknowledges. Yet *PSR* is no mechanical transportation of "Maoist" and Marxist categories to Philippine society; it is, instead, a creative synthesis of Marxism with unique Philippine realities. Even the *Far Eastern Economic Review*, the Hong

Kong-based international business weekly, had to acknowledge
that *PSR* was a "work of flawed brilliance."

Fifteen years after the first edition came out, PSR continues to elicit controversy. Filipino Marxists continue to debate
whether the Philippine countryside continues to be "semi-feudal,"
as Guerrero claimed, or has become dominated by the capitalist
mode of production. The lavish praise of Mao, admiration of the
Chinese Cultural Revolution, and endorsement of the old Maoist
characterization of the Soviet Union as "social imperialist" seem
strident and incongruous today, but all great works are affected by
the spirit of the times. And in the late 1960s, the Chinese Cultural
Revolution and Beijing's challenge to Moscow as the center of
world revolution were a source of inspiration to a whole generation of progressives in both the East and the West. Mao inspired
a generation of Philippine leftists to go back to the country's
long-standing revolutionary tradition and offered a set of theoretical categories and methodological principles with which they
could re-examine their own society and formulate a revolutionary
program.

But the demands of making a complex national revolution
in the succeeding years pushed the left to transcend its Maoist
theoretical beginnings and develop understandings, methods and
policies appropriate to the Philippine context. This process of
theoretical maturation was accompanied by the CPP's move in the
late 1970s to a position of non-alignment and strict independence
from both China and the Soviet Union—a development which
could only be accelerated by China's de facto alliance with the
U.S. and its call for the continued maintenance in the Philippines
of the bases which the CPP was fighting to oust.

If Guerrero's aim had been simply to provide a historical and
structural analysis of Philippine society, his work would already
stand as no mean achievement. But, like Lenin, Guerrero draws
his inspiration from Marx's 11th Thesis on Feuerbach: "The philosophers have only interpreted the world in various ways; the
point, however, is to change it."

Changing Philippine reality means, first and foremost, completing the national democratic revolution, which is "a necessary
stage in the struggle of our people for social justice, whereby the
freedom of the entire nation is first secured so that the nation-
state that has been secured would allow within its framework the

masses of the Filipino people to enjoy the democratic rights to achieve their social emancipation."

Unlike the democratic revolution of the "old type" led by the bourgeoisie, the national democratic struggle is a democratic revolution of the "new type" led by the most advanced social class in the era of imperialism, the working class. The Filipino national bourgeoisie, like other Third World capitalist elites, can no longer be entrusted with leading the democratic revolution because it has proven "flabby," inconsistent, and subservient in the face of imperialist hegemony. Thus, the Philippine national democratic revolution, while distinct from the socialist revolution, nevertheless looks forward to the latter.

In Guerrero's view, there are three indispensable weapons in the national democratic struggle. The first is the leadership of a "rectified" or purified Communist Party. The second is armed struggle based on a strategy of "protracted people's war," wherein a proletarian-led peasant army builds up its strength in the Philippine countryside (which contains 70 percent of the population) and advances "wave upon wave" to encircle the urban bastions of the Philippine government. Finally, there is the national united front, which seeks to unite all "patriotic classes and strata with an objective interest in overthrowing U.S. imperialism and feudalism into a powerful social and political force."

In the volatile atmosphere of the late 1960s, when the McCarthyist superstructure was breaking down, nationalism was reawakening in student ranks, the Vietnamese people 700 miles away were fighting the mightiest power on earth to a standstill, peasants were demanding land, and workers were marching for higher wages. . . *PSR* was heady stuff. DGs (discussion groups) organized around *PSR* became the main mechanism for the integration of thousands of students into the ranks of the burgeoning national democratic student and youth organizations which spearheaded the effervescent mass demonstrations that preceded the imposition of martial law on 21 September 1972.

In the countryside, *PSR*, translated into different vernacular languages, became the basic course in the political education of peasant recruits into the New People's Army. For mindful of the experience of the PKP, where peasant millenarianism overwhelmed proletarian ideology, the leadership of the CPP and NPA was determined that its peasant cadres would internalize working-class ideology. In *PSR*, Guerrero warned that, with the increasing intensity of the Philippines' unresolved social contradictions, the ruling class would be increasingly tempted to shift from formal democratic means of control to a more openly repressive, fascist form of state.

In September 1972, the Marcos faction of the elite imposed martial law, both to seize absolute power and to freeze the social conflicts which were gradually unravelling the neo-colonial order. By then, however, two of the three basic revolutionary institutions had been re-established: the CPP was set up on 26 December 1968 and the New People's Army was formed with sixty-eight men and thirty-five rifles on 29 March 1969. And during the dark days of the early martial law period in 1973, the third institution, the preparatory commission for the national united front, the National Democratic Front, was organized in Manila.

By 1974, the NPA was operating in twenty guerrilla fronts on the main island of Luzon. It was, however, hard-pressed by encirclement-and-suppression campaigns carried out by the Armed Forces of the Philippines (AFP). Though it was solidly rooted in peasant populations, the NPA was in danger of being ousted by the AFP's superior military force from its two main areas of operation in Cagayan Valley and the Bicol peninsula.

It was at this point that the leadership's theoretical skills came to the rescue of the revolution. *Specific Characteristics of Our People's War*, which appeared in 1974, posed the fundamental military problem confronting a fledgling guerrilla force battling against the superior resources of the Philippine military: "[W]e have to fight within narrow fronts because the entire country is small and its countryside is shredded." Amado Guerrero responded with two strategic prescriptions which sought to adapt the Chinese and Vietnamese strategy of people's war to an archipelagic country. First, the NPA had to create multiple guerrilla fronts throughout the archipelago instead of focusing its energies on creating just one central base area, as Mao did in Yenan. This would have the effect of forcing the enemy to disperse his superior force to several major islands, thus stretching it thinly. Second, it had to exploit the mountainous character of the Philippines to maximum advantage. By skillfully operating from the mountain ranges which "sew up" and crisscross the major islands, the NPA could exert political and military influence on the various lowland provinces which bordered each range. The spirit behind these strategic innovations was profoundly dialectical, profoundly Marxist; it was to turn geographic constraints into advantages.[18]

Guided by this strategy, NPA armed propaganda units (APUs) fanned out from Luzon to the other major islands of the archipelago in the mid-1970s. In the early stage of organization, the bulk of the APU's work was non-military political work, such as popular education, land reform, health delivery, cleaning out local crime, and mass organization-building. With the formation and deployment of increasing numbers of semi-legal teams (SLTs) to carry out political organization, however, the APU's mass work became secondary to its military functions. In Samar, Negros, Panay, and Mindanao, this pattern of patient, solid based-building tested in Luzon was repeated innumerable times: win local confidence by tackling issues of local concern, expand the people's political consciousness by showing the systemic character of social problems, recruit, build mass organizations, specialize and form regular NPA units. Only when solid organizing had been carried out and regular NPA units formed could the latter initiate "tactical offensives" to gain arms from the enemy on a regular basis.

Mindanao, the country's second largest island, illustrates the explosive potential of the NPA "formula." From one APU in 1974, NPA strength grew to twenty full-fledged guerrilla squads spread out over five fronts in 1978. As of 1984, numerous "undersized companies" or "oversized platoons" had replaced the squads and were deployed to ten guerrilla fronts covering 2,200 town centers. NPA expansion in Mindanao, by drawing AFP units from other parts of the country, provided much-needed breathing space for expansion and consolidation of NPA fronts in Luzon and the other major islands. The formation of guerrilla bases is most advanced in Mindanao. In contrast to guerrilla zones, which are contested areas, bases are secure sanctuaries of NPA control which AFP troops either cannot penetrate at all or, if they do succeed, cannot encamp in.

CPP and NPA leaders view the bases' political infrastructure, made up of governing committees linking up different "sectoral" mass organizations, as the local embryos of a future national revolutionary government. The guerrilla bases also host military training centers for NPA regulars. This function will become increasingly important as the NPA increases its recruitment in response to the heightened tempo of the civil war. CPP-NPA strategists have acquired a reputation for carefully calibrating their advances to their actual or projected strength. Nonetheless, the revolutionary momentum is such that they estimate that the NPA has passed from the early sub-stages to what they term "the strategic counter-offensive substage of the strategic defensive." This military concept describes a correlation of forces in which the Marcos army is rapidly losing its strategic advantage nation-wide to the NPA. In this developing phase, company-sized NPA units (about a hundred fighters) will become the norm, replacing guerrilla squads as the standard fighting unit, with some advanced [areas] beginning to field battalion-sized formations by the end of the period. In terms of warfare, this period will see a transition from small-scale guerrilla offensives to the primacy of regular mobile warfare, complemented by guerrilla actions.

So extensive is the revolutionary movement's politico-military infrastructure in the countryside that there is widespread confidence that it will be able to pass from the strategic defensive to the "strategic stalemate"—a status of rough parity with the Philippine military—in three to five years' time. In a recent interview, the imprisoned Jose Maria Sison stated that in the next few years, "at the cumulative rate the NPA is gaining strength, it shall have control or influence over about 50 percent of the 1500 municipalities in the country and will be able to easily concentrate companies and even battalions to wipe out army units in most of the country."

That this was no idle boast was shown by the recent battalion-sized formations (500 men and women) which staged spectacular arms-gathering raids on AFP command posts and armories in Western Mindanao and Negros Island. Painting the expected scenario, Sison continued: "Right now, the NPA can wipe out or disarm entire army platoons in various parts of the country. In the strategic stalemate stage, the annihilation of enemy companies or battalions in single operations or campaigns will become commonplace. There will be temporary repeated seizures of big towns, provincial capitals, and small cities to wipe out or disarm army units." Sison's predictions appear to be rooted in hard military realities. Even now, the real ratio of NPA to army strength is 1:6, a perilously low figure from the perspective of U.S. officials, who consider a 1:10 ratio as the ideal. This is because after one deducts the 20,000 troops deployed against the insurgent separatist Moro National Liberation Front (MNLF) in Western Mindanao, there are only 60,000 combat troops countering the 10,000 NPA regulars with high-powered rifles. To achieve parity with the army, NPA strategists estimate, according to some reports, that they will need 25,000 regulars. This is seen as within reach. It will entail, among other things, a sharp escalation of attacks on army units and installations to gather arms. Equally important is the laying down of the extensive political infrastructure needed to support a vastly expanded people's army.

The rapid development of the war in the countryside has thrown a new light on the relationship between the armed struggle in the countryside and the legal, semi-legal, and clandestine mass struggles in the cities led or influenced by the National Democratic Front. "While it is our principal task to wage a protracted war in the countryside," Guerrero stressed in *Specific Characteristics . . .*, "it is our secondary task to develop the revolutionary underground and the broad anti-imperialist and democratic mass movement in the cities." He continued: "We should excel in combining legal, illegal and semi-legal activities through a widespread and stable underground. A revolutionary underground developing beneath democratic and legal or semi-legal activities should promote the well-rounded growth of the revolutionary forces, serve to link otherwise isolated parts of the Party and the people's army at every level and prepare the ground for popular uprisings in the future and for the advance of the people's army."

Working under extremely dangerous conditions in the early years of martial law, when the average working career of urban organizers was said to be less than six months before they got too "hot" and had to be redeployed to the countryside or another city (if they had not already been caught), National Democratic Front organizers had, by 1975, laid the basis for a militant workers' movement. This launched a year-long wave of over 400 strikes which challenged the regime's promise of a docile, strike-less work force to foreign investors. Work among the lower ranks of the Catholic clergy built up a strong network of recruits and supporters in a stratum made receptive to new concepts of Christian social doctrine by Vatican II. Among lawyers, medical workers, teachers, professionals, and students, similar networks of supporters and sympathizers were forged. As in the countryside, the organizing principle was the same: champion justice issues of particular concern to a sector, like rises in students' tuition fees; organize and boldly lead mass struggles around these issues and stretch the limits of legality set by the regime; raise political consciousness by linking the various issues as abuses emanating from a system of fascism supported by U.S. imperialism.

By the time of the Aquino assassination on 21 August 1983, the NDF had built up an impressive intersecting array of "sectoral," "cause-oriented" organizations cooperating at the legal, semi-legal, and illegal levels. Thus, a great number of the massive, sustained nationwide demonstrations, pickets, and marches which shook the cities in the months after the brazen murder [of Aquino] were not simply spontaneous. Sustaining the varied expressions of people's anger was a sophisticated and firm scaffolding that had been creatively and carefully constructed over the previous decade. Many of the five hundred or so cause-oriented sectoral organizations nationwide are influenced by the NDF and they provide it with a strong base with which to negotiate alliances with other parties in the urban opposition. One such broad alliance, the recently established *Bayan* coalition led by former Senator Lorenzo Tanada and supported by the cause-oriented groups, is seen by many as a major effort to formalize a broad united front with diverse class forces. Urban mass actions now have a direct relationship to the armed struggle. Intensified urban protest, by drawing army forces from the countryside, takes the heat off NPA units working in adjacent rural areas. And, when breathing space is needed to accelerate urban organization, the NPA steps up its tactical offensives against the Marcos troops, forcing the latter to request assistance from urban garrisons.

The city of Davao, the Philippines' third largest, has become the major experimental area for the direct coordination of open mass actions by urban sectoral organizations, clandestine urban guerrilla warfare by "armed city partisan" units (ACPs), and NPA tactical offensives carried out in the rural outskirts of the metropolis. As one NDF leader put it, "The armed struggle in the countryside and the people's struggles in the cities are two faces of the same war." The influence of the "Nicaraguan model" on a revolutionary movement that puts a premium on absorbing new lessons and innovating is obvious.

The capacity to absorb, experiment, and innovate is related by many observers ... to a principle of organization laid out in *Specific Characteristics. ...* : "centralized leadership and decentralized operations." This was prompted by the need, under conditions of archipelagic guerrilla warfare, for cadres who are of sufficiently high quality to find their own bearing and maintain initiative not only within periods as short as one or two months ... but also within periods as long as two or more years, in case the enemy chooses to concentrate on an island or a fighting front and blockade it. With the premium placed on self-reliant local units, CPP and NPA training has stressed the development of strong ideological commitment as well as rigorous internalization of dialectical methods of analyzing, breaking down and resolving problems. Every cadre, in short, is expected to be a leader, and the sort of blind unthinking loyalty to the party leadership that was cultivated by the PKP is strongly discouraged not only as undemocratic but also as disastrous in the conduct of revolutionary war. Trained to trust the method of analysis instead of relying on mere authority, the CPP and NPA are said to enjoy a vibrant inner party democracy that would be the envy of other Leninist organizations, where the organizational principle of democratic centralism has been severely skewed on the side of centralism, and democracy has been replaced by bureaucracy. Sympathetic observers have frequently remarked on CPP members' faith that a collective tackling of a problem "all-sidedly" with dialectical methodology can arrive at the right line.

Periodic "criticism and self-criticism" is meant to toughen the "class stand" and to hone one's grasp of theory and method. Advancement to positions of greater responsibility depends on theoretical and organizational competence as well as firmness of class stand, all of which are assessed by an individual's different present and past collectives. The principle of self-reliance and the cadres' internalization of "scientific method" has enabled the CPP and NPA to absorb body blows which have crippled bureaucratic Leninist parties. Whereas the Huk Revolution never recovered from the capture of the PKP Secretary General and most of the "Politburo-In" in October 1950, the NPA insurgency has kept expanding despite the arrest of over half the Central Committee of the CPP in the mid-1970s. Well-trained subordinates capable of thinking on their feet simply stepped into the roles of those captured, and the arrest of some of these successors simply led to others filling their shoes. Thus, Marcos' celebrated boast in 1977 that the "back of the Communist insurgency" was broken with the capture of many of its original leaders was swiftly shown to be the illusion of a dictator who failed to discern the true character of his revolutionary antagonists. For the dictator and his U.S. backers, the revolution has become a hydra-headed creature which cannot be decapitated.

The armed revolution launched by the CPP and the NPA has entered its seventeenth year, with its leaders cautiously confident of gaining the strategic initiative vis-a-vis the government in a few more years. There continue to be major obstacles on the path to a successful completion of the national democratic revolution. For one, there is the question of arms. More youth want to join the NPA than can be accommodated because of the lack of arms, say movement sources. While increasing arms-gathering raids on the AFP will probably meet the demands of firepower for a few more years, this method will soon prove inadequate. The shift to regular mobile warfare on the plains of Luzon and Mindanao when the correlation of forces reaches the strategic stalemate and the NPA moves to the strategic offensive will demand a larger and more stable flow not only of small arms but also heavy weaponry, like howitzers and mortars. Should the NPA try to procure its arms from external sources, it will have to contend with the likelihood of a naval blockade by the U.S. Seventh Fleet. Then, there is the looming threat of direct U.S. intervention should the demoralized AFP collapse. While American public opinion at present will probably not sanction the sending of ground troops, the strength of the "Vietnam Syndrome" a few years hence cannot be taken for granted, especially with the continuing rightward motion of the U.S. electorate. But if the past is any indication, we should expect the revitalized Philippine left to produce innovative responses to these and other constraints and threats.

Rarely has a revolution suffering a strategic defeat recovered in the period of time it took the Philippine revolution to revive and move once again to a position of relative strength. It took fifteen years to move from devastating defeat in 1954 to the re-establishment of the CPP in 1968 and the founding of the NPA in 1969. And it has taken 16 years for the NPA to grow from a hardy band of 68 men to a nationwide force of 15,000 regulars who are pressing the AFP to a debilitating stalemate....

In conclusion, two factors appear especially decisive. One is the CPP and NPA's capacity to fuse revolutionary discipline with strong initiative from cadres at all levels of the movement. The other is the consistent employment of theory to illuminate practice and chart out the road to state power. All the key junctures in the revitalized left's history—the forging of the program of the National Democratic Revolution, the struggle leading to the re-establishment of the party in 1968, the adoption of the archipelagic guerrilla strategy in the mid-1970s, the interaction of the advancing rural armed struggle, the united front in the cities, and the urban mass protests in the mid-1980s—serve to illustrate the continuing relevance of Lenin's assertion: "Without revolutionary theory, there can be no revolutionary practice...."

Theory, Practice, and History in Synch?

Was this a biased, ideologically informed narrative that was divorced from reality? Was it cock-eyed optimism? Both? It might be useful here to see what some other quarters were saying at roughly the same time this piece was written for the left-leaning academic audience that constituted the readership of the *Third World Quarterly*.

After years of routinely repeating the Marcos regime's severely understated figures on the strength of the party and the NPA, the Pentagon sounded the alarm in February 1984, when it informed the House of Representatives Subcommittee on Asia-Pacific Affairs that about one-fifth of the Philippines' 40,000 villages were influenced by an estimated 10,000 NPA regulars. "We do not know how many non-combatant NPA supporters there are among the Filipino people but NPA efforts to build more support in the countryside have been most impressive."

Surprised by the Pentagon's volte-face on the strength of the Philippine insurgency, the U.S. Senate Foreign Relations Committee sent its own team to investigate the situation in the summer of 1984. Titled *The Situation in the Philippines*, the Senate report painted a bleak prospect for U.S. policymakers. The insurgency, it asserted, kept growing despite the fact that it was receiving "little or no outside support." It was widespread: the NPA units operated in sixty-two of the country's seventy-three provinces and "challenge the AFP Forces of the Philippines] across the length and breadth of the Philippine archipelago." The authors could not conceal their respect, if not admiration, for the CPP-NPA when they discussed the reasons why the insurgency had reached this point. They attributed this to three principal factors: a brilliant military strategy, superior image-building, and an innovative organizational principle. The guerrillas' strategy of creating multiple guerrilla zones and bases throughout the Philippine archipelago instead of a few central base areas had devastating consequences for the Philippine Army, since it denied the latter the opportunity to mass its forces for concentrated attacks and stretched it to the breaking point by forcing it to cover many small guerrilla fronts in the country's nine major islands. The NPA's mass support among peasants was attributed, not mainly to terror, as in standard right-wing analysis, but to the fact that it "has carefully and effectively cultivated the image of being a 'Robin Hood.' So effective have they [the guerrillas] been, in fact, that many local people we talked to even used the term when describing the NPA's activities." But it is for the NPA's organizational principle of "centralized leadership and decentralized operations" that the writers reserved their highest—though understated—praise. This was not a movement that one could bait with the old anti-communist stereotype about politburos monopolizing decision-making, thinking and initiative. The power of the insurgents, the authors discovered, lay precisely in the fact that rank-and-file units were encouraged to think, decide, exercise initiative, and be creative while carrying out the thrust of the overall military and political program:

> Operating successfully requires a high order of discipline as well as individual initiative. . . Many we interviewed feel that this is one of the NPA's great achievements. They credit the NPA's national recruitment scheme for much of the success. It brings in both new intellectuals from the campuses and young people from areas under its influence, and tests them under battlefield conditions. The best of the new and old are then sent to expand the revolution into new areas.[19]

The U.S. Senate Foreign Relations staff and I were coming from opposite perspectives, they from a counterrevolutionary one, I from a revolutionary one. Yet we had the same conclusion: the Philippine left had become a powerful revolutionary force that constituted a mortal threat to the status quo.

For me, at that period of my life, theory, practice, and history were in synch and headed in a single direction towards one inevitable conclusion. Victory was the movement's destiny. I was under a hypnotic spell, and so were a great many of my contemporaries, and only in 1986, with the EDSA Uprising and its aftermath, were we able to snap out of it. It probably is not easy for either our parents' pro-American generation or our children, who lack an inspiring vision for their country's future, to grasp this experience that so galvanized my generation.

4. "Behind Enemy Lines"

USING THE TERM given to bastions of counterrevolutionary activity, Washington, DC, was a "white area"—indeed the whitest of areas since it was the nerve center of the U.S. empire. But it was different from white areas in the Philippines under the Marcos dictatorship, since it was the capital of a liberal democracy where free speech was respected, and a free press thrived. While activists could not underestimate the ability of the surveillance capabilities of the U.S. state, unlike in Manila, one could not just be arrested and clapped into jail or "disappeared." Due process was something the U.S. government had to pay attention to at home even as its military and police aid enabled Marcos to violate it at every turn.

Working in the U.S. meant you had to use freedom of speech and freedom of the press to erode the legitimacy of the Marcos dictatorship in the eyes of the American people and expose the complicity of the U.S. government in supporting a repressive regime. This made Washington as much a battlefield as the rural areas in the Philippines, though the main weapon to be deployed was different. The way the Vietnamese liberation forces waged their struggle on two fronts, militarily at home and by weakening support for the Vietnam War among the American people provided a model. The recipe for victory was winning on both fronts.

Raising the Dictator's Profile

Our problem in the 1970s and early 1980s was the relatively low profile of the Philippines in the consciousness of the American public. Marcos was seen as a bad guy, but the need to deal with him was low on the priorities of both the government and the people. The challenge was how to raise Marcos' profile as a bad guy and make Americans pressure their government to cut off the supply of weapons as well as the economic assistance that allowed him to stay in power.

In making U.S. support for Marcos controversial, we had to work mainly on Congress, since administrations from Richard Nixon to Ronald Reagan saw Marcos as a "strategic ally." Even Jimmy Carter, who made respect for human rights one dimension of his foreign policy, resisted efforts to cut aid to the dictator. But we also had to work on ordinary citizens to pressure their representatives in the capital to cut or reduce aid. So visible opposition on the ground was necessary to make them hear the message.

Protests were, of course, very important to maintain visibility, but since there were already protests and demonstrations across the U.S. on a wide range of causes, most of which could draw so many more people than an anti-Marcos demonstration or picket, we had to make sure the forms of protest we chose were high impact ones. Having led successful protests like the occupation of the Woodrow Wilson School at Princeton, I discovered I had a forte for innovative actions that attracted attention, especially that of the media. Three of these stand out in my memory.

Disrupting Imelda's Kennedy Center Attendance

The first involved Imelda Marcos, the First Lady, who came to attend a concert being given by her protégé, pianist Cecile Licad, at the Kennedy Center in Washington, DC. This was in November 1981. It was a most difficult time for us, with then President Ronald Reagan being solidly behind his friend, Ferdinand. We needed to do something to underline to Washington's political class that the opposition was alive and well in the Philippines. What better way to do this than by staging a political protest *inside* the John F Kennedy Center for the Performing Arts? Since there had never been a political protest within the sacred watering hole of America's culturati—indeed, probably no protest of significance *inside* a Washington, DC, venue for the arts since John Wilkes Booth assassinated Abraham Lincoln at the Ford Theater in April 1865—our action would surely attract attention.

So I, along with Jon Melegrito, Odette Taverna, Ric Polintan, and Pacita Bunag, dressed in our best outfits—mine being a worn tweed blazer—and paid for tickets that cost a fortune since we wanted the best seats from which to heckle Marcos. Banners calling for the downfall of the dictatorship were tucked under our coats as we made our way past the unsuspecting ushers to our seats. We wait until after the end of the first number, which, if my memory serves me right, was a piano concerto by Beethoven. The rest of the story was carried by the *Washington Post* the next day.

Angry demonstrators staged a brief demonstration in an aisle of the Kennedy Center Concert Hall last night, protesting the presence in the presidential box of Imelda Marcos, wife of Philippines President Ferdinand Marcos. She came to hear Philippine pianist Cecile Licad in her National Symphony debut.

The interruption occurred immediately after the opening number. Four young men and women rushed down the aisle, then turned and faced the box where Marcos was sitting next to pianist Van Cliburn. One of them shouted, "We have an unwelcome guest in the house!" after which the others began chanting, "Down with Marcos! Down with Marcos!"

Marcos remained seated throughout the episode. Several ushers quickly grabbed the protesters and wrestled them, still shouting, out of the hall. They were arrested and charged with disorderly conduct and released, according to U.S. Park Police.[20]

The Miss Piggy Protest

To gain media attention during those dark days, we had to experiment with different kinds of protest. "Protest-cum-comedy" became one of my specialties and one of my partners in crime was the late anti-Marcos fighter Charito Planas, who was in exile in the U.S. in the late '70s and early '80s.

Walden and Charito Planas—Ferdie the Sick Frog and Meldy the Piggy, respectively—stage the skit at the headquarters of the International Monetary Fund in Washington, D.C.
COURTESY OF *PHILIPPINE NEWS*

Among our most memorable skits was one where I dressed up as Kermit the Frog and Charito was costumed as Miss Piggy. This was sometime in 1982. Dropped off by a battered VW Beetle belonging to journalist John Kelly at the International Monetary Fund headquarters at 19th St and Pennsylvania Avenue NW in Washington, DC, Miss Piggy and I strutted regally to the receptionist and asked to see Jacques de Larosiere, the Managing Director, "to arrange for a loan to my bankrupt regime." Trying her best to maintain a straight face in the presence of two Sesame Street characters, the lady asked who we were, at which point I barked, "Can't you see I'm Ferdinand Marcos, president of the Philippines, with my wife Imelda."

By this time, a large crowd of IMF bureaucrats had gathered in the lobby, some bewildered, some in stitches, some urging the receptionist to let us in. The poor woman was in a quandary and a standoff ensued, until the Washington DC police arrived to spoil the fun and whisk poor Kermit and Miss Piggy off to the precinct.

The protest became legendary in activist circles, and ever since I've been associated with the Sesame Street character. Asked what made me dress up like a frog to stage such an unconventional protest, my ready answer was, "Desperate people do desperate things."

The National Press Club Protest

We never ran out of tricks to destabilize the Marcos regime and its agents and supporters in the U.S. For instance, I did not use the Kermit costume at a press conference we held when Marcos made a state visit in 1982, but I did something just as effective that also passed into anti-dictatorship lore. The jampacked audience at the National Press Club at 14th St Northwest in Washington, DC, was crawling with Marcos agents and supporters. I welcomed the audience in English, saying, "Thank you all for coming, especially our Filipino compatriots who are here with the presidential delegation." I then asked the audience's permission to translate my words of welcome in Tagalog and proceeded to say with a pleasant smile, *"Putang ina niyo, may araw rin kayo,"* or "You sons of bitches. We're gonna get you bastards soon." Oblivious to the linguistic exchange that was going on, the non-Filipinos in the mainly American audience later complimented me on how graciously I had welcomed the Marcos people, even as the latter stomped out of the room in thinly disguised anger.

Seizing the San Francisco Consulate

Civil disobedience was part of our repertoire. Acts of civil disobedience were not just meant to call attention to the dictatorship and U.S. support for it. We also saw them as "propaganda of the deed," acts that, by defying Marcos and the U.S., would instill courage in others in the Filipino community to step forward and publicly declare their opposition to the regime.

The boldest act of civil disobedience we carried out was the seizure of the Philippine Consulate in San Francisco to protest the rigged elections to the interim *Batasan Pambansa*, or National Assembly, on April 13, 1978.

I convinced six comrades—Deborah Kaufmann, Vee Hernandez, Steve Wake, Rev Lloyd Wake, Wilma Cadorna, and Sylvia Kimura—to join me in this action. Shortly before picketers arrived at the consulate at 447 Sutter Street, each of us sneaked separately into the building on the excuse that we were renewing our passports or seeking Philippine visas. We then ordered the staff and visitors, including the Consul General, to leave the premises. Surprisingly, they hurriedly complied, thinking we were armed. Once they were out, we shut the main entrance to the consulate on the fourth floor, then holed up in the Consul General's reception area and office, barring the door with a sofa and chairs. Then we waited.

The San Francisco police arrived an hour after we seized the place and, using a bullhorn, called on us through the locked door to surrender peacefully. We said we would not surrender but we were not armed. This exchange, during which we were informed of the various crimes we would be charged with—including resisting arrest, criminal trespass, and unlawful assembly—went on for about an hour. Meantime, more and more demonstrators were gathering on the sidewalk below, chanting "*Marcos, Hitler, Diktador, Tuta* [running dog]," the street was blocked off, and police car sirens were blaring.

The police gave us an ultimatum, saying that they would smash the door and arrest us in five minutes if we refused to give up. At that point, Deborah, Vee, Steve, Lloyd, Wilma, Sylvia, and I and I sat down on the floor of the Consul General's office and linked arms. True enough, the SWAT team came barging in. All I remember of the next few minutes was being forcibly separated from the others, pulled up with a baton under my jaw, handcuffed, dragged through the hallway and led down four flights of stairs, finally coming out of the building to a mix of cheers and the curses of the police. The *San Francisco Chronicle* reported that "Walden Bello ... was carried out by a policeman with a hammerlock on his neck."[21] We were booked at the closest police station, where we waited for hours until we were released on bail.

Two days later, when I went to the City College of San Francisco, to meet my students for the part-time course I was teaching on Philippine history, I was summoned to the office of the dean. The dean asked me what I had been doing when I was supposed to be holding classes on April 13. The action had been front-page news and televised, so there was no use beating around the bush. "Seizing the Philippine Consulate," I said. And where were the students I was supposed to be teaching that morning?, he asked. "I brought them to the demonstration," I answered. At that point, he told me I was out of a job for "endangering the welfare of our students." I had expected this but, having been dismissed from two jobs earlier in my life, I was unfazed, having accepted the reality that the price of activism included being deprived periodically of gainful employment.

Walden being dragged out of the Philippine Consulate in San Francisco after leading a nonviolent takeover to protest against the Marcos dictatorship.

The San Francisco protest was significant not only for its being the first and only time a Philippine consulate in the United States had been seized by anti-government protesters, but also for the trial and imprisonment that came after, in October 1978. After pleading not guilty and going through four tedious days of jury selection and cross-examination of witnesses, Judge Richard Figone found us guilty of criminal trespass and said he was giving us a suspended sentence.[22] At that point, the six of us stood up and I declared, "We are not recognizing the authority of this court," and proceeded to walk out. At that point, Figone angrily ordered the U.S. marshals to seize us and issued a new sentence of 45 days in jail.

Remanded to the San Francisco County Jail in San Bruno, I was strip-searched and provided the standard prison outfit of blue shirt and jeans, then brought to the minimum-security section of the jail. Steve and I shared a cell in the men's quarters, while Vee, Deborah, Wilma, and Sylvia were kept in the women's section. After two days, we declared our pre-arranged plan to go on a hunger strike until we were released.

The first three days of the hunger strike were the most difficult. By the fourth day, my body had adjusted, though I went through the day light-headed and in a haze. When we woke up each morning for the next few days, we found dozens of packets of orange juice stacked outside our cell that had been donated as an act of solidarity by some of the other inmates.

Daily, demonstrators from the Anti-Martial Law Coalition assembled outside the prison chanting slogans seeking our freedom. Rumors spread across the inmate population that "the revolutionaries are going to break in and let all of us out," as one inmate told me. Several more days passed, with me getting more and more light-headed each day. Then the warden told us we were being released. Success! Apparently, we later learned, he had reported to his higher-ups that the inmates were being made restless by our presence and the demonstrations outside, and he feared this could lead to disturbances unless we were released.

We regained our freedom after two weeks. Steve and I joyfully reunited with our women comrades outside prison walls to cheers of "*Marcos, Hitler, Diktador, Tuta*" from the welcoming crowd. Madge picked me up and, along with other friends, we headed towards 24th Street in San Francisco to get what I had been dreaming of those nights in jail: a giant *carnitas* burrito. God, it tasted so good! My digestive system, however, experienced a shock, and I was very sick for the next few days. Ever since then I cannot eat a *carnitas* burrito without conflicting feelings of extreme pleasure and great apprehension.

One of the things we in the United States were able to do better than people in the Philippines was to access and spread certain types of information about what was going on in the Philippines, where strict censorship prevailed, blocking out human rights violations and U.S. assistance and policy towards the Marcos regime. One of the first major contributions of vital information gathering was publication of the book *Logistics of Repression: The Role of U.S. Assistance in Consolidating the Martial Law Regime in the Philippines*, which I edited with Severina Rivera. The key articles in that collection that came out in 1977 detailed the yearly allocations of military grants and sales going to Manila as well as the different weapons and weapons systems. In the preface to the book, the eminent anti-imperialist scholar Daniel Boone Schirmer wrote: "How long will the people of the United States allow their government to throw its weight and U.S. taxpayers' dollars behind a one-man dictator who tramples on human rights—against those Filipinos who speak out for freedom? That is the question this book puts before us."[23]

How We Robbed the World Bank

There was, however, a big lacuna in the area of economic aid. The bilateral economic aid going to Marcos was relatively small, but that going via the World Bank was massive, an average of over $400 million a year in the mid- and late seventies. This meant that the U.S. was coursing most of its assistance via the World Bank, which it controlled. World Bank lending and activity in the Philippines, however, was relatively opaque. What were the programs being funded and set up? Were they related to counterinsurgency? What sort of development was being promoted? The only information that we got were sanitized press releases. We were stumped, and we finally decided that we had no choice but to get the information from within the bank itself.

At first, we slowly formed a network of informants within the Bank. These were acquaintances, liberals with a conscience. These people started to occasionally bring us some documents, but this was a tedious—although necessary—process. One World Bank officer, the late Edgardo Rodriguez, took great risks to smuggle out sensitive documents. Still, the information was not enough, so we thought that it was necessary to resort to more radical means. So, my associates and I investigated the patterns of behavior of Bank people, and we realized that there were some periods in the year when there was nobody in the Bank: Thanksgiving, Christmas, New Year, July 4, Memorial Day, etc. On those days and over a period of three years, we went to the Bank pretending that we were returning from a mission, unshaven, with our ties askew, and that we were just coming off the plane from Africa, India, etc. The security guards always asked for our ID's and when we pretended to fumble for them and as we looked so tired, they said "Ok, just enter." It always worked. It's hard to imagine today, but security was quite loose in those days.

Once we were inside, we were like kids let loose in a candy store. We took as many documents as we could—not only on the Philippines but on countries like Korea as well—and photocopied them using the Bank facilities. This happened over a period of three years!

There was one close call. While I was rifling through documents at the World Bank's office on the Philippines sometime in 1979, I heard the footsteps of someone coming towards the office. They stepped in front of the office, where the door was locked and the lights were out. I prepared to be discovered. My mind flashed to accounts of Gordon Liddy and his pals being discovered by a security guard at the Watergate years earlier. I was hurriedly preparing a story to explain my presence when I heard the footsteps receding from the door. Close call, but to show what bravado we had in those days, I stayed two more hours, taking and photocopying several hundred pages—our richest haul to date.

It was after a heist on Thanksgiving Day in November 1980 that we decided to call a halt to our expeditions. This was after we obtained the document, "Political and Administrative Bases for Economic Policy in the Philippines," which came to be known as the Ascher Memorandum after its author William Ascher, a World Bank consultant from Johns Hopkins University. The report warned that the Marcos regime was marked by increasing instability "which could result in the lifting of martial law under a parliamentary system in which President Marcos, even if initially situated as Prime Minister, would have serious difficulty remaining in power or a military government."[24] This was explosive. We released it first to my friend John Kelly's contact, Jerry Landauer of the *Wall Street Journal*, then to the wider U.S. press and to the underground in the Philippines. The exposé of the report led to a great strain in the relations between Marcos and the World Bank and was the first indication that things were not that good between the United States and the dictatorship.

The documents—ultimately coming to some 6000 pages on practically every Bank-supported project and program in the country—provided an unparalleled look at the workings of a close relationship between two non-transparent authoritarian institutions, the World Bank and the Marcos regime. They revealed World Bank President Robert McNamara's decision to make the Philippines a "country of concentration" to which the flow of Bank assistance would be greater than that to a developing country of a similar size and income level. They showed how the Bank successfully convinced Marcos and his technocrats to focus on industrializing for export markets instead of for the Philippines' domestic market on the grounds that the latter was too small, owing to great poverty and inequality.

But the documents also revealed contradictions between the Bank and Marcos. The Bank's technocratic, pro-market agenda eventually came into conflict with Marcos' predatory posture. The key issues, as the Bank saw it, were:

1) Agrarian reform. The Bank sought to create a class of smallholders that would serve as a conservative base against radicalization. Marcos resisted this since he did not want to alienate his base of local landed elites.

2) The effective implementation of export-led industrialization. Marcos, in the Bank's eyes, neglected this even as he dragged his feet in bringing down tariffs and dismantling quotas.

3) Marcos' cronies. The Bank wanted to disempower them since they were cornering and channeling to their monopolies the bulk of the massive credit from foreign banks being given to the regime—money that was enabled in great part by the seal of approval that the World Bank itself gave Marcos. Marcos, needless to say, wanted their preservation, whether due to personal regard or for political protection.

The World Bank papers showed how things came to a head in the early eighties, when in the midst of the global recession occasioned by the Third World debt crisis, the Bank imposed a technocrat-led cabinet headed by Cesar Virata in an effort to discipline the cronies. Equally important, the Virata cabinet was meant to supervise a new type of loan, one that was meant to bring decisive pro-market reform across all key sectors of the economy. This was termed structural adjustment. The Philippines was one of the five guinea pigs, the others being Turkey, Kenya, Turkey, and Bolivia.

And how could the papers not contain a reference to Imelda Marcos? Imelda, one World Bank officer told McNamara, "has identified herself with a few showcase projects, which we consider ineffective and which are a bit of a joke among knowledgeable Filipinos."[25]

To the embarrassment of both the Bank and the Marcos regime, we held press conferences to expose the juicy documents piece by piece, beginning in December 1980, with the explosive Ascher Memorandum vividly warning of brewing instability. Then eventually, we came out in 1982 with the book *Development Debacle: The World Bank in the Philippines.*[26] My co-authors were Elaine Elinson, David Kinley, Robin Broad, David O'Connor, and Vincent Bielski. I remember writing for four frenzied months in the winter of

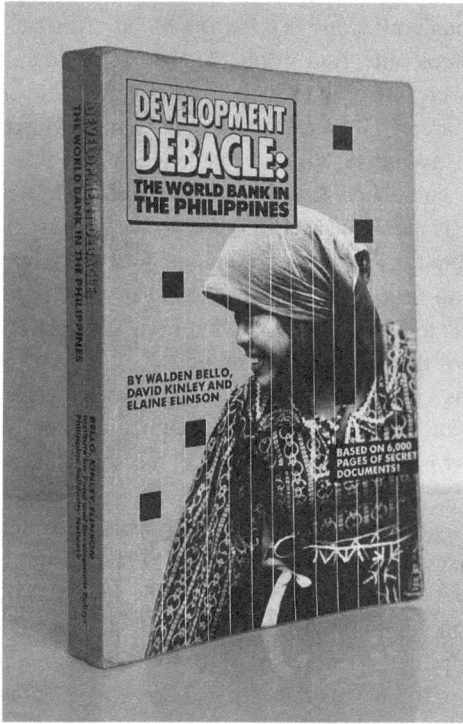

The book *Development Debacle,* based on thousands of pages of confidential documents stolen from the World Bank by Walden and his colleagues, became an underground bestseller in the Philippines and was said to have contributed to the downfall of the Marcos regime.

1981, hardly sleeping and subsisting mainly on coffee, cigarettes and Doritos, and napping at the office on Dupont Circle. That historic circle was marked by very busy traffic, and I recall praying every day that I would not be hit by a car until after I finished writing the book. This was the only time in my post-Christian life that I prayed, not to save me from hell but to make sure the book was finished, whether I ended up in heaven, hell, or in limbo.

The book was published in the U.S. by the Institute for Food and Development Policy, and its various editions eventually sold some 20,000 copies. Upon publication in the U.S., the book circulated in the underground press in the Philippines, becoming what the principal Philippine publisher, the late Joaquin Po, told me was most likely the biggest bestseller in the history of Philippine publishing. More important, the book, many told me, played a key role in the political education of the middle class, especially after they became an active political force in the aftermath of the assassination of Benigno Aquino, Jr, in 1983. When I returned to the Philippines in the late eighties, many people to whom I was introduced had two related reactions—that *Development Debacle* was central to "raising" their consciousness and that they had thought all along that I was a bloody American!

The book also called Marcos' attention to me. This had implications for my Ilocano parents, who were more than just friends of Marcos; my mom was distantly related to Marcos' mother, Dona Josefa Edralin Marcos, who sometimes paid a visit to my parents' island residence. According to my mother (who, incidentally, composed the "Ferdinand Marcos March" played at Marcos' inauguration as president in 1965), Marcos asked my dad if he could not do something about my being in the opposition. My parents had always known better than to try to tell me what to think, and he told Marcos, said my mother, that his telling me to stop what I was doing would do precisely the opposite. Marcos then dropped the matter.

Development Debacle was not just a political tract. It was a serious academic study, almost each sentence of which was documented from the purloined documents. But it was not simply the empirical material that was critical but the theoretical framework in which the facts were deployed. It was a flexible—some would say, syncretic—political economic paradigm that drew not only from Marxism but from Keynesianism, the structuralist theory associated with the great Argentine economist Raul Prebisch and the United Nations Commission for Latin America, the related school of "dependent development" exemplified in the work of Theotonio dos Santos and Fernando Henrique Cardoso, the work on the "fiscal crisis of the state" of James O'Connor, and the emerging "developmental state" approach pioneered by Chalmers Johnson. It was a paradigm I would later refine to understand the dynamics of the "newly industrializing countries" (NICs) of East Asia.

Development Debacle was the only comprehensive study of any country based purely on internal World Bank papers. The likely reason for the absence of other comprehensive country studies was the appearance of the book itself. Security was tightened considerably at the World Bank, so that every visitor had to be carefully cross-examined on what her or his business was, and the bank staffer being visited had to come down to meet the visitor. The story of what the Bank was doing in other countries was now locked away in its vaults.

We were not able to tell the real story about how we got the documents until 10 years afterward—in 1992—when the statute of limitations for criminal prosecution in the U.S. had lapsed. My associates and I could have gotten 25 years in jail had we been caught breaking into the Bank, though at that time, we would most likely have been released on parole after a few years. Nor did the Bank file charges of theft against us, probably worried that it could easily turn into a highly publicized trial that would not only indict its relationship with a repressive dictatorship and possibly lead to additional exposures—but also demonstrate to the countries of the world the laxity of the security of their data.

We were able to establish a network of sympathizers not only at the World Bank but at the U.S. State Department and at the Treasury. In the ten years the network was active and sending us confidential information, we only suffered one setback, and that was because of a lapse on my part. In 1987, long after *Development Debacle* had come out and a year after Marcos was overthrown, a sensitive confidential World Bank document reached me. I thought it was important enough to be shared with the press right away. So we held a press conference where we circulated the document. Unfortunately, we had in our haste failed to perform the usual thorough inspection of the document to make sure it did not have marks that would lead Bank security officers to trace who leaked it to us. The 12 copies that were circulated had, indeed, been marked, and when someone in the audience—probably sent by the Bank—sent his copy to Bank security, they easily traced it to the mid-level official that had provided the document to us and who had been one of our most fervent supporters.

He was immediately dismissed, being given no opportunity to be heard. He floated around for several years, finally getting into another international agency. He never talked to me again, and to this date I am haunted by my responsibility for his having been derailed from a promising career as an economist.

Reflections on Document Theft

Looking back at those years, one wonders if stealing or unauthorized access to confidential documents has become easier or harder. Today, much of this is done electronically by hacking into an agency's account. So nowadays, the process is more technologically sophisticated. In the 1970s and 1980s, a "prehistoric" period when the internet or even email did not yet exist, getting classified stuff was more labor intensive, and tracing leaks and leakers was a matter of tracking hard copy, as the Bank security did in the case of my contact. But being physical—like sneaking into a bank or an office like we and the Watergate burglars did—the process was much more risky and with greater negative consequences than when pursued digitally today, when one has many ways of covering up one's electronic tracks. Back in the day, if you were caught. then the game was up, *habent corpus tuum*. They got your body, buster!

But whether the means are physical or virtual, getting access to classified documents via electronic hacking or stealing them, the bigger issue is the relation between the law and the truth. The law may help bare the truth or hide it, and in the tension between the two, the activist's commitment must be to get at the truth, even at the price of breaking the law. Not surprisingly, I am an ardent supporter of Julian Assange and Edward Snowden. Addressing the issue of our breaking and entering the World Bank at the International Studies Association's Conference in San Francisco in 2008, when I was named the International Studies Association's Outstanding Public Intellectual, I said, "the decision we had to make was not easy. It is never easy to decide to break the law not only because of the penalties involved but because we all are so deeply socialized to follow the law. But we felt that we had no choice. Otherwise, the truth would have been buried for a long, long time."[27]

One of the more positive consequences of taking on the World Bank and writing *Development Debacle* was the forging of close personal, political, and academic ties with a number of progressive academics. Perhaps the most significant and lasting has been my relationship with the eminent wife and husband team of Robin Broad and John Cavanagh, with whom I have worked closely until today, not only on the Philippines but also in other areas, like the emergence of the newly industrializing countries and environmental rights.

International Solidarity Work for the National Democratic Front

My work with the CPP and the National Democratic Front was not limited to within the United States. It meant cooperating with other party units in other countries to further Marcos' international isolation. Perhaps the most ambitious international undertaking I participated in was the Permanent People's Tribunal (PPT) on the Marcos dictatorship that was held in Antwerp, Belgium in 1980. This was a joint venture between the NDF and the Moro National Liberation Front (MNLF) which saw me and Joel Rocamora, then head of the Southeast Asia Resource Center in Berkeley, fly to Antwerp, Belgium, to join activists from the Philippines to provide testimony on the human rights abuses and anti-democratic practices of the Marcos regime as well as Washington's escalating support for it. Coordinating the two-day introduction of the NDF to the world as government-in-waiting were seasoned activists Louie Jalandoni, Connie Ledesma, Brid Brennan, and Malu Padilla, all of whom were based in Utrecht, Netherlands, which served as the de facto headquarters of the movement's international arm. The Dutch allies they brought to Antwerp included solid supporters like Evert de Boer and

Thea Fierens, a charming comrade who later became a member of the Dutch Parliament for the Labor Party.

The PPT consolidated the NDF's ties with leading European and American luminaries, many of whom had become important political figures in the international resistance to the Vietnam War. Among them was Richard Falk, an international law expert from Princeton University who was becoming one of the world's leading advocates of an international order built on respect for human and environmental rights. Falk, who served as head of the panel of judges, had been introduced to the Philippine struggle when we invited him to be part of a human rights investigating mission to Manila in 1977, along with former U.S. Atty General Ramsey Clark, Peter Weiss, head of New York's Center for Constitutional Rights, and Don Luce of Clergy and Laity Concerned. That 1977 mission and the PPT served to solidify a decades-long commitment on his part to the cause of human rights and democracy in the Philippines. Nearing 90 years old in 2020, he nevertheless summoned up the energy to become one of the outspoken international advocates for the release of Senator Leila de Lima, who had been imprisoned on trumped-up charges by then President Rodrigo Duterte.

The PPT also marked the NDF's major international push to establish links with western and developing country governments as well as national liberation movements. It also marked the establishment of more direct control of solidarity activities and organizations by the NDF. A CPP-NDF team was sent to the U.S. to oversee this process beginning in 1981. With KDP engaged more and more in party building for socialist struggle in the U.S., asserting direct control of solidarity activities was seen as a necessity by the NDF. Though largely amicable, this process of separation from KDP and organizations allied with it like the Coalition against the Marcos Dictatorship (CAMD) was not without its tensions, especially since KDP insisted on the right to independently organize solidarity activities for the Philippines among its members and allies. By 1985, this process of separation and reorganization was largely completed, with the creation and consolidation of three major organizations with close ties to the NDF: the Alliance for Philippine Concerns (APC) that worked in the Filipino community, the Church Coalition for Human Rights in the Philippines that focused on lobbying in Congress, and the Philippine Solidarity Network (PSN), whose task was to build support in the broader U.S. public.

Then in 1986, the EDSA Uprising took place, shaking this carefully constructed network, as it did the entire CPP-NDF movement in the Philippines.

5. EDSA, or The Revolution Derailed

I MET Benigno ("Ninoy") Aquino, Jr., only once, and that was some-time in 1981 during his brief exile in the United States. Aquino was Marcos' main political rival, whom the dictator released from jail and allowed to go into exile in the U.S., thinking his stature as a symbol of opposition would be diminished if he was out of the country. I spent an afternoon talking to him in Washington, DC, but all I remember of our discussion is that he was mainly listening as I shared my views about the Reagan administration's policy towards the Philippines and the state of the anti-Marcos movement in the U.S. But one could feel his charisma and sense the combination of hatred for Marcos and great ambition burning within him.

"It's Aquino or Me"

Aquino's assassination by agents of the regime on August 21, 1983, however, affected me profoundly, both personally and politically. Having been separated and divorced from Madge, I was visiting Houston, Texas, with Lizzie J., my girlfriend at the time, spending time with her mother and father, who were likely to be my future in-laws. Her father was a high execu-tive in one of Texas' leading oil companies. After a lovely lobster dinner the second night, we were driving home when the news came on that Ninoy had been shot dead on the tarmac of the Manila International Airport. When we reached her parents' home, I told Lizzie that I was sorry to have to spoil our visit, but I had to rush to Washington, DC, in the morning because the world had turned upside down. She got very upset and said I had to choose between "Aquino and me." I chose Ninoy, and that was the end of our relationship. Lizzie was not being unreasonable. She had really prepared for months for this tryst with her parents, and all she was asking was to postpone my going to Washington for a week. It was not the last time that I would put my sense of political obligation over what was personally the right thing to do. In any case, I will never know whether Ninoy's unexpected death derailed me from a happy marriage or saved me from a bad one. I am certain one thing though: the lovely Lizzie was lucky.

The Manila Middle Class Enters the Scene

The political fallout from the Aquino assassination was, however, far more consequential than its impact on me. The killing shook the country's middle class into opposition, providing a base for the elite opposition. The Roxases, Osmeñas, Lopezes, and other families disenfranchised by Marcos were invigorated, and they began to distance themselves from the left, with which they previously had established active lines of communications owing to their desperation. Unlike in Chile, where the left that was in power was seen as the main threat to its interests, the middle class in the Philippines viewed the dictatorship as the principal enemy and joined with the traditional elite on a program of "democratization." The National Democratic Front and the network of political formations and civil society organizations allied with it were no longer seen as the only effective opposition to Marcos. A liberal mass opposition had spontaneously been triggered by Aquino's death, and within the next few months, it became a stronger force than the left.

The left responded cautiously to this new actor, joining forces with it in street mobilizations but unaccustomed to surrendering the leading role in these escalating protests. The Marcos regime was just as surprised as the left, and cracks began to show in the once formidable iron fist, with discontent beginning to simmer in the military and civilian elites that had previously exhibited unqualified loyalty to the dictator.

This also surprised Washington, but it adjusted to the new political configuration much quicker and more effectively than the left or Marcos. Being in Washington, with sources of information in Congress, State Department, and the Treasury Department, I was able to monitor the changes in the U.S. government's policy towards the Philippines though, like my comrades at home, I did not fully appreciate their implications. They certainly did not shake our conviction that the armed struggle or people's war would be the decisive force that would end the dictatorship. It was only after the EDSA Uprising in 1986 that I was able to piece together and write the only comprehensive, nuanced picture of the fluid interaction between U.S. policy and the post-Aquino assassination developments on the ground in the Philippines. I am retelling it here.

It was in late January 1985 that one of our contacts at the State Department sent me what turned out to be one of our most important intelligence coups: the National Security Strategy Directive on the Philippines (NSSD), which reached our hands shortly after it was adopted as policy.

Marcos as Part of the Solution

The essence of the NSSD was its now classic formulation:

> While President Marcos at this stage is part of the problem, he is
> also necessarily part of the solution. We need to be able to work
> with him and to try to influence him through a well-orchestrated
> policy of incentives and disincentives to set the stage for a peace-
> ful and eventual transition to a successor government.[28]

The NSSD revealed that "pragmatists" in Washington's national security establishment were getting impatient with President Ronald Reagan's
ideological approach towards Marcos—unwavering support simply because
of the latter's strong anti-communism. A loose "Inter-Agency Group" set up
after the Aquino assassination, I later learned, had moved to forge a common approach after Admiral William Crowe, Jr., chief of the U.S. Pacific
Command, came back from a visit to Manila with an alarming report on the
growth of the insurgency.

Should Marcos prove uncooperative, the NSSD recommended that
Washington "send signals that non-cooperation ... delayed disbursement of
funds, delayed program approvals, negative votes in multilateral forums"
would result, and that it "discreetly publicize the fact that cooperation is
not forthcoming on matters important to the welfare and security of the
Philippines," with the expectation that "these signals should increase pressure on Marcos from the public opposition, business leaders, and even his
close associates."[29]

At this stage, Washington's approach was one of "cueing in to initiatives pushed by the business class and the middle class," which were seen
as the "ultimate arbiter of the succession." Nor was the end the overthrow
of Marcos. Rather, it was to force him to share power.[30] "Ultimately," as
Undersecretary of State Michael Armacost was later to describe it, "our
role was one of helping Marcos reach the right conclusions from events and
developments."[31]

"Should Marcos prove uncooperative," the NSSD recommended that
Washington "send signals that non-cooperation" would delay "disbursement
of funds ... program approvals, negative votes in multilateral forums" and
"discreetly publicize the fact that cooperation is not forthcoming on matters
important to the welfare and security of the Philippines," with the expectation
that "these signals should increase pressure on Marcos from the public opposition, business leaders, and even his close associates." At a large inter-agency
gathering at the National Defense University in late July 1985, officials from

the State Department, Pentagon, and the intelligence agencies heard a panel recommend that "while the United States should not work for the overthrow of Marcos, it should take an open view about his removal from office."[32] It was around this time that the pragmatists came around to a consensus that Marcos had to be really pushed to hold "free and fair elections."

That was the message to Marcos that Senator Paul Laxalt brought to Manila in mid-October 1985, along with a toughly worded message from President Reagan that he stop "screwing up" the counterinsurgency effort. That was followed by an orchestrated outpouring of administration statements that sounded an apocalyptic note. Typical of this was the warning to Congress by Paul Wolfowitz, Assistant Secretary of State for East Asian and Pacific Affairs, that "time is running out, but time is not being used well." Only "dramatic action" would "turn back the tide of communist insurgency."[33]

Washington Pushes Marcos to Stage an Election

On November 3, in response to mounting pressure from Washington, Marcos dramatically announced on U.S. television that he had decided to hold presidential elections sooner than in 1987, when they had originally been scheduled. On November 6, on the occasion of a visit by Richard Holbrooke, the tough-talking former Assistant Security of State for East Asia, Philip Kaplan, Chargé d'Affaires at the U.S. Embassy, assembled key leaders of the anti-Marcos political parties and, according to a confidential Embassy cable,

> emphasized the need for the opposition to get its act together given the limited time left before the campaign starts, if the election is going to be held on January 17 or some date soon thereafter. He said the U.S. cannot get involved in the issue of the date of the election—this was something to be worked out in the Philippine political process. The charge emphasized that what we can do— and are doing—is to press for free and fair elections.[34]

The cable also revealed that "both the charge and Holbrooke ... underlined the importance of avoiding being portrayed as anti-bases or soft on communism. These postures would not play well in the United States."[35]

The State Department pragmatists had apparently come to the conclusion that an electoral victory by the elite opposition would be in the best interests of the United States. As early as February 1985, Ambassador Stephen Bosworth had cabled Washington:

If the opposition should succeed in uniting behind a single candidate, and that candidate should be elected president, what would be the overall impact on U.S.-RP relations? Based on our frequent contact with most of the opposition leaders, our judgment at this time is that the opposition could be expected to act responsibly and that the U.S.-RP relationship would prosper.[36]

The electoral campaign leading to the February 7, 1986, elections provided an arena for mobilizing Filipinos in support of the candidacy of Corazon Aquino, widow of Benigno Aquino, Jr. The U.S. strategy during the elections was, in the words of Michael Armacost, to "encourage the constraints" on Marcos by sending an observers' delegation from the U.S. Congress, encouraging western media coverage, and pressing Marcos to set up the legal framework for free elections.

U.S. funding of various opposition initiatives was less visible to the public. U.S. government funds, for instance, went to NAMFREL.[37] This reincarnation of the citizens' electoral watchdog body during the Magsaysay period was set up to neutralize Marcos' Commission on Elections. U.S. funds, Armacost later revealed, also went to the Catholic Church-run Radio Veritas via the Asia Foundation, a well-known conduit of Central Intelligence Agency and State Department money.[38]

Even the cautious Pentagon exerted its own forms of political pressure. Given the widespread expectation that Marcos would use the Armed Forces of the Philippines (AFP) to steal the elections, Richard Armitage, Assistant Secretary of Defense for International Security Affairs, appealed to the military to disobey Marcos if he used them to subvert the electoral process:

> The AFP would be faced with a supreme challenge during the electoral process. At stake would be nothing less than the credibility of the AFP and, in particular, the honor of its officer corps. The conduct of the Philippine military during this critical period would determine whether the AFP is, in fact, loyal to the Constitution and a true pillar of support for the democratic process, or whether the AFP is a more perverse entity, bent on a course which will accelerate the spiral of instability.[39]

The NDF's Fateful Decision

While the United States was actively intervening in favor of the opposition, the National Democratic Front acted out of character. Its non-doctrinaire, flexible, and innovative approach to political mobilization and organizing had been key to its rise in the previous 18 years. When Marcos called for snap elections, the NDF correctly saw that the U.S. was behind the strategy and that the goal was to deprive it of leadership of the anti-dictatorship movement. But after heated debate on the contention of some in its ranks that this particular election was different and that people were, in fact, taking it seriously as a means to oust Marcos, it then went on to cavalierly dismiss the elections as another "meaningless contest among reactionaries." The NDF leadership then made the fateful step of calling for a boycott of the elections, a move that elated the Americans. It was a major blunder. The key consequence was that the Left sat on the sidelines during the fast-moving developments that followed Marcos's fraudulently claiming "victory" in the February 7 elections.

The United States, however, nearly squandered this gift from the Left. In the critical period following Marcos's theft of the February 7 elections, Ronald Reagan, still undecided on Marcos's fate, hesitated, remarking that the elections had been marred by "fraud on both sides." This brought to a boil the frustration of State Department and CIA officials with Reagan and the ideologues around him. Veteran diplomat Philip Habib was sent on a last-ditch effort to set up a "power-sharing arrangement" between opposition candidate Corazon Aquino and Marcos, but events could no longer be contained within the State Department script of an eventual peaceful transfer of power to the elite opposition.

On February 22, Defense Minister Juan Ponce Enrile, AFP Chief of Staff Fidel Ramos, and the Reform the Armed Forces Movement (RAM) staged their mutiny with an initial strength of only 200 out of 250,000 troops, after their plans for a coup were discovered by Marcos. Thousands of civilians, mainly from the middle class, rushed to Camp Aguinaldo on EDSA (Epifanio de los Santos Avenue) to protect the vastly outnumbered rebels after hearing the plea of Cardinal Jaime Sin that was aired by the U.S.-financed Radio Veritas. Marcos was not, however, going to allow the civilians to stop his army from crushing the rebels and made preparations to move against them. He was prepared to shed blood. At that point, under pressure from the pragmatists of the national security establishment, Reagan finally relented and told his old, trusted ally to step down.

Shorn of the principal basis of his power—support from Washington— the hated dictator had no choice. The Americans stepped into the power vacuum. On February 25, under cover of darkness, the shell-shocked Marcos and his entourage were ferried by U.S. helicopters to Clark Air Base and from there to exile in Hawaii. "We played a constructive role in getting him out of the country," Undersecretary of State Armacost recounted frankly later on: "He wanted to go North [Marcos's stronghold in Ilocos Norte], but this would have provoked civil war since there were elements in the military still loyal to him."[40]

The State Department and CIA pragmatists breathed a sigh of relief that Reagan, due to their pressure, had finally cut his buddy loose. But it was a near thing. As William Sullivan, a former envoy to Manila, put it, they had "saved the Reagan administration from its own worst instincts and stopped it from snatching defeat from the jaws of victory."[41]

EDSA: "Off-script but OK"

Washington's aim had been to derail the Left with an electoral strategy that would eventually transfer power peacefully from Marcos to the opposition. The plan went somewhat off-script with the EDSA Uprising, but in the view of its authors, that was a good thing. Yet, the EDSA event would have been for naught had Reagan, warned that blood would be on his hands if he continued to stand by Marcos, not acceded to the pragmatists' pressure.

To John Monjo, one of the State Department's team that orchestrated things on the ground, "the coming to power of the Aquino government constitutes a setback for the insurgency because . . . [the] principal propaganda target of the communists, the Marcos regime, is gone."[42] Michael Armacost, Monjo's higher up, for his part, boasted in a speech before a packed crowd of foreign service officers eager to listen to one of Washington's major foreign policy successes in years: "Our objective was to capture . . . to encourage the democratic forces of the center, then consolidate control by the middle and also win away the soft support of the NPA. So far, so good."[43]

Armacost thought he was in a session that was supposed to be off-the-record. I had been mistakenly invited to the session and, bound by no such rules, I was happy to record all his damning remarks.

EDSA's Impact in the U.S.

Reflecting developments in the Philippines, the Filipino community in the United States was in a state of constant excitement and movement since the Aquino assassination. As in the Philippines, the elite opposition represented by the Movement for a Free Philippines was reinvigorated and it threw itself behind Corazon Aquino's candidacy with gusto when Marcos announced the holding of snap elections. The KDP also supported Aquino's candidacy as an important event that could lead to a drastic weakening of the Marcos regime, if not its demise. In contrast, along with the NDF and its allied formations, I upheld the boycott position, my mind telling me in good

Leninist fashion that there was no way the U.S. would abandon a dictatorship that protected its interests while my instincts were nonetheless in turmoil as I observed Washington's increasingly fluid responses to the developing situation. There was a good chance Washington would eventually force a Marcos-opposition compromise or joint rule—but would it allow Marcos to go under? Heck no!

What we in the NDF did not take into consideration or underestimated were the intervention of the middle class on the ground, the strong institutional influence of the Church, and the splits in the Marcos camp. Neither did the U.S. initially, but it adjusted quickly and skillfully so that, in ordering Marcos not to fire on the people gathered at EDSA and ferrying him out of Malacanang Palace to Hawaii, it identified itself with the forces of liberal democratic restoration. In contrast, the Left was left out in the cold.

Taking Over the Embassy...for the New Government

When the smoke cleared on Feb 25, 1986, for me the facts on the ground were that there has been a successful uprising. With Manila being 12 hours ahead of Washington, DC, at 6 am, as Marcos was being flown out to Hawaii, I shelved my doubts about the elections and rushed to the Philippine Embassy on Massachusetts Avenue along with John Cavanagh. Whatever my feelings were about the events in Manila, no one was going to rob me of the opportunity to possess the object of my greatest desire. The two of us took possession of the building, ordering the stunned and dejected staff to leave the place. They complied and filed out peacefully. Unlike my seizure of the Philippine Consulate in San Francisco in 1978, the police did not come to eject us, though some plainclothes Americans tried to stop other people from joining those of us already celebrating with champagne and cigars in the Ambassador's office. But the crowd was irresistible. Totoy and Elsie Castrence, the generous hosts of our Washington Forum meetings over the years, Dante Simbulan, Doug Cunningham, and Becky Asedillo of the Church Coalition for Human Rights in the Philippines, World Bank executive Gadoy Rodriguez, journalist John Kelly, Jon Melegrito and Odette Taverna of the Coalition against the Marcos Dictatorship, Corinne Canlas, Rene Nachura, Pancho Lara, and so many others that I had worked with for years to bring down the dictatorship, filtered in as the day wore on. At around 3 pm, I met the official representative of the new government, Sonny Alvarez, and turned over the Embassy to his care.

The *New York Times* recorded the day's events:

"As a representative of the Filipino opposition and in the name of the Filipino people—we are taking over this Embassy," shouted Walden Bello, a professor who has been exiled from his homeland for 13 years.

Mr. Bello said the crowd was quickly pushed out of the building by American Secret Service agents who said that President Ferdinand E. Marcos had not yet given up.

An hour later, the doors swung open again—and this time they would not close. President Marcos had left the Philippines and the exiles here who have been lobbying Congress and the White House for years began thinking about their return home.

Charito Planas, who said she was imprisoned in 1977 for 14 months, came back to the embassy because it was a way of celebrating on Philippine territory. Just six months ago, Miss Planas and Mr. Bello had been arrested for protesting in front of the embassy.

But today they were part of a crowd that assembled in the office of Ambassador Benjamin T. Romualdez for a champagne toast. The ambassador was said to have left the United States about a week ago.

As the day wore on at the embassy, the curious came to see for themselves the visible symbol of power changing hands. Filipinos shyly walked into the foyer and looked, wide-eyed, at the inside of the building, looking up at the rectangular blank spots on the walls where portraits of President Marcos had been.

Inside was scattered the detritus of a regime in collapse. On the floor of the ambassador's office, a pile of shredded paper was spread next to the shredder. Embassy officials apparently did not have time to throw it away.[44]

Mixed Feelings, Beer, and a Whisper

Yet as I went home to my room at the house on Kilbourne Place Northwest that I shared with four wonderful comrades working in solidarity organizations for progressive movements in Latin America—Jeannie Walsh, Martha Tannenbaum, Mary Anne Buckley, and Cathy Sunshine—I had very mixed feelings, indeed, a heavy heart, about the events of the last 24 hours. On the one hand, I felt relieved Marcos was gone. On the other hand, I was deeply disturbed that my fears had come to pass. As in the 1950s, when Col Edward Lansdale, the CIA's man in Manila, had outmaneuvered the old Communist Party (PKP) in its bid for power, Washington had played a decisive role in bringing about a liberal democratic restoration that I felt deep in my gut would again derail the Left.

I would piece the full story of the successful U.S. intervention afterwards. That evening all I had were questions. Where did we go wrong? Would we be able to recover?

Could we have adopted a different strategy than boycotting the elections and emerged on our feet? I was not in a position to know then, being in the U.S., but in the aftermath of the elections, many party units, observing the massive ferment on the ground, had urged the party leadership to join the insurrection in EDSA instead of rigidly sticking to its stand that the U.S. would not abandon Marcos. Had it done so, it could rightly have claimed to be part of the movement that ousted the dictator and placed it in an advantageous position to influence the composition of the Corazon Aquino government and the direction of the post-EDSA period.

But these were "ifs" that dawned on me much later as I learned about the conditions on the ground in Manila during the days of the uprising. That evening after our seizing the embassy in Washington, DC, all I wanted was to drown my contradictory feelings. I grabbed a bottle of beer from the fridge and fell asleep on the couch with the lights on. I was gently awakened by a woman's touch, I don't remember whose, and a voice that whispered in my ear, "Congratulations."

6. The Movement Disarmed

THE SHOCK to the NDF that the February uprising had delivered wore off slowly. It was inevitable that the shattering of its basic assumption that the U.S. would not allow Marcos to be dislodged would trigger an internal debate on such issues as whether a more open, "parliamentary struggle" had now to be prioritized over the armed struggle, and on what kind of armed struggle, if not—did it mean a continuation of a protracted people's war strategy of surrounding the city from the countryside or initiating a Nicaragua-style insurrection centered in the urban areas? After years of operating on a tight leash, it was inevitable that there would be a degree of political and organizational loosening in the National Democratic movement.

The new liberal democratic regime had a contradictory character. It was certainly open and democratic, but the military took advantage of its legitimacy to repress the Left, which could no longer depend on the liberal elite and the middle class to defend it. One of the leading lights of the Left, the young, charismatic Lean Alejandro, was ambushed and killed, the CPP was destabilized by successive captures of its top people and their replacements, and paramilitary groups were set up to neutralize NPA expansion operations.

The NDF network in the U.S. remained in place, but it was inevitable that, as in the Philippines, the same organizational and political liberalization would set in after years of tight discipline. I set about building a new family with a new partner, the outwardly collected but inwardly incandescent Marilen Abesamis, who had been sent over by the party in the early eighties. This meant I now had to abandon the activist lifestyle of self-imposed poverty and take on a steady job.

Fortunately, my having done a lot of writing even while being a full-time activist, and especially the reputation that came with the publication of *Development Debacle*, made it relatively easy to land a research and analysis job at the San Francisco-based Institute for Food and Development Policy, also known as Food First, that had been founded by the prominent anti-hunger scholars Frances Moore Lappe and Joe Collins. For the first time in 13 years, I had a full-time job! At Food First, I began to catch up on economic and political development issues in the rest of the world. The Philippines, however, remained a central concern of mine in the late eighties and early 1990s.

Coming to Grips with Liberal Democracy

My thinking was shaken loose from its theoretical and political cage by the boycott debacle, as was my unqualified submission to the party's authority. As in the Philippines, the event had triggered a "let a hundred flowers bloom" atmosphere among activists in the U.S. that could not be contained by the organizational principle of democratic centralism. The theoretical and political direction of my thinking was reflected in an assessment of the six years of the Corazon Aquino presidency of which I was the principal author that was presented at the Forum for Philippine Alternatives conference in the Bay Area in 1993. It was based on observations on trips to the Philippines I made in 1988 and 1989 and on my permanent return there in the early nineties

Essentially, I wrote, what transpired during Corazon Aquino's six years was that the Philippine elite had abandoned the "exceptional state"—the Marcos dictatorship—and returned to what was actually its traditional form of rule: formal democracy. During the American colonial era, the U.S. had introduced liberal democracy as a mode of governance. Most of the elite readily assimilated it because it provided them with a means of peacefully competing for political power while uniting them against radical efforts from below to change the political and social structure. Marcos had sought to monopolize power in his faction of the elite, which turned significant sections of the ruling class against him and his cronies. In a very real sense, therefore, the post-EDSA system was the restoration of a regime inherited from the U.S.

The process of restoration took six years and could only be said to have been completed with the passage of electorally legitimized presidential authority from Corazon Aquino to Fidel Ramos in 1992.

What were the principal features of the restored liberal democratic regime?

Tentatively, I asserted that firstly, power had been demonopolized and dispersed among many factions of the elite. The accumulation of power and authority by the central state bureaucracy characteristic of the Marcos era had been reversed, with much power and authority devolving first to Congress, then, under the slogan of "decentralization," to regional and local government units controlled by regional elites. Even the Philippine military's centralized control over the use of force that it had enjoyed under Marcos in the seventies and eighties had diminished, with the reemergence of huge private armies and the growing effective control over local units of the Armed Forces of the Philippine by local warlords.

Second, the central mechanism for determining who ruled was the electoral struggle, which provided different factions of the elite the opportunity to succeed one another in office in a relatively non-violent way.

Third, the glue of the system was the exercise of "cultural or ideological hegemony," that produced the consent of the governed, and that was elicited and constantly reproduced via mass participation in periodic elections, where citizens did choose their representatives, but for the most part from opposing factions of the elite. Cultural hegemony was the missing element in Sison's analysis, which in orthodox Marxist fashion saw the system as cohering only owing to coercion by the state. Liberal democracy, introduced by the Americans after pacifying the country at the turn of the 20th century, was a powerful ideological-political antidote to class antagonism.

Nonetheless, this hegemony was reinforced by the fact that the elite's control over economic resources in a system in which running for even the lowest municipal office was an expensive affair ensured that most of those who contested political office would come only from the ranks of the elite or middle-class politicians beholden to the elite. It also gave the elites the ability to secure the consent of the government through vote-buying that made a furious comeback in the immediate post-EDSA years.

Finally, the exercise of force continued to be an important mechanism to assure the stability of the system, but it was systematically deployed as the principal instrument of rule only when the support for the government had largely evaporated.

Trapped in the Net

The dynamics of liberal democracy were very different from authoritarianism as a form of regime, but unfortunately, the CPP-NDF continued to act in the same old way. Imagining the enemy to be essentially the old dictatorship albeit with a democratic mask, it fell back on what it regarded as the tried and tested formula: tight, centralized, hierarchical organizing, with a focus on intensifying the armed struggle, with a significant part of the leadership opting for an urban insurrection in place of the old strategy of "protracted people's war." Both approaches were, however, equally questionable in the new circumstances, and I likened them to "a battering crew trying to ram what they perceive to be a wooden gate, only for the gate to open as they rush in, straight into an elastic net that ensnares them."

Many activists I worked with, among them Joel Rocamora, Francisco Nemenzo, and Ronald Llamas, had similar ideas, though they might have expressed them in slightly different ways. Certainly, I was greatly influenced in my assessment of the new situation by the work of the Italian Marxist

Antonio Gramsci, especially his emphasis on ideological hegemony, and the structuralist Marxist, Nicos Poulantzas.

The Purge

But it was not only the political paradigm of the CPP-NPA that forced me to rethink my own commitment to it. Equally if not more important was a grim development whose full scale would only emerge in dribbles throughout the late 1980s: the internal party purges that came to be called collectively "*Kampanyang Ahos*" or Operation Garlic. Aimed at ferreting out people suspected as "deep penetration" military agents (DPAs), *Ahos* apparently ran out of control and resulted in the execution of several thousand party cadres. The CPP eventually called the campaign "madness," and this was not surprising since it took the lives of some of the party's most seasoned operators.

Massive purges, as opposed to leadership purges such as those undertaken by the Chinese Communist Party before it won the civil war, usually take place after a movement seizes power. What was strange about *Ahos* was it happened *before* it came to power. In an effort to get at the causes of this inexplicable tragedy, I carried out in-depth interviews in Manila sometime in 1990 with officials or ex-officials of the CPP National Commissions, the NPA General Command, and the NDF national leadership. But the key interviews were made with lower-level party cadres who had participated in the purges, either as victims or executioners. A major factor, it seemed, was paranoia that took on a life of its own, as deaths, loss of territories, and battlefield defeats were attributed to the work of hundreds of agents within the ranks. I got a sense of how out of control it became when interviewing one young activist who was intimately involved in the campaign in a region in Mindanao. I wrote up her account thus:

> At first, she was recruited mainly to be one of the recording secretaries.
>
> Then, step by step, she became a judge as the head of the committee began to regularly consult her on the guilt or innocence of the people being arrested, most of whom she knew. At this point, she said that she gave a guilty verdict not only because she felt they were guilty but also because she felt that the campaign committee head *wanted* her to say they were guilty, and she could not afford not to do so for fear of her own security. Soon she was being asked to participate in torturing people during the interrogation, and she felt compelled to hit the victims for fear that had she refused, the finger of accusation would be pointed at her. Paranoia

became normal, the number of victims mounted, and she became resigned to eventually becoming a victim herself.[45]

The campaign had run out of everyone's control even as everyone felt compelled at the same time to fuel it, and it was not surprising that it ended, like the French Revolution's Reign of Terror, with the party member most responsible for the executions—the head of the campaign committee—himself being executed. She survived, but was scarred for life.

In the report I wrote, which was the first empirical investigation of the *Ahos* campaign, I reported that there was no evidence of a devilishly successful government plot to insert hundreds of secret agents into the party and the NPA. A large part of its response was paranoia, though paranoia by itself was not a sufficient explanation.[46] It could have been contained but for three factors. One was Marxism's very instrumental view of people, that is, its lack of a developed concept of individual rights; in other words, it saw individuals as having rights only by virtue of their membership in the right classes, or, failing that, their holding the right politics. Thus, if an individual is suspected or judged to be a "class enemy," he or she does not have an innate right to life, liberty, and respect, and what happens to her depends purely on the tactical needs of the moment. A second, related factor was the absence of institutions for the dispensation of justice in the CPP or NPA, which led to ad hoc committees being formed and arbitrary rules being adopted. The third, I said, was not to underestimated: this was the lack of "guidelines for the preservation of common sense"—common sense which would tell you that it would be endowing the AFP with superhuman powers to think that over a number of years, "it could infiltrate hundreds of people within the revolutionary movement who would not reveal themselves but behave day-to-day as earnest revolutionaries, who were so good that they fooled their wives, children, and closest friends."[47]

The report, which was eventually published in the journal *Kasarinlan*, was an honest-to-goodness effort to introduce reforms to an organization to which I still belonged. In retrospect, I was perhaps naïve, but in the fluid situation within the movement in the late eighties, one could probably not be faulted for optimism.

My investigation of *Ahos* left a very strong imprint on me. Growing up, I really had not given much thought to the rights of the individual, perhaps because they were not the focus of the Catholic ethical education that I received, which emphasized the individual's duties to god, not one's rights. The privileged place of individual rights that would have been the ethical cornerstone of a secular liberal education in France or the United

States, reflecting the centrality of the liberal democratic revolution in these countries' historical development, was not something I had been exposed to. The humanist existentialism that I adopted when I broke with the Church did make the individual subject the source of value, but still in an abstract, philosophical sense.

Thus, when I became a Marxist, it was quite simple to glide to the perspective of class rights reigning supreme over individual rights, which were dismissed as "bourgeois" and were mainly to be invoked as a propaganda weapon against the dictatorship. All the time I was with the Communist Party, had I been ordered to commit an act that violated someone's right to life or other rights, I would have received this as a political decision, something to be judged mainly in terms of its political efficacy. Did it or did it not advance the revolution? Would it not simply play into the hands of the authorities, thus delaying the triumph of the cause? For me and the cadres, those were the critical questions.

Ahos was a rude shock. Being confronted with the sheer scale of the purges of people being regarded as "counterrevolutionaries" and therefore stripped of class rights or reduced to beings with no human rights bludgeoned me into an ethical crisis, eventually pushing me to the position that individuals had rights beyond class rights and they derived this from their being simply human beings and were not gifts bestowed on them by the party or by a supernatural being. I had the sense of having fortunately escaped being in the position of being an executioner sitting in judgment of his peers in those blood-soaked fields. Even more damning, I knew I would have acted in the same way as they had. As I contemplated the executioners and victims of the *Ahos* campaign, it dawned on me: there, but for the grace of God, go I.

The final count of cadres executed was around 2,000. This contributed to party membership falling abruptly from 9000 to 3000. In his assessment of the overall situation of the revolutionary forces after *Ahos*, Joma Sison said that "the resultant devastation was unprecedented in the entire history of the Philippine revolution. Never has the enemy inflicted so much damage to the revolutionary forces in so short a period of time."[48] He connected the *Ahos* killings to the election boycott error and the wrong political line that he claimed was operative even before the debacle, that is, the substitution of an insurrectionary strategy for that of protracted people's war. In his view, this combination produced "setbacks that were already clear in 1984 and then in self-destruction from 1984 onward.... They wrought destruction at a rate and in absolute numbers the enemy had never before achieved frontally in so short a time."[49] By the early 1990s, the movement's rural mass base had been reduced by 40 percent relative to its size in 1986. Who were to blame? Forces who had seized the leadership of the CPP while they and others who adhered to the "right line" were in jail.

"Reaffirm" and the Great Split

In December 1991, from Utrecht in the Netherlands, where he had taken refuge during the Aquino years, and writing under the pseudonym Armando Liwanag, Sison issued his analysis of the state of the movement since the EDSA Uprising. Titled "Reaffirm Our Basic Principles and Rectify Errors," the document hit the Left like a sledgehammer. In that document, while acknowledging the above-indicated factors, he ultimately attributed the crisis of the movement to a leadership that had "deviated" from Marxism-Leninism. "Reaffirm," as it came to be called, cut short the "let a hundred flowers bloom" atmosphere of the late eighties and initiated a vicious split between "reaffirmists" and "rejectionists" which, after 30 years, has not been healed. Instead of reinvigorating the Left, this debate took it further downhill to marginalization from the mainstream of politics.

Like his previous writings, "Reaffirm ..." was comprehensive and well argued, showing flashes of Sison's old brilliance. It was convincing, that is, if your mind was still confined within the Marxist-Leninist paradigm that he had fleshed out over the previous 20 years and was not given pause by the movement's recent self-immolation. With most party and NDF cadres operating still largely within that framework, it was not a surprise that "Reaffirm" was welcomed by the majority as putting an end to the confusion and drift in the ranks triggered by EDSA and its aftermath. By 1990, however, I had largely abandoned that paradigm, forced out by political realities that it could not explain. Gramsci's emphasis on the role of ideological or cultural hegemony in the production of mass consent had shaken me loose from the Leninist focus on the role of coercion as the basis of class rule. "Reaffirm" saw ideology largely in instrumental terms, as a process of manipulation, whereas it was really something that the masses themselves participated in reproducing through their willing participation in elections and other liberal democratic processes. Coercion certainly was important as instrument of rule, but it was secondary to securing hegemony, as demonstrated by the effectiveness of liberal democracy.

Moving on

After playing an active role in the debate in the late eighties, principally in the U.S., I began to move to other concerns than the line of struggle in the Philippines, feeling nothing good could come from a struggle that was beginning to take the form of fratricide. To be honest, I was getting frustrated by the internal crisis that had the Philippine Left in its grip. I had begun to view international developments outside of just a Philippine lens. My being at Food First had afforded me the chance to familiarize myself with the Bretton Woods multilateral system, structural adjustment programs throughout the Global South, the emergence of the newly industrializing countries, and corporate-driven globalization, which was then taking off. It was liberating to see the world beyond the Philippines. I felt like I was returning to an internationalist side that had been neglected since my PhD work on Chile.

I could not, however, escape monitoring the vortex of the debate even as I retreated from active participation in it. My views on the role of the elite's reassertion of ideological hegemony via liberal democracy were attacked as a "Gorbachevite" deviation. My comments on Marxism's lack of appreciation for individual rights were seen as coming from a "bourgeois" standpoint. I was in the process of being classified as a counterrevolutionary and class enemy, but the full force of the Reaffirmist attack on me would not come till the mid-2000s, triggered by my reaction to a "diagram" that came out in the CPP's theoretical journal, *Ang Bayan*. That is, however, an episode that we'll come to in Chapter 15.

I left the party sometime in 1989 or 1990. Unlike my recruitment in 1974, my departure from the party was marked by no ritual. It came as an almost natural outcome of a prolonged process of alienation that began with the EDSA Uprising and was accelerated by my investigation of the *Ahos* purge. But frustration combined with sadness since the party had been, after all, my political family for 15 years, where I had cut my political teeth, where comrades were not only comrades but friends, sometimes partners.

That said, my departure was not the end of my deep engagement with revolutionary change. I simply entered a new phase.

Looking Back

My participation in the National Democratic Movement and the Communist Party of the Philippines from the early 1970s to the late 1980s was the high point of my political life. It was all-consuming. It was a time when I was willing to give up my life for a cause had the opportunity presented itself. It was an experience, a high, that would never be recaptured. Fighting the dictatorship under an organization that demanded all from us was the romance of my generation, one that is not easy to communicate either to those who came before us or those who have come after.

It is an experience that fills me with nostalgia. It remains memorable despite its having been banished post-EDSA by the cold facts of analysis and history. And what are these?

First of all, Jose Maria Sison's *Philippine Society and Revolution* and earlier writings did have their flaws, many of which were recognized in retrospect. Their main appeal was in their providing what seemed to be a comprehensive political and theoretical paradigm for a generation that was waiting for something like it.

Second, the birth of the National Democratic Revolution and the imposition of the Marcos dictatorship had triggered a Newtonian reaction, as the re-founded Communist Party of the Philippines offered an organizational framework that was able to harness the anti-dictatorship energies of Philippine youth.

Third, because of its focus on the armed struggle, its fixation on the Maoist strategy of surrounding the city from the countryside, and its rigid conviction that the U.S. would never abandon Marcos, the Left was derailed and disarmed by the return of the ideology and practice of elite democratic politics, a process that was cleverly supported by the pragmatists in the Washington foreign policy establishment.

Fourth, instead of recognizing the new conditions of struggle and making a bootstrap effort to recover from its decision to boycott the 1986 elections, the Communist Party of the Philippines/National Democratic Front/New People's Army (CPP-NDF-NPA) bloc "reaffirmed," under Sison's leadership, the old Maoist strategy, with disastrous consequences.

Fifth, while the CPP-NDF-NPA did engage electorally, its practice was unfortunately fatally compromised by sectarianism that led it to regard other sectors of the Left that it could have allied with as "counterrevolutionaries," in the worst Stalinist fashion. Name-calling and shrill rhetoric magnified by the bullhorn became the order of the day, with critics like me invariably tagged as "CIA agents" whose public appearances were subjected to disruption.

Sixth, there was no real change in the internal party institutions of administering justice after the devastating *Ahos* purge, with the reaffirmed leadership simply blaming some former party leaders of "deviations," an outcome that was personally disappointing since I had invested much effort and time in doing a personal investigation of the causes and processes of the tragic event and coming out with concrete recommendations to prevent their repetition.

Finally, there was little appreciation of the need to theoretically and politically re-envision the Left and the socialist project in the post-1989 era. The party and its subordinate organizations were caught in a time warp, frozen in the thinking and practices of the late sixties and seventies. Its view of the political economy of the country, for instance, continued to be that of a semi-feudal, semi-colonial society, whereas the rapid expansion and penetration of capitalist relations even before the Marcos era made it more like the dependent capitalist formations of Latin America that thinkers like Theotonio dos Santos, Francisco Henrique Cardoso, and Andre Gunder Frank wrote about.

The evolution of the CPP from promise to demise paralleled my personal political transformation from a relatively uncritical partisan of the revolution to a critical revolutionary subject. In retrospect, I would say that there have been four phases to my life as an engaged intellectual. There was my existentialist phase during my college years, where existentialism became the vehicle of a secular revolt as an individual against religious mysticism. Then, when I was at Princeton and in Chile, I became a Marxist and activist, but one who thought and worked independently, not as part of an organization. Then came those 15 years, 1974–89, when my subjectivity was totally submerged in the collectivity, the Communist Party of the Philippines, where I was unconditionally and uncritically obedient to central party decisions— yes, in the stereotyped manner of a party member governed by democratic centralism.

My departure from the party in 1989–90 marked the emergence of a critical subjectivity in relation to the collective that was paralleled by a philosophical and political valuation of the rights of the individual vis-a-vis the bigger movement even as I recognized their complementary relationship. It did not mean a relapse into the independence of the engaged intellectual, but the adoption of a more critical stance towards a revolutionary organization even as one recognized and prized the latter's indispensability. I am in this fourth phase today—part of a movement, part of progressive organizations at various times, but not uncritically so.

7. Becoming an International Activist

MY ANALYTICAL and political work on the Philippines during the Marcos regime engendered a profound interest in three geopolitical issues whose scope went beyond the Philippines: the relationship between U.S. policy and forms of political regime in the Global South, the structure and dynamics of the U.S. empire, and the institutions and workings of late 20th century global capitalism. Even as the focus of my political work remained the Philippines, my analytical work and writings went beyond it. Ever since my PhD, where I compared counterrevolutions in Chile, Italy, and Germany, my mind had a strong inclination towards comparative analysis—and indeed, towards uncovering what had been done wrong by the movements they crushed.

A Comparative Perspective on Empire

Beginning with a long essay titled "Elite Democracy and Authoritarian Rule" that I wrote in 1983, I explored the changes in U.S. policy towards countries in the Global South, focusing initially on the question of what accounted for Washington's increasing preference for authoritarian regimes over liberal democratic governments in the 1970s and 1980s. This was especially evident during the administration of Ronald Reagan, where it was promoted as the "Kirkpatrick Doctrine," after Reagan's ambassador to the United Nations Jeane Kirkpatrick, who famously argued that "the fabric of authority unravels quickly when the power and status of the man at the top are undermined or eliminated. The longer the autocrat has held power, and the more pervasive his personal influence, the more dependent a nation's institutions will be on him. Without him, the organized life of the society will collapse, like an arch from which the keystone has been removed."[50]

Washington was an ideal place to explore these ideas in the early 1980s, and especially critical was the Institute for Policy Studies, which I was invited to join as a research associate by John Cavanagh. IPS hosted many researchers doing work on Reagan's foreign policy and the Kirkpatrick Doctrine and discussion with them helped me discern the similarities between

U.S. policy in the Philippines and other countries, particularly in Latin America. The process was not, however, divorced from activism since I was also absorbing insights from activists involved in solidarity work around El Salvador, Nicaragua, and Guatemala. In our household at Kilbourne Street, which I shared with activists doing work on Latin America, many sparkling after-dinner discussions were the source of deeper understanding of the roots and dynamics of Reagan's aggressive support for vicious right-wing gangs like ARENA in El Salvador and the Contras in Nicaragua.

As the 1980s progressed and, as in the Philippines, country after country got rid of military or executive dictatorships, I discovered how flexible Washington could be in relating to countries in the Global South, deserting authoritarian regimes and identifying itself with liberal democratic movements, the better to be able to control or influence them. The transition in the Philippines was reflective of a broader shift that also manifested itself in Brazil, Argentina, Chile, and South Korea. A comparative perspective helped me see that the key consideration that guided U.S. policy as to its preference for a type of political regime was preventing the Left from coming to power, and if either authoritarianism or liberal democracy failed to secure this, then there was still the final solution: military intervention, as in Nicaragua, with the sponsorship of the Contras during the Reagan years.

Of course, these shifts were not done in an instrumental fashion, but arrived at through policy debates among different factions of the U.S. elite, with positions often coinciding with the liberal versus conservative or Democratic versus Republican divide, but with the outcome dependent on which position was most persuasive to the elite as a whole as the type of regime that would best serve U.S. interests.

"American Lake"

One of the more productive intellectual relationships I had was with Peter Hayes, an Australian energy specialist, and Lyuba Zarsky, an activist from the San Francisco Bay Area. I had hooked up with them during the campaign to derail the Bataan nuclear power plant in the late seventies, coming up with the study "500-mile Island: The Bataan Nuclear Reactor Deal."[51] We then formed the Nautilus institute to look at military and energy issues in the Pacific. We worked for three years on a project to document and analyze the development of the U.S. military presence in this vast oceanic expanse. I remember spending summers at the residence of Peter and Lyuba in Amherst, Massachusetts, running in the morning, then jumping into a nearby lake, before spending the day writing, then having dinner where we exchanged our insights (or lack of them) for the day. The result was the 1987 book, *American*

Lake: The Nuclear Peril in the Pacific, published by Penguin which, at over 500 pages, was and remains the most comprehensively documented survey of the force structure and dynamics of the U.S. military in the Pacific and its evolution since the late 19th century.[52]

Co-writing *American Lake* brought home to me the centrality of the military dimension of the U.S. presence in the Pacific and enabled me to see the Philippines as part of a transnational garrison state in the Western Pacific that extended from Japan and South Korea in the North, then from Guam and the Philippines to Australia in the South Pacific, supported from a vast rear area, Micronesia. It underlined how the Second World War had drastically reshaped the political geography of the Western Pacific, with the creation of semi-sovereign offshore or peninsular states from which the U.S. could project power onto the Asian landmass. It led me to a close examination of the U.S. wars in Asia and how those wars, beginning with the subjugation of the Philippines at the turn of the century, gave an insight into the heart of the American imperial enterprise: into the convoluted twinning of settler colonialism, genocide, slavery, capitalism, and racism. As I articulated it a few decades later in one of my most-read reflections on the United States:

The military is an institution of American society, and as such its origins and development have been centrally influenced by the political economy of U.S. capitalism.

The political economy of the U.S. is built on two "original sins." One was the genocide of Native Americans, the main function of which was to clear the ground for the implantation and spread of capitalist relations of production. The second was the central role played by the slave labor of African Americans in the genesis and consolidation of U.S. capitalism.

These original sins have had such a foundational role that the reproduction and expansion of U.S. capitalism over time have consistently reproduced its racial structures.

So powerful were its racial impulses that providing the legitimacy necessary for capitalist democracy to function necessitated the radical ideological denial of its racial structures. This radical denial was first inscribed in the Declaration of Independence's message of radical equality "among men" that was drafted by the slaveholder Thomas Jefferson. Later it appeared in the ideology that the mission of U.S. imperial expansion was to universalize that equality among the non-European, non-white societies.

The deadly interplay of racism, genocide, and radical denial at the heart of American white society has been reproduced in that society's military, and it has been especially evident in America's Asian wars.[53]

Writing *American Lake* with Peter and Lyuba also led me to have a more nuanced view of the U.S. empire, moving me away from the mechanistic Marxist view of economic corporate interests (the "base") determining state policies (the "superstructure"). While the reproduction of the U.S.-dominated global capitalist system was the ultimate objective, I gained appreciation of this process as having three "relatively autonomous dimensions": a military/strategic dimension, a corporate economic dimension, and a political/ideological dimension, made manifest in the promotion of "missionary democracy." Unlike in Latin America, where corporate interests were dominant, strategic expansion pushed by the U.S. military, in particular the Navy, had primacy in the Pacific. Indeed, the interests of U.S. corporations in East Asia were often subordinated to the imperatives of military expansion or political stabilization, as my later studies of the economies of South Korea, Japan, and Southeast Asia would then document.

Activism accompanied analysis. The mid-1980s saw the U.S. brazenly move to convert the trusteeship for the key island groups in Micronesia it had received from the United Nations—the Marshall Islands, Palau, and the Federated States of Micronesia—into formally dependent states via the so-called Compact of Free Association. Being in Washington, I assisted in the formation of the (short-lived) U.S. Pacific Network that was aimed at informing the American public about the terrible legacy of high cancer rates from nuclear bomb testing at Bikini and other atolls in the Marshall Islands, seeking to make people aware of the social disintegration that resulted from their economic and financial dependency on the dole from Washington, and exposing the Compact as simply another form of colonialism.

Among the people I worked with were the Palauan activist Roman Bedor and the remarkable Marshall Islands campaigner, Darlene Keju-Johnson, who died of breast cancer that resulted from genetic complications stemming from radioactive fallout from the 67 nuclear tests that she and her people were exposed to in the late forties and 1950s. Also part of the hardy band whose energies made up for our small number were the anthropologist Glenn Alcalay, Austrian activist Ingrid Kircher, and the film-makers Marybeth Brangan and Jim Heddle. We knew there was little support for independence among the Pacific islanders, so we were pushing for such concrete and attainable objectives as Washington's acceptance of responsibility and payment of reparations for the genetic damage to people created by nuclear testing, more popular participation in governance, and support for the reinvigoration of local economies that would lessen the deadening dependency on welfare from Washington.

My work opposing nuclear power in the Philippines and supporting Pacific Islanders in their struggles for atomic reparations brought me into contact with other organizations seeking to stop nuclear testing and the massive U.S. military presence in the Pacific, among them Greenpeace, of whose international board I became a member in the early 1990s. These organizations came together in the Nuclear Free and Independent Pacific Network (NFIP) in the early 1980s. This loose coalition made up in spirit what it lacked in numbers. One of its victories was New Zealand's ban on the entry of nuclear-capable warships under the government of David Lange, which earned the ire of the U.S. and caused it to be downgraded from being a U.S. "ally" to a "friend." When I was given the Right Livelihood Award in 2003, it was a source of great pleasure to me that among my co-recipients that year was David Lange, who told me at the awards session in Stockholm that his only regret was that few other countries had followed New Zealand's lead in banning nuclear-capable ships.

The Food First Years

It was the system of global capitalism—the process of accumulation, trade, the financial system, and the multilateral institutions that served as the political canopy assuring U.S. domination of the system—that became the focus of much of my work when I joined Food First, or the Institute for Food and Development Policy, as a research associate in 1987. At last, my research and writing was not something I did in between political assignments. Now I was being paid to do it and full time, with a decent salary at that! Nearly 15 intense years of anti-dictatorship organizing and solidarity work in Washington had taken its toll on my sanity and personality, and I was more than willing to jump at the excuse provided by the fall of the *ancien regime to* leave the city of power and take other trips without feeling guilty.

My new partner Marilen Abesamis and I lived, along with her two daughters from a previous relationship, Ami and Annette Ferrer, in a house in Richmond, across the Bay from San Francisco. I either commuted to work on BART, the Bay Area Rapid Transport system, or drove across the Bay Bridge to the Food First office that was located near the busy 16th Street and Mission intersection in San Francisco before it moved to 9th Street. "South of Market" served as the "proletarian quarters" of the city in contrast to the area north of Market Street, with its lovely hills, grand residences, antique trams, and breath-taking views of San Francisco Bay.

Food First was founded in 1975 by Frances Moore Lappe and Joe Collins. Lappe had gained prominence as the author of the best-selling *Diet for a Small Planet*, a pioneering cookbook appealing to the health- and environment-conscious liberal American middle class. She and Collins then went on to write *Food First*, which located the roots of global hunger in the corporate control of much of the production, trade, and retailing of food. By the time I joined it in 1987, Food First was a bustling non-profit operation of some 25 people, with a popular line of books that not only dealt with the food system but also with other key issues in development, the World Bank and the international Monetary Fund, and people's movements for change. One of its best-sellers was *Development Debacle,* which I had co-authored five years earlier.

Food First was a collection of brilliant and strong-willed personalities that included Medea Benjamin and Kevin Danaher and, as is often the case, putting such people together could trigger a volatile clash of ideas, visions, and ambitions. Having just been involved in the struggle on the Philippine Left, I was not about to get myself drawn into another internal conflict and tried my best to hole up on the third floor of the new Food First office on 9th Street, and focus on my research while ignoring the conflicts that were taking place in the executive suites on the second floor. That, I found, was impossible, and soon I was taking sides in acrimonious conflicts. Sometime in 1988, Medea and Kevin left, going on to found the hugely successful Global Exchange and, much later, to Medea's establishing the influential CodePink with Jodie Evans. Then Joe Collins departed, also under strained circumstances. Then Frankie announced her intention to close Food First and move to the East Coast to found an institute focused on coming out with innovative ideas on popular democracy and promoting them. At that point, in 1989, I was asked by the staff to assume the executive directorship so we could keep the Institute open. Frankie agreed to leave but not close down Food First, and over the next few years, I put a lot of effort into stabilizing the organization, with the indispensable assistance of staffers Marilyn Borchardt and Martha Katigbak and board members Crosby Milne, Steve Hellinger, and Robin Broad. This involved supervising the physical transfer of Food First from San Francisco to a house across the Bay in North Oakland near the University of California at Berkeley.

Managing Food First allowed me to develop new skills in organizational and financial management, including how to tap funds from the U.S.'s network of progressive funders. I made sure, however, to keep management and fundraising subordinate to my research and writing priorities. I also had to make sure the increasing number of speaking commitments I had to fulfill as the head of one of the U.S.'s leading independent progressive research outfits did not fly out of hand, since they involved a great deal of travel and energy.

There were engagements that could not be avoided. One of them was my attending the United Nations Conference on the Environment and Development in Rio de Janeiro in June 1992, where I did most of the listening during a brief meeting with then Malaysian Prime Minister Mohammed Mahathir as he articulated his controversial position that developing countries should not be subjected to environmental standards that would prevent them from rapid industrialization. I could not focus on what he was saying, though, since my mind was distracted by the contrast between my image of him as a big man and the realization that he was actually shorter than me. I was much less unfocused during my interventions at various sessions of the historic

Walden in a debate with Robert McNamara, former World Bank president, at Notre Dame University, Indiana.
COURTESY OF INSTITUTE FOR FOOD AND DEVELOPMENT POLICY

conference. In one of which, titled, "Who Will Rule the World after UNCED: The World Bank, the UN, or the People?", I called for the resignation of Larry Summers, then chief economist of the World Bank, for advocating the transfer of polluting industries from the rich to the poor countries on the ground that this made economic sense.[54]

Probably the most memorable of these engagements was the debate I had with the former president of the World Bank, Robert McNamara, at Notre Dame University in South Bend, Indiana, on March 20, 1992, where we found ourselves on the same panel dealing with issues on development.[55] It was an opportunity I had long been waiting for. I sparked the debate when I claimed that structural adjustment programs promoted by the World Bank had been the central factor driving down per capita income in Africa in the late 1980s to their level at the time of decolonization in the 1960s and depressing per capita income in Latin America below its level in 1980. I added that "the World Bank has become a debt collection agency, facilitating the astonishing transfer of $155 billion worth of financial resources from the South to the North between 1984 and 1989."[56] McNamara's response was to say he would "caution the heads of government of India, Tanzania, and Argentina before accepting the picture of the World Bank drawn by Mr. Bello. I am sure they will tell you that the World Bank has played a positive role in the economic development of their countries."[57] He provided the opening I had been look-ing for, enabling me to say directly to his face, "Mr McNamara, you yourself designated the Philippines as a 'country of concentration' when you were head of the Bank, and you provided the Marcos dictatorship with $6 billion worth of World Bank money, but when Marcos was overthrown in 1986, 70 percent of Filipinos lived under the poverty line, in contrast to 40 percent at the beginning of the dictatorship in 1972."[58]

Deconstructing Structural Adjustment

I did two major studies while heading up Food First. The first was on structural adjustment, which was the first truly global comparative study I did, drawing on the experiences of more than 15 countries in Africa, Asia, Latin America, and from the United States. Some analysts, including the late Peter Gowan, have called *Dark Victory: The United States, Structural Adjustment, and Global Poverty* my "most influential" book. The question that I sought to answer in the book was why, despite the rosy pronouncements of the World Bank and the IMF, there were hardly any successful cases of adjustment lead-ing to sustained and comprehensive economic growth. What I then did was to show, using the actual experiences of a number of developing countries, how to the contrary, the interaction of different key elements of the structural adjustment formula, notably cutting wages, reducing government spending, devaluation, and export orientation had led to the economy becoming "stuck in a low-level trap, in which low investment, reduced consumption, and low output interact to create a vicious cycle of stagnation and decline, rather than a virtuous circle of growth, rising employment, and rising investment, as originally envisaged by World Bank theory."[59]

An extraneous factor or agent, like government incompetence or "anti-development culture" or lack of political will, was not needed to explain why the model did not work across different societies. The internal logic of structural adjustment inexorably led to stagnation instead of growth. What you needed was an external agent, the state, to counteract the systemic logic leading to stagnation, but it was precisely this agency that was being taken away in the structural adjustment formula.

Chile, a country that I had continued to monitor as the post-Allende counterrevolution took place under Gen August Pinochet, provided my main case study of how neoliberalism created havoc in an economy. On the occasion of Margaret Thatcher's death in April 2013, I wrote an article for the *Guardian* that detailed the failure of the free-market policies that were implemented in Chile by Pinochet, Thatcher's ideological soulmate:

> The Chilean strongman's free-market policies that the Iron Lady admired indeed transformed his country's economy, but in ways that could hardly be considered a success except among doctrinaire followers of the University of Chicago economist Milton Friedman. Pinochet's programme subjected his country to two major depressions in one decade, first in 1974–75 when GDP fell by 12%, then again in 1982–83 when it dropped by 15%. Contrary to ideological expectations about a positive correlation between free markets and robust growth, average GDP growth in 1974–89—the radical phase of the Pinochet revolution—was only 2.6%. By comparison, with a much greater role for the state in the economy during 1951–71, Chile's economy grew by an average of 4% a year.[60]

By the end of the radical free-market phase, I noted, "both poverty and inequality had increased significantly. The proportion of families living below the 'line of destitution' had risen from 12% to 15% between 1980 and 1990, and the percentage living below the poverty line, but above the line of destitution, had increased from 24% to 26%. By the end of Pinochet's regime, about 40% of Chile's population, or 5.2 million in a population of 13 million, was poor." In terms of income distribution, "the share of national income going to the poorest half of the population declined from 20.4% to 16.8%, while the share going to the richest 10% rose dramatically from 36.5% to 46.8%."[61]

Moreover, once one of the most industrialized countries of Latin America, Chile was deindustrialized, with the combination of erratic growth and radical trade liberalization resulting in "'deindustrialization in the name of efficiency and avoiding inflation," as one economist described it. Manufacturing's share of GDP declined from an average of 26% in the late

1960s to 20% in the late 1980s. Many metalworking and related industries went under in an export-oriented economy that favored agricultural production and resource extraction."[62]

What came to be packaged as structural adjustment or the "Washington Consensus" and generalized throughout the Global South, I pointed out, was a set of free market policies that had actually failed in the country that had served as the experimental site to exemplify them, at the price of great suffering and political repression. With its blueprint being seriously flawed, it was not surprising that there was hardly any case of structural adjustment that could be claimed as a success in the over 70 countries in the Global South where it was implemented.

Engaging the NICs

The other major study I worked on while heading up Food First was on the phenomenon of "newly industrializing countries." The so-called NICs were the rage of development economics in the late 1980s and 1990s, before the Asian Financial Crisis of 1997–98. With their high rates of growth, South Korea, Singapore, Taiwan, and Hong Kong were seen as providing the key to escaping underdevelopment for many countries. Along with Japan, they were seen as constituting a region of rapid growth that would prove likely to displace the United States and Europe in the coming 21st century. In the late 1980s, the increasingly obvious failure of both the Marxist collectivist model of development and the traditional nationalist strategy of import-substitution industrialization lent particular urgency to the need to investigate the question of whether the NIC model, in fact, offered a viable future for developing countries.

My quest to explain the dynamism of the NICs took me on a long three-month trip to Asia in the summer of 1988. But before I went to the first stop in my study, Singapore, I went to the Philippines, my first trip back since I left for graduate school in 1969. Aside from visiting my parents and friends, I was brought to visit an area controlled by the New People's Army near Sariaya, Quezon Province. Being still a member then of the CPP, I was briefed on such matters as the size of the mass base of the CPP/NPA in the province, how many squads of the NPA there were, and the number of enemy detachments there were, along with their unit designations. It was all very detailed. After two days, I was dropped off at a bus station in a "white area," where I took a bus to Manila. There I met a number of people in the NDF and CPP leadership, like Satur Ocampo, his wife Carolina Malay, and Ricardo Reyes.

After two weeks in Manila, I flew to Singapore to begin my study. My interviews and documentary research confirmed what other analysts had already pointed out in the debate on the role of the market versus the state in the development of the NICs. The state was all-pervasive, whether it was in trade, finance, labor relations, transport, and infrastructure, such as the provision of export-processing zones to attract foreign capital with tax holidays and other incentives. Where I thought the original contribution of my research lay was in its depiction of the Singapore model as a partnership between the state and transnational capital at the expense of Singaporean private capital, whose interests were subordinated to those of the TNCs. The political regime there was very central not only in creating the productive infrastructure for capital but also in producing and reproducing the social conditions for the stable reproduction of the system of production.

Singapore was—and continues to be—authoritarian but not in the same crudely repressive way as the Marcos dictatorship. The government did have blunt instruments for dealing with dissent, and it used them. But rather than rely mainly on repression, the People's Action Party regime led by Lee Kuan Yew controlled the island state in sophisticated but eminently effective ways. Potential critics were coopted into the system by recruiting them as candidates for Parliament. For the most part, people were not tortured or jailed for speaking against the regime, but their professional life and activities would be scrutinized and even the slightest hint of illegality could be used to destroy your career (as one university professor who dared to speak out against the PAP discovered to his dismay, when the authorities found he had mailed his wife's thesis to the U.S. using the funds of the public university he was teaching at to pay postage costs, which was technically illegal).

But most impressive was the way the PAP was able to integrate social welfare and political containment, and nowhere was this more evident than in the country's public housing program. A key promise of the PAP was housing for everyone. It went a long way to delivering this, largely via owner occupied units, but it did this by eliminating the traditional village clusters differentiated by ethnicity or race and mixing Chinese, Malay, and Indian families in the same housing complex. The housing program was an example of the PAP's "genius": to gain legitimacy and promote political stability, it did deliver the goods, but it also simultaneously demobilized and converted the population into a pliable mass by destroying class, communal, and residential solidarities and "reintegrating" people into officially sanctioned and controlled collectivities.

The visible hand of the state was just as present as the invisible hand of the market, and it was everywhere, including in population policy where a frankly eugenicist and elitist policy entrenched incentives for the better educated to have more children and disincentives designed to discourage the poor—and non-Chinese—from having more.

After three weeks, my interviews were complete, I was very tired, and I was very bored by Singapore's controlled society, and flew on to my next stop, Taiwan.

I flew into a Taipei that was bustling with democratic energy. The first democratic elections ever had just been held under the president from the Kuomintang Party, Lee Teng Hui, the first native Taiwanese leader of the Republic of China, a pariah state that was in existence owing mainly to the continued protection of the United States but whose economy was seen as a model of dynamic growth by development economists. Members of the opposition, the Democratic Progressive Party (DPP), escorted me around like an official visitor. People were eager to be interviewed and unlike in Singapore, they were not afraid to have themselves recorded and identified.

As in Singapore, the state played a very strong role in directing development, as a number of political scientists had pointed out. What particularly impressed me was the role of land reform in Taiwan's growth. Land reform, promoted by both the Kuomintang (KMT) and the United States in order to head off the Communists' appeal to the peasants, created a dynamic internal market that served as the engine of industrialization. This was in marked contrast to the Philippines where the U.S. continued to support the landed elite and its largely fraudulent agrarian reform programs. This was the main lesson that Taiwan had for developing countries, I concluded: the political will to enact radical land redistribution.

Another important observation I had was that the state was an important actor, but its favors were unevenly divided between KMT-connected firms and families or "mainlanders" that had taken refuge in Taiwan upon their defeat by Mao Zedong in the civil war in the late 1940s and those controlled by native Taiwanese, with the former enjoying extensive government protection. Indeed, I observed in the population at large a deepening rift between the native Taiwanese and the "mainlanders" and sensed that at some point in the future, the DPP, whose main base was the native Taiwanese, would gain power.

Interestingly, though, the most vivid memory I had of my month of doing research on the island was my strolling to Taipei's main market at midnight, where I witnessed a cobra versus mongoose fight to the death. For two hours, I was entranced by the mongoose killing one cobra after another, with its deft footwork and sure instinct of when to land the death blow. After every cobra gladiator was killed, the man running the show split it open and poured its blood into a glass and sold it to spectators, telling them it would improve their sexual performance. After the mongoose's 15th victim, I decided it was time to go home, but not after fending off the man's insistent offer to improve my sexual prowess with cobra blood. Viagra was not yet available then, so cobra blood was apparently popular in Taipei for males suffering from Erectile Dysfunction Disorder.

I arrived in Seoul to the news of students leaping from the top of Myundong Cathedral in spectacular suicides to demand democratization. The whole country was aflame with democratic protest, and workers were in the lead, launching thousands of strikes over a three-year-period. This was shaking what I later termed the system of "command capitalism" created by the dictator Park Chung Hee that was an alliance between the military-controlled state and the private conglomerates known as *chaebol* that the state had itself created in its project of breakneck industrialization from the 1960s to the 1970s.

This partnership was Exhibit A for those who distrusted the standard economic explanation of the priority of market forces in development and served as an antidote to the neoliberal thinking that had gained dominance in economics in the 1980s. What most of these admirers—which included technocrats in the Chinese Communist Party that were then shaking off Maoist thinking—ignored were the costs associated with the system. In my interviews, I saw how the massive exploitation of workers had built the system and, to keep them in place, an extremely repressive state had come into being. Even in the workplace, the management mimicked military hierarchy. In the process, an insurrectionary working class had been created, and bitter class conflict became the Achilles Heel of the system, making political stability well-nigh impossible. My study also highlighted other costs or flaws, including the erosion of agriculture, the difficulties posed by technological transformation from labor intensive manufacturing to high tech production, and the environmental crisis.

Workers often gathered in groups to talk to me, in one instance, telling management representatives who wanted to break up the meeting to go to hell. Traffic was hell—*kyotongchiok* in Korean—but I used a motorcycle, with a daredevil driver, Chang Shin-wan, who doubled as my interpreter, who got me to my appointments almost invariably 10 minutes early. If a cobra-mongoose fight was imprinted in my memory in Taipei, in Korea the impression made was on my palate, which appreciated how kimchi, the Korean delicacy, could differ from region to region, from town to town, indeed from household to household.

My one month in Korea forged long-lasting ties with workers' unions, student activists, progressive media, and Church people, who invited me back several times to do public speaking on my book with Stephanie Rosenfeld, *Dragons in Distress: Asia's Miracle Economies in Crisis,* which was published in 1990.[63]

Dragons was later said to have predicted the Asian financial crisis of 1997–98. It did not. In fact, there were no sections on the financial sector in Singapore, Taiwan, and Korea. What it did was to draw attention to the structural weaknesses of the NIC model—a phenomenon that later received the term "middle income trap"—which were just as critical in undermining the NIC model as the financial crisis, as Robin Broad, John Cavanagh, and I were later to argue in an article for *Foreign Policy* titled "Development: The Market is not Enough."[64] Stephanie and my analysis in *Dragons* drew much inspiration and ideas from the work of many scholars of development, in particular, Bruce Cumings and the late Chalmers Johnson, author of *MITI and the Japanese Miracle,* from whom I would later receive the unexpected accolade of being "the world's best guide to American exploitation of the globe's poor and defenseless."

From Moscow to Pyongyang

It was during my years at Food First that I was able to visit countries that were then termed the "socialist bloc." These were years when the old centralized socialist model was being reformed in the Soviet Union. *Glastnost* (political reform) and *perestroika* (economic reform) were the bywords when I visited Moscow with a group of academics led by Princeton Professor Richard Falk in October 1988. Alexei Arbatov, one of the Soviet leader's top advisers, exuded optimism when he lectured us on how the Soviet Union's national security rested on three pillars: military power, economic power, and political and diplomatic relations. Since Stalin's time, he said, achieving military security had been emphasized, "to the detriment of the economy and the Soviet Union's political relations with surrounding states." This focus on military security had "compromised Soviet security, and the aim of *perestroika* and the new diplomacy is to bring into optimal balance the three pillars of our national security."[65] Gorbachev and his people never got to achieve that "optimal balance" since the process of reform ran out of control. In slightly over three years' time since my visit, Gorbachev, Arbatov, *glastnost*, and *perestroika* were history and in their place rose the troubled New Russia presided over by the drunken Boris Yeltsin and later, Vladimir Putin.

The visit to Vietnam in 1992 was unremarkable except for a near diplomatic incident I provoked in Hanoi. As a board member of the international aid organization Oxfam America, I was invited to join Ngo Vinh Long, a Vietnamese resident of the U.S. who had been one of the stalwarts of the anti-war movement, to examine Oxfam's projects in Vietnam. I was given the royal treatment, though I was careful to tell my government hosts I was a member of Oxfam's board, not its staff, and therefore had no say in decisions to fund projects. That principle of separation of powers was, not surprisingly, something that went over their heads since their experience of organizational structure was that the party was a monolithic entity that controlled everything. The trip brought me to Hanoi, Ho Chi Minh City, and Songbe Province. In Hanoi, a grand banquet was held, with the deputy mayor himself in attendance. A man in his late forties, the deputy mayor approached me while I was savoring delicious pho. He had probably not been briefed on my politics since he said with a wide smile, "I think Mrs. Marcos is very beautiful." I nearly choked on my noodles, then answered angrily, "No fascist is ever beautiful." Then followed the most impressive diplomatic somersault that I had ever witnessed. Not missing a beat, he pointed to my pho and replied warmly, "How are your noodles? Do you like pho? It is our national dish."

This incident highlighted to me the changes happening in Vietnam, where privatization was the name of the game, corruption was spreading as fast as capitalism, and the days of international solidarity were long over. Except for a few, hustling for assistance in the form of projects was what I was treated to by the officials I met, and there was little reference to the war, which was a closed chapter to most. My later visits were different, as I will relate in Chapter 17.

The most memorable visit to a non-capitalist country I made while at Food First was the one I made to North Korea in the summer of 1989. It was one from which I almost returned not to the "Free World" but to a South Korean jail.

Perhaps owing to my advocacy of labor rights and democratic rights in Korea, I was invited in June 1989 to join a three-week "long march" in North Korea to promote the unification of the divided peninsula by the organization Young Koreans United (YKU). To get to North Korea, we had to go through Beijing, and I took advantage of the one-day layover to go to Tiananmen Square, where the deadly suppression of democracy activists had taken place three weeks earlier. It seemed to be business as usual. In Beijing, we boarded a North Korean civilian aircraft for Pyongyang, where we disembarked without our passports being stamped. After a day in Pyongyang with our "minders," we were loaded into buses and brought to the border with Manchuria. There we viewed Mount Paektu, which our guides told us was the birthplace of the Korean people. We thought it was just a viewing, but our hosts brought us on a two-hour hike up the mountain, to a point where we could see the spectacular shimmering lake below that, we were told, had been created by a volcanic eruption. The sight was worth the effort and perspiration to get to the ridge.

Over the next few days, we travelled back to Pyongyang, stopping in a few towns along the way. We got to know our hosts better and found that they were like young people everywhere. The men spent much of their time trying to make an impression on the women in our delegation, and the women joked with ease with foreign males. After two days, I felt enough at ease with them to make a joke. I asked one of our minders why even the toilet in our hotel room had a portrait of the Great Leader Kim Il Sung. I was then on my third glass of soju and proceeded to answer my own question. Is that to remind you that he's watching as you perform your bodily function so you better not waste any time and get it out fast? The guy burst out laughing, but immediately caught himself, remembering he was after all a representative of the great Democratic People's Republic of Korea.

We had meetings with officials and ordinary people, part of which were orchestrated, part spontaneous. As far as I could ascertain, people felt very strongly about the division of their country, and their anger at the U.S. was very real. By the end of the second week, however, boredom was catching up with me. When we got back to Pyongyang, I was ready to do something crazy, like composing a song. The melody was hijacked from the hit song "New York, New York," and so were the lyrics, except for a few strategic replacements:

> *Start spreading the news*
> *I'm arriving today*
> *I want to be a part of you*
> *Pyongyang, Pyongyang*
> *I'm longing to be*
> *Making love to you*
> *So I could get the most of you*
> *Pyongyang, Pyongyang*
>
> *I don't want to wake up*
> *From a dream that never ends*
> *Where I am the toast of the Party*
> *Top of the Politburo ...*
> *Seoul's nothing at all*
> *But a little shithole*
> *I'll make a brand new start of it*
> *In old Pyongyang*

If I can make it there
I'll make it
Anywhere
It's up to you
Pyongyang, Pyongyang

It would not have won the Grammys for best adapted lyrics, but members of the delegation loved it, as did my North Korean hosts (and minders). I remember one evening when, fortified by soju and kimchi, I sang it at our table, to wild applause (or was that a soju-induced illusion?).

Despite its Stalinesque architecture, I liked Pyongyang. But I was bored and was more than happy when we left to continue our journey south, towards the 38th Parallel. When we got to Wonsan, the whole city, it seemed, turned out to welcome us as we marched down its broad main thoroughfare. It was in Wonsan, with schoolgirls shrieking and chanting anti-imperialist slogans, that we felt what the Beatles must have felt. It was also in Wonsan that three of us managed to give our minders the slip, and for about an hour we wandered about un-minded until we realized when talking to people that they knew no English and we knew no Korean. We were soon located by our minders, who were laughing at our silly attempt to get away and telling us that it was the people themselves who turned us in when they saw three strange foreigners wandering about who were trying to communicate in some weird language.

By the time we reached the DMZ, we had been thoroughly primed to view the American and South Korean troops that we saw through the binoculars as the enemy. There had been no formal lectures, nothing that seemed in the least like brainwashing. We had simply bonded with our hosts over the course of three weeks, shared meals, joked, and flirted. It was while peering through the binoculars that I felt the 38th Parallel like a long gash in my heart and felt the pain Koreans felt at being a divided nation.

The end of the journey to the 38th Parallel culminated with a historic crossing into South Korea by the 21-year-old South Korean student leader Lim Soo-Kyung and a Catholic priest, the Rev Moon Ik-hwan, on August 15. At a time that South Koreans were strictly banned from going to North Korea, Lim and Moon had travelled there via third countries. They faced certain arrest and jailing in South Korea were they to cross the DMZ.

I had been approached and asked if I would like to join them. Given my experience in civil disobedience, the idea appealed to me. It would mean certain arrest and jail. It could have meant being jailed in South Korea for espionage. But two things deterred me. Was this really an action—getting arrested and jailed—that was a priority? This had to do with Korean unification, not the Philippines, for which I would not have had any second thoughts. Also important was my family back in San Francisco. Was it really responsible to do something that I had not consulted them about and lose the job that supported them? So this time, I declined, and instead went to the two brave souls who were about to cross the most militarized border in the world to voice my personal support. As anticipated, Lim and Fr. Moon were arrested a few minutes after they crossed into South Korea, and later sentenced to ten years in jail, three of which were served.

Lim, whose radiant face I remember as she bid us goodbye, later became a member of the National Assembly.

Living in and Leaving the Bay Area

Being based in the San Francisco Bay Area meant being located in a place where the cityscape and nature often combined in breath-taking ways, one whose leisurely feel was so different from power-driven Washington, DC. It was also a space where Left and liberal political culture mingled intimately with the drug culture and with liberal sexual mores. It was the most liberal enclave in the whole country.

I avoided hard drugs like cocaine and heroin, but did occasionally smoke pot, which I, like most of my peers, felt should be decriminalized. I gave up pot, however, after a weird experience. After visiting my good friends Jim Heddle and Marybeth Brangan in Bolinas, the fabled town about 30 miles north of San Francisco, I had to drive back to the city on Route 1, which was famous for its zigzags. I was a bit high, and while driving, the thought kept on entering my head, wouldn't it be great if I were to just sail off with this car into eternity? I had a hell of a time keeping my mind and arms on the wheel negotiating the curves and was greatly relieved when I got to the Golden Gate Bridge.

And, oh yes, one should not fail to mention those "party stimulants" like ecstasy, also known as atom, which were harmless but made a sexual or emotional liaison very memorable indeed.

After crisscrossing the Pacific for five years as head of Food First even as I reintegrated back to the Philippines and Asia, I felt the organization was secure enough to be handed to the newly appointed executive director, Peter Rosset, by the beginning of 1994. I joked to friends that my Food First experience made me realize the perils of permanent revolution and the virtues of stability. It was with not a little sadness that I said goodbye to people I had worked with for two decades, first as a Filipino activist, then as the leader of a progressive U.S. NGO.

8. The Neoliberal Challenge

THE YEARS I was in Food First, 1987–1994, witnessed a sea change in international relations, with the collapse of the Soviet Union and the Eastern European satellite economies, the emergence of the United States as the sole superpower, the rise of the NICs, China's push to integrate itself into the capitalist world, the universalization of structural adjustment or doctrinaire free market economics, and a sharp rise in global trade and transnational corporate investment. The years thereafter saw some of these trends come together and gather momentum in what came to be known as "globalization." Confronting globalization and its challenges became the focus of my energy during this period, when I moved permanently back to Asia.

I returned not to one fixed point in Asia but to two: the Philippines and Thailand. I joined the faculty of the University of the Philippines at Diliman, Quezon City. At the same time I co-founded and guided the activist think tank Focus on the Global South in Bangkok. This "bi-location" between two cities, made possible by their relatively short distance from each other by air, allowed me to engage in the national debates on key issues in the Philippines at the same time that I was able to keep track of and engage in key global developments from Thailand.

Back to Academe

After 20 years, I went back to academic life, being invited to serve as a professorial lecturer at the sociology department of the University of the Philippines at Diliman in 1994. I had what was called a lateral appointment, meaning I did not have to go up through the ranks. Profs Randy David and Cynthia Bautista were instrumental in securing faculty approval; there was no opposition. I guess I was seen as a special case, having the reputation of being an activist, but one with a wide range of academic outputs despite not having been a full-time academic and as one able to keep some distance between his advocacies and his analytical work. I was granted tenure after three years and promoted to full professor. I welcomed the teaching, and the department pretty much gave me the space to teach what I wanted. These included sociological theory, political sociology, environmental sociology, and social change.

Students at UP were very different from those at Ateneo de Manila University, at least from the purely male Ateneo thirty years earlier. Most were competitive achievers, the process of winnowing beginning with the tough UPCAT entrance exams, which only 10 percent of those who took it passed. Spoon-feeding was alien to the place. It was sink or swim. Unlike students in the United States, where I had done part-time teaching in places like the University of California at Berkeley, students accepted the grades I gave them with stoicism. During the 15 years I taught at the University of the Philippines (UP) I do not remember anyone complaining about their grades. I became known for treating undergraduates like graduate students and giving them long reading lists. When I was asked why, I said it was because "UP students are extraordinary. They can take a lot of punishment." I was only half kidding, but that was usually the end of the conversation, since no self-respecting UP undergraduates would admit they could not live up to my demands. Indeed, I tended to be less strict with my graduate classes since there were many students there who had not undergone the rigor of the UP undergraduate education. At least where students were concerned, UP was a meritocratic institution, probably the only meritocratic institution most of them would ever be exposed to in a society where there were few other such institutions, if any.

The focus of the faculty was on teaching, and the greatest satisfaction for many was to get a high rating on the student evaluation scores. Teaching was so demanding that there was often little time for research and writing for the junior faculty. People who had gone away for a few years to do graduate work in the U.S. or Europe found themselves taking a long time upon return to complete their dissertations owing to the demands of teaching.

In contrast to the meritocratic student regime, however, the relationships among the faculty were often ridden with politics and academic jealousies, and promotions could be delayed if one was too outspoken about one's views or politics. In many cases, it did not pay to have views that diverged from departmental orthodoxy, unless one was regarded as obviously brilliant. Competition for administrative positions was fierce, leading me to suspect that academic politics was a substitute for the real politics outside university walls for people who could not stomach the demands of the latter. Academic and personal rivalries, which were often intertwined, were more notorious in some departments than in others. Here, UP was not that different from the typical U.S. university. Where it did differ from western universities, at least the leading ones, was that it seemed to place relatively little value on one's publications or research history, despite periodic efforts by some university leaders, such as university president Francisco Nemenzo, during his term, to encourage it via monetary incentives. You did not perish if you did not publish. For many, attaining tenure was the end of academic striving and it was easy to fall into the trap of being consumed by teaching and engaging in the tempting game of academic politics. I think it is this relative scarcity of publications in world-class journals by its faculty that accounts for UP's relatively low rankings in global or Asian university indices despite the fact it produces first-class graduates.

I had no cause to complain. There seemed to be an unspoken under-standing among my colleagues that, having multiple commitments outside the country, I was not to be loaded with administrative tasks, including serving as chairperson of the department. They were also tolerant of my using my own resources to hire teaching assistants, not only to grade papers but to teach in my place when I was on one of my international forays. UP had no funds for teaching assistants. I was lucky to have a number of TA's who combined analytical acuity and the capacity to absorb my demands with accessibility to students—Marissa de Guzman, Marylou Malig, Julie de los Reyes, and Mara Baviera—the first three of whom would join me in Bangkok as members of the staff of Focus on the Global South.

There was only one serious altercation I had with my colleagues, but it was a big one and happened towards the end of my teaching at the university. This was the decision of the majority to deny tenure to a brilliant, published junior faculty member, Sarah Raymundo, for her outspoken progressive politics. But there was an upside to this distressing development. Our finding ourselves on the same side in defense of academic excellence led to a pro-ductive academic relationship and wonderful friendship with Ging Gutierrez, the sociology department's resident criminologist, whose congenial exterior was accompanied by a first-rate mind and who introduced me to the fabulous films of the Hong Kong movie director War Wong-kai.

The Advent of Globalization

The early and mid-1990s were a time when neoliberalism was trium-phantly marketed as the blueprint for the new world order, following the dissolution of the socialist bloc. Capitalism was not only unrivalled, but it was seen as entering a new phase, where nation-state economic border controls like tariffs, quotas, and restrictions on capital flows would fall, and with them would vanish the distinct national capitalist configurations they sheltered from the magic elixir of competition. Globalization, or the global integration of production and markets, which was not a term one encountered in the 1980s, entered the lexicon in the 1990s.

Eliminating barriers to trade and investment was not, however, an automatic process. The unhampered flows of trade and capital needed political assistance, and this was provided by transnational multilateral institutions that would set the rules of the new world order. Of these institutions, the International Monetary Fund and the World Bank existed prior to the 1990s, and their work in preparing the ground for globalization via structural adjustment programs that dismantled government obstacles to the free flow of goods and investment across borders was important. But what was needed was an overarching set of rules to which all governments would bind themselves. The World Trade Organization, which was negotiated from 1986 to 1994 in what was known as the Uruguay Round, would provide these rules, covering at first trade and trade-related matters like intellectual property rights, but expanding to cover direct investment, portfolio investment, government procurement practices, and trade facilitation practices. It was an ambitious agenda, so it is no wonder that the new organization was seen as the "crown jewel of the multilateral system," as one of its leaders later put it.

That was the vision. What the vision did not communicate was that the prime beneficiaries of such a borderless world where goods and capital flowed effortlessly and efficiently were the transnational corporations, most of them based in the West. Any indication of the power relations that this would entrench was simply absent in this paradigm.

Shuttling between my teaching job in Quezon City in the Philippines and Focus on the Global South in Bangkok, Thailand, and traveling to so many countries for speeches, conferences, and popular gatherings as an analyst and activist, provided me with opportunities to witness, ponder, and increasingly oppose neoliberalism and corporate-driven globalization.

Opposing Neoliberalism in the Philippines

The Philippines was an ideal place to confront the new trends in global capitalism. The first post-Marcos years saw the administration of Corazon Aquino rocked by around seven military coup attempts. People's hunger for stability made them focus on the political transformation taking place from a dictatorship to an elite democracy and pay relatively less attention to the new government's economic policies. Yet the latter exercised such a great influence and placed iron constraints on the future of the reestablished democracy.

The most important of these policies was the decision to repay in full the Marcos regime's debt of $26 billion. Under pressure from the international banking elite led by John Reed of Citibank, the IMF, the World Bank, and leading technocrats, Aquino adopted the so-called "model debtor policy" that would allow the government to access international capital markets for new debt to pay off the increasingly onerous interest payments on the old debt. This was against the advice of the head of the National Economic Development Authority (NEDA), Solita Monsod, who had written, along with her colleagues at the University of the Philippines, that, "The search for a recovery program that is consistent with a debt repayment schedule determined by our creditors is a futile one and should therefore be abandoned."[66] Nevertheless, the Aquino administration continued following the Marcos era decree that placed the automatic appropriation of what was due for servicing the foreign and domestic debt as the budgetary priority.

The structural adjustment program was inherited from Marcos by Aquino, thus constraining further the economic policy space of the new administration. But it was not until 1992, when the administration of Fidel Ramos took over from Aquino's, that the Philippines felt the full impact of the "neoliberal revolution." The brunt of this offensive hit the two most important sectors of the Philippine economy: manufacturing and agriculture.

Executive Order 264, masterminded by Cielito Habito, head of the National Economic Development Authority under Ramos, sought to bring down tariffs on all but a few sensitive products to 5 percent or below by 2004. The model for this radical reform was the Chilean tariff reform under the dictator Augusto Pinochet, which brought tariffs down to 11 percent and under. If the Chileans could put 11 percent as the upper limit, then the Philippines could set it at 5 percent! What doctrinaire Filipino technocrats saw was Chile's growth rate, not the deindustrialization and enormous social crises subsequently induced by its free-market policies.

And indeed, as in Chile, deindustrialization swiftly followed the tariffs reform in the Philippines. The list of industrial casualties included paper products, textiles, ceramics, rubber products, furniture and fixtures, petrochemicals, beverages, wood, petroleum oils, and clothing accessories. The textile industry shrank from 200 firms in the late 1970s to less than 10. The world-class shoe industry centered in Marikina vanished, and along with it, the leather tanning industry of Meycauayan, Bulacan, which lost its pre-tariff liberalization reputation of being the "armpit of the country." Ten years later, the head of the Department of Finance of the administration of Gloria Macapagal Arroyo gave the definitive judgment on tariff liberalization: "There's an uneven implementation of trade liberalization, which was to our disadvantage." While consumers may have benefits from tariff cuts, tariff liberalization "has killed so many local industries."[67]

The Battle over WTO Ratification

I had a more direct role in the debate over the direction of the Philippine economy in the fight over the future of agriculture. To join the WTO in 1995, the Philippines had to sign about 60 agreements, annexes, decisions, and understandings. These were known as a "single undertaking." For the Philippines and most under developing countries, the most important was the Agreement on Agriculture (AOA). The AOA required the Philippines to eliminate quotas on the import of all commodities except rice, allowing a certain amount of each commodity to enter the country at a low tariff rate—the so-called "minimum access volume"—with the amount increasing over time. In pushing for the ratification of the WTO by the Senate, the Ramos administration tried its best to assure Filipino farmers that the AOA was designed to make them more efficient producers by exposing them to more competition.

I worked with a number of committed researchers and organizers to oppose the administration's drive to commit the Philippines to the WTO and AOA. Among them were Francisco Lara, Au Regalado, Jocey Cajiuat, Omi Royandoyan, Menchie Flores, and Riza Bernabe. We worked to expose the real purpose of the AOA, which was to bring about much greater foreign penetration of the domestic market. We found that when it came to rice farmers, corn farmers, pig raisers, and other livestock producers, we did not need to do much persuading. They saw that agribusiness giants in the U.S., European Union, and Canada were on the lookout for developing country markets on which to dump their surpluses and regarded AOA as one of their chief instruments to do this. Filipino farmers knew that they did not stand a chance of survival against such subsidized agro-industries while they received no assistance at all from a government whose coffers had been stripped bare by structural adjustment.

This was a battle where, from the government's side, every tactic was fair, including conjuring unbelievable statistics out of thin air by a WTO-USAID-paid economist, Ramon Clarete, who claimed that the Philippine agricultural sector would produce 500,000 new jobs a year if the country joined the WTO! It was a battle fought not only with mass protests but also via competing articles and rejoinders in newspapers like the *Philippine Daily Inquirer* and on radio. We proposed a nationally televised debate, but the secretary of trade, Rizalino Navarro, and other technocrats declined, knowing their projections and statistical fabrications would not hold up in a public exchange in which there was much national interest.

But there were still hesitations in the Senate, which had to vote on ratification, so fearmongering became the administration's strategy in the final stages of the national debate. Unless it joined the WTO, the senators were warned, the Philippines would become another North Korea, isolated from world trade and friendless. It was, we later learned, an argument that was used in the ratification process in other developing countries that were worried about the survival of their agricultural sector. The U.S. government, we learned, was the source of the farcical North Korea argument. This was not surprising since the U.S. was the greatest champion of the new multilateral organization.

As expected, the WTO treaty was ratified. We had, however, made it clear to the country that there would be those of us who would not go willingly into that good night. As one of the country's most popular newspaper columnists, Conrad de Quiros, put it, our command of the facts and, especially, my challenge to the government to debate our side, "helped thrust the issue into the public mind and made the treaty one of the most hotly debated topics in the country. No small feat in a country that would rather debate whether the Brunei beauties should be banned or not."[68]

The results of our implementing the AOA were as to be expected, and they showed up rather early. All areas of agriculture—corn, rice, vegetables, hog raising, and poultry—were rapidly destabilized by high levels of import penetration, mainly by EU and U.S. products. In the years prior to our joining the WTO in 1995, our annual agricultural trade was most often in surplus. The last time the country's agricultural trade was in surplus was in 1993. Since it joined the WTO in 1995, its agricultural trade went into deficit, growing from $149 million in 1995 to $960 million in 2005 to a whopping $7,867 billion in 2019. Far from increasing by 500,000 a year, employment in agriculture dropped from 11.2 million in 1994 to 10.9 in 2001 to less than 10 million in 2016. With little incentive to remain in a dying sector, the rate of emigration to the city and abroad increased sharply, leaving behind a rapidly aging work force.

Financial liberalization and privatization of water provision and energy generation and transmission accompanied the radical transformation of the country's trade in goods and manufactures. But by the early 2000s, the failure of the neoliberal revolution in the Philippines to deliver on its promises of lower cost, greater efficiency, economic growth, and widespread prosperity could no longer be denied.

The erosion of the manufacturing and agricultural sectors left the fragile service sector and labor export as the main absorbers of employment. With over 20 to 40 percent of government expenditures going to interest payments annually and only 12–16 percent to capital expenditures, the government, normally the biggest investor in any economy, was virtually eliminated as a stimulus of growth for the economy. Between 1990 and 2010, the Philippines' rate of growth, at 1.5 percent, was the second lowest in Southeast Asia.

Not surprisingly, at the turn of the century, close to a third of Filipinos lived under the poverty line and the Gini coefficient at .44, showed it to be one of the most unequal societies in Asia. These and other indicators were brought together by Herbert Docena, Marissa de Guzman, Marylou Malig and me in 2004 in the book, *The Anti-Development State: The Political Economy of Permanent Crisis in the Philippines,* which was an effort to analyze the failure of neoliberal economics.

The Anti-Development State

The Anti-Development State and *State of Fragmentation,* which Focus came out with a decade later, aimed to do for the first decades of the EDSA Republic what *Development Debacle* had done for the Marcos era: provide a comprehensive coherent critique of the country's political economy.[69] We argued that by eroding the country's agricultural base and the manufacturing sector and radically reducing government spending, structural adjustment had made the economy dependent on economic activity that had little capacity to produce significant employment, added little productive value, or was marked by instability, such as fly-by-night "business processing outsourcing" activities like call centers, real estate, and financial speculation. The fragility of these activities was underlined by the downspin of the economy during the Asian Financial Crisis of 1997–98.

At the same time, the privatization of essential services like energy and water left much of the population, especially the poor, subject to the worst of all possible worlds: higher prices and worse services. The result was continuing high levels of inequality and poverty and growing mass indebtedness as people sought to supplement their deteriorating incomes. Poverty was exacerbated by the continuing high population growth rate that was not curbed by family planning as was the case in other countries in Southeast Asia, owing to the opposition of the Catholic Church.

Even when the economy registered significant GDP growth, as it did after 2010, this mainly reflected volatile activity in the real estate and financial sector, not in steady employment-generating growth in agriculture and manufacturing. With the economy producing mainly marginal jobs for the majority of the work force, the government had to resort to promoting the export of labor, and it. It did so on massive scale, so that by the first decade of the 21st century, some 10 million Filipinos were working overseas.

"Naturalizing" Neoliberalism

What we failed to address in the two books, however, was why there has been so little resistance to the neoliberal restructuring of the economy despite its obvious limitations and failures. I later advanced five major reasons for this.

First, for a long time, corruption, especially in the form of crony capitalism under Marcos, was seen as the main reason for the underdevelopment of the country. Accordingly, with its emphasis on the market instead of politics as the driver of the economy, neoliberalism could be sold as an "antidote" to corruption. The government's presence in the economy, especially its regulatory apparatus, was, in this view, the primordial source of corruption, with businesses seeking advantage, not through market competition, but via special favors from officials in return for bribes.

Second, neoliberal practices were institutionalized in decrees and laws as well as in international agreements and institutions like the World Trade Organization, thus making reversing them an extremely difficult task.

Third, neoliberalism was not simply an external imposition. It was internalized by the support of a whole generation of Filipino economists and technocrats who studied in U.S. universities or worked at the World Bank and IMF at a time that Keynesianism had been displaced as the reigning economic paradigm, its credibility undermined by its failure to address the stagflation that hit western economies in the 1980s. Coupled with the collapse of the socialist states of the Soviet Union and Eastern Europe in the late 1980s and early 1990s, the discrediting of Keynesianism made public opinion critical of economic alternatives and discourses where the state figured as a key actor. Neoliberalism became become synonymous with economics, itself. As a future president of the Philippines, Gloria Macapagal Arroyo, an economics graduate, told my colleague Joy Chavez in a 1992 interview, "Imposed, maybe in one way, but on the other hand, the mainstream decision-makers—the technocracy and policymakers—also internally believed in that. So there's a confluence of policy direction."[70]

The prominent role of World Bank and IMF-backed technocrats did not mean that the country's economic elites did not play a role in promoting and institutionalizing neoliberalism. There was wider ruling class support for neoliberalism, as evidenced by the support for it by representatives of the influential Makati Business Club, which brought together influential domestic corporate elites like the Zobels and foreign transnational corporate elites. What seemed to have been the case was that there was broad diffuse support for neoliberalism as a weapon against the Marcos cronies, and this backing remained so long as "neoliberal reforms" did not result in initiatives to demonopolize the sectors these elites dominated, such as real estate and banking and finance. Neoliberal measures were mainly focused on tariff reform, weakening labor, deregulation, and privatization, so the oligarchy found them congenial. But when it came to taking a leading role in ideologically promoting neoliberalism, the corporate elite left that largely to the technocrats and economists, though the Makati Business Club would occasionally weigh in at strategic junctures.

Fourth, while critics of neoliberalism were able to point to specific sectoral failures of neoliberalism, they were not successful in their effort to connect those failures to one another, that is, to show that neoliberalism was a system, an ideologically coherent set of ideas and policies that eliminated any policy space and doomed the economy across the board to recurrent crises and stagnation.

Fifth, there was no credible alternative to neoliberalism as a paradigm after the fall of socialism and the discrediting of Keynesianism. It was only in the mid-1990s that the developmental state model, which attributed a central role to the state in the success of Japan, South Korea, and Taiwan, offered an alternative paradigm and, being mainly advanced by political scientists, it did not register in the line of vision of Filipino technocrats and economists in ideological thrall to the new orthodoxy. Not surprisingly, even after its being discredited internationally after the 2008–09 global financial crisis and its multiple failures to deliver on its promises locally, neoliberalism remained the default mode in economic policymaking.

The Philippine Tragedy

By the end of the 20th century, Chile was the most neoliberalized economy in the Global South. The Philippines was a close second. But especially over the last decade, neoliberalism has not only been intellectually discredited in Chile; it has been challenged by a popular revolt. Sebastian Edwards, a World Bank economist observing the uprising, provided the following eyewitness account of the uprising that lasted weeks:

> On October 18, 2019, and to the surprise of most observers, massive protests erupted throughout the country. Demonstrations were triggered by a small increase in metro fares—thirty pesos, or the equivalent of four cents of a dollar. But the rallies were about much more than the fare increase. Hundreds of thousands of people marched in several cities and demonstrated against the elites, corporate abuse, greed, for-profit schools, low pensions, and the neoliberal model. Demonstrators asked for debt forgiveness for

students and free universal health services. . . . Although most of the demonstrations were peaceful, some turned violent. There was arson, destruction of public and private property, and looting; more than twenty metro stations were set on fire during the first few days of the protests. The police responded with unjustified force and were accused of multiple human rights violations.[71]

Can such a revolt against neoliberal policies take place in the Philippines? I certainly hope so, but I doubt it, at least not in the short term. As in Chile, neoliberalism has been proven false by the facts on the ground but, both among the elites and people of the Philippines, it reigns supreme. In a very real sense, it has become "naturalized," an ideology that can seemingly only be dislodged by an economic calamity greater than the calamity of neoliberalism itself. In that lies the Philippine tragedy.

9. Global Battlefields

I GRAPPLED with neoliberalism not only at the national level but also internationally. Focus on the Global South, which was co-founded by Kamal Malhotra and myself, became the key medium for my work in the international front.

I had met Kamal when he was a senior staff member of Community Aid Abroad in Australia, and we were surprised to find out that we had the same idea of setting up an institute that would combine research, advocacy, and activism on region-wide issues of great relevance to Asia. The organization would not only engage in critical analysis but it would serve to catalyze alternatives in close association with people's movements. We agreed that, given our common experience and interest in South and Southeast Asia, the organization would be located somewhere in these two regions.

Founding Focus

We ultimately chose Bangkok to be the location of its head office, owing to Thailand being in the Global South, Bangkok being a communications and transportation hub, and Thailand's reputation of having a friendly NGO culture that did not, however, "suck" a regional organization into focusing on local priorities, unlike Manila.

Thai friends like Professors Suthy Prasartsert and Surichai Wan-Geao were instrumental in getting the planned institute to be affiliated with the Chulalongkorn University Social Research Institute. This was an important consideration, given our concern that Focus have some "protection" from political interference. With our institutional base secured, Shea Cunningham, my research assistant from Food First, accompanied me and Kamal to Bangkok to set up Focus in 1994 and 1995. Before long, we had an organization with subsidiary offices in Manila and New Delhi and a staff complement of nearly 20 people by the end of the 1990s.[72] We were fortunate to have an A-Team from the very start.

The totally fortuitous establishment of headquarters in Bangkok allowed Focus a ringside view of the first major crisis of the era of corporate-driven

Focus on the Global South, which Walden cofounded in Bangkok, Thailand,
achieved international renown for its advocacy of deglobalization.
The photo shows the cover of the Brazilian edition of Walden's book
Deglobalization: Ideas for a New World Economy. The Economist credited
Walden for introducing the concept to the global development discourse.

globalization, the Asian financial crisis of 1997–98. With its 9–10 percent
average GDP growth in the late 1980s and early nineties, Thailand was
known as the "fifth tiger," after Taiwan, Hong Kong, Singapore, and South
Korea. Global capital was flowing into Thailand, eager to take advantage of
the seemingly never-ending "Asian miracle." Bangkok was a debtor's rather
than a creditor's market in the early 1990s, with so many foreign banks and
funds falling over themselves to lend to Thai enterprises, banks, and finance
companies, whatever the reputation—or lack of it—these entities had.

A Ringside Seat in the Asian Financial Crisis

Thailand had benefited from the inflow of Japanese capital in the late
1980s as Japanese industries transferred many of their operations to labor-
cheap Southeast Asia. In the early 1990s, however, this stream began to taper
down. Bank capital and other forms of speculative capital were eager to enter
Thailand but needed assurance of both profitability and financial stability.
Thai technocrats devised a policy package that consisted of eliminating

capital controls as advised by the IMF, fixing the rate of the baht relative to the dollar at 25 baht to 1 dollar, and offering domestic interest rates substantially above rates in the United States.

Billions of dollars flowed in. The only problem was that it went mainly to investment in real estate, so that a glut of investment resulted with some $20 billion worth of new residential and commercial property remaining unsold. Monuments to the real estate investment folly were evident everywhere, among them a massive but virtually deserted residential complex near the Dong Muang International Airport and the sleek but empty thirty-story towers in the Bangna-trat area of the city. On both sides of the majestic Chao Phraya River bisecting the metropolis, scores of unfinished high-rises stood alongside still cranes.

Foreign portfolio investors found that the companies and banks they had loaned to had a heavy load of non-performing loans. Worried, many called in their loans through the spring and early summer of 1997 and moved to change what they received into dollars at the 25:1 rate. Worry turned into panic and to sustain the dollar/baht peg, the Central Bank released its dollar reserves into the market. But after throwing in $32 billion of its $39 billion holdings, it found the pressure to devalue simply too great, what with currency speculators joining the free for all to make money from the devaluation of the baht. When the baht was allowed to float to seek its "true" market value on July 2, 1997, the feeling in Bangkok was that it was the end of the world, with investors, local and foreign, now stuck with loads of "worthless" baht.

Like the epicenter of an earthquake, the collapse of the baht triggered the collapse of the other Southeast Asian currencies; even up north, in South Korea, the levels of debt incurred by the *chaebol* or conglomerates were shown to be unsustainable and the financial system went into a downspin.

The Asian Miracle had some to a screeching halt.

But what came after made things even worse. The IMF assembled billions of bailout money for Thailand, Indonesia, the Philippines, and Korea, but most of these funds went to bail out foreign investors and not to rescue the troubled economies. In return for the bailout money, the IMF demanded emergency economic measures whose principal condition was to radically cut government spending which, instead of arresting the collapse of the private sector, accelerated it, driving countries into recession and millions into poverty. With its push to eliminate capital controls, its bailing out foreign investors, and its ill-advised cutbacks in government spending, the IMF suffered a loss of credibility in Asia from which it never recovered. This was only to be expected given the terrible human consequences of the crisis. At least 1 million people fell into poverty in Thailand and 21 million in Indonesia. In Korea, the trend of declining poverty rates between 1975 and

1995 was sharply reversed in 1998, and the recession led to a suicide rate in 1998 that was nearly 60 percent higher than in 1997.

When the financial crisis broke out, I was in the midst of completing a book on the political economy of Thailand, based on interviews of scores of Thais from all walks of like. The book, which eventually came out with the title *A Siamese Tragedy: Development and Disintegration in Modern Thailand*, co-authored with Shea Cunningham and Li Keng Poh, and trans-lated into Thai by Suranuch Thongsila, my future wife, touched only slightly on finance and focused mainly on the structural fissures opening up owing to the strategy of foreign capital-intensive, rapid growth: the crisis of the farm-ing sector, growing inequality, the uncontrolled environmental degradation, and the increasing difficulties faced by the manufacturing sector as it tried to move towards more technology-intensive production. The financial sector boom had covered up these crises. Now the cover was blown, and the crises that had been percolating but had been ignored by technocrats, the business press, and the local media were exposed. How could these happen when all the signs of danger were there for all to see?

That is when I realized the power of a paradigm of growth to capture minds across the social spectrum by filtering in only aspects of reality friendly to the model and screening out data that did not fit it. As I wrote in my post-mortem of the Asian financial crisis:

> A global network of investors, journalists, investment analysts, and academics were locked into a psychology of boom, where growth rates, expectations, analysis, advice, and reporting interacted in a mutually reinforcing inflationary fashion, charac-teristic of manic situations. Just as in the case of the Cold War lobby in the U.S., there was a whole set of actors that—perhaps half consciously, one must concede—developed an institutional interest in the maintenance of the illusion of a never-ending Asian bonanza so that, whether in the press, in the boardroom, or in the academy, alternative viewpoints were given short shrift.[73]

The IMF's Avenging Angel

Doing a critique of the disastrous policies of the IMF—its push for financial liberalization that was one of the triggers or Asian Financial Crisis followed by its imposition of austerity programs on the troubled econo-mies—was not the only response of Focus on the Global South to the crisis. We were determined to do a high-profile action that would call the attention of the world to the Fund's dreadful mistakes. As if in answer to our prayers,

According to Walden, the throwing of a pie on the face of outgoing IMF managing director Michel Camdessus was the most cost-effective action he was involved in, the only investment being the USD1 it cost to buy the cherry pie at a 7-11 store.

Michel Camdessus, the IMF chief who had called the shots during the crisis, scheduled a trip to the epicenter of the crisis, Bangkok, to attend the meeting of the United Nations Conference on Trade and Development (UNCTAD) in February 2000 to give a farewell speech as head of the Fund.

We decided to give him a farewell he would never forget. We brought into our plans Robert Naiman, then an economist with the progressive Washington, DC, think tank Center for Economic Policy Research, who was attending the conference. He agreed to be our avenging angel. The *Associated Press* reported what happened next:

> The outgoing chief of the International Monetary Fund got a rude retirement present today when an American anti-free-trade activist penetrated security at a trade conference and hit him with a pie in the face.
>
> Moments before Michel Camdessus was to deliver his last speech as IMF chairman, the activist hurled a fruit-and-cream pie inside the hall where some 190 nations are holding the U.N. Conference on Trade and Development.
>
> The action left Camdessus—seen by many activists as Public Enemy No. 1 for dictating financial policies to poor

countries—and Thailand's tough-talking security officials with pie on their faces.

The pie-thrower, who identified himself as Robert Naiman, 34, of Washington, D.C., said he performed the stunt to give the IMF chief "a friendly reminder of what we think of his policies and to give a warning to his successor we expect different policies."[74]

Naiman's act proved to be very popular in Thailand, which was in the throes of an IMF austerity program, so that the government decided not to press charges against him. It was one of Focus' most cost-effective acts of non-violent protest, our only capital outlay being the 50 baht or one dollar it cost me to buy Naiman's weapon, a cheap cherry pie, at the 7–11 store at the conference site.

The ADB's "Honolulu Handshake"

Camdessus was not the only multilateral top dog that was on the receiving end of Focus' innovative protest tactics. The head of the Asian Development Bank, Tadao Chino, got the "Honolulu Handshake" when we descended on breezy Oahu, Hawaii, to protest the agency's 34th Annual General Assembly in May 2001. Like its bigger partner, the World Bank, the ADB was itself on the cutting edge of globalization while promoting in particular the interests of Japanese capital. It also had a terrible reputation of funding large environmentally damaging capital-intensive projects and plunking them on communities with no consultation at all. We were determined to communicate our concerns to Chino, who agreed to emerge from the Honolulu Convention Center to receive a petition from the 1500 protesters. My Focus colleague Shalmali Guttal and I hatched a plan with a Thai activist, Miss Dawan, to ensure that Chino would get our message. Dawan had come to Hawaii to tell the Bank to defund the Samut Prakarn Wastewater Management Project in Thailand, which threatened irreparable damage to a sensitive coastal ecosystem and was ridden with corruption.

Chino expected a perfunctory meeting, in which the civil society delegation would hand him a petition after which he would scamper back to the safety of the convention center and his retinue of assistants. What he did not expect was that Dawan would not release his hand once he had offered it to her in a handshake, no matter how hard he tried to withdraw it. Her firm but gentle grip allowed me to read aloud the collectively written petition to a captive Chino. I took my sweet time reading it. And despite the demands of Chino's assistants that the police break up the meeting—since the ADB president, they said, had come to receive a written petition, not to hear it read aloud to him—the police were pretty much unable to do anything, to the glee of the media who recorded the sight of a befuddled, scared bureaucrat trapped in an unscripted situation.

The statement, signed by 50 non-governmental and people's organizations from throughout the Asia Pacific region, read in part:

> The Asian Development Bank ... is an institution that is now widely recognized as having imposed tremendous sufferings on the peoples of the Asia-Pacific. In the name of development, its projects and programs have destroyed the livelihoods of people, brought about the disintegration of local and indigenous communities, promoted the sharp rise of inequality, deepened poverty, and destabilized the environment.
>
> We, representatives of peoples, communities, and organizations throughout the region, have had enough of this destruction in the name of development. We have had enough of an arrogant institution that is one of the most non-transparent, undemocratic, and unaccountable organizations in existence.
>
> The people of the region want the ADB out of their lives ... and yield the space for others to promote alternative strategies of development that truly serve the people's interests."[75]

All the relieved Chino could promise, once Dawan gently released his hostaged hand after 15 long minutes, was the same old mantra that ADB officials had been reciting to critics for years: "Your views will be taken into account." Still, it was a small victory in the fight for bureaucratic transparency and the prospect of their possibly being publicly held to account and shamed for their actions may have weighed on them somewhat, going forward.

Facing the Enemy in Davos

When it looked like East Asia was on the verge of a recovery from the depths of the recession provoked by the crisis, I was invited in February 2001 by the organizers of the World Economic Forum to Davos, Switzerland, to share my views on trends in the region after the crisis in a panel that included Gene Sperling, the head of U.S. President Bill Clinton's Council of Economic Advisers. "There is now growing disillusion with a pre-crisis model marked by high growth rates, massive dependence on foreign capital, export orientation, and indiscriminate integration into the global economy," I asserted. "We have learned that we need capital controls," I added, "to deter speculative attacks on the currency, deflate financial bubbles before they get serious, and stabilize an economy in financial turmoil." I then called attention to the region's great distrust of the IMF owing to its having been central in bringing about the crisis and making it worse. I then proposed three immediate measures: "immediate dismantling of the IMF's structural adjustment and stabilization programs in Asia and throughout the developing world; immediate reduction of the IMF staff to 200 from 1000; and the creation of a Global Commission on the Future of the IMF, which would decide whether to radically transform the institution or, as I would prefer, decommission it."[76]

I might as well have been talking to a wall. Few in that audience of tech tycoons, financiers, economists on the make, and media personalities on that wintry afternoon high on the Swiss Alps were listening. The only one who I am sure was listening was a good friend, Marybeth Brangan, an environmental activist who had also been invited to Davos in a token nod to the anti-nuclear power movement. Most of the rest still seemed trapped in that psychology of boom that I had discerned in Thailand before the day of reckoning. Certainly, on Wall Street and in Washington, the Asian Financial Crisis was seen as no more than a hiccup in the integration of global capital markets. I had accepted the invitation to go to Davos partly to get the press to take a more critical look at globalization. But the media people present were still caught up in the triumphalism of neoliberalism. Indeed, most of them celebrated how what *Time Magazine* called the "Committee to Save the World"—U.S. Federal Reserve Chairman Alan Greenspan, Treasury Secretary Robert Rubin, and Treasury Undersecretary Larry Summers—"contained the crisis" and allowed globalization to proceed. It was a terrible underestimation of the turbulent underside of financial liberalization that would later take down the U.S. economy in 2007 and 2008 and leave the reputations of all three members of that "Committee" in tatters.

Trade liberalization and financial liberalization were the two main prongs of globalization. Our being on the ground observing the struggle against the WTO in Manila and the financial meltdown in Thailand provided us with a fund of first-hand experience that undergirded our analyses and proved critical as the debate over globalization sharpened. Focus was not just a think tank. We conceived our role as a producer of analyses that would assist people's movements in understanding and mobilizing against neoliberalism and globalization. In carrying out this institutional mission I racked up millions of air miles traveling to about 60 countries in all five continents to do teach-ins, attend conferences, engage in high-profile debates, and participate in or lead demonstrations in the period from 1994 to 2005. The most significant of these were the meetings and mobilizations against the World Trade Organization, World Bank, the IMF, and the G-7. My compulsive pen produced a constant stream of articles through these years, providing a documentary record that was far more comprehensive and detailed than any diary could ever be.

From Corporate Triumphalism in Singapore...

Our main preoccupation was the World Trade Organization. I still don't know why I was invited to the first ministerial meeting of the WTO in Singapore in December 1996. But I saw other known civil society critics of the WTO there, like Martin Khor of Third World Network, so I figured that we were asked to attend to impress on us that a new era was at hand, that the WTO was going to be the institution that would shape the new order, and that it was useless to resist. The corporate presence at the Singapore meeting was massive, with businesspeople outnumbering officials of governments. To prevent any untoward events in this celebration, we were told gingerly by Singapore officials not to engage in "processions," as if pronouncing the world "demonstrations" might conjure one up in the protest-free city state.

Contentious issues, especially those about the opening of the markets of developing countries and the role of labor standards in trade, were mentioned in ministerial speeches, but these were subordinated to the note of triumphalism and celebration surrounding the birth of the WTO and its becoming the third leg of the multilateral system, joining the International Monetary Fund and the World Bank that had been born over 50 years earlier, at the historic Bretton Woods Conference in New Hampshire in 1944. As a number of speeches by representatives of the dominant governments stressed, the division of labor among the three, formally affirmed in "cooperative agreements" signed among them, was that the WTO would preside over the establishment of a "rules-based global trading system," while the IMF would ensure freedom of capital flows and the World Bank would play the leading role in transforming the economies of developing countries along free market, neoliberal lines. And to whet the imagination of the corporate executives present, the EU contingent laid out its vision that trade was only the first area to be liberalized by the WTO. The organization would soon extend its ambit to investment, government procurement, competition policy, and trade facilitation, which were baptized as the "Singapore Issues" or "New Issues."

If you listened closely to the speeches of delegates from the Global South, however, you could hear rumblings of concern that their countries would be disadvantaged by the new dispensation, which appeared to be aimed mainly at prying open their markets to commodities from the Global North. Muted in Singapore, these representatives of developing country governments would speak more loudly at the Third Ministerial in Seattle three year later. Joining them would be a cacophony of voices from global civil society demanding respect for workers' rights, denouncing the plight of small farmers, and protesting the rape of the environment by corporate capital.

...to the Battle of Seattle

When I flew into Seattle in late November 1999 for the Third Ministerial Meeting of the WTO, I did not expect it to be the historic event it turned out to be. I had come mainly to give a talk at the teach-in sponsored by the International Forum on Globalization, an organization that brought together leading anti-globalization activists from different parts of the world, formed under the leadership of the late Jerry Mander, a successful advertising professional turned critic of the corporations, and John Cavanagh, executive director of the Institute for Policy Studies (IPS). There was an overflow crowd at the evening event, and familiar faces in the anti-globalization set like Vandana Shiva, Martin Khor, Maude Barlow, Sara Larrain, Vicky Corpuz, Anuradha Mittal, Susan George, and Lori Wallach had the audience on their feet applauding loudly all evening.

The mood was electric and combative, and I reflected that in turn. In my intervention, I invoked an image from the great sociologist Max Weber, saying the aim of the powers behind the WTO was to create an "iron cage" to trap the countries of the Global South in underdevelopment. "It's about luring us into free trade in order to grab our markets with their corporate monopolies," I said, referring in particular to the Agreement on Agriculture. I ended my ten-minute intervention with the words, "The future of corporate-driven globalization will depend on what we do here in Seattle." That was a rhetorical flourish. Little did I realize that it was a prediction of what would happen in the next few days and thereafter.

It was raining at daybreak on the first day of the Ministerial. I was billeted at the same hotel as Tomoko Sakuma, an activist from Japan that I had befriended in Singapore, and we set out together to see what was going on. With no central coordination, different groups of activists were positioning themselves at the different sites where delegates would be meeting, including the main venue, the Seattle Convention Center, as well as at the entrances of some hotels where delegations were housed. The plan, also spontaneously and democratically evolved, was to use peaceful, non-violent means to block delegates from finding their way to the conference sites.

Very early on, the Seattle police were teargassing and pepper-spraying different clumps of people that had their arms linked. Some of the groups being attacked by the police had sat down on the pavement and, covering their faces with wet cloth to ward off tear gas and pepper spray, they refused

Police using pepper spray to disperse demonstrators during the Battle of Seattle in November 1999. Walden was beaten up by a policewoman during the protest.

CREATIVE COMMONS

to move. I spotted one group that was being broken up with clubs by the police and recognized Medea Benjamin of Global Exchange. At that point, the same reflex that had made me jump to join people sitting in at the Institute for Defense Analysis at Princeton nearly three decades earlier kicked in. I rushed to prevent a burly policeman from manhandling Medea, a person of slight build. Before I knew it, I was being wrestled to the ground by another officer, who then picked me up and hurled me several feet away, following this up by beating me with a club on my back, my buttocks, and my legs. I scrambled away somehow and when I looked back, the officer had taken off his helmet and I saw that the person who had thrown me as if I were a leaf was a policewoman! By some miracle, my head had escaped blows from her club, but in the course of the next few hours, other parts of my body began to throb with pain.

I got away but lost Tomoko in the confusion. By late morning, the police violence against peaceful demonstrators had turned into a full-scale police riot. Peaceful marches, including one involving several thousand trade unionists, were gassed and disrupted by police, some of them mounted on horses. I somehow got into a march headed towards the famous Pike Place Market at Seattle Harbor, but it was charged by police, and we scattered. Small skirmishes between unarmed demonstrators and police continued throughout the day and it was only nightfall and rain that cleared the battle-field that Seattle had become of warring sides. I was relieved to find Tomoko back at the hotel, unhurt but with eyes still smarting, like mine, from the teargas that still wafted throughout the entire city. We hugged each other like long-lost friends.

The massive street protests that continued over the next two days, though with less intensity, developed a synergy with the official meetings of the Ministerial. Delegates from many developing countries had arrived in Seattle resentful that the U.S. and the EU planned to use the Seattle Ministerial to launch the "Millennium Round." Most had not yet finished changing their domestic laws and constitutions to make them compliant with the commitments they had made to the Uruguay Round's 60 agreements, decisions, and understandings, and here were the powerful governments seeking to subject them to more demands to liberalize their trade and trade-related practices. They were especially incensed at the U.S. and EU's refusal to seriously deal with their massive trade-distorting subsidies in agriculture and instead focus on pushing the developing countries to open up their economies even more to their exports.

Emboldened by the 50,000 protestors clashing in the streets with police and calling for abolishing the WTO, developing country delegates strongly resisted efforts by the EU and U.S. to steamroller them in committee discussions. This led to a failure to come out with points of agreement that would be brought together in a consensus statement. The U.S. and EU had their own disagreements, especially in agriculture, contributing to the stalemate. Even a visit by President Bill Clinton failed to move the negotiations forward. The WTO's method of decision-making was by consensus, and by the end of the second day there was no consensus in sight. The Ministerial had collapsed! The de facto alliance between civil society in the streets and developing country representatives in the Seattle Convention Center had produced an outcome of massive significance: a defeat for the promoters of globalization.

For me, Seattle was a game-changer in more ways than one. One of its most important lessons was how collective action—the decisive intervention of masses of people—can "make the truth true." I tried to capture this dimension of what had passed into legend as the "Battle of Seattle" ten years later, in the depths of the global financial crisis of 2007–2008:

> It is now generally accepted that globalization has been a failure in terms of delivering on its triple promise of lifting countries from stagnation, eliminating poverty, and reducing inequality. The current *deep global downturn*, which is rooted in corporate-driven globalization and financial liberalization and the

ideology of neoliberalism that legitimized them, has driven the last nail into the coffin of globalization.

But things were very different over a decade ago. I still remember the note of triumphalism surrounding the first ministerial meeting of the World Trade Organization in Singapore in November 1996. There, we were told by representatives of the U.S. and other developed countries that *corporate-driven* globalization was inevitable, that it was the wave of the future, and that the sole remaining task was to make the policies of the World Bank, International Monetary Fund, and the WTO more "coherent" in order to more swiftly get to the neoliberal utopia of an integrated global economy.

Indeed, the momentum of globalization seemed to sweep away everything in front of it, including the truth. In the decade prior to Seattle, there were a lot of studies, including UN reports, that questioned the claim that globalization and free market policies were leading to sustained growth and prosperity. Indeed, the data showed that *globalization and pro-market policies were promoting more inequality and more poverty* and consolidating economic stagnation, especially in the global South. However, these figures remained "factoids" rather than facts in the eyes of academics, the press, and policymakers, who dutifully repeated the neoliberal mantra that economic liberalization promoted growth and prosperity. The orthodox view, repeated ad nauseam in the classroom, the media, and policy circles was that the critics of globalization were modern-day incarnations of Luddites, the people who smashed machines during the Industrial Revolution, or, as Thomas Friedman disdainfully branded us, believers in a flat earth.

Then came *Seattle*. After those tumultuous days, the press began to talk about the "dark side of globalization," about the inequalities and poverty being created by globalization. After that, we had the spectacular defections from the camp of neoliberal globalization, such as those of the financier George Soros, Nobel laureate Joseph Stiglitz, and the star economist, Jeffrey Sachs....

True, neoliberalism continues to be the default discourse among many economists and technocrats. But even before the recent global financial collapse, it had already lost much of its credibility and legitimacy. What made the difference? Not so much research or debate but action. It took the anti-globalization *actions of masses of people in the streets of Seattle*—which interacted in synergistic fashion with the resistance of developing country representatives in the Sheraton Convention Center and a police riot, to bring about the spectacular collapse of a WTO ministerial meeting—to translate factoids into facts, into truth. And the intellectual debacle inflicted on globalization by Seattle had very real consequences. Today, the *Economist*, the prime avatar of neoliberal globalization, admits that the "integration of the world economy is in retreat on almost every front," and *a process of "deglobalization"* that it once considered unthinkable is actually unfolding.

Seattle was what the philosopher Hegel called a "world-historic event." Its enduring lesson is that truth is not just out there, existing objectively and eternally. Truth is completed, made real, and ratified by action. In Seattle, ordinary women and men made truth real with collective action that smashed an intellectual paradigm that had served as the ideological warden of corporate control.[77]

From Seattle onwards, I felt myself as a participant in a movement that was on a roll. Those years passed like a long, hot summer, probably because the decisive events in which I took part almost invariably took place in the months of June to early September.

The Prague Debate

After Seattle, the next big mobilization I found myself in was the fall meeting of the World Bank and the IMF that was held in Prague in late summer in 2000. Some 10,000 people came from all over the Europe to do a repeat of Seattle, that is, prevent it from taking place.

The day before the World Bank meeting opened, the issues that had brought thousands of people to Prague were the subject of the famous debate on Sept 23, 2001, at the historic Prague Castle, immortalized in Franz Kafka's novel *The Castle*. On one side were Horst Kohler, IMF managing director, World Bank President James Wolfensohn, George Soros, the financier, and Trevor Manuel, South Africa's finance minister. On the other side were Katrina Liskova, a representative of militant Czech NGOs, Ann Pettifor, head of Jubilee 2000 in the United Kingdom, and me. The debate was chaired by Mary Robinson, United Nations Human Rights Commissioner and former President of Ireland.

Czech President Vaclav Havel—the leading personality who had top-pled the Communist regime in then Czechoslovakia a decade earlier and to whom I was Introduced shortly before the debate started—told me, between puffs on his cigarette, that "I asked you to be part of this debate because your side deserves to be heard."

Knowing that his country was being subjected to structural adjustment by the IMF, I was determined not to disappoint him. Sensing that Wolfensohn and Kohler underestimated the opposition and had not really prepared, I took the offensive in a prepared speech, saying at the outset, "I did not realize I would be sitting this close to James Wolfensohn. I guess this is what you call combat at close quarters." The *Washington Post* was on hand to record what happened next.

Although he has been a head of state for more than a decade now, Vaclav Havel still has the instincts of the playwright he once was, for creating great political theater.

This morning, Havel set his latest play on the grounds of Prague Castle in a building constructed by the Habsburgs for playing badminton. There, with Havel looking on, the heads of the International Monetary Fund and the World Bank—in Prague for their semiannual meetings—heard directly from critics who accused them of coddling tyrants, despoiling the environment and spreading poverty.

"Yes, Mr. Wolfensohn, under your watch you helped to legitimize the Suharto dictatorship [of Indonesia], and that is something the world will never forgive," said Walden Bello, a Philippine scientist and human-rights activist, addressing World Bank President James Wolfensohn, who was sitting beside him.

Minutes before, Katrina Liskora, a Czech student, told Horst Koehler, the German who is head of the IMF, that if the World Bank and IMF had applied their current economic policies to Europe after World War II, "we'd still be living with food rationing today."

And by the end of the 90-minute session, the chairman of Friends of the Earth International told Wolfensohn that he and his colleagues—in their enthusiasm for building dams in Third World countries—were personally responsible for killing 400 people and displacing 10 million more.

Although these complaints have been heard before, they rarely have been delivered in a setting at once so intimate and so public. And not surprisingly, Wolfensohn and Koehler took it all a bit personally.

"I must say that when we go to work every day, we have a rather different view of what we do," replied Wolfensohn, a former investment banker with a long history of philanthropy and civic activism. "We don't think we're responsible for the fact that there's global warming or that there are 3 billion people who live on less than $2 a day. We're not a world government."

"I have a heart, but I also must use my brain to find solutions," said Koehler at another point, making clear that his view that economic policy requires more than just empathy.

Surprisingly, it was Ann Pettifor, an advocate for Third World debt relief, who delivered the most spirited defense of the international bankers, albeit a left-handed one. Her point was that it was really U.S. Treasury Secretary Lawrence H. Summers and the European finance ministers who effectively set the rules of global capitalism.

After the formal presentations, the actors left the stage and continued their dialogue while strolling the shaded grounds of the castle. Billionaires such as George Soros mixed with backpack-carrying student protesters, while South Africa's finance minister sipped wine with human rights activists from Indonesia.

At times it all had a surreal quality as tuxedoed waiters passed drinks while occasional music was provided by roving bands of gypsy fiddlers, chanting monks and a flutist strolling around with a basket over his/her head.

When it was all over, Havel said he was satisfied that the gathering had helped civilize the dialogue between the globalizers and their critics, but he had no illusion of heading off the massive street demonstrations planned for Monday.

"We are only in the first act," the playwright-president said. He wouldn't say how he thought it would turn out.[78]

The second act proved to be an even more militant sequel. Prague lived up to its billing that leaders of the anti-globalization movement had promised it would be. With demonstrations and street battles trapping delegates at the Congress Center or swirling around them as they tried to make their way back to their quarters in that beautiful city's famous Old Town, the agenda was, as one World Bank official put it, "effectively seized" by the anti-globalization protesters. When a large number of delegates refused to go to the Congress

Center in the next two days, the convention had to be abruptly concluded, a day before its scheduled ending.

Prague was not all politics. The evening after the debate, I joined Suranuch ("Ko") Thongsila and the late Gadoy Rodriguez, who was part of a small delegation from the Asian Development Bank, for dinner at a small restaurant near the historic Charles Bridge spanning the Vitava River. They laughed when I told them that Soros had approached me after the debate and said he was embarrassed that Kohler and Wolfensohn had performed "terribly." I had convinced Ko to interrupt her business trip to Spain to come to Prague so she could meet Gadoy, my best friend. There appeared to have been chemistry between them, and things seemed to be proceeding smoothly with my matchmaking plan. Little did I know that, as in the movie *When Harry Meets Sally*, nothing would emerge from my good intentions and I, the purported matchmaker, would be the person who would end up with the lovely Ko ... 13 years later!

The Battle of Genoa

Less than a year after the Prague protests, I was in Genoa, Italy, with my Focus colleagues Shalmali Guttal and Nicola Bullard, to participate in teach-ins at the invitation of Vittorio Agnoletto, Rafaella Bollini, and other leaders of the Genoa Social Forum. Having recently reclaimed the post of prime minister, Silvio Berlusconi, whose name had already become synonymous with corruption, was hosting the summit of the Group of Seven plus Russia, then known as the G8. With some 250,000 people streaming in from all over the world, Genoa went down in history as the biggest of the anti-globalization events and the most violent.

Thursday, June 21, 2000, was devoted to teach-ins. Among those who attracted the biggest crowds were movement gurus Susan George of the Transnational Institute and Frenchman José Bové, better known as the man who had dismantled a McDonalds restaurant—McDonald's Golden Arches, found throughout the world, were the ubiquitous reminders of the globalist project at the turn of the century.

The next day's activities began, in leisurely Italian fashion in contrast to Seattle's on-time activism, at around 2:15 pm with a column of around 8,000–10,000 people, led by the famed Italian specialists in civil disobedience, the *Tute Bianche*, marching down the Via Tolemaide, with marshals using megaphones announcing, "This is a nonviolent march. We believe in nonviolence."[79] The goal of the marchers was to reach the twenty-foot wall of iron that the authorities had erected around the Group of Eight meeting site at the Piazza Ducale about two kilometers away.

We never reached the wall. At the foot of the hill, at the intersection with Via Corsino, *carabinieri* hidden in a small side street started firing tear gas in an unprovoked attack that scattered the advance ranks of the march where there were many reporters and television crews.

Everything happened so quickly. The Battle of Genoa had begun. Throughout the next four hours, the battle unfolded in the narrow side-streets and the small piazzas of the Corso Torino area, with the battle lines shifting constantly. The police would attack with teargas, vans and armored personnel carriers. The protesters would retreat, then come back with stones and bricks ripped from the pavement. Huge trash bins were turned over to serve as barricades. "*Genova Libera! Genova Libera!*" would erupt from the crowd every time the police were forced back.

The image that black Friday embedded in my mind was that of a police van careening down the Via Giovanni Tomaso Invrea, moving crazily from one side of the narrow street to the other in pursuit of protesters. I flattened myself against the wall, and it missed me by two feet. Another six inches and it would have mowed down the man beside me. "*Assassino, assassino*," people screamed as the vehicle stopped a few yards away. A bald *carabinieri* opened the door and glared at us.

Being in constant motion, either running away from the police or running towards clumps of fellow protesters that were reforming themselves, is what my body remembers of those hours that seemed to pass by so quickly. Had it not been for my daily running regimen of seven kilometers, I would have folded quickly that hot summer day. I still could not keep up with my colleague Christophe Aguiton of ATTAC, who seemed to be in different places at the same time.

At 4:20 pm, I had my first glimpse of an injured man being carried away by the first aid personnel of the *Tute Bianche*. It was at around the same time that one person was shot dead by carabinieri in the same vicinity. Ambulance sirens blared constantly. Later I would find out that about 150 people had been injured during the day—about fifty of them being members of the media.

I also learned later that there were acts of civil disobedience throughout the day, the most dramatic apparently being that of a woman from the so-called "Pink Bloc" of marchers who tried to scale the steel wall to place grappling hooks on it, only to be hosed down brutally by the police when she had nearly reached the top.

To the dismay of some, the anarchists—the so-called "Black Bloc"—were also around. Despite efforts by mainstream demonstrators to dissuade them with dramatic pleas for nonviolence, they went about burning a couple of cars, including an Alfa Romeo. They also moved down Genoa's beautiful seafront drive, the Corso Italia, selectively breaking windows—breaking those of banks and car companies while leaving those of restaurants untouched. "Capitalism kills" with an anarchist logo alongside was painted on walls. The antics of the Black Bloc were, however, few and mild compared to those of the *carabinieri*, who staged a riot, as in Seattle.

The most dangerous part of that long summer day occurred at around 5:30 pm, when several hundred of us were able to reassemble and march down a very narrow street, ranged from the solid wall of buildings on one side of the street to that of the other side. There was hardly any space to breathe. At that point, the *carabinieri* unleashed a barrage of tear gas bombs. Had we panicked, there would have been a stampede, and in such crowded quarters, many would have been trampled to death. But our ranks did not break, discipline and solidarity tying us together as we chanted a slogan made popular in Chile 30 years earlier, *"El pueblo unido, jamas sera vencido. The people united will never be defeated. Il popolo unito vincera."*

In contrast to Friday, the next day seemed to be relatively peaceable... until the evening. At around 11 pm, while I and several media people were filing stories, the police barged into the Genoa Social Forum press center in search of "anarchists." *"Prensa, prensa,"* we shouted, our hands held high, as baton-wielding *carabinieri* pushed us and commanded us to sit on the floor. We were captives for the next hour, but things were worse at the high school next door which served as temporary quarters for people coming from out of town. About 200 police in full riot gear crashed into the building, rounding up Nazi-style about twenty young people suspected of being "anarchists."

Twenty years later, one of those who was apparently trapped with me at the media center that evening, the Italian sociologist Paolo Gerbaudo, wrote in the American Left-wing publication *Jacobin*, about how my ideas were still not in the mainstream of the motivations of most of those who came to Genoa but would be in the decade to come:

> The people gathered at the media center that day included Walden Bello, a Filipino economist and environmentalist whose theory of *de-globalization* was becoming influential at the time. Since the 1990s—a decade which had seen the NAFTA agreement, European economic integration, and trade liberalization under the aegis of the World Trade Organization—there had been much debate on the Left on how to approach the global era. For some, economic globalization and its superseding of nation-states was an irreversible tendency. Yes, its nefarious effects had to be

attacked—but its progressive aspects should be reclaimed, pursuing global justice and global democracy as a higher form of universalism.

Bello's approach was more blunt. True to its popular name, the anti-globalization movement had to fight for outright "de-globalization," an overall reduction in planetary economic interconnectedness and a re-localization of economic processes. For Bello . . . de-globalization would mean taking away power from transnational corporations and re-empowering local communities and citizens. It would prioritize equity and environmental sustainability over growth.

Looking back, he wrote in 2021, "At the time of the Genoa protests, any talk of a break from globalization appeared to many as an unrealistic if not outright dystopian prospect. However, twenty years later, this is precisely the course that history is taking."[80]

Setback in Doha

A month and a half after the Battle of Genoa, 9/11 happened. The U.S. and WTO immediately seized on the event to urge a disoriented world that ensuring a successful fourth ministerial of the WTO was one way to fight terrorism—in much the same way President George W. Bush told Americans to go shopping a day after the fateful event. The location, Doha, Qatar, was also unfavorable, and not only because it was deliriously hot during the day. The feudal monarchy that ruled the small desert country was able to limit the number of genuine NGOs granted visas to about 60. Deprived of that synergy between mass mobilizations and developing country delegations, the 30 or so governments that made decisions in non-transparent meetings called the "Green Room" (after the Director General's conference room in the WTO headquarters in Geneva) were able to successfully play a game of divide and rule to launch a new trade round, the so-called Doha Development Round, a process that was captured in detail by Focus staffer Aileen Kwa in her book with Fautomata Jawara, *Behind the Scenes at the WTO.*[81]

Still, Medea Benjamin of Global Exchange, Anuradha Mittal of Food First, and I were able to organize an NGO protest despite the super-paranoia of U.S., Qatari, and WTO officials. Standing on both sides of the entrance to the huge Al Dafna Hall at the Sheraton, the protesters carried a common sign that read "No Voice at the WTO," calling attention to the lack of transparency, democracy, and civil society input in the decision-making processes of the organization. Once most of the delegates had filed in, the demonstrators started chanting "What do we want? Democracy!" An effort by Jose Bove, the famous French anti-McDonalds activist, to lead the demonstrators into the hall was initially countered by Qatari security forces. A few moments later, however, they were allowed in. Fulfilling a pledge made at an open session earlier in the day by the Qatari Crown Prince, the authorities detained none of the activists. It was a small ray of light in what appeared to be a major setback for the forces fighting globalization.

Indeed, Doha was a big blow to us, and in more ways than one. To placate developing countries and global civil society, Clare Short, the development minister of Tony Blair's Labor government in the United Kingdom, had successfully campaigned to have the round of trade negotiations launched in Doha labeled the "Doha Development Round." A number of international NGOs like Oxfam were unfortunately taken in by this devious attempt to cover up the main goal of the WTO, i.e. to further open up developing country economies, ban technology acquisition by them, and prevent them from undertaking industrial policy. Though with good intentions, Oxfam sought to use trade negotiations to get the developed countries to grant duty-free access to the agricultural products of the least developed countries. This was, I argued, a big mistake, since it would legitimize the WTO and distract us from the main objective, which was to derail it and render it dysfunctional from further liberalizing developing country agriculture and industry, which had already been destabilized by the previous Uruguay Round.

In the debate that ensued, Oxfam maintained its position, though it said that while disagreeing with me and Focus, "Oxfam holds the work of Walden Bello in the highest regard. He has played a central role in challenging the legitimacy of global institutions that place corporate profit and the self-interest of Northern governments before the imperative of poverty reduction. We also recognize the enormous contribution made by Focus in mobilizing support for change."[82] It sounded like a concession even before the fisticuffs had begun.

But Oxfam's position was overtaken by events. Its push to get the Global North to get the WTO to grant tariff privileges to LDC exports did not even reach first base, since it was the strategy of making the WTO dysfunctional as a mechanism of trade liberalization that prevailed, not so much by plan but by the concatenation of events and the convergence of interests during the following WTO ministerial meeting, the fateful Fifth Ministerial in Cancun in 2003.

Walden joins Maude Barlow of the Council of Canadians (left) and
Anuradha Mittal of Food First in celebrating the collapse of the Fifth
Ministerial of the World Trade Organization in Cancun, Mexico.

LICENSED BY AGENCE FRANCE-PRESSE

Collapse in Cancun

When the Fifth Ministerial Meeting of the WTO convened in Cancun,
Mexico, in September 2003, countries from the Global South showed that
they had learned from the divide and conquer tactics of the Global North
in Doha. Intransigence on the part of the EU and U.S. to cut their massive
agricultural subsidies provoked the formation of a united front, the G20, led
by India, Brazil, South Africa, and China, to ensure that there would be no
retreat by the developing countries from their demands for substantial cuts
in all forms of agricultural subsidies deployed by governments in the Global
North. Another group, the Group of 33 developing countries, formed around
the demands against tariff reductions for imports that would compete with
"special products" they produced and for "special safeguard mechanisms"
against highly subsidized agricultural exports from the global North. Another,
even larger grouping formed around resistance to the efforts by the rich

countries to begin negotiations on the "New Issues," that is, to use the WTO to liberalize investment, competition policy, government procurement, and trade facilitation. When some developed countries nevertheless signaled their unwillingness to drop the "New Issues" from the negotiating agenda, several G 90 members walked out, leading the Ministerial to collapse like a house of cards. Again, the consensus rule—which the rich countries had originally promoted, confident that this democratic concession would not prevent them from obtaining a coerced consensus from the poor countries—proved, as in Seattle some three years earlier, to be the Achilles Heel of the WTO.

Civil society was a central part of the equation of collapse. Within the Cancun Convention Center, civil society organizations like the South Center, Third World Network, and Focus on the Global South provided invaluable advice to the developing country delegations. Outside the center, lightning demonstrations flared throughout the three days of the meeting, the climax of which was Korean farmer Lee Kyung Hae taking his own life by stabbing himself in the heart while on top of one of the barricades to protest the marginalization of small farmers. The suicide took place just a few feet from where my good friend, Anuradha Mittal, and my Focus colleague, Marylou Malig, were standing. We were stunned and horrified, as were the other demonstrators. So were the official delegates, who observed a minute of silence in his memory. Indeed, given the intensity of the North-South conflict, it was likely that Lee's taking his life in what the French classical sociologist Emile Durkheim would have called "altruistic suicide" was one of the ingredients that led to the walkout of developing country delegates and the subsequent collapse of the ministerial.

There continued to be ministerial meetings after Cancun, but after its collapse there, the WTO ceased to be the main avenue for the U.S. and EU's efforts at trade liberalization. Robert Zoellick, the U.S. Trade Representative, warned, "The rhetoric of 'won't do' overwhelmed the concerted efforts of the 'can do.' 'Won't do' led to the impasse.... As the WTO members ponder the future, the U.S. will not wait; we will move towards free trade with can-do countries."[83] Zoellick was as good as his word: the U.S. focused its efforts at forging bilateral free trade agreements. So did the EU, which sugarcoated such anti-development initiatives as "economic partnership agreements."

Showdown in Hong Kong

The Asian Financial Crisis delivered the first big shock to the globalist project. Seattle exposed its dark side in the most dramatic fashion. The battles of Prague and Genoa globalized resistance and Cancun delivered a near-fatal blow to the corporate global trade agenda promoted by an organization that

Mike Moore, one of its directors general, had described as the "jewel in the crown of multilateralism." Even before the Global Financial Crisis of 2008 demonstrated how unfettered capital flows could bring the world to the brink of financial collapse and Covid 19 exposed the fragility of TNC global supply chains, globalization was in trouble, undone by its false assumptions as well as by the global resistance of ordinary people.

The final act in my personal duel with neoliberalism and globalization was yet to take place. On February 28, 2019, a few months before Covid 19 shut down the world for three years, I was invited by the *Economist*, the ideological font of free trade, to debate Robert Koopman, the chief economist of the WTO, at the Asia Trade Summit in Hong Kong. Billed as the "Great Trade Debate," the Oxford-style 20-minute debate took place before an audience made up largely of corporate executives and government delegates.

Never one to refuse a challenge, I used the opportunity to compress what I had been saying about free markets, free trade, and globalization over the last thirty years into a five-minute speech (that went overtime to six minutes):

> I am all for trade. But I am not for "free trade," because it's a bad idea and bad policy.
>
> Free trade is in real trouble today. But the promoters of free trade brought this on themselves. However, it is not because they have been tepid in their defense of free trade, as the description of this debate has it. They have been guilty of far greater sins.
>
> The first sin is hypocrisy. Free trade ideologues have enshrined the WTO as the so-called "jewel in the crown of free trade and globalization." Yet, the WTO promotes monopoly, not free markets, in its key agreements. The Trade Related Intellectual Property Rights Agreement (TRIPS) seeks to restrict the diffusion of knowledge and technology and reserve for giant corporations the fruits of technological innovation by significantly tightening patent rules.
>
> The Trade Related Investment Measures (TRIMS) agreement was meant to preserve and expand the markets of the existing automobile giants by outlawing local content policies that had enabled developing countries like Korea and Malaysia to develop their motor vehicle industries—industries which had, in turn, been central to the comprehensive industrialization of these economies.

The Agreement on Agriculture (AOA) has been nothing but an instrument to pry open developing country markets to highly subsidized agricultural products from EU and the United States.

Free trade is simply a euphemism for the corporate capture of international trade.

The second sin of the free trade ideologues is that what they've promoted is pure ideology. They say that countries that practice free trade are the ones that have successfully developed. Wrong. In fact, whether it was Germany and the United States in the 19th century, Japan and Korea in the 20th century, and China in the 21st century, protection of the domestic market, export-subsidies, domestic content requirements, investment regulations, unrestricted technological acquisition from foreign firms, currency management, and informal and formal import barriers were critical to industrial development.

(Yes, China's growth was export-oriented, but let's not kid ourselves. China did not engage in free trade but in managed trade that included a healthy dose of creative currency management and tremendous export subsidies.)

On the other hand, those countries that allowed themselves to be fooled or were bullied by the apostles of free trade and forgot the creative role of the state, like Mexico, the Philippines, and much of Africa, bit the dust.

The third sin of the free trade ideologues is disseminating as true very questionable conclusions from bad research. There is, in fact, little or no evidence that, as the World Bank claims, "countries that used large tariff cuts to open their trade to the beneficial effects of globalization have seen more poverty reduction than those that have not."

Don't take it from me. Take it from the celebrated task force of top economists co-chaired by Nobel laureate Angus Deaton from Princeton that was formed to evaluate the research on the impact of trade liberalization and globalization being conducted by the World Bank, the main institutional advocate of free trade. In a scathing review, the panel wrote: "[M]uch of this line of research appears to have such deep flaws that, at present, the results cannot be regarded as remotely reliable, much as one might want to believe the results." The Bank's evidence, they said, was "chosen selectively, without supporting argument, and empirical skepticism selectively suspended."

Bringing up the dubious quality of World Bank research is important because most of the free trade lobby, including the WTO, has relied on it in their advocacy.

On the other hand, what does solid research reveal?

First, that greater global integration through trade has greatly increased inequality within countries and, if you take out the very exceptional case of China, increased inequality among the global population of households and individuals.

Second, that globalization has created in both the Global North and the Global South intra-country polarization between domestic regions that prosper from trade and those that are driven to greater poverty by trade.

Third, that globalization has had differential impacts on the developing world, with East Asian countries benefiting from it because of their prior protectionist policies and managed trade during the period of globalization, and Latin America, Africa, and the Middle East drawing little benefit or indeed suffering from it. It is not only regions of the U.S. and Europe that have suffered deindustrialization from Chinese products but manufacturing industries in Mexico, Brazil, and Africa.

Fourth, free trade, by encouraging more unbridled consumption, is a key driver of increased carbon emissions and overwhelms whatever gains are made by greater energy efficiency. I am not only talking about transportation but the creation of global value chains with big carbon footprints.

Is the answer to withdraw from global trade, as the free traders have caricatured our position? No, it is to go back to a system like the General Agreements on Tariffs and Trade (GATT), which promoted trade but was flexible enough to allow countries policy space to develop and to preserve their intricate social contracts by preventing commodity dumping, environmental dumping, and social dumping.

Like the ideologues of centrally planned "socialism," the ideologues of free trade ignored all this and tried to impose a one-size fits all model on everyone. They produced not the best of all possible worlds but Donald Trump.[84]

Surprisingly, the audience judged me the winner, unanimously. These were people from business, government, academia, and media who would

Walden talks to the media after he and others disrupted the opening of the
World Trade Organization's Sixth Ministerial Conference in Hong Kong

COURTESY OF ASSOCIATED PRESS

not have given me and my ideas the time of day 20 years earlier. Indeed, the world had turned upside down.

Still, our victory over free trade and the WTO was largely limited to the realm of intellectual debate. When it came to concrete policymaking, policies guided by neoliberal assumptions continued as the default mode, even for technocrats who could see they were not working. Part of the reason was that these policies had been institutionalized in constitutions and laws in scores of countries and multilateral agreements, making initiating anti-neoliberal moves difficult, if not impossible, even if one wanted to. Part was that although the anti-globalization movement was effective in pointing out the flaws of specific sectoral neoliberal policies and institutions, what it was much less effective in doing was exposing how these policy failures were connected to one another because neoliberalism was a coherent ideological system based on wrong assumptions that doomed the economy across the board to permanent instability and crises.

Finally, an important part of the reason for the resilience of neoliberalism despite its failures was the inability of alternative paradigms advanced by progressives to gain traction beyond narrow circles. These included paradigms that, among other things, would justify activist government, promote community participation in economic decision-making, place the environment at the center of economics, and champion other values than narrow efficiency such as gender equality.

Yet reality would eventually break through the neoliberal fog, and for many this happened not in intellectual debate but in relation to global realpolitik: the rise to economic primacy of China's managed capitalist economy, where market forces were harnessed by a powerful developmental state to politically and socially determined objectives, like radically reducing poverty, building a supra-modern national transportation structure in record time, and the determined rapid acquisition of technology, all of which placed the state in a central role. By the time of Joe Biden's presidency, thanks partly to Donald Trump's savaging of free trade during his term in office, neoliberalism had become a bad word in U.S. policy circles, and the state had to step in in a major way if the U.S. were not to be left behind by China.

For much of the Global South like the Philippines, most of Africa, and much of Latin America, however, neoliberalism imposed by technocrats linked to the IMF and World Bank continued to reign, though its days were numbered ... hopefully.

10. Alternative Futures

SOMETIME in the middle of 2000, Focus on the Global South received an invitation from the late Gustavo Codas, Maria ("Maisa") Mendonca, Chico Whitaker, and other friends in Brazil to participate in a projected "World Social Forum" that would be held in the city of Porto Alegre early in 2001. The idea was to have a global counterpoint to Davos. It was irresistible.

The Porto Alegre versus Davos Debate

The organizers of the WSF had this great idea of kicking off events with a televised trans-Atlantic debate. Billed as a "Dialogue between Davos and Porto Alegre," the ambitious $1 million production involving four satellite hookups, aimed to explore if there was common ground between the annual elite gathering in Davos and the newly launched World Social Forum in the medium-size southern Brazilian city. Since I had been to Davos the previous year, I was requested to make the opening statement for our side.

When I arrived at the studio for the debate with George Soros, the financier, and other representatives of the elite in Davos, Switzerland, a visibly shaken Florian Rochat of the Swiss delegation was waiting for me.[85] The Swiss are known for being impassive, but Florian was trembling.

"They are arresting protesters in Davos," he told me. "They're killing democracy in our country. Our friends there are asking you to support them in calling for the shutting down of the World Economic Forum."

That request drove out any lingering desire to be "nice" in the coming exchange. I obliged with the following: "We would like to begin by condemning the arrests of peaceful demonstrators to shield the global elite at Davos from protests."

"I was in Davos last year, and believe me, Davos is not worth a second visit. I am here in Porto Alegre this year and let me say that Porto Alegre is the future while Davos is the past. Hemingway wrote that the rich are different from you and me, and indeed, we live on two different planets: Davos, the planet of the super-rich, Porto Alegre, the planet of the poor, the marginalized, the concerned. Here in Porto Alegre, we are discussing how to save the planet. There in Davos, the global elite is discussing how to maintain its hegemony over the rest of us."

The press termed the next 90 minutes not a debate but an emotional exchange of personal insults. But I and the other panelists were simply reflecting the non-conciliatory mood toward the Davos crowd of most of the 12,000 people who flocked to Porto Alegre.

Perhaps the outcome of the duel between Davos and Porto Alegre was best summed up by George Soros: "The excessive precautions were a victory for those who wanted to disrupt Davos. It was an overreaction. It helped to radicalize the situation."

On his performance in the televised debate with Porto Alegre, Soros commented: "It showed it is not easy to dialogue." Then he added, "I don't particularly like to be abused. My masochism has its limits." Soros had apparently been thrown off-balance when Hebe de Bonafine, representing the Argentine organization of the mothers of the disappeared, *Las Madres de la Plaza de Mayo,* screamed at him across the Atlantic Divide, "Mr. Soros, you are a hypocrite. How many children's deaths have you been responsible for?" That Soros had, in the course of the debate, made some utterances regarding the need to mitigate the negative impacts of globalization did nothing to endear him to the Porto Alegre crowd, who saw him mainly as a finance speculator who had made billions of dollars at the expense of economies in the Global South.

Observed the *Financial Times*: "Such uncomfortable experiences seem temporarily to have scrambled his ability to deliver pithy sound bites."

But Soros was not alone in flubbing his lines. Soon after my opening statement, Bernard Cassen of *Le Monde Diplomatique* leaned over and told me: "Walden, it wasn't Hemingway who said the rich are different from you and me. It was Scott Fitzgerald."

That first WSF in Porto Alegre set the style for its successors over the next decade. "Another world is possible" was the forum's slogan. Porto Alegre lived up to it, with its thousands of participants, mainly from Latin America, engaged not only in drawing up strategies of resistance to globalization but in elaborating as well alternative paradigms of economic, ecological and social development.

Militant action was not absent, with José Bové and the Brazilian Movement of the Landless (MST) leading the destruction of two hectares of land planted with transgenic soybean crops by the biotechnological firm Monsanto.

There was another important symbolic dimension: while Seattle was the site of the first major victory of the transnational anti-corporate globalization movement—the collapse amidst massive street protests of the third ministerial meeting of the World Trade Organization—Porto Alegre represented the transfer to the South of the center of gravity of that movement. Proclaimed as an "open space," the WSF became a magnet for global networks focused on different issues, from war to globalization to communalism to racism to gender oppression to alternatives. Regional versions of the WSF were spun off, the most important being the European Social Forum, the African Social Forum, and the Asian Social Forum; and in scores of cities throughout the world, local social fora were held and institutionalized.

The World Social Forum

The WSF performed three critical functions for global civil society:

First, it represented a space—both physical and temporal—for this diverse movement to meet, network, and, quite simply, to feel and affirm itself.

Second, it was a retreat during which the movement gathered its energies and charted the directions of its continuing drive to confront and roll back the processes, institutions, and structures of global capitalism. Naomi Klein, author of *No Logo*, underlined this function when she told a Porto Alegre audience in January 2002 that the need of the moment was "less civil society and more civil disobedience."[86]

Third, the WSF provided a site and space for the movement to elaborate, discuss, and debate the vision, values, and institutions of an alternative world order built on a real community of interests. The WSF was, indeed, a macrocosm of so many smaller but equally significant enterprises carried out throughout the world by millions who told the reformists, the cynics, and the "realists" to move aside because, indeed, another world was possible ... and necessary.

The WSF and its many offspring were significant not only as sites of affirmation and debate but also as direct democracy in action. Agenda and meetings were planned with meticulous attention to democratic process. This was before the Zoom era, so it was no mean feat that through a combination of periodic face-to-face meetings and intense email and Internet contact in between, the WSF network was able to pull off events and arrive at consensus decisions. At times, this could be very time-consuming and also frustrating, and when you were part of an organizing effort involving hundreds of organizations, as we at Focus on the Global South were during the organizing of the 2004 WSF in Mumbai, it could be very frustrating indeed. But this was direct democracy, and direct democracy was at its best at the WSF. One might say, parenthetically, that the direct democratic experiences of Seattle, Prague,

Genoa, and the other big mobilizations of the decade were institutionalized in the WSF or Porto Alegre process.

The central principle of the organizing approach of the new movement was that getting to the desired objective was not worth it if the methods violated democratic process, if democratic goals were reached via authoritarian means. Perhaps Subcomandante Marcos of the Zapatistas best expressed the organizing bias of the new movements: "The movement has no future if its future is military. If the EZLN [Zapatistas] perpetuates itself as an armed military structure, it is headed for failure. Failure as an alternative set of ideas, an alternative attitude to the world. The worst that could happen to it apart from that, would be for it to come to power and install itself there as a revolutionary army."[87] The WSF shared that perspective.

What was interesting was that there was hardly any attempt by any group or network to "take over" the WSF process. Quite a number of "old movement" groups participated in the WSF, including Leninist "democratic centralist" parties as well as traditional social democratic parties affiliated with the Socialist International. Yet none of these put much effort into steering the WSF towards more centralized or hierarchical modes of organizing. At the same time, despite their suspicion of political parties, the "new movements" never sought to exclude the old parties and their affiliates from playing a significant role in the Forum. Indeed, the 2004 WSF in Mumbai was organized jointly by an unlikely coalition of Marxist-Leninist parties and social movements like the *Narmada Bachao Andolan* that opposed the Narmada River Dam, a set of actors that were not known for harmonious relations on the domestic front.

Perhaps a compelling reason for the modus vivendi of the old and new movements was the realization that they needed one another in the struggle against global capitalism and that the strength of the fledgling global movement lay in a strategy of decentralized networking that rested not on the doctrinaire belief that one class was destined to lead the struggle but on the reality of the common marginalization of practically all subordinate classes, strata, and groups under the reign of global capital.

The WSF was, however, not exempt from criticism, even from its own ranks. One in particular appeared to have merit. This was the charge that the WSF as an institution was unanchored in actual global political struggles, and this was turning it into an annual festival with limited social impact.

There was, in my view, a not insignificant truth to this. Many of the founders of the WSF interpreted the "open space" concept in a liberal fashion, that is, for the WSF not to explicitly endorse any political position or particular struggle, though its constituent groups were free to do so. Others disagreed, saying the idea of an "open space" should be interpreted in a partisan fashion, as explicitly promoting some views over others and as openly taking sides in key global struggles. In this latter view, the WSF was under an illusion that it could stand above the fray, and this would lead to its becoming some sort of neutral forum, where discussion would increasingly be isolated from action. The energy of civil society networks derived from their being engaged in political struggles, said proponents of this perspective. The reason that the WSF was so exciting in its early years was because of its affective impact: it provided an opportunity to recreate and reaffirm solidarity against injustice, against war, and for a world that was not subjected to the rule of empire and capital. The WSF's not taking official stands on the Iraq War, on the Palestine issue, and on the WTO was said to be making it less relevant and less inspiring to many of the networks it had brought together. I was partial to this view.

This is why the Sixth WSF held in Caracas in January 2006 was so bracing and reinvigorating: it inserted some 50,000 delegates into the storm center of an ongoing struggle against empire, where they mingled with militant Venezuelans, mostly the poor, engaged in a process of social transformation, while observing other Venezuelans, mostly the elite and middle class, engaged in bitter opposition. Caracas was an exhilarating reality check.

President Hugo Chavez captured the essence of the conjuncture when he warned delegates in Caracas about the danger of the WSF becoming simply a forum of ideas with no agenda for action. He told participants that they had no choice but to address the question of power: "We must have a strategy of 'counter-power.' We, the social movements and political movements, must be able to move into spaces of power at the local, national, and regional level."[88]

Developing a strategy of counter-power or counter-hegemony did not mean lapsing back into the old hierarchical and centralized modes of organizing characteristic of the old Left. Such a strategy could, in fact, be best advanced through the multilevel and horizontal networking in which the movements and organizations represented in the WSF had excelled in advancing their particular struggles. Articulating their struggles in action meant forging a common strategy while drawing strength from and respecting diversity.

After witnessing how the Kenyan government and commercial interests were able to coopt the Seventh World Social Forum in Nairobi in 2007 and blunt its radical message, I wrote, "Many long-standing participants in the Forum are asking themselves: Is the WSF still the most appropriate vehicle for the new stage in the struggle of the global justice and peace movement?

Or, having fulfilled its historic function of aggregating and linking the diverse counter-movements spawned by global capitalism, is it time for the WSF to fold up its tent and give way to new modes of global organization of resistance and transformation?"[89]

My answer came in the form of the Global Financial Crisis that broke out in 2008, provoking the rise of the Occupy Movement in the U.S., the *Indignados* Movement in Spain, and the Anti-Austerity Movement in Greece in 2010. This was followed by the Arab Spring in 2011. Just as the anti-globalization movement had helped bring about the WSF in the early 2000s, so too did the huge tent of the WSF house diverse social movements that then broke out of its confines when globalization and authoritarianism entered their latest crises. There were continuities as well as breaks in these successive incarnations of the spirit of anti-capitalism and democracy.

I met many impressive people in the years I was active in the WSF. Two of them were Naomi Klein and Hugo Chavez.

Naomi Klein Deconstructs Contemporary Capitalism

When Naomi came up to me at the first WSF in Porto Alegre in February 2001 and modestly handed me her book, with the quiet dedication "to Walden, with respect and solidarity," little did I know that I was receiving a stick of dynamite.

Before our meeting, I had, of course, heard of Naomi Klein and had read somewhere that her *No Logo* was fast becoming the anthem of the anti–corporate globalization movement.[90] But nothing had prepared me for the dizzying intellectual experience of going through the book. I was so impressed I gave it one of the most enthusiastic reviews I have written.[91]

Naomi's essential point in *No Logo* was that capitalism in the age of globalization is the age of the brand, the logo. Logos are everywhere, staring at you during your most private moment in the john; invading once clearly delineated public spaces like schools; becoming, like the Nike swoosh, the centerpiece of athletic and cultural spectacles. We live in a "branded world" where taste, cultural standards, and ultimately even values are increasingly defined by megabrands like Nike, whose swoosh has come to represent the ultimate in athletic style and whose slogan, "Just Do It," identified Nike with the assertion of individuality.

The age of the brand, Naomi asserted, witnesses the evolution of a new relationship between the producer and its product. Originally, brands were meant to assure the quality of the product; today the brand has detached itself from the product to become, instead, the selling point.

This was deconstruction of capitalism at its best.

Naomi Klein, a central figure in the anti-globalization movement, endorses Walden's vice-presidential bid during the 2022 Philippine national elections.

Naomi and I kept in close touch over the years. I also reviewed her book *The Shock Doctrine: The Rise of Disaster Capitalism.*[92] She called me "the world's leading no-nonsense revolutionary," a description that embarrassed me not a little but that provided a staple line for people introducing me to an audience before my speeches, and made me the exception to her rule of not endorsing people running for elected office by supporting my run for vice president of the Philippines in 2022.[93]

The Larger-than-Life Hugo Chavez

Unlike in the case of Naomi, I have not been in touch with Hugo Chavez for the simple reason that he passed away in 2013.

I first met Chavez in August 2002, when I attended an international conference in Caracas, Venezuela. My account of that meeting read:

> At a banquet for participants at an international conference the next evening, Hugo Chavez, President of the Bolivarian Republic of Venezuela, is at his social, disarming best. Upon being introduced to me, he takes me by the hand, pretending to lead me in the Filipino bamboo dance "tinikling", which he says he learned during a state visit to the Philippines during the presidency of Joseph Estrada. And far into the evening, he talks expansively on a wide range of topics, from his being saved and re-installed by the poor in Miraflores, the presidential palace, during the failed coup of April 11–13, to his dream of integrating the petroleum industries of Venezuela, Brazil, and other oil producers in Latin America.[94]

Venezuelan President Hugo Chávez, who read Walden's books and called him "mi padre," offered Walden refuge in Venezuela when he was declared a "counterrevolutionary" by the Communist Party of the Philippines.

CREATIVE COMMONS

When I next met him in at the World Social Forum in Porto Alegre—I believe it was 2003—he greeted me, "*Mi padre*," and said he learned a lot from me. I was dubious about this and thought he was simply buttering me up, like any two-bit politician. Then he started telling me what he learned from *Development Debacle, Deglobalization,* and *Dark Victory*. I was stupefied; the guy actually read my stuff! He actually asked me detailed questions about assertions I made in those books, leaving me a bit red in the face since I didn't remember what I had written and ended up fumbling my responses. Like many exceptional individuals, Hugo had an eye and memory for detail.

About two years later, we met again, this time again in Caracas. He told me he was seriously concerned about my safety since he had heard that the Communist Party of the Philippines had marked me as a "counterrevolutionary" and targeted me for elimination. He invited me to cool off in Venezuela, telling me he would take me on a tour of the whole country. Thank you, I said, but he shouldn't worry since I was dealing with a bunch of space cadets, though crazy ones. He asked me what a "space cadet" was. I tried my best to explain, then he said, "Ahh, *un pendejo*," and roared with laughter. It was a moment of levity but we both knew we were dealing with pretty serious stuff—the not very nice consequences of being labelled a "counterrevolutionary" by former comrades.

In January 2006, during the World Social Forum in Caracas, he had several of us sit with him on stage and introduced us one by one. When it came to me, he declared grandiloquently that "in his veins runs the blood of Asian martyrs." I didn't know whether to laugh or crawl under my chair, while he went on to construct an image of me that, wow, I wish was true!

The next day, at a forum of representatives of social movements, he asked me what I thought about what was happening in Venezuela. I don't know what came over me, but I made use of the occasion to criticize his government for going back on its promise not to sign the Declaration of the World Trade Organization Ministerial Meeting in Hong Kong in December 2005, which would have led to the third collapse of a WTO ministerial, one that would have been the last nail in the coffin of that anti-development mafia dominated by the North. "As a revolutionary, you can't go back on your word," I said. He was silent, offering no defense. And that was the last time I got invited to Caracas. The guy was great, but he could not take criticism.

I didn't take that personally, though, since nobody could kick the U.S. in the ass like he did. He did and got away with what we all wanted to do, and he entertained us in the process, with unparalleled humor, as when he ascended the rostrum at the United Nations General Assembly where U.S. President George W. Bush had spoken the day before and declared that he still smelled the sulfur that was the odor of *el diablo*.

When he died, I wrote an obituary titled "I'll Miss Hugo:" "Goodbye, Comandante Hugo. You were a class act, one impossible to follow. Wherever you are right now, give 'em hell."[95] The article would later be used by people who hated me to discredit my politics, especially when Venezuela descended into deep crisis under Chavez' successor. My response, which always took them aback, was always to affirm that "I miss the guy."

Deglobalization: The Evolution of an Idea

In the discussion of alternatives to capitalism at the World Social Forum, Focus and I became identified with the term "deglobalization." The *Economist* cited me—in a disapproving context—as having coined the term.[96] I plead guilty. Deglobalization was never meant as a neutral term. It was conceived in political struggle. If globalization was what we were opposing, then we had to counter it with the strongest idea possible: deglobalization. When we advanced it, deglobalization was a vision, a strategy, not a description of an empirical reality or process, as it is used now to describe current trends away from globalized production and global supply chains or "reshoring," though we foresaw these.

This did not mean it was simply a slogan. It was a program, the main points of which were refocusing the economy back on production for the domestic market rather than for export markets, resubordinating the market to society, reasserting cooperation over competition, replacing the pursuit of narrow efficiency with that of social effectiveness, and allowing for a diversity of ways of organizing the economy rather than fitting all economies into one mold, as per the neoliberal template. It was also an idea that sprang from a rich intellectual tradition, associated with the Hungarian thinker, Karl Polanyi.

In his classic book *The Great Transformation* that came out in 1944,[97] Polanyi wrote that the unregulated market championed by neoliberals emerged from a process of "disembedding" the market from the broader social system, so that market relations came to drive the whole system. But he also argued that this disembedding was the first phase of a "double movement." When the disembedded market began to run out of control, creating tremendous social crises, society reasserted its supremacy over the market. The second phase occurred after the Great Depression of the 20th century, in the shape of strong state intervention to "re-embed" the market in society.

Inspired by Polanyi's double movement, the deglobalization paradigm called for a second re-embedding of the market in society after the crisis unleashed by the unfettered market under neoliberalism. "Something fundamentally similar is necessary today, with the current crisis of neoliberalism," I wrote. "Unlike classical socialism, degobalization does not call for the abolition of the market and its replacement by central planning. What it does call for is the 're-embedding' of market relations in society, meaning that social relations must reflect the subordination of market efficiency to the higher social values of community, solidarity, and equality. The market's role in exchange and the allocation of resources is important, but this must not only be balanced but subordinated to the maintenance and enhancement of social solidarity. The state and civil society must not only act to balance and guide the market but, in place of the invisible hand as the agent of the economic common good must come the visible hand of democratic choice. In place of the economics of narrow efficiency, we propose what we might call "effective economics."[98]

Stockholm, December 2003

Deglobalization was the theme of my acceptance speech when in 2003, I was named the recipient of the Right Livelihood Award, also known as the Alternative Nobel Prize, along with fellow Filipino Nicanor Perlas and former New Zealand Prime Minister David Lange, who had been responsible for his country's ban on the entry of nuclear-armed warships, a tremendously brave act. The reason for my getting the award, according to the official citation, was "[f]or his outstanding efforts in educating civil society about the effects of corporate globalization, and how alternatives to it can be implemented." Addressing the audience at the Swedish Parliament in Stockholm on December 8, 2003, I said,

... [A]bove all, we must change the rules of the global economy, for it is the logic of global capitalism that is the source of the disruption of society and of the environment. The challenge is that even as we deconstruct the old, we dare to imagine and win over people to our visions and programs for the new.

Contrary to the claims of the ideologues of the establishment, the principles that would serve as the pillars of a new global order are present. The primordial principle is that instead of the economy, the market, driving society, the market must be—to use the image of the great Hungarian Social Democrat Karl Polanyi—"reembedded" in society and governed by the overarching values of community, solidarity, justice, and equity. At the international level, the global economy must be deglobalized or rid of the distorting, disfiguring logic of corporate profitability and truly internationalized, meaning that participation in the international economy must serve to strengthen and develop rather than disintegrate and destroy local and national economies.

The perspective and principles are there; the challenge is how each society can articulate these principles and programs in unique ways that respond to their values, their rhythms, their personality as societies. Call it post-modern, but central to our movement is the conviction that, in contrast to the belief common to both neoliberalism and bureaucratic socialism, there is no one shoe that will fit all. It is no longer a question of an alternative but of alternatives.

But there is an urgency to the task of articulating credible and viable alternatives to the global community, for the dying spasms of old orders have always presented not just great opportunity but great risk.

At the beginning of the 20th century, the revolutionary thinker Rosa Luxemburg made her famous comment about the possibility that the future might belong to "barbarism."

Barbarism in the form of fascism nearly triumphed in the 1930s and 1940s.

Today, corporate-driven globalization is creating so much of the same instability, resentment, and crisis that are the breeding grounds of fascist, fanatical, and authoritarian populist movements.

Globalization not only has lost its promise but it is embittering many. The forces representing human solidarity and community have no choice but to step in quickly to convince the disenchanted masses that, indeed, as the banner of World Social Forum in Porto Alegre proclaims, "Another world is possible." For the alternative is, as in the 1930s, to see the vacuum filled by terrorists, demagogues of the religious and secular Right, and the purveyors of irrationality and nihilism.

The future, dear friends, is in the balance.[99]

Walden (third from right) is one of two Filipinos (the other being Nicanor Perlas, second from right) to receive the Right Livelihood Award in 2003.

COURTESY OF RIGHT LIVELIHOOD FOUNDATION

The evening after the award ceremonies, my wife Marilen, my step-daughter Annette and our good friends Robin Broad and Rebecca Ratcliffe and I had dinner in a lovely restaurant in the center of Stockholm. We were later joined by Philippine Ambassador to Sweden, Victoria Bataclan, who pulled the surprise of the evening when she revealed she had been part of the First Quarter Storm, the historic Philippine student protests of 1970. There were snow flurries that night, but that did not disrupt my feelings of near-perfect bliss. It was a memory that remained vivid and precious in later years, after my marriage to Marilen ended in 2006, a victim of too many absences owing to political commitments as well as personal differences.

In its later iterations after my Stockholm speech, deglobalization was translated from principles into a concrete program that came to include, among others, activist trade and industrial policies, land and income redistribution, de-emphasis on economic growth in favor of improvement in equity and environment enhancing policies, and the creation of a "mixed economy" that included community cooperatives, private enterprises, and state enterprises.

Some called what we were proposing a non-capitalist economy. We did not object. More critical commentators said we were anti-capitalist. We did not deny it. But what we did do was seek common ground with other exciting emerging paradigms such as Food Sovereignty, Ecofeminism, Eco-socialism, Degrowth, and "Buen Vivir"—the last being a paradigm incorporating the perspectives of indigenous communities in the Andes.

Deglobalization and the Far Right

During the second decade of the new century, things became more complicated in terms of the public's reception of the deglobalization paradigm. The situation in France, for instance, was interesting. Arnaud Montebourg, a member of the Socialist Party, ran for president under the banner of *demondialisation*, with one account noting that "the utopia of demondialisation is all the more appealing as Montebourg points out that it's not a rich-man's dream of keeping the poor at bay, crediting Walden Bello, the Princeton-educated Filipino writer, politician, and a man of the South for the concept."[100] Montebourg was later appointed minister of reindustrialization in the government of President Francois Hollande, though, as far as I know, he never got to seriously implement a program of deglobalization.

On the other hand, the French far right led by Marine Le Pen of the National Front embraced deglobalization, but it cleverly mixed valid working-class anxieties about globalization with anti-European Union and anti-immigrant sentiments. As one account noted, Le Pen "carries the idea [of] globalization further, as she advocates an exit by France from the euro and erection of barriers at France's borders. Her plan, a one-country-versus-all approach, makes no economic sense, but carries strong nationalistic and emotional appeal."[101]

What was happening was that themes we had articulated, among them the subordination of trade to the social good, the expansion of social protection, and the re-embedding of the market in society were being articulated within an ideological framework that privileged the dominant social group and marginalized large numbers of people on the basis of their race, ethnicity, nationality, or culture. Deglobalization was being hijacked to provide legitimacy to anti-migrant politics. The right was appealing to community, but its concept of community was very different from that of the progressive tradition. As I later pointed out,

For the right, community is determined by race, ethnicity, and blood. It is narrow in terms of who is included in it rather than expansive. For us, community is principally a matter of shared values that transcend differences in blood, gender, race, class, and culture. Community tends towards continual expansion and incorporation of people that share the same values. ... Central to this interpretation of community is the assumption that all people are entitled to the full range of political, civil, economic, social, and human rights, including the right to join a desired community. This does not mean that there are no procedural rules governing the acquisition of citizenship or migration. It does mean though that these rules and regulations are guided by a fundamental openness towards accepting those who wish to join a community.[102]

I called the far right's embrace of anti-globalization or deglobalization the "right eating the Left's lunch," since the Left had originated the critique, but it was the extreme right that was able to use it with resounding success to capture the hearts and minds of a great number of those working-class women and men dislocated by and resentful of corporate-driven globalization.

As the deglobalization paradigm entered its third decade, we who had launched it faced the ironic situation of having been vindicated in our critique of globalization yet fighting to wrest the perspective and the program from the clutches of forces that had opportunistically seized deglobalization as the battle cry to popularize their reactionary agenda.

11. Jousting with Empire

I TUNED IN to CNN just in time to catch the second plane slam into the second tower of the World Trade Center. Like most, I was stunned by the horrific act. I realized deep down that this would be an event that would have an impact on the course of my life. When I learned a few hours later that one of the planes was United Air Lines Flight 175 which had left Boston for Los Angeles, I was doubly stunned. That was the very same flight I used to take during the years I was on the board of Oxfam America from the late eighties to the late nineties; I would get off in LA and transfer to the trans-Pacific flight to Tokyo as I made my way back to Manila. Since the Oxfam board met in the first half of September every year, had I continued on the Oxfam board, there was a good chance that I would have been on that flight. In any event, I felt extremely lucky.

9/11 was, of course, the topic of every conversation for weeks. What was noticeable was that many I talked to were ambivalent about it. And not just progressives and activists. A very good friend, the late Dick Ng, who was usually apolitical, told me, "It was terrible, but the Americans had it coming." At the popular MBK shopping mall in Bangkok, T-shirts with Osama bin Laden's face with the twin towers being hit in the background were selling like hotcakes, though I didn't see anyone wearing it.

Che's Strategy Executed by Osama

As the U.S. launched its invasion of Afghanistan a few weeks after 9/11, in an effort to understand bin Laden's motives in launching such an assault that was not within the realm of the imagination, I wrote:

> The September 11 attacks were horrific and heinous, but from one angle, what were they but a variant of Che Guevara's "foco" theory? For Guevara, the aim of a bold guerilla action is two-fold: to demoralize the enemy and to empower one's popular base by getting the cadres to participate in an action that shows that the all-powerful government is indeed vulnerable. The enemy

is then provoked into a military response that further saps his credibility in what is basically a political and ideological battle.

For bin Laden, terrorism is not the end but a means to an end. And that end—a vision of Muslim Asia, rid of the American economic and military power and corrupt surrogate elites, and returned to justice and Islamic sanctity—is something that none of Bush's rhetoric about defending civilization through revenge bombing can compete with. . . .

Washington has put itself in a no-win situation. If it kills bin Laden, he becomes a martyr. If it captures him alive, freeing him will become an intense focus of Muslim resistance, while capital punishment would be effectively prevented by the likelihood that it would set off massive revolts throughout the Muslim world. If the U.S. fails to kill or capture him, he will secure an aura of invincibility, as somebody favored by God and whose cause is therefore just. Ironical and perverse as this may sound, the Washington-bin Laden conflict is becoming a battle of spirit versus matter, righteousness versus might.[103]

I make no claim to predictive powers, but what unfolded over the next 20 years was not unlike what I had suggested: Washington had placed itself in a no-win situation. Taking off partly from Paul Kennedy's concept of "imperial overstretch," I was in the beginning of the process of developing a theory of overextension. While globalization was overreach on the economic front by U.S. corporations, overextension was overreaching on the military and political front by a unipolar power, the U.S. government.

To get an objective view of what was happening on the ground in Afghanistan, Focus conceived the idea of sending an International Peace mission to that country. It was not until May 2002, however, that one of the Focus staff, Marco Mezzera, was able to visit Afghanistan, where he witnessed the chaos of the first period of the U.S. occupation. Not satisfied with the praise for the U.S.-led invasion he was hearing in Kabul, Marco journeyed to the rural areas, where he heard a different story:

During a meeting in early May with a group of tribal leaders from the district of Pul-i Alam, Logar province (only about 70 km south of Kabul), their leader . . . Sheri Khan, cast a different light on one of the most obscure and reclusive periods of Afghan history. In words that elicited expressions of agreement from the gathering of Pashtun elders, he calmly explained, "Security during the Taliban was very good. There were no weapons around at that time, while now the people who are ruling us have reintroduced weapons." He further recalled that women and children would stay outside until late in the evening, along the main road that leads to Kabul, without fearing for their safety. Something unthinkable before the Taliban brought order to the region, and something still to be verified in the current times of political transition.[104]

What Marco was observing was something that would become more obvious in the months and years to come: that support for the Occupation forces was very tenuous outside Kabul.

The reason we could not immediately send someone to Afghanistan was that we were overtaken by events. For the next step in President George W. Bush's "War on Terror" struck much closer to home: his sending of U.S. Special Forces to the island of Basilan in the southern Philippines to help the armed forces of the Philippines go after the radical Islamic group Abu Sayyaf in January 2002, slightly over three months after he invaded Afghanistan.

The Basilan Mission

In response, Nicola Bullard and the Focus staff quickly assembled a team of 13 international peace activists to go to Basilan, among them Matt Wuori, a member of the European Parliament; the late Aijaz Ahmad, a leading Pakistani intellectual; Victoria Brittain, a correspondent for the *Guardian*; French activist Pierre Rousset; Etta Rosales, a prominent member of the Philippine House of Representatives; and the prominent Filipino critic of U.S. bases, Roland Simbulan. I went with the team, along with Nicola and Marco.

Basilan was a largely Muslim area where the government had a tenuous presence. There was a strong presence of several secessionist movements owing to a sense among people of being second class citizens in the predominantly Christian country, the same feeling that had led the Abu Sayyaf to engage in kidnapping for ransom activities to establish an Islamic state. The government, however, had only one response, the iron fist, and for this it was receptive to the U.S. offer to send Special Forces, supposedly to train Filipino troops combat the Abu Sayyaf.

It was clear from the outset that officials of the national government, the local government, the military, and the U.S. did not like us around. The National Security Adviser of President Gloria Macapagal-Arroyo described the mission members as "people of doubtful credentials" and "imported military bashers." Decrying the mission as a "shameful act of foreign inter-vention in our internal affairs," he urged the immigration bureau to bar all entering foreigners whose only goal for visiting the country is to "find fault and destroy the image of the country."

But if there was no cooperation from the authorities, people were willing to talk to us and tell us about human rights abuses. In an effort to get at what was really happening, we did intensive interviewing and, against the advice of the authorities who told us we would be "kidnapped by terrorists," even went to the village of Tabuk, birthplace of Abu Sayyaf founder Abdurajak Janjalani, and the community where scores of civilians had been arrested on suspicion of links with the Abu Sayyaf. Here, the mission members had free, off-the-cuff, face-to-face interactions with the residents of the predominantly Muslim community. We found out that sixty-two suspected Abu Sayyaf members had been illegally detained. They included a pregnant woman, an old woman aged 70, and two children. The people we interviewed claimed they had been held in the Basilan provincial jail for six to seven months despite the fact that warrants for their arrest had not yet been issued.

We then moved to Tabawan, where the U.S. Special Forces were camped. After initially saying he would meet us, the colonel leading the contingent did not show up, though his second in command admitted that Filipino troops did not really need training in marksmanship and medical evacuation, which was the rationale for their presence. We told this officer we did not believe the official line that the Special Forces would be able, in combat, to maintain the distinction he was making between firing in self-defense, which they were allowed, and firing in attack mode, which they were banned from doing.

After three days, we left Basilan, leaving by ferry at Lamitan instead of returning to Isabela, the provincial capital, by land owing to credible threats that some warlord groups linked to the local government planned to waylay the unarmed peace mission, which the Philippine military had refused to provide with an escort, and blame the Abu Sayyaf for the deed.

At the press conference in Zamboanga City upon the completion of the mission, I said, speaking for the rest of the mission, "All of us in the mission condemn the atrocities committed by the Abu Sayyaf; in fact, we spent our last day in Basilan listening to the testimonies of Abu Sayyaf victims in Lamitan. However, the military cannot adopt Abu Sayyaf tactics to destroy the Abu Sayyaf, not only because this is immoral but also because engaging in warrantless arrest, torture, and the killing of innocents is the surest way of creating more recruits for the Abu Sayyaf."[105]

As for the U.S. Special Forces, we told the press that they were not providing any "value-added" in the fight against terrorism. So why were they in Basilan? Aijaz Ahmad summed it up best for different audiences he spoke to: "With the technology available, the U.S. doesn't need to build the kind of bases they used to have here," he told students at the University of the Philippines. "They only need the infrastructure that will be serviceable to them when they want it, when they need it." He asserted, "The Americans want to return to a position of power that they used to occupy here." In 1992, the U.S. had withdrawn from its big bases, Subic Naval Base and Clark Air Force Base after the Senate's rejection of a new bases treaty. Ahmad saw the new U.S. logistical facility in Zamboanga and the Special Forces camp in Basilan as actually the first steps on the road back to a major military presence in the Philippines. He passed away a few years ago but Ahmad's words were prescient. Over 20 years after the Basilan mission, the U.S. now has nine bases throughout the Philippines—contained within nominally Philippine bases, along the lines of the arrangement he predicted.[106]

To Baghdad and Back

Over a year later, late in March 2003, I was on my way to Baghdad, along with Filipino members of Congress Etta Rosales and Hussin Amin, Pakistani MP Zulfikar Gondal, Indonesian labor activist Dita Sari, TV cameramen Jim Libiran and Ariel Fulgado, and Focus staffer Herbert Docena. The team had been assembled by Herbert in record time and we called ourselves the "Asian Peace Mission." Our objective was to join other similar missions in Baghdad that aimed to stop the American invasion threatened by Bush, Jr, and show solidarity with the Iraqi people. By the time we assembled in Dubai on March 11 and flew by Emirates to Baghdad, Secretary of State Colin Powell had made his notorious UN Security Council presentation claiming the existence of nuclear weapons in Iraq and an invasion of the "Coalition of the Willing" was almost certain. But there was still a chance, no matter how slight, that peace delegations rushing to Iraq could cause Bush to think twice.

When we got off in Damascus on the morning of March 11 to take a connecting flight to Baghdad, we were told that our commercial flight to the Iraqi capital had been cancelled along with all other flights owing to the impending invasion. We faced being stranded in Damascus as the invasion unfolded. A frenzied few hours followed as we sought an alternative way to get to the Iraqi capital. Just when we were about to give up, a Syrian approached Herbert, the coordinator of the trip, to tell him he could get all seven of us on a blockade runner, a private aircraft that smuggled goods to Iraq that had been banned by the United Nations embargo. For a fee, of course. We accepted without hesitation and boarded the sealed and darkened aircraft.

After what seemed to be an eternity, the smugglers' plane descended and landed in Baghdad International Airport, where we were welcomed by Iraqi officials and Philippine and Indonesian Embassy officials who had somehow heard of our coming. One of them was Consul Grace Princesa who expressed relief we had arrived but told us firmly that this was not the best time to come to Iraq.

The next morning, we were ushered into the foreign ministry where we were welcomed warmly by Iraqi authorities, who nevertheless seemed puzzled that so many foreigners were coming to Iraq despite the impending invasion. As head of the delegation, Etta Rosales expressed the solidarity of the Filipino people with the Iraqis, followed by similar statements by MP Gondal and Dita Sari. Over the next few days, we were brought to hospitals where we were shown children suffering from malnutrition owing to the embargo of essential goods, schools where pupils carried on as usual, and civil defense facilities.

I realized that even in times of crisis, entrenched habits die hard. We were billeted at the Palestine Hotel, which stood over Firdoz Square, with its big statue of Saddam, the one that would be pulled down later by crowds when the Americans reached Baghdad. Seeing the impressive square, I could not resist doing my early morning seven-kilometer run that even below freezing temperatures in Europe had not been able to stop me from doing. On the first morning, I was stopped by troops who obviously thought it strange that a foreigner would be thinking of jogging when a war was about to break out. I gave them the peace sign, and for lack of anything else to say, I said, "Friend of Saddam." At that point, they told me to proceed and never stopped me again the next few days.

On March 15, a worried Consul Princesa told us it was time for us to leave. Etta told her that we still had to visit the holy city of Karbala. At that point, the consul said, "Madame, this is not the time to play tourist," and pulled out her ultimate weapon, which was to tell us that she would not leave Baghdad until Congresswoman Rosales left, because those were the instructions from the Philippine ambassador, who had already left for Jordan. Her career would be on the line if she deserted Etta and her motley, crazy crew. That did it. We abandoned the plan to visit Karbala and acquiesced to the consul's plan to charter two GMC vans to make the 10-hour trip to Damascus two days' later. Prices for vehicles were doubling by the day as the expected D-Day approached and diplomatic staffs and others were eager to leave, but Herbert Docena, resourceful as always, was able to secure two vehicles for $1000 each.

The next day proved to be the most poignant one for me. We visited Baghdad University. In an article I wrote when we reached Syria, I recounted the events of that day.

It was cool and sunny when we set out early this morning to meet with students at Baghdad University. As it has been over the last few days that we have been here, the city appeared to be going about its business in the usual fashion. Some sandbags have been placed on some street corners and in front of some government buildings, but this city is not physically on war footing.

At the College of English, it is most definitely springtime. Coeds are chatting cheerily and they smile as we pass. "We are intent on finishing the syllabus, war or no war," says Professor Abdul Jaafar Jawad. He tells us that during the Gulf War of 1991, he was discussing a doctoral dissertation with a student while American and British warplanes were bombing Baghdad. Jawad's determination to carry on despite the approach of war is shared by the students at his department. Students at a class on Shakespeare are discussing Romeo and Juliet when we interrupt them. No, they say, they don't mind answering some questions from the Asian Peace Mission.

They are carrying on with Shakespeare, but their answers show that morally they are on war footing. What do they think of George Bush? "He is like Tybalt, clumsy and ill-intentioned," says a young woman in near perfect English.

What do they think about Bush's promise to liberate them? Another coed answers, "We've been invaded by many armies for thousands of years, and those who wanted to conquer us always said they wanted to liberate us."

What if war comes, how would they feel? Another says, "We may not be physically strong, but we have faith, and that is what will beat the Americans."

A young professor tells me, "I love teaching, but I will fight if the Americans come."

These are not a programmed people. Saddam Hussein's portrait may be everywhere, but these are not programmed answers. In fact, we have hardly encountered any programmed responses from anybody here in the last few days.

Youth and spring are a heady brew on this campus, and it is sadness that we all feel as we speed away, for some of those lives will be lost in the coming war.

As one passes over one of the bridges spanning the Tigris River, one remembers the question posed by Dr. Jawad: "Why would today's most powerful industrial country wish to destroy a land that gave birth to the world's most ancient civilization?" It is a question that no one in our delegation can really answer. Control of the world's second biggest oil reserves is a convenient answer, but it is incomplete. Strategic reasons are important but also incomplete. A fundamentalism that grips the Bush clique is operative, too, but there is something more, and that is power that is in love with itself and seeking to express that deadly self-love.

An American journalist I met at the press center said the people were carrying on as usual because they were in deep denial of the power that will soon be inflicted on them. I wish he had been with us when we visited the campus earlier in the day, to see the toughness beneath the surface of those young men and women of Baghdad University. Like most of the Iraqis we have met over the last few days, they are prepared for the worst, but they are determined not to make the worst ruin their daily lives.

Tomorrow afternoon, March 17, the date of the American ultimatum for Iraq to disarm or face war, we in the Asian Peace Mission will be traveling by land on two vans flying the Philippine flag to the border with Syria. Dita Sari, the labor leader from Indonesia, was offered a ride to the border this evening by the Indonesian ambassador, who was very concerned about her safety. She refused, saying she would leave only when the mission left. We are leaving late and cutting it close because all of us— Dita Sari, Philippine legislators Etta Rosales and Husin Amin, Pakistani MP Zulfikar Gondal, Focus on the Global South associate Herbert Docena, our reporter and cameraman Jim Libiran and Ariel Fulgado, and myself—feel the same compulsion: we want to be with the Iraqi people as long as possible.[107]

We headed out of Baghdad at noon on March 17, part of a long procession of cars and busses trying to get to the border with Syria. We covered the 840 kilometers in nearly 9 hours, with two brief breaks, traveling on Iraq's impressive superhighway that cut through the desert between the two ancient centers of the Arab world, Baghdad and Damascus. Consular officials met us in Damascus and told us about Bush's speech delivering an ultimatum to Saddam to leave the country a few hours before we arrived. After visiting the stunning Al-Hamidiyeh Souq, the famous covered bazaar, to buy souvenirs, we left Damascus on March 19, a few hours before the invasion began, and when we landed in Dubai, we caught the first wave of troops leaving Kuwait on CNN.

Overextension

At an anti-war conference in Jakarta two months after the launch of the American invasion, I delivered a more refined version of my theory of overextension about which I had first begun to think when the U.S. invaded Afghanistan in 2001. Because it laid out in an uncanny way almost exactly what would transpire over the next two decades, I am reproducing key sections of it here:

> After its successful invasion of Iraq, the U.S. appears to be at the height of its power. One can understand why many feel the U.S. is supreme and omnipotent. Indeed, this is precisely what Washington wants the world to think.
>
> No doubt, the U.S. is very powerful militarily. There is good reason to think, however, that it is overextended. In fact, the main strategic result of the occupation of Iraq is to worsen this condition of overextension.
>
> Overextension refers to a mismatch between goals and means, with means referring not only to military resources but to political and ideological ones as well. Under the reigning neoconservatives, Washington's goal is to achieve overwhelming military dominance over any rival or coalition of rivals. This quest for even greater global dominance, however, inevitably generates opposition, and it is in this resistance that we see the roots of overextension. Overextension is relative—an overextended power may in fact be in a worse condition even with a significant increase in its military power if resistance to its power increases by an even greater degree.
>
> If a stable, pro-U.S. order in the Middle East is Washington's goal, then that is nowhere in sight. What is likely instead is greater instability that will tempt Washington to employ more military power and deploy more military units, leading to a spiral of violence from which there is no easy exit. . . . [108]

Among other things, I also wrote,

> One actor will be central in all this: China. As the American
> economy is mired in stagnation and Washington is overextended
> militarily and politically, China will grow in relative strength. The
> unilateralists will grow more and more preoccupied with China's
> growing strength and will sharpen their political and ideological
> competition with Beijing. At the same time, their options will
> continue to be limited given Wall Street's increasing financial
> stakes in China, American corporations' increasing dependence
> on investment in that country, and the U.S. consumers' escalating
> reliance on imports from China, from low-tech commodities to
> high-tech goods. Washington will not find an easy exit from its
> Chinese conundrum.[109]

Second Superpower

On February 17, 2003, the *New York Times* came out with its famous
article asserting that, "The fracturing of the Western alliance over Iraq and the
huge antiwar demonstrations around the world this weekend are reminders
that there may still be two superpowers on the planet: the United States and
world public opinion. In his campaign to disarm Iraq, by war if necessary,
President Bush appears to be eyeball to eyeball with a tenacious new adversary: millions of people who flooded the streets of New York and dozens
of other world cities to say they are against war based on the evidence at
hand."[110] The *Times* was reacting to the massive global mobilization against
the coming U.S. invasion on February 15. Focus and I felt ourselves to be part
of that other superpower.

Over the next few years after the invasion, I traveled to Jakarta, Beirut,
London, Athens, New York, Mexico City, Johannesburg, Istanbul, Sao Paolo,
Porto Alegre, and other cities to participate in anti-war conferences, demonstrations, and mammoth rallies. It was not the easiest time to travel since,
following the example of the newly established Department of Homeland
Security in the U.S., governments throughout the world tightened up on airport security, resulting in long queues and interminable questioning by suspicious airport personnel. In the U.S., the Department of Homeland Security
finally consolidated nationwide arrest records, so that every time I entered
the country, my multiple arrests for civil disobedience during my anti-Marcos
activities in that country would pop up on the immigration officer's computer
screen, leading to tedious questioning under "secondary screening."

But the rallies were invigorating and really made you feel an organic part of a global resistance. The one image that, for some reason, stuck in my memory as emblematic of those many demonstrations was one where thousands of us marched, militantly chanting, "U.S. and UK, out of Iraq now," into Trafalgar Square, with the statue of Nelson, the epitome of British imperialism, looming over us.

I made my own little personal protest against the Iraq War sometime in 2005, if my memory serves me right, when I walked into the U.S. consulate in Bangkok and surrendered the green card that I had maintained for easy entry to and occasional work in the U.S. since President Ronald Reagan—of all people!—gave me political asylum in 1982 for my anti-Marcos activities. When the consular official asked me why I was giving up my permanent residence in the land of the free, I answered that it was to protest the U.S. occupation of Iraq. She seemed surprised and asked me to wait. When she returned, apparently after consulting a superior, she asked me to explicitly write down the reasons why, and when I asked why this was necessary, she said, "Well, it's usually the other way around, people would do anything for a green card, and we just want a record that what you're doing is voluntary and we didn't coerce you to do it."

Judgment Day in Istanbul

The high point of my involvement in the movement against the Iraq War was my participation in the final session of the World Tribunal on Iraq (WTI) that was held in Istanbul June 24–27, 2005. By this time, Focus on the Global South had achieved the reputation of being the Southeast Asian outpost of the global anti-imperialist movement. Fortunately, we had a superb management team to keep things together in Bangkok while some of us on the program staff went on extended missions.[111]

The WTI was global civil society working together at its finest, and I was honored to participate in it. This event was the culmination of two long years of 20 sessions of hearing evidence on the atrocities and abuses of democratic and human rights and breaches of the principles of national sovereignty by the U.S. government and Bush's Coalition of the Willing. The hearings were held in different parts of the world, including London, Mumbai, Copenhagen, Brussels, New York, Japan, Stockholm, South Korea, Rome, Frankfurt, Barcelona, Tunis and Geneva. The tribunal consisted of a 15-member Jury of Conscience and a 54-person Panel of Advocates.

The Jury of Conscience was chaired by Indian novelist Arundhati Roy and composed of prominent activists from around the world. Two Americans, David Krieger, president of the Nuclear Age Peace Foundation, and feminist author Eve Ensler were jury members. The jury also included Chandra Muzaffar, Malaysia's leading human rights advocate and noted author, as well as two internationally respected Turkish intellectual personalities, Murat Belge and Ayse Erzan.

The Panel of Advocates was led by the distinguished specialist in international law, Richard Falk, and Turgut Tarhanli, dean of the Bilgi Law School in Istanbul, who organized the fifty-four presentations offered to the jury. Describing the advocates and their presentations, Falk said, "they came from a wide range of backgrounds, and the presentations included some incisive analyses of international law issues by such respected world experts as Christine Chinkin of the London School of Economics; Amy Bartholomew of Carleton University, Ottawa; Barbara Olshansky, Assistant Legal Director of the Center for Constitutional Rights, who made a gripping presentation of the gruesome record of abuse of detainees and prisoners held by the U.S. Government since 9/11; two former assistant secretary generals of the UN (Denis Halliday & Hans von Sponeck), both of whom had resigned in the 1990s to protest the genocidal effects of UN sanctions in Iraq. There were accounts of the devastation and cruelty of the occupation by several seemingly credible eye-witnesses who had held important non-government jobs in pre-invasion Iraq; a moving presentation of why he turned against the Iraq War by Tim Goodrich, a former American soldier and co-founder of Iraq Veterans Against the War; and overall assessments of how the Iraq War fit into American ambitions for global empire by such renowned intellectuals as Samir Amin, Johan Galtung, and Walden Bello. Their presentations combined an acute explanation of the strains on world order arising from predatory forms of economic globalization with the view that the U.S. response to 9/11 was mainly motivated by regional and global strategic aims and only incidentally, if at all, by antiterrorism."[112]

I was asked by Falk to deliver the indictment of the British government and other members of the Coalition of the Willing. I was not unhappy with the assignment since I found Tony Blair, the prime minister who led Britain to war, to be even more repugnant than Bush, Jr. The latter was, in many ways, a blockhead who swallowed the lies fed to him by his *eminence grise,* Dick Cheney. Blair was a hypocrite and a liar, parading as a champion of freedom and democracy while knowing that Saddam Hussein possessed no weapons of mass destruction, contrary to the American claim that served as the rationale for the invasion. I focused my remarks on the contradiction between the confidential "Downing Street Papers" that continually reasserted that there was no credible evidence that Saddam possessed weapons of mass destruction and Blair's bold public claims that his intelligence had unquestionable evidence that Saddam did. I then went on to document British killings of unarmed civilians, particularly in Basra, as well as torture and sexual abuse of suspected Iraqi resisters. Why did Blair commit a third of the UK's armed forces—65,000 soldiers—to war? I showed that from the beginning, Blair's shared goal with the Americans was regime change, and that it was important not to break with Washington, even though France and Germany had done so, because he saw the alliance with the U.S. as a condition for his fundamental foreign policy goal of "projecting British power." I concluded that evidence collected by the two-year tribunal underlined "the special burden of guilt of the government of the United Kingdom."[113]

Drawing on two years of truth-gathering, the three days of truth-telling in Istanbul drew, in compelling detail, a portrait of an illegitimate and unjust war that was perhaps the most comprehensive ever done on the Iraq war. On the last day of the tribunal, the novelist Arundhati Roy, head of the Jury of Conscience, observed that her thoughts and actions would categorize her as an "enemy combatant" in the U.S. government's view.[114] As I joined the applause for the jury's decisions, I thought, yes, why not, we are all enemy combatants now, and proud of it.

Standing Up to Israel

One cannot go to the Middle East and seriously grapple with its many challenges without encountering the oppressive reality of Israel, an apartheid state that not only has its jackboot on the neck of the Palestinian people but is a threat to its Arab neighbors as well. This fact seared itself permanently in my consciousness when Focus led a 12-person international solidarity mission to Lebanon in mid-August 2006. We had been asked by friends in Beirut to come and witness what Israel was doing to their country and how the Lebanese were resisting. We put together a 12-person team of prominent civil society personalities, and with logistics expertly coordinated by Herbert Docena, the members of International Civil Society and Parliamentary Mission flew to Damascus, then proceeded by land to Beirut. Among the team members were Brazilian labor leader Kjeld Jakobsen, Indian journalist Seema Mustafa, Indian peace activist Kamal Chenoy, and parliamentarians Mujiv Hataman of the Philippines and Mohammad Salim of India, and farmer leader Gerard Durand of Via Campesina.[115]

By the time we arrived in Beirut, the Israelis had been pounding South Beirut for nearly 30 days but had nonetheless been fought to a standstill in Southern Lebanon. As an excuse for its aggressive actions, Israel said that Hezbollah, the radical Islamic force that had a carved out a strong presence in Lebanon, had staged a cross-border raid and kidnapped two Israeli soldiers.

But everyone saw through that rationale and knew that the aim of the Israeli invasion and bombing was to crush Hezbollah before it became a force that could stand up to it.

Our friend Nahla Chahal and our other hosts lost no time in bringing us on a tour of South Beirut in the morning of August 13, one day before a ceasefire between Israel and Hezbollah and the government of Lebanon would take effect. The destruction was horrific. Whole high-rises had been reduced to rubble; whole neighborhoods were flattened. While the Israelis had issued advance warnings to the population to leave weeks earlier, this was the economic equivalent of the collective punishment that the Nazis had dealt whole communities in occupied Europe when German troops had been killed by resistance forces. South Beirut was a Hezbollah stronghold, so non-combatants must be punished for "sheltering" Hezbollah fighters—that was the logic. But as in rural Southern Lebanon collective economic punishment simply stiffened the resistance. Hezbollah retaliated with guerrilla raids and long- and medium-range rocket attacks deep into Israel.

As around 20 of us, including media people covering our mission, poked around the ruins of a 12-story building in the neighborhood of Haret Hreik, I came across a teddy bear, a child stroller, and books. One had to be careful not to slip and fall throughthe cracks of ruined structures. The silence was eerie; these were streets that only a month before had been bustling with traffic, noise, and life. We were also mindful of the Israeli drones hovering overhead since all we could go on, in terms of assurance, was the expectation that Israel would not dare fire on civilians and foreigners investigating the wreckage and create another crisis on top of the one it already had. They would hold their fire until after we left. Sure enough, two hours after our departure, the Israelis again bombed the neighborhood we had visited, apparently with no other aim than to make the rubble bounce. I would be reminded of those scenes of destruction I witnessed in South Beirut 17 years later, when a vengeful Israel went on a massive bombing and killing spree in Gaza after being humiliated by the October 7, 2023, Hamas' attack and followed this up a year later with massive bombing of Beirut once again.

After our visit to South Beirut, we went on to Beirut University General Hospital. We briefly interviewed Firas Chahal, a 27-year-old man suffering internal and external wounds after being thrown out of a minibus when an Israeli jet bombed the bridge at the Casino du Liban. Confined in a nearby room was Khaleek Mahmoud, a 68-year-old grandmother whose legs were shattered after the roof of her house collapsed on her when Israeli warplanes pounded her village in South Lebanon. "Israel is a tyrannical state," she told us. "You should go down there and see for yourselves."

After visiting the hospital, we hurried to the Ecole El Ghoul in downtown Beirut, which served as temporary quarters for 355 people from 66 families from the South. One million Lebanese had been displaced by the war, so the conditions of the people we met were typical of those of a full third of the country. "The integration of the refugees into old neighborhoods brings its share of problems," said Nahla Chahal. "The Hezbollah, however, is trying its best to provide the social services to support the people in this school."

Children and adolescents filled the courtyard and greeted our delegation with glee, taking advantage of every photo opportunity. For a few moments, confronted by this sea of smiles, the war seemed far away. The younger ones readily broke out into cheers when Vijaya Chauhan, one of our delegation members who worked with women and children in India, waved and talked to them. Then they broke into a chant that invoked the name of Hezbollah leader Hassan Nasrallah that translated roughly into "Nasrallah, we're with you/ You can bomb Tel Aviv."

We then spent most of the afternoon with Lebanese NGOs assessing the scale of the humanitarian and ecological disaster and looking ahead to post-cease fire cooperation. Even as two massive blasts interrupted our discussion, our Lebanese hosts kept talking, assuring us that the sounds came from Israeli Navy boats shelling South Beirut a few miles away.

At dinner at a restaurant later that evening, the ongoing sounds of explosions in South Beirut did not deter people at a nearby table from continuing to carouse loudly. The Israelis were bombing up till the last minute to terrorize the Lebanese. It was not working. They were very angry, but the Lebanese were used to war and were not about to let it get in the way of living their lives. They are brave, stoic people, I thought.

The next morning, at around 6 am, I was roused from bed by two massive blasts. They sounded very close, though they were probably coming from South Beirut. I was in a hotel in Central Beirut, which being Christian and cosmopolitan, the Israelis had exempted from the shelling. With the ceasefire due to take effect in less than an hour, the Israelis were still trying to get their punches in. These guys are unbelievable, I thought. But they had already lost.

The bittersweet mood in Beirut on the day when the ceasefire took effect was perhaps best expressed that morning by Rahul, a taxi driver, who told me, "We won, but at what cost? So many people displaced, so many dead, so many buildings destroyed." The final toll of this war was still being counted but experts from NGOs said it was likely that the death count would go above 1400, and the economic damage would reach $6 billion.

But Hezbollah were still standing. They had accomplished what was hitherto thought impossible, so I decided to make a detailed account of what people told me and what my impressions were during that historic day and the rest of my stay in Beirut.

As soon as the cessation of hostilities came into effect at 8 am, cars and vans and trucks started to roll down to the South as people who took refuge in Beirut and other parts of the country went back to their homes. "They'll most likely find their houses gone, but their lands will still be there and there's really no place like home," said Anwar El Khalil, an MP representing the area of Marieyoun, the site of the strafing of a civilian convoy by Israeli planes last week, who himself was eager to return home. With a full third of the country's inhabitants having been displaced from their homes, a massive civilian movement was expected to bring traffic along the country's main highways to a crawl in the next few days.

There was no doubt about who the loser was in the war. Everyone we talked to on that day of national pride agreed with the editorial in the *Daily Star*, Lebanon's liberal English language paper, that asserted, "The Israeli government has been discredited and serious wrinkles in the U.S.-Israeli relationship have been exposed. The Israelis now have to contend with a political arena that is in disarray." With even members of the government of then Prime Minister Ehud Ohlmert saying Israel had lost the war, the Jewish state was indeed plunged into its worst political crisis in years

In Lebanon the situation was different. In the thirty-day war, most of the country's political groups and most of the country's population came together to support the struggle against Israeli aggression led by the Shiite Muslim-led organization. First among these was the country's Maronite Christian President Emile Lahoud, who was not shy about praising "the leadership of Hezbollah in the national resistance."

Everybody acknowledged that Hezbollah's sterling military performance was the source of what the *Daily Star* called the "unprecedented level of solidarity" of Lebanese society today. Domestic critics who, at the start of the war, accused Hezbollah of dragging Lebanon into war by capturing two Israeli soldiers for prisoner-exchange purposes were quiet in those heady days of national pride.

If anything had been put to rest by the events of the last 30 days, it was the lie that the Hezbollah was a terrorist organization. Deliberate Israeli targeting of civilian targets while Hezbollah fighters focused on fighting Israeli soldiers put the shoe on the other foot. Indeed, there was now a massive clamor among international civil society groups to try the Israeli political leaders and the army for war crimes and state-sponsored terror.

It had not only been Hezbollah's military prowess that was on display but also its tremendous capacity to provide welfare services, in this instance, for the country's displaced population. Indeed, in a country whose social services, especially for the poor, are very backward, Hezbollah's social infrastructure was a model of efficient modernity. It ran, for instance, 46 medical centers and a hospital.

Hezbollah experts explained to us that there were three main reasons for Hezbollah's victory. One was the employment of rockets to neutralize Israeli airpower and give Hezbollah an offensive air capability without airplanes. The second was the Hezbollah's use of guerrilla warfare, which stymied an Israeli Army used to fighting conventional Arab armies. Third was the Hezbollah fighter who was "not only a guerrilla trained in self-reliance but is also filled with ideological conviction that he is on the right track."

Beirut on the evening of 14 August was a city filled with sorrow and pride, with the latter clearly dominant. Throughout the city, there were motorcades celebrating Hezbollah and its General Secretary, Hassan Nasrallah. Everyone tuned in when Nasrallah came on television at nine o'clock to announce what he considered a "tremendous strategic victory for Lebanon" and announced Hezbollah's preparedness to withdraw its fighters behind the Litani River.

As he spoke, a high official of the Lebanese Communist Party, perhaps the epitome of secular politics in Lebanon, said of the man who was the face of Islamic politics, "There is our Arab Che Guevara—with a turban. . . . "

But my time in Beirut during that visit was not all spent in politics. It was then I really got to appreciate how good Lebanese food was, even if it was not accompanied by the superb local red wine when we were eating with folks from Hezbollah, who were serious about respecting the Muslim ban on alcohol. I also got to appreciate what a lovely, cosmopolitan city Beirut was. Most impressive of all was the Beirut Corniche, a three-mile-long esplanade along the city's coastline. As in Baghdad, I could not give up my daily seven-kilometer run, and I discovered that the Corniche was probably the best stretch in the world for a brief run. On my last day, I ran to the end of the esplanade and onto the beach, which was deserted. It was then that I noticed what seemed to be an Israeli drone in the sky above. For a moment, I was disoriented. Was the war really over?

But no drone was going to spoil my running. So I cursed it, gave it the finger, and ran on and on until I hit the rocks at the edge of the city's shoreline.

The shining unity of that day did not last long. Before long, Lebanon's sectarian conflicts reemerged, and with it another cycle of violence. Also, the Hezbollah, according to some analysts, eventually followed a path of being responsive more to the interests of Lebanon's economic elite than those of its mass base and adapting to instead of opposing neoliberal policies. But one thing Hezbollah's victory did was to make it clear to Israel that it was not in its interest to ever invade Lebanon again.

Eighteen years later, in September 2024, that lesson appeared to have been forgotten as Israel followed up its ongoing campaign against Hamas in Gaza with a punishing bombing campaign against Hezbollah that leveled parts of South Beirut and killed Nasrallah, along with thousands of civilians. Had Israel forgotten its earlier defeat at the hands of Hezbollah? With the death of many senior Hezbollah commanders, many western commentators regarded the organization as finished. But having witnessed its resilience and its deep roots in the population during that brief visit in 2006, I had no doubt Hezbollah would bounce back from the loss of the "Arab Che Guevara."

"The Most Wanted Man in Lebanon"

Beirut's reputation for being the crossroads of politics of the diplomatic and the not so diplomatic kind is well deserved. If you wanted to meet the people who were carrying the fight to Israel, the folks the Israelis were really, really pissed off about, you went to Beirut to find them. In late 2004, I made an anti-imperialist conference on the Iraq War the cover for a meeting with Hamas, the radical Muslim Palestinian political force that was carrying the fight to Israel inside Palestine and Israel the same way the Hezbollah was doing it in Lebanon. Not surprisingly, though Hezbollah was Shiite in its sectarian affiliation and Hamas was Sunni, the two were close allies. It was via Hezbollah that I and my fellow Focus staffer, Marylou Malig, an expert in making impossible things happen, got an appointment to see Hamas' top agent in Lebanon.

The meeting took place a day after we visited Sabra and Shatila, two refugee camps for Palestinians in Beirut that had been the site of the horrendous 1982 massacre of thousands by Christian Phalangist allies of Israel under the watchful eyes of the Israeli Defense Forces commanded by Ariel Sharon. Though over 20 years had passed, memories of the massacre were still fresh among the people we met, and sites were marked and slogans were painted to remind residents and visitors of the bloody affair.

As we drove frantically through Beirut's hilly streets to make sure we were on time for the interview with Usamah Hamdan, someone in the car remarked: "Well, I hope the Israelis don't decide to kill him today, while we're meeting him." The gallows humor was prompted by the fact that Hamdan was reputed to be the most wanted man in Lebanon, one who had been marked for assassination by Israel.

As we neared the secret interview site, Marylou was still fidgeting with her headscarf, which, being Christian, she was not used to wearing. This was upsetting our interpreter, who suspected Marylou was just trying to look pretty for a historic occasion. At that point, one of the Hezbollah guides commented, "You're beautiful, don't worry, very beautiful." Fortunately, before those comments could ignite an argument between the two Lebanese, the secular female interpreter and the Hezbollah male guide, we reached our destination.

Knowing it would be historic, I took detailed notes of the meeting that I later put together in this article for the progressive Indian magazine, *Frontline*.

Usamah Hamdan is the representative of Hamas, the Palestinian Islamic Resistance Movement, in Lebanon and Syria. Hamas is associated in many people's minds with "suicide bombings" of Israeli military and civilian targets. Widely condemned as a terrorist tool, the bombings have altered the military situation considerably, leading one Hamas leader to describe suicide bombing as the Palestinians' "F-16." Israel has retaliated by systematically assassinating leaders of Hamas and other groups in the Palestinian resistance. A member of the Central Committee of an organization that is said to be Israel's Enemy No. 1, Hamdan has seen many of his comrades fall victim to Israeli operatives, including Hamas' last two top leaders, Sheikh Ahmed Yassin and Abdel Aziz Rantisi, both of whom were killed within a month of each other by helicopter-launched missiles earlier this year.

Following the twin suicide bombings that killed 16 Israelis in Beersheba on August 31, the Israeli government reiterated its policy of reserving the right to strike at Hamas leaders living outside Palestine. Hamdan is one of the likely targets, as is the currently top-ranking Hamas figure, Khaled Maashal, who lives in Damascus, where most of Hamas' strategic planning is done, according to the Israeli government. Indeed, a few weeks after we did this interview, on September 26, senior Hamas official Ezzedin al-Sheikh Khalil, was assassinated by Israeli agents in a car bombing in Damascus.

When we enter the interview site in a suburb of Beirut, we are asked to hand over our mobile phones—a wise precaution since the Israelis have been known to locate their prey via signals emitted by the phones. Surprisingly, however, the security seems light, with hardly an armed bodyguard visible in the premises.

We are prepared to see an older man, but Hamdan looks like he is in his late 30s. Hardly looking at all like the stereotype of the terrorist, he is cordial, sharing a number of jokes with our party while treating us to an impromptu breakfast of cheese-filled pita bread and strong coffee. After a few minutes, he tells us he is ready to answer any questions we may have. "You can be as frank as you want," one of our interpreters tells us, and we begin the interview:

Israel says it is withdrawing from the Gaza and much of the West Bank—how does Hamas view this? Do you consider this a victory?

I believe any withdrawal from our land, no matter how small it is, is a victory for the Palestinian people. But the Israelis want the Palestinians to pay a political price. They want us to give up the right of return [to Israel]. They want to keep one-fourth of the West Bank. We will not accept these conditions. We will continue our resistance. We have sacrificed for the last 56 years. What difference will another 10 to 15 years make?

Israel is continuing to build the "separation" wall despite global opposition. How does Hamas plan to deal with this?

The World Court of Justice made the right decision. It is most important because Israel really just wants to take the land. They are taking 21 percent of the West Bank bordering Jordan, but there are no security problems there. The international community has to continue pressuring Israel to stop and to destroy what has already been built. They plan to complete the wall by March 2005. They are building one kilometer a day, and they say it will take them 250 days to complete it. And they think of everything, like painting the wall with "artwork' so that people cannot write on it. But this wall will not prevent our resistance or put a stop to our activities.

Suicide bombing has been widely condemned. Others have said it is no longer effective. What do you think?

First, we do not call it such. And it is only one of the many tactics we use. We will use it when it is effective for a specific time and place. We choose the right place and time for this. People should realize that there are many cinemas, buses, coffee shops in Israel, but we choose only a few specific places and at specific times. We do this as a message to the Israeli government that if there is no security for the Palestinian people, there will be no security for the Israeli people. There will be none until there is a complete withdrawal from all occupied land, until there is an end to the occupation. In the last four years this has only been 12 percent of our operations—this is not a major tactic.

How does the Hamas view and relate to the PLO and the Palestinian Authority?

First, the Palestinian Authority. This was a result of the Oslo Agreement. We rejected the Oslo Agreement because it changed the objective from that of securing Palestinian rights to that of providing security for the occupation. Thus, we did not participate in the presidential elections. Now, the peace process is deadlocked. The Israelis occupied 45 percent of the Gaza. Oslo did not solve the problem.

But we will not fight the Palestinian Authority; Israel is the enemy. In fact, we help the Palestinian Authority by providing services for our people. Throughout the years, we have assisted with millions of dollars for infrastructure and services. We will not participate in the Palestinian Authority but we help out in the political process in our own way.

On the PLO. This was established in 1964 by the Arabs who wanted to turn Palestine from an Arab issue into a Palestinian issue. The PLO has become corrupted. We no longer know its real structures. It no longer has any real political vision. But we don't allow ourselves to be used in the struggles within the PLO, for instance, in the recent efforts by some to promote [Palestinian Prime Minister] Ahmed Qureia, at the expense of Arafat.

But if there is reform and there is a Palestinian leadership elected on a clear and acceptable basis, we would be open to sharing power with the PLO.

Israel has a policy of assassinating leaders of Hamas. How do you personally feel about this since you are on their list? Do you feel like you're living under a death sentence?

I am on two lists, one with six names and another with 12 names. But I am living my own life normally. I eat breakfast with my children, I always try to do this because this is when I can talk to them and ask them about their day and their plans. I visit my friends and my friends visit me. I just recently went out with my children to swim in the sea. You just die once, and it can be from cancer, in a car accident, or by assassination. Given these choices,

I prefer assassination. My friends are more worried for me than I am.

The brief interview ended with Hamdan telling us that he looked forward to inviting us soon to a "liberated Palestine." As we bade goodbye, we had the distinct impression that this young, intelligent leader of one of the Palestinian resistance's most feared organizations, knew he was living on borrowed time. By this time, Marylou was comfortable with the previously troublesome headscarf and all of us had a sense of accomplishment, having succeeded in interviewing Lebanon's most wanted man. We also breathed a sigh of relief, glad that Hamdan's security had protected us from a possible Israeli assassination attempt and/or that Israel had decided to postpone its attempt to assassinate Hamdan that day, allowing us all to live another day.[116]

It was probably in May 2009, shortly after I joined the Philippines' House of Representatives, that I was invited by Hamas and other Palestinian organizations to visit Gaza. This was not an invitation to refuse, and I flew to Cairo and joined other guests that would enter Gaza at Rafah. Our buses were filled with goods for the people of Gaza that could not reach them otherwise, owing to an ongoing land and sea blockade imposed by Israel. Rafah was the only point where we and the goods could get into Gaza. But at the last minute, most likely owing to Israeli pressure, the weak-kneed Egyptian Mubarak government decided to revoke the permission it had granted us to journey to Gaza. Hamdan's invitation to me to visit his homeland would have to wait.

Reading that interview with Hamdan almost two decades later, I could not help feeling how little has changed since then. Israel remains an intransigent apartheid state; indeed, it has become more aggressively annexationist. Hamas remains determined to liberate the Palestinian people. Resistance has been passed on to a new generation of Palestinians.

Indeed, on October 7, 2023, as I was putting the finishing touches to this book, Hamas launched a massive rocket and ground attack on Israel and showed both Israel and the world at large that the struggle for Palestinian freedom was alive and well. There was widespread condemnation in the U.S. and Europe of the killing and hostage-taking of civilians but very little appreciation for the sufferings that the Palestinians had suffered for over seven decades.

A month after the attack, something caught my eye in a *New York Times* article on what motivated Hamas to launch it. It was the name of the man we had interviewed nearly 20 years ago in Beirut! Hamdan attributed Hamas' move to Israeli efforts to evict Palestinians from their homes in East Jerusalem and Israeli police raids of the al-Aqsa Mosque in Jerusalem's Old City.

That was a turning point, Osama Hamdan, a Hamas leader based in Beirut, Lebanon, told *The Times*. Instead of firing rockets over issues in Gaza, Hamas was fighting for concerns central to all Palestinians, including those outside the enclave. The events also convinced many in Hamas that Israel sought to push the conflict past a point of no return that would ensure the impossibility of Palestinian statehood.

"The Israelis were only concerned with one thing: How do I get rid of the Palestinian cause?" Mr. Hamdan said. "They were heading in that direction and not even thinking about the Palestinians. And if the Palestinians did not resist, all of that could have taken place.[117]

I was elated. The Israelis had not yet managed to eliminate him! They must have tried several times over the last 20 years, but he had foiled them. It was then that I realized how deeply invested I had become not only in the life of this man, who had told us that he preferred death by assassination, but in the cause of Palestinian freedom and sovereignty.[118]

In an article I wrote after the October 7 attack, as the Israelis prepared to invade Gaza in retaliation, a move that would eventually take thousands of Palestinian lives, I laid out my concerns about the way the western press was dealing with the Israel-Palestine conflict:

First, there is among progressives and liberals a tendency to blame both Israel and Hamas in equal measure for the violence. This is a false equivalence. When it comes to violence, Israel is a thousand times more responsible and accountable for violence than Hamas since it created the conditions whereby many Palestinians have come to the conclusion that violence is the only way they can secure their rights.

Second, there is, also among progressives and liberals, a tendency to separate Hamas from the Palestinian people. They're deluding themselves. The only reason Hamas can carry out such bold military operations is because it enjoys tremendous support among Palestinians. When Israel says it is out to eliminate Hamas, what it is really saying is that it is prepared to commit genocide by killing off the mass base of Hamas, the Palestinian people, who will constantly reproduce the children who will join the organization.

Third, some of us may find some of Hamas' methods ethically unjustifiable. I do. But I find them understandable. Understanding is the first step towards dialogue, towards a peaceful solution. But Israel does not even want to understand, to acknowledge the reasons why Palestinians have been cornered into committing the acts they condemn out of desperation. And the West as a whole is guilty of the same refusal to understand the fundamental injustice of the Palestinian situation. As in the past, the apartheid state and its defenders have in recent days resorted to the inflammatory rhetoric of the Holocaust to shut down any debate.[119]

I then asked my readers to conduct a thought experiment, "if you were a young Palestinian, faced with a situation where except for a handful, Israelis refuse to even hear your case, where dialogue and negotiations with you are alien words in the vocabulary of the Israeli state, where the president of the most powerful country on earth says he backs Israel 100 percent and is prepared to give Israel all the weapons it needs to perpetuate a fundamental historical injustice, what would you do?"[120]

Osama bin Laden's Vision Prevails...

When the mad scramble for the exits that was the U.S. withdrawal from Afghanistan was taking place in late July and early August 2021, I attempted to understand the reasons for the total debacle of the 20-year-long intervention in the Middle East and how it had unfolded. I began by revisiting two articles I wrote at the beginning of my engagement with the anti-war movement. One was the piece I wrote over twenty years earlier, when Bush, Jr. made the fateful decision to invade Afghanistan in response to 9/11. The other article was written two months after the U.S. invasion of Iraq in 2003.[121] In those two pieces, I had stressed three points. The first was that Osama bin Laden was able to provoke the U.S. to an unending military commitment to the Middle East. The second was that this would result in what I termed "overextension." The third was that once committed, the U.S. would find it very difficult to withdraw and the condition of overextension would worsen, sapping the resources of the empire. The U.S. adventure unfolded almost exactly as I had projected early on, and looking back in 2021, I detailed how the disaster unfolded.[122]

Bin Laden operated with something like Che Guevara's "foco theory." Guevara believed that direct engagement of the enemy was necessary to show peasants that guerrillas could defeat the military and encourage them to join the revolution. Bin Laden, operating on a global stage, saw the September 11 events as an act that would expose the vulnerability of the "Great Satan" and inspire Muslims to join his jihad against it. "It was therefore necessary," he wrote, "to break the fear of this false god and destroy the myth of American invincibility that has taken over the hearts of Muslims. It was necessary to do something so that Muslims may wake up from their mindlessness and overcome their weakness. . . ."[123] He underlined "the importance of drawing the enemy to Afghanistan so that we could subject him to a war of attrition thar will damage his economy, morale, human resources."[124] 9/11 would create many fronts and lead to the overextension of U.S. military power as Washington would move to put out many fires. Bin Laden had played a central role in evicting the Soviet Union from Afghanistan, and,

> [N]ow, as he targeted the only remaining superpower, he told Muslims they could redeem all the humiliation they felt. All it required was violence—violence that wasn't just permissible, but holy. Bin Laden sought to force America to abandon its grip on the Muslim world. Knowing by now how superpowers work, all he needed was to provoke it into unsustainable military campaigns.[125]

It did not quite work out that way. Instead of being inspired, most Muslims were horrified and distanced themselves from the terrible deed. Still, bin Laden lucked out, thanks to George W. Bush and the neoconservatives who had come to power with him in Washington in 2001. For them, Osama's attack was a god-given opportunity to teach both America's enemies and friends that the empire was omnipotent. Ostensibly waged to go after the "roots of terror," the invasions of Afghanistan and Iraq were in fact what the Romans called "exemplary wars." Their aim was to reshape the global strategic environment to fit Washington's so-called "unipolar" status following the demise of the Soviet Union.

Disappointed with his father's reluctance to finish off Saddam Hussein during the 1990–91 Gulf War, George W. Bush initiated these invasions as the first steps in a demarche that would eliminate the so-called rogue states, compel greater loyalty from dependent states or supplant them with stronger allies, and put strategic competitors like China on notice that they should not even think of vying with the United States.

Disregarding the lessons of Vietnam and the British and Soviet debacles in Afghanistan, the Bush administration drove the United States into two unwinnable wars against highly motivated insurgents in the Middle East, as bin Laden watched with satisfaction, one might well have presumed, were he indeed living unperturbed in the peaceful garrison town of Abbottabad in

Pakistan. It was not exactly the scenario he had envisaged, but he was not about to quibble if the Bush administration, owing to its drive for unipolar hegemony, placed the United States on the road to overextension, which was, after all, his strategic aim.

Prolonged occupation demanded boots on the ground, and as Deputy Secretary of State Richard Armitage saw it, "The Army, in particular, [is] stretched too thin . . . fighting three wars—Afghanistan still, Iraq, and the global war on terrorism." At the height of the Iraq War, defense analyst James Fallows wrote, it was "only a slight exaggeration to say that today the entire U.S. military is either in Iraq, returning from Iraq, or getting ready to go." Most of the Army's maneuverable brigades were overseas, and those left in the United States were too few to maintain the contingency reserve or the training base necessary. Even the famed Special Forces were degraded, with their actual numbers in the field coming to hundreds at the most. Lack of human resources led the high command to call on the Reserves and the National Guard. As might be expected, morale plummeted, especially as tours of duty were extended and casualties mounted in lands to which these part-time soldiers had never expected to be assigned.

And as the prospect of prevailing in the battlefield became more and more distant, public support for the Iraq and Afghanistan expeditions, which was very limited right from the start, went up in smoke.

Even as the U.S. was bogged down in Afghanistan and Iraq, Israel, the Euro-American settler colony in the Middle East, Washington's only solid ally, was being challenged by new actors. In Gaza, Hamas took over as the dominant force following Israel's withdrawal in 2005–2006 and began to implement its military plan to eventually dismantle the apartheid state.

In Lebanon, Hezbollah, allied with Hamas, carried out border raids against Israel that resulted in 2006 in Israel's invasion of Southern Lebanon and bombing of South Beirut. Hezbollah's resistance, however, forced a withdrawal of Israel after a month, under the cloak of a UN-brokered ceasefire, inflicting an outcome that even members of the Israeli government regarded as a defeat for the apartheid state. Both Hamas and Hezbollah were part of the new, reinvigorated stream of Muslim political radicalism of which Osama's Al Qaeda was also a part, that increasingly displaced secular liberation movements like the Palestine Liberation Organization in the Arab world. But, unlike Al Qaeda, Hamas and Hezbollah had a solid mass base on the ground. These comrades in arms were much closer to national liberation movements than to transnational fundamentalist jihadists like Al Qaeda and ISIS, focused as they were on gaining power within their societies, as was the case with Hezbollah, or creating a nation-state, which was the priority of Hamas.

Barack Obama came to power in 2009 promising an end to the Middle East wars. In Iraq, the bulk of U.S. forces were withdrawn during his first term, but thousands of marines and Special Forces personnel were reintroduced to fight against the Islamic State, whose growth had been provoked by the U.S. presence in the Middle East. Even as this was happening, what had been a key U.S. objective in Iraq—a stable non-sectarian pro-U.S. state—collapsed as the Iraqi Shiite government aligned itself with Iran, against whom the United States was colluding with the Israelis in a high-tech effort to sabotage Tehran's nuclear energy program.

Obama also began an open-ended intervention in the Syrian civil war, deploying Special Forces and airstrikes that eventually enmeshed the United States in a multi-cornered confrontation with the Islamic State and other jihadists, Syrian forces, and Russian troops. The Democratic president, ironically a recipient of the Nobel Peace Prize prior to the Syrian venture, in fact expanded the U.S. military reach to North Africa during the Arab Spring in 2011, unilaterally enforcing with its NATO allies a "no fly zone" featuring attacks on Libyan defenses that resulted in hundreds of civilian deaths and massive air support of the ground campaigns of anti-Qaddafi rebels. The intervention left Libya with no centralized government, and the country lapsed into an anarchy that persists until the present, another American-made disaster.

In Afghanistan, Obama added 33,000 troops to the 68,000 already in the country when he came to office, thinking this "surge" would cripple the Taliban. The surge failed, but he maintained 8,400 troops in the country. In fact, Obama expanded the war to Pakistan, using drones to assassinate Taliban leaders and jihadists operating from bases near the border with Afghanistan; this computer-managed war took the lives of hundreds of innocent civilians that the military termed "collateral damage." He also sent Special Forces on raids deep into Pakistan, the most prominent example being the one to Abbotabad that killed bin Laden in 2011, though by this time, this was mainly a PR event with no strategic value.

In contrast to Bush II, who preferred "boots on the ground," Obama, as the *New York Times'* David Sanger put it, embraced "hard, covert power," alluding to the necessity of a "'light footprint' that enables [the United States] to fight its wars stealthily, execute its operations with the speed of the bin Laden raid, and then avoid lengthy entanglements." Like Bush II, who had never experienced war firsthand, Obama brought to his brand of war-making an "aggressiveness" that people around him found "surprising."

Obama, though, did appreciate the fact that being bogged down in the Middle East was sapping U.S. power by provoking disaffection at home and alienation from America abroad. Fighting so-called "asymmetric warfare" with irregulars like the Taliban and the jihadists could go on forever, and Obama wanted to shift the global U.S. military strategy to one that was more congenial to its perceived strength in conventional warfare instead of counterinsurgency. The grand new design was the "Pivot to Asia" that involved the deployment of the bulk of the U.S. naval strength to the Indo-Pacific area to contain China. Reorientation was easier said than done, however, as extrication from the Middle East morass was made impossible by the strength of interests that made up the War on Terror/Counterinsurgency lobby.

Though it was mainly his blistering interpretation of America's economic and social crises that brought Donald Trump to power, a not negligible role was played by his appeal to anti-war sentiment, with him continually reminding people during his campaign for the presidency in 2015 and 2016 that his rival, Hillary Clinton, had voted for the invasion of Iraq in 2003 when she was a senator. In office, however, he ended up destabilizing the Middle East even more. There was, first of all, his unqualified support for Israel, which led him to a major move that infuriated the Arabs: the transfer of the U.S. embassy from Tel Aviv to Jerusalem. Then he reversed the one tension-lessening achievement of Obama by taking the United States out of the Iran nuclear deal that had put effective checks on Tehran's development of weapons-grade uranium in return for a relaxation of economic sanctions. Finally, he gave a blank check for weapons purchases to Saudi Arabia, enabling the benighted kingdom to wage its cruel intervention in the civil war in Yemen.

Trump occasionally remembered, however, that eliminating boots on the ground was one of his major campaign promises, so that the country could focus on "America First." But, as in the case of Bush II and Obama, both of whom had an inferiority complex when dealing with generals owing to their lack of combat experience, draft dodger Trump also deferred to the military. After he decided to end the Obama-era intervention in Syria by withdrawing 1,000 U.S. troops in early October 2019, he caved in to the military's pushback. Over a month later, the head of the U.S. Central Command stated there was no "end date" on Washington's intervention in Syria and the presence of 2,500 American troops in neighboring Iraq.

Like Obama, Trump was passive-aggressive, eager to show the generals that he could be as macho as they were. The most notorious display of this behavior was when he flagrantly disregarded international law and ordered the assassination of Qassem Soleimani, a top Iranian general, at Baghdad International Airport in January 2020, against the advice of the top brass and the U.S. intelligence elite.

Faced with passive resistance on the part of the generals, Trump ended up keeping thousands of troops in Afghanistan during his term in office, but, mindful of the consequences of not keeping his promise by the 2020 elections, he directed the military in February 2020 to withdraw all troops by November 2020. Again, the military procrastinated, with the support of the War on Terror lobby, the deadline passed, and Joe Biden inherited some 3,500 troops and Special Forces personnel still in the country when he took office in January 2021.

The same pressures from the military to stay the course engulfed the new president, but by the time he ascended to office, not only was there no popular support for continuing the forever wars, but they were, he realized, a severe distraction from the real threat to the U.S. strategic position, which was China. The 20 years between the invasion of Afghanistan and the start of his presidency had seen China become the world's second biggest economy, possessing a military which, while still far from parity with U.S. military power, appeared headed in that direction.

When he decided in 2021 to withdraw from Afghanistan, Biden was not motivated by concerns for global peace but by an urgent desire to reframe U.S. strategy and refocus it on China, where the U.S. could rely on a strategy of containment, chiefly by naval power, which its forces were far better geared to carry out than chasing after popular insurgents or engaging in nation-building where the conditions did not exist for success, as in Iraq, Afghanistan, and Syria. That Biden was no peacenik but a warmonger would be shown in his provocative moves to bait China in the South China Sea and Taiwan a few months after the Afghanistan withdrawal and in his bellicose rhetoric affirming Washington's determination to fight to the last Ukrainian in its duel with Putin.

Extricating from the Middle East was, however, easier said than done. Instead of military engagement, Washington tried to put together a diplomatic rapprochement among Israel, Saudi Arabia, and the smaller Arabian Gulf states like Qatar in order to stabilize the region. The Hamas offensive into Israel in October 2023, however, blew up this plan for regional stabilization, since the Saudi government and the other reactionary Arab states could not afford to come to a deal with Israel while the latter was slaughtering another Arab people, the Palestinians. The U.S. stood even more isolated than when it withdrew from Afghanistan over two years earlier, now condemned by the whole Arab world, indeed by the whole world, as it provided the Israelis with weapons to commit genocide in Gaza. Meanwhile, its rival, China, allied with the Global South and successfully promoted a peacemaking diplomacy that contrasted with Washington's unqualified support for Israel's genocidal military offensive.

In short, Osama bin Laden's strategy of provoking U.S. overextension was successful. Indeed, he succeeded beyond his wildest dreams, for one of the reasons overextension occurs is that it is infernally difficult to shed old priorities; that means everything becomes a priority. Few have been the empires that have been able to unclench their fists and let go of self-destructive commitments.

But bin Laden was not only able to provoke the U.S. to a condition of military overstretch abroad. 9/11 pushed the American public into a state of fear and panic that the national security elite, conservatives, and reactionaries used to successfully push radical measures domestically that violated constitutionally guaranteed rights. These exacerbated the already deep political divides in the citizenry, severely destabilizing the country and producing the most polarizing figure in recent American history: Donald Trump.

Osama bin Laden's vision and methods were not shared by many, certainly not by me, but let's give the devil his due: 9/11 was a heinous crime but who can deny that it triggered a chain reaction that weakened the empire considerably?

But I cannot end this discussion of bin Laden simply on the political plane. I am also a sociologist, and from this standpoint, my takeaway from the dynamics of the 9/11 era is that individuals cannot simply be regarded as personifications of objective social forces—a perspective shared by most orthodox social scientists. Individuals do count, and some, in fact, have had an outsized imprint on history, their actions serving as the trigger that moves it from one track to another. Bin Laden is one of those figures that deserves the description "Napoleonic." As Nelly Lahoud, the U.S. intelligence analyst who came out with the most detailed study of inner workings of Al Qaeda under bin Laden's direction, conceded, "Though the 9/11 attacks turned out to a Pyrrhic victory for al-Qaeda, Usama still changed the world and continued to influence global politics for nearly a decade after."[126] If the U.S. is the confused and groping global power with a sick economy that it is today—one that has been, moreover, reduced to a dog being wagged by the Zionist tail—that is, to a not insignificant degree, due to bin Laden.

We Made a Difference

Still, the forces that bin Laden set in motion with 9/11—the varied resistance movements in Afghanistan, Iraq, and Syria—were not alone in degrading and eventually defeating U.S. power. Global civil society, the global movement against empire, also played a key role, that of delegitimizing the imperial venture and isolating the United States, just as it had the globalization project. The forever wars could have lasted longer had there been popular support for them. The movements against the American empire destroyed that possibility.

Along with so many others, we in Focus on the Global South made a major and long-term commitment to that battle against empire, providing analyses, organizing demonstrations, speaking in unending series of mass meetings, participating in peace missions and war crimes tribunals. As part of a collective global effort, we made a difference.

We made a difference, but where is that second superpower, global civil society, now? Like the disappearance of the anti-war movement after the U.S. withdrawal from Vietnam, the dissipation of the global movement following the end of the massive American presence in Iraq has been seen as a structural weakness of progressive movements by some analysts. The same observation has been made of the anti-globalization movement of roughly the same period.

Is it impossible to institutionalize these movements of protest and opposition? While it is true that organizational continuity is difficult to maintain over time, the memory of movements' successes remains strong, inspiring a new round of mobilization when the next crisis emerges. Collective memory of success in undermining the U.S. military adventure in the Middle East provided some of the energy for the massive global outburst of protests against the Israeli assault on Gaza in 2023. So had the rise of the Occupy Movement following the global financial crisis of 2009 drawn on the memory and tactics of the anti-globalization movement a decade earlier. Indeed, it is sometimes the case that the lessons of earlier movements get appropriated in surprising, sometimes troubling ways, as is the case with Trump's "America First Movement," which has a strong element of opposition to U.S. military deployments abroad as well as to neoliberalism, but then this facilitates the racist and fascist tendencies that also animate it.

12. From "Counterrevolutionary" to Congressman

IF I REMEMBER correctly, I was running along Riverside Drive in New York City when I received the call from the Philippines. It was late April 2009, and I was in the Big Apple to participate in the annual Left Forum at Pace University at a session alongside the prominent Marxist scholar David Harvey and other progressives. "You have to come home at once. You have been proclaimed a winner of the 2007 elections and you have to be sworn into office as Akbayan's second representative in the House," an excited Arlene Santos, then Akbayan's Secretary General, told me from Manila.

As I turned off my cellphone, I had the feeling that the intense and exciting decade of shuttling between teaching at UP, heading up Focus on the Global South in Bangkok, and participating in anti-globalization and anti-imperialist events throughout the world was about to end. This call to return to Manila could not have come at a more inopportune time since the global financial crisis had erupted the previous year, ushering in a grand debacle for globalization and an opportunity to promote alternatives to now more receptive ears throughout the world.

As I had told *Al Jazeera* at the Ninth World Social Forum in Belem, Brazil, a few weeks earlier, "What has happened now is in fact the sum of our fears, but at the same time I think that the WSF held out a hope; a hope that there could be a different world from the kind of neo-liberal capitalism world that Davos represented . . . I think that people are now looking to the World Social Forum more than ever for the kinds of alternatives that we need, to be able to restructure the world now that neo-liberalism has failed, now that capitalism is in severe crisis, now that the whole system has lost its legitimacy."[127]

But at the end of that seven-kilometer run at Riverside Park, my mind was clear as to where my responsibility lay, and that was to enter the brave new world of the House of Representatives of the Philippines. At that point, Focus had robust programs dealing with globalization, climate, trade, peace, and democracy, which were headed by top-flight activists. Meena Menon was on top of our India program, Joy Chavez headed the Philippine program, Shalmali Guttal led our work on the Mekong region, Jacques Chai Chongthomdi had succeeded Aileen Kwa as our representative in Geneva, Dorothy Guerrero had been recruited to work on climate and China, and Nicola Bullard and Chanida Bamford were at the helm at the headquarters in Bangkok. I did not feel indispensable, so after serving as executive director for 12 years, I stepped down, confident in the future of Focus, and reoriented the focus of my life back on the Philippines.

Detachment and Reflection

After the battle over the ratification of the ill-fated Senate decision to join the WTO in the mid-1990s, I had distanced myself from activist engagement in Philippine politics, focusing instead on anti-globalization and anti-imperialist work outside the country, operating mainly out of Focus in Bangkok but shuttling to Manila to teach, with much of my load being devolved to my capable TA's. My engagement with the Philippines was mainly academic. I led a Focus team that dissected the neoliberal political economy and produced the book *The Anti-Development State: The Political Economy of Permanent Crisis in the Philippines*, an exhaustive analysis of the economy of the post-martial law period, the main points of which were discussed in Chapter 11.[128] But to be honest, I was disgusted with elite-dominated politics while repelled at the same time by the internecine struggles on the Left.

Relative detachment also gave me the opportunity to reflect more deeply on the dynamics of Philippine politics. In an article titled "Yellow and Black (With Apologies to Stendhal)," I contended that representative democracy, as articulated by an Englishman, John Locke, was the ideology of the Philippine ruling class, one that it had enthusiastically absorbed from Locke's American heirs during the colonial era because it enabled them to compete relatively peacefully for power while at the same time uniting them against challenges from below.[129]

The U.S. burst into the local scene at the turn of the 20th century, and the liberal democratic institutions it brought with it from that period were also eagerly adopted by the local ruling class. These American imports included the Chicago-stye machine politics that was built on the exchange of jobs and social security for the long-term loyalty of the voter to the "boss" and his party.

When machine politics was transplanted to the Philippines, it was easily absorbed into the patron-client culture of the regional and local elites. But machine politics fueled by personal loyalties also became an avenue for political and social mobility for the lesser elites and the upper middle classes. Indeed, in many parts of the country, machine politics translated, as in Mayor Daley's Chicago, into virtual dictatorship periodically legitimized by votes that were mobilized, bought, or coerced by the superior organizational resources of *arrriviste* members of the elite that owed their position to their mastery of mass electoral politics.

I found the work on political clans of Al McCoy of the University of Wisconsin very helpful and wrote that "a strong undercurrent of the evolving system was the tension that developed between what he called the 'patrician' elite families whose power was largely on inherited wealth and privilege like the Aquinos and the Osmenas, and the 'provincial' elites whose power lay more in their ability to master the electoral machinery." The former were more inclined to play by the existing rules of the game that protected their wealth and traditional privileges, the latter to modify the rules so they could translate political advantage into wealth and status. What I called the "yellows" had their bastions in institutions such as the Makati Business Club, Liberal Party, and Catholic Church hierarchy, while the bulwark of the "blacks" were up-and-coming local dynasties that became masters at accumulating power by combining control over government resources with a populist appeal. The Aquinos, Osmenas, and Roxases I identified as belonging to the yellow current, the Marcoses and the Estradas to the black.

The failure of the "yellow" presidencies of Cory Aquino and Fidel Ramos to address the massive problems of poverty and inequality provided fertile ground for the populism of the "blacks," and no one was able to exploit this more fully in the post-EDSA system than Joseph "Erap" Estrada, who was elected president in 1998. Of all Philippine presidents, Erap owed his position least to class and money, though he had been patronized by the rich and was himself of no mean wealth. He owed it to his unsurpassed ability to translate into political power the star power that he had accumulated in that most democratic of institutions, the entertainment media.

Estrada's libertine lifestyle, shady friends, and corrupt practices such as receiving a cut from the numbers game *jueteng*, left him vulnerable to an attack from the yellows, and the struggle between the two currents in the elite led to Estrada's impeachment trial in the Senate and, though this did not result in his conviction, he was ousted from power in January 2001 when the military withdrew its support from him.

Relative detachment from politics was not total detachment. I was pulled back briefly to the thick of Philippine politics during the tumultuous mobilizations in Epifanio de los Santos Avenue—the famous EDSA of the 1986 Uprising—in 2001. The party I belonged to, Akbayan, took a stand against Estrada during the impeachment process, shocked as we were by the massive evidence of corruption in high places. In January, we took part in the so-called EDSA II mobilization against Estrada that went on for weeks, but with some discomfort since we found ourselves side by side with people who were mainly from the elite and the upper rungs of the middle class.

Estrada's lower class base erupted when he was arrested in late April 2001 on corruption charges and for a week, massive crowds converged at the EDSA shrine in what came to be known as "EDSA III," with anti-yellow politicians firing them up. This led to a massive confrontation on May 1, with thousands marching towards Malacanang Palace where, before they were disbanded, they engaged in pitched battles with the military in an effort to overthrow the government of Gloria Macapagal-Arroyo. Being the chairman of Akbayan, I gave a speech in support of the beleaguered Arroyo administration in a morning-after rally at the contested EDSA Shrine, but it was a tepid one since my political moorings had been shaken by the massive support for Estrada in the streets and lower-class districts on Metro-Manila.

I poured out my churning thoughts and feelings in an article published five days after the May 1st riot, the key point of which was that for a whole week the country had experienced class warfare, and we, most of the Left, were on the wrong side class-wise. When all is said and done, I wrote,

> [O]ne would be hard put to deny the truth that the vast majority of those who went to the EDSA Shrine and later marched to Malacanang were mainly motivated by resentments against the rich, by feelings that a terrible injustice had been done to their hero, Joseph "Erap" Estrada, by a sense that they were acting to protect the constitution and democracy. To say that they were simply manipulated by cynical politicians is to express a half-truth and to do the masses a great injustice.
>
> How a corrupt lout masquerading as a man of the masses like Estrada was able to capture the fierce loyalties of the poor, downtrodden, and marginalized will be the subject of many studies in political psychology in the months and years to come. But the reality is that, for all their vast corruption and incompetence while in office, Estrada and his backers have been able to do something that has eluded the Left for decades, and that is to organize the people along class lines into a powerful mass movement.[130]

Mass politics had finally come to the Philippines but it did so with a vengeance, not as the class alliance between the working class and the peasantry that the parties of the Left had worked for but as a populist coalition between the urban and rural poor, brokered by party bosses with a strong grip on the electoral machinery and headed by a charismatic personality whose populist rhetoric and style was second nature. "Unless the Left looks at the recent crisis with humility, as an opportunity to learn and revitalize itself," I concluded, "the fire next time might not only sweep away the elite but also decimate the progressive movement, rendering it ... forever irrelevant."[131]

These words proved prophetic. Backing Arroyo eventually proved to be a mistake for the Left, for she proved to be an even more fabulously corrupt figure than Estrada. Allowing one's party to be played by the two opposing currents of the elite had catastrophic results, but what was the way out? That was the million-dollar question.

As things quieted down after EDSA III, I refocused on international engagements.

"Counterrevolutionary"

A few years later, I was thrust back, rudely, into national reality. This was in 2004–2005, when the December 2004 issue of *Ang Bayan*, the principal organ of the Communist Party of the Philippines (CPP), singled me out as a "counterrevolutionary." My name was listed in a diagram alongside 13 other names of individuals who were either living or dead. Two of the people in the "counterrevolutionaries" list, Arturo Tabara and Filemon Lagman, had already been assassinated, the former just three months before. Another one, Ricardo Reyes, was being hunted down by operatives of the Communist Party and New People's Army (NPA) and had been forced to go into hiding.[132] Perhaps the most spectacular assassination had been that of Romulo ("Rolly") Kintanar, former head of the NPA, whose name was not on the list, perhaps because he had already been killed at a restaurant near UP nearly two years before, with the NPA publicly taking responsibility.

I and Rep. Etta Rosales, who was also on the list, decided that the best defense was offense, so we exposed what we believed the diagram to be: a hit list. Having been part of a Marxist-Leninist organization, we knew that being branded a "counterrevolutionary" meant one was beyond the pale, one was fair game. Our exposé triggered a bitter polemical exchange, with the CPP denying the diagram was a hit list. But it was too late, since people could not understand publicizing a list of living and dead activists and branding them counterrevolutionaries if one did not have malign intent. The CPP diagram made international news, and even President Hugo Chavez of Venezuela became worried about my safety, so that he invited me, as I wrote earlier, to "cool off" in Venezuela.

Jose Maria Sison and I exchanged such pleasantries as, "Is Mr. Sison so out of touch as not to realize that the informed reader need not be a card-carrying party member to know that in fundamentalist Marxist Leninist parties like the CPP, being branded 'counterrevolutionary' is practically a death sentence, with the only question being the time and place when the party will carry it out?"[133] In response, Sison characterized me as "a well-behaved and obedient citizen of the violent state of the U.S.-lining comprador big bourgeoisie and landlord class. He is also a highly paid hack whose air miles of traveling and hotel bills can compete with those of high-ranking officials of the U.S. State Department."[134]

I don't know if Sison believed what he wrote about me. I suspect not, but he was imprisoned in a role as *pontifex maximus* of the Philippine Revolution and had to behave accordingly. But precisely because he was at the top of the CPP hierarchy, it is impossible that he did not have anything to do with my designation as an enemy of the people. I did not take it personally, and I was glad when the polemics died down so I could concentrate on my teaching, writing, and public speaking. But I had been branded a "counter-revolutionary" and that was a point of no return for the National Democrats.

Had I been just a lone Leftist intellectual, the CPP would probably not have bothered about me if not for the fact that I was the National Chairman of Akbayan, and Akbayan was posing a very serious threat indeed to the NDF's claim to be the only force entitled to represent the Left. It was our presence in Congress that they saw most threatening, for it gave us a platform to project the politics of a new Left. One must point out though that not all of my former comrades in the NDF behaved towards me in a hostile fashion. Satur Ocampo, one of their leading political personalities, never let political and ideological differences get in the way of a warm personal demeanor towards me and never said anything negative about me, even as many of his comrades were excoriating me as a "CIA agent."

Anyway, my polemics with the CPP tapered off after a few weeks (though my being harassed by the party's exuberant youth activists both in the Philippines and the U.S. would continue off and on). For the next two years, I was again immersed in non-Philippine engagements, going on anti-globalization and anti-war speaking tours but also serving as a visiting professor at the University of California at Irvine, UC Santa Barbara, St Mary's University in Halifax, and the State University of New York at Binghamton, New York— and, always, compulsively writing, writing, writing. Then I decided to run for Congress on the Akbayan ticket in the national elections of 2007.

Akbayan and the New Left

Akbayan was founded in 1998 as a party of the Left from some currents of the so-called "rejectionist" wing of the pre-1992 National Democratic Front and political formations that were broadly Social Democratic, but not anti-Communist in orientation. Key in its formation were two very skilled political entrepreneurs, Ronald Llamas and Joel Rocamora. Two important ideological inspirations were the socialist luminary Francisco ("Dodong") Nemenzo and his wife, feminist advocate Ana Maria, popularly known as Princess.

Akbayan, or, roughly, "shoulder to shoulder," in Tagalog, held pretty much the same main advocacies as the CPP-NDF and its allied organizations such as the Makabayan, or Nationalist, Bloc—that is, agrarian reform and labor rights. Where it was distinctive was its democratic socialist orientation, which meant it did not see the armed struggle as the main way to come to power, putting the emphasis instead on electoral participation. It had a democratic as opposed to "democratic centralist" decision-making process; and was more flexible when it came to building alliances with non-left forces. It also saw the struggle for women's rights, LGBTQ rights, indigenous rights, and the environment as proceeding in parallel to and not subordinated to the class struggle. When it came to the U.S., it was as sharp in its opposition as the CPP and NDF, though the latter saw it as a Trojan Horse for Washington.

I was not active in the process leading up to the founding of the party, so I was surprised though honored to be asked to be the national chairman of the new party, and I accepted when I was assured it was not going to be a day-do-day management job but more like an honorary one.

Akbayan became a national actor via the party-list system. In their concern to have some secure representation for the "marginalized sectors," the framers of the post-Marcos 1987 Constitution had reserved 20 percent of the seats in the House of Representatives for people representing these social groups who would be elected at a national election via a party-list system, the other 80 percent being elected at the local district level via the usual first-past-the-post system.

By 2009, when I received the call in New York, Akbayan, which had registered as both a party and a party-list, had already participated in four national elections. With articulate tribunes like Etta Rosales, Mayong Aguja, and Risa Hontiveros, it had achieved national recognition for its advocacies of land reform, political reform, workers' rights, indigenous rights, and gender rights. Along with other party-lists like Bayan Muna and Sanlakas, Akbayan had brought a strong pro-people voice to an institution, the House of Representatives, whose seats were mainly filled by people out to protect their dynastic interests and where the operative principle was "I scratch your back, and you scratch mine, and let's all enjoy our pork barrel allocations, and to hell with everything else." These progressive parties may have had limited cooperation with one another, indeed disliked one another, but they were viewed by traditional politicians and those not familiar with their internecine struggles as collectively *ang kaliwa,* the Left.

Joining the 14th Congress

When I decided to run as a candidate for Akbayan in the 2007 elections, it was from a variety of motives. I was a political activist constantly in fights with those in power, and it didn't seem right to criticize unless I had the experience of being in public office and confronted the constraints it placed on officeholders. There was also the challenge of how to use my election to advance a progressive agenda in an essentially conservative institution. There was also personal ambition, the (dubious) prestige of being a member of Congress. All this came together in the dream of being a "tribune of the people."

According to the formula used to allocate 20 percent of congressional seats among those party lists that had participated in the 2007 elections, I did not make the cut; only Risa Hontiveros did. Well, that's that, I said, and with the satisfaction of having tried for the dubious distinction of being a congressman and failed, I ended my brief electoral pursuit of a position for which, deep inside, I knew I was probably congenitally unfit. Or so, I thought.

The Supreme Court had other ideas. In 2009, it ruled that the traditional formula for allocating party list seats was flawed and introduced a new, more complicated mathematical formula that entitled Akbayan to one more seat. Under the new rule, 29 candidates in the 2007 elections, including myself, were judged qualified to join the House.

I took the first available flight to Manila, stopped briefly at the house to don my *barong tagalog,* the traditional Filipino long-sleeved shirt, and rushed to the House for a collective oath-taking. To my horror, I found myself standing beside former general Jovito Palparan, who had gained notoriety as "the butcher" during the presidency of Gloria Macapagal Arroyo. Palparan had left a trail of extra-judicial executions and "disappearances" of activists in his various assignments, including those of two UP students, which many of us in the UP faculty had publicly condemned.[135] As I mumbled my words, I realized he might try to shake my hand upon completing the ceremony. I momentarily toyed with the idea of hitting him in the face instead, but that would create a scandal on my very first day in Congress. So right before repeating the words "pledge faithful obedience to these rules . . . ," I stepped back and turned quickly to the left, as he lifted his hand to try to shake mine. He then turned to the fellow on his right, but too late—the guy, probably also unwilling to shake Palparan's hands, had also scampered quickly away, leaving the Butcher with his hand in the air.

I quickly assembled a staff from members or sympathizers of Akbayan.[136] A few days after I was sworn in, I was immediately pulled into legislative combat, engaging Rep Mark Cojuangco of Tarlac, the son of notorious Marcos crony Danding Cojuango, in a duel that lasted for three nights. The occasion was the second reading of his bill seeking to revive the Bataan nuclear power plant that had been mothballed for years owing to safety reasons. Since, as an activist in the U.S., I had been part of the campaign to stop this dangerous Marcos project, my friends in civil society felt it fell on me to stop Cojuangco. I was surprised to see him familiar with different aspects of nuclear power—the public health, safety, and economic dimensions—so the debate boiled down to a contest between opposing data, like the cost of nuclear power relative to other means of energy generation, the geological characteristics of the proposed nuclear power site, and the impact on public health of a possible meltdown. We would debate far into the night, adjourning at 10 pm, when there were only four or five people left in the plenary hall and we two gladiators were absolutely exhausted. A news article summed up my position in the debate:

> Walden Bello, Akbayan party-list representative and the most vocal critic of the rehabilitation move in the lower house, said that even after more than 2 decades, the old problems of the BNPP [Bataan Nuclear Power Plant] had not been resolved. Bello enumerated 3 persisting problems of the plant: 1) nuclear waste disposal, 2) geological hazards, and 3) unfinished debt payments. Bello and [former Rep] Etta Rosales both claim that, even now, the country is still paying the BNPP debts as the money used to pay-off the initial debts came from loans made by the national government. If rehabilitated, they say, the BNPP will become another fiscal nightmare. "Rehabilitating the plant is throwing good money after bad money," Bello said.[137]

Debate was suspended after three nights, and it was not resumed before the ending of the 14th Congress, so I felt a sense of accomplishment, though I developed a healthy respect for my younger opponent. Unfortunately, as one account after the ending of the 14th Congress noted, "In the final session of the previous Congress, Mark Cojuangco got so riled up by the failure to have his bill approved that he nearly collapsed from high blood pressure."[138] There have been periodic attempts by Cojuangco to reopen the nuclear plant since then, but the Fukushima disaster in Japan in 2011 has practically killed off nuclear power as an option in the Philippines.

The Agrarian Reform Extension Struggle

I was also dragged immediately into the fight to extend and expand agrarian reform. Owing to its many loopholes, the original Comprehensive Agrarian Reform Program (CARP) of 1988 remained in large part unimplemented. It had mainly distributed public land to land reform beneficiaries and very little private land, which was the best land in the country. Landlords also simply refused to obey the weak Department of Agrarian Reform, with some resorting to sheer terror undertaken with impunity.

Under the leadership of Rep Edcel Lagman of Albay Province and Akbayan Rep Risa Hontiveros, CARPER, or the Comprehensive Agrarian Reform with Extension Bill, sought to speed up the redistribution of private land by allocating new funding, end legal obstructionism at the local level, and plug other loopholes.

The legislative battle unfolded in the midst of mass mobilization by peasants from Luzon to Mindanao. Time was of the essence since funds for the compulsory acquisition of private lands would not be available beyond 2008. What gave the pro-land reform extension forces the upper hand was an epic 1700-kilometer march in November 2007—from Sumilao, Bukidnon, to the presidential palace in Manila—by fifty-five farmers demanding redistribution of 144 hectares of land to which they were entitled. The long march brought agrarian reform back to the center of national consciousness and provided the spark for the counteroffensive against the landlord bloc's drive to kill land reform in Congress.

Put on the defensive, the landed bloc in Congress set in motion a strategy of not frontally opposing CARP but disemboweling it. Cutting off funding for compulsory land acquisition—the *sine qua non* of successful agrarian reform—was the central element in the landlords' strategy and, in a nip-and-tuck battle in the House, their representatives nearly succeeded in doing this when they voted in mid-December of 2008 to extend CARP for six months without authorizing funding for compulsory acquisition of the remaining private lands.

Buoyed by popular support, the pro-peasant forces in Congress fought back, and over the next few months, succeeded in forcing a final debate in plenary of House Bill 4077 (the CARPER bill).

The climactic battle was fought in and out of Congress, as farmer organizations staged sit-ins twice at the lobby of the House of Representatives' plenary hall and, on the final evening, broke through the North gate of the Batasan (House of Representatives) complex, leading to scuffles with the police and the arrest of nearly a hundred of them as the House debated, then approved the bill in a photo finish on the evening of June 3, 2009, before it went into recess.

Used to being on the outside in the street, this time I was on the inside, delivering a speech in support of the legislation where, if I recall it right, I said, "Democracy is on trial here. If we don't deliver what the people desire, then our days as an institution are numbered."

It was in the battle for CARPER that I learned the lesson that the perfect can be the enemy of the good. It was not perfect legislation, but it achieved its main purpose of extending agrarian reform, providing compulsory acquisition of the remaining 1–1.5 million hectares of private land, with funding to the tune of P150 billion. Still, there were provisions that landlords could use to stall the process of land redistribution at the ground level which we had to concede, though in diluted form, to get the legislation through. As I said in my post-mortem analysis,

> The battle over CARPER went down to the wire. It was class politics taking the form of rough legislative struggle and maneuver, and in the end, the pro-reform forces were forced to choose between passing a bill many provisions of which were a significant improvement over CARP but which carried one menacing provision, and seeing the agrarian reform process stall. I believe that given the balance of forces in the country today, those who voted for CARPER made the right choice. This was the best piece of agrarian reform legislation we could come up with at this historical juncture, given the correlation of class power. But the contingency element looms large: whether CARPER becomes truly a vehicle for advancing reform will depend on whether pro-reform forces can create, at the local level, the critical political mass involving farmers, progressive elements at the Department of Agrarian Reform, the Church, and other groups that would overcome the rearguard actions of the landed class to delay the inevitable. To paraphrase an old legal saying, the facts on the ground will constitute nine-tenths of the law.[139]

Five years later, with CARPER a wreck, a topic I will touch in Chapter 18, I was no longer sure about that maxim about the perfect being the enemy of the good.

Those last few months of the 14th Congress were not all about learning the legislative ropes. I became part of an opposition effort to impeach President Gloria Macapagal Arroyo for corruption, I went to Maguindanao to offer my condolences to the families of the 58 people massacred by the ruling Ampatuan family in that province in the infamous "crime of the century"—the first of many such missions of condolence I would undertake in the next few years to comfort the loved ones of victims of impunity and urge the local police to bring to justice those responsible. I also went to Vienna during the congressional break to try to get the Austrian government to cancel an illegitimate loan extended to the Philippines—one of the most quixotic missions I ever undertook, since neither the government nor the Austrian banks believed in debt forgiveness.

Campaign Season

The campaign period, which is held once every three years, leading up to the May national elections, is the time when democracy is most evident in practice in the Philippines, when its aspiring rulers present themselves in a beauty contest before the people culminating in election day, after which top-down elite rule resumes for another three years. Much as Akbayan was uncomfortable in a process that had been mastered to a T by traditional politicos, we had to participate in it, and after four campaigns, the party had developed an impressive campaign machinery.

The 2010 campaign was my first real campaign. Crisscrossing the country—since party-list members of Congress were elected on a nationwide, not district-wide, basis—required stamina since rest days were rare. It brought me into contact with the poorest parts of the country, to dirt-poor rural villages and the innermost recesses of urban poor settlements where housewives, taking a break from their day-long struggle to keep their families together, often did not appreciate your interrupting their gambling to introduce yourself—and who could blame them? For the most part, I had only encountered the poor in their roles as drivers, salesgirls, janitors, or waiters. It was only when I went to their makeshift houses with galvanized iron roofs in foul-smelling alleys that I fully realized the devastating impact of poverty and severe inequality not only on one's economic status but on one's dignity. If F. Scott Fitgerald could write, "The rich are different from you and me," so could I say as a child of the middle classes that "the poor are different from you and me."

The campaign also made me feel how much of a stranger I was in my own country since I had to speak in Tagalog or Pilipino to connect with people, and practically all the public speaking I had done in my life was in English—even in Congress, where interpellations and speeches were delivered in English, except to score a rhetorical point to remind one's dozing colleagues that one was a Filipino.

My party-mates were amused when I said, "*Ibababa namin ang presyo* [we will bring down the price] *ng droga*," using the Tagalog word for illegal drugs instead of the right word, which was *gamot*, or medicines. "You've won the addict vote," people kidded me throughout the campaign.

But if speaking in Tagalog was rough for a mind that thought in English, Ilocano was even harder. A visit to my parents' hometowns in the Ilocos region to gain Ilocano votes was obligatory, so for the first time in my life, this boy from Manila got to visit his ancestral roots, where pro-Marcos sentiment was still strong, especially in Ilocos Norte. The last time I had spoken Ilocano was when I was growing up, so switching from my smattering of Ilocano to Tagalog to English (as a last resort) before crowds of several hundred in Piddig, Ilocos Norte, my mother's hometown, and Santa, Ilocos Sur, where my father was from, was an ordeal, though the audience was sympathetic to someone they considered one of them, even if he had opposed the great son of the "Solid North," Marcos. When I was linguistically in knots, they urged me to "say it in English," never in Tagalog, which, of course, most of them knew how to speak.

Akbayan Joins Hands with the Liberal Party

The Akbayan Congress in Antipolo in late 2009 was historic, since we entered into an alliance with the Liberal Party (LP) on a platform of reform, the centerpiece of which was a crusade against corruption. At the time of the Congress, Senator Mar Roxas was expected to be the LP's presidential standard bearer, but he later decided to throw his support to Senator Benigno Aquino III, the son of Ninoy and Cory Aquino. Remembering our backing during the EDSA II mobilization of Gloria Macapagal-Arroyo, who turned out to be formidably corrupt, I thought that joining a coalition with an elite party on a platform of reform was not objectionable so long as one stuck to one's principles, did not shelve one's progressive program while a member of the coalition, and reserved the right to criticize one's partners if they strayed from the coalition program. The Liberals assured us they supported agrarian reform, higher wages for labor, women's rights, and LGBTQ rights, along with a crusade against corruption. When my party mates assured me that being in a coalition with the Liberals would not prevent me from criticizing our partners if they departed from a program of reform, I lent my support to the formation of the coalition, whose chief slogan came to be "*Kung walang korap, walang mahirap*" ("Without corruption there would be no poverty"). But Ric Reyes, who had played a central role in the early years of Akbayan, did not. He walked out of the congress and left the party. So did another party pioneer, Joel Rocamora, though in his case, it was owing to internal party differences. These were painful separations.

The LP-led coalition won the elections, and in the new administration, Ronald Llamas joined the Cabinet as Political Secretary and Etta Rosales was appointed Commissioner of Human Rights. With Risa Hontiveros having decided to run—unsuccessfully—for senator, I was now the leader of Akbayan in the House, with Kaka Bag-ao joining me as the party's other representative. I was also named chairperson of the Committee on Overseas Workers Affairs.

The Great Reproductive Health Debate

The 15th Congress was dominated by one legislative struggle: the great battle over the Reproductive Health Bill. It was probably the one time in Congress' history where an ideological or cultural struggle took precedence over legislation having to do with economic interests, political interests, personal interests, or national security. The protagonists were the people of the Philippines and the powerful 2,000-plus-year-old Catholic Church. And the people prevailed.

The RH Bill was first introduced in the House in 1999, but for nearly 12 years, the Church lobby kept it bottled up in the Committee on Population. Thus, when the bills made it past the Committee on Population early in 2011, legislators and civil society organizations supporting RH were ecstatic, for the RH bill had blasted its way to the plenary and appeared to have the momentum. What made the difference was the women's movement's influence. The original thrust of advocacy for family planning supported by the state emphasized fertility control or population management for development, which had top-down, technocratic connotations. Over the years, family planning was reoriented as an issue of women's control over their bodies, as a health issue, as a question of individual freedom and choice.

It would, however, take another year and a half before the bill was turned into law. During this period, the most exciting and dramatic struggle in the country's parliamentary history unfolded, with both sides deploying all the arguments and tactics they could muster to outmaneuver the other.

The provisional vote count in both the Senate and the House favored the bill, but instructed by the bishops, the anti-RH legislators resorted to delaying tactics, including repeated long interpellations or the threat of a quorum call to prevent the bill from coming to a vote or, failing that, pushing the vote as close as possible to the 2013 elections in order to make pro-RH legislators waver in the face of the Church hierarchy's threat to turn voters against them at the polls.

Indeed, the Roman Catholic hierarchy waged a massive campaign against the bill. This included the mobilization of parish priests to inveigh against the bill in their weekend sermons, and the spread of disinformation about the RH.

The main thrust of the Church's propaganda was to paint contraception as a vital step on the slippery slope towards abortion—indeed, to make contraception indistinguishable from abortion. Contraceptive pills were rhetorically denounced as "abortifacients."

Another debating strategy was to deny that a high fertility rate and a high population growth rate in a low-growth economy like the Philippines constituted obstacles to development.

The fast and loose use of statistics marked the arguments of anti-RH advocates, along with really outrageous claims, like the assertion that condom use in Thailand caused the spread of AIDS. Or that the RH bill was part of a U.S. plot "to keep down the population of developing countries"—the so-called "Kissinger Doctrine." Or that it was all part of a conspiracy of the big foreign pharmaceutical companies to expand the local market for artificial contraceptives.

When it was pointed out that most other religions and religious denominations in the country either favored or did not oppose the bill, the argument was simply brushed aside with the claim that 80 percent of the population owed fealty to Rome.

That these arguments did not cut any ice in both chambers is due to the fact that the pro-RH forces did a good job shooting them down and mustering strong arguments in support of the bill. Particularly effective in the floor debates were the following arguments:

- The RH bill was built on the basic democratic principle of freedom of choice;
- Access to family planning was essential to maternal and child health;
- Survey after survey had shown a significant majority of respondents favoring family planning, including artificial contraception;
- Poor respondents, by a large majority, favored access to government-provided or facilitated family planning methods, including condoms, pills, and other methods of contraception;

- The 450,000 abortions that took place yearly could be significantly cut down by access to contraceptives;
- Income level was negatively correlated with family size, meaning the bigger the family, the poorer it was;
- Effective family planning was a central element in any strategy to promote development and reduce poverty.

Rep Edcel Lagman shouldered the brunt of the debate while Rep Janet Garin of Iloilo oversaw the floor strategy. I relished engaging in the exchange, jousting with congressmen like Jackie Enrile of Cagayan and Victorino Dennis Socrates of Palawan. Enrile, who was sympathetic to my views, appeared to me to be mainly interested in showing his anti-RH father, Senator Juan Ponce Enrile, that he was taking the arguments of both sides seriously. Socrates insisted that a "demographic winter" would befall the Philippines as it did the U.S. owing to the use of the pill, to which I responded: "I think that this whole issue of the pill having created the decline of the United States is, [on] the face of it, really silly. To think that the U.S. was brought down by the pill, which is our Gentleman's theory of history, please—I would like to say to the Gentleman that this [was] a very complex process in which economic and political forces were the central factors."[140] Socrates's demographic winter argument was just one of the other's side's assertions that lent a surreal air to the debate. Then there was another congressman's contention that condoms were useless as prophylactics against HIV-AIDS since the AIDS virus was allegedly so microcosmic that it would penetrate the latex condom.

My main contribution to the debate, however, consisted of a four-part series of articles aimed at both Congress and the public that was published in the *Philippine Daily Inquirer*, the leading daily newspaper, showing the strong correlation between family planning and the better economic performance of Vietnam, Thailand, and Indonesia, and the correlation between uncontrolled population growth and failed development in the Philippines.

Based on intensive field visits I made to the three countries in 2011, I argued:

What accounts for the difference in the performance of the four economies? Economic policy? Hardly, since all four countries followed export-oriented economic strategies over the last four decades. Structural adjustment? Not really, since all four economies were subjected to some variety of market-oriented reform, though it is arguable that adjustment was milder in our neighbors than in our country. Asset and income redistribution? No, since as in the Philippines, state-promoted asset and income redistribution programs in Thailand and Indonesia were either weak or nonexistent. Corruption? Again, all four countries have been marked by high levels of corruption, with Indonesia being a consistent top-notcher in annual surveys. There is, in fact, one very distinctive feature that separates the Philippines from its neighbors: unlike our country, Vietnam, Indonesia, and Thailand managed to rein in the growth of their populations through effective state-sponsored family planning programs. And while successful family planning is not the whole story, economists and demographers have a consensus that it is an essential element in the narrative of economic advance in our neighboring countries.[141]

In the lead-up to the vote, the Catholic hierarchy, dressed in scarlet robes and sporting zucchetto skull caps, made a show of force in the House, hoping to intimidate us infidels into submission. Our forces in the gallery and outside the gates of the Batasan, countered them, clad in purple or sporting purple ribbons.

On Dec 12, 2013, the decisive vote on the RH bill took place. When the presiding officer, Rep. Lorenzo (Erin) Tanada III, arrived at my name in the roll call and asked for my vote, I replied in the affirmative and walked towards the rostrum to explain my vote. He then posed the standard question, "What is the pleasure of the gentleman from Akbayan?" To which I replied, "I hesitate to answer that question since 'pleasure' has become a controversial word during the last few days' debate." A ripple of laughter went through the plenary hall as the exhausted participants in the long debate were reminded of the anti-RH's side impassioned warnings that sexual hell would break loose should they pass the bill.

The House passed the RH bill by a vote of 113 to 104. There would be a third reading, but we knew we had won.

While the media was focused on the partisans of the RH Bill in Congress, the force that brought victory was the women's movement, with leaders like Risa Hontiveros, Junice Demeterio Melgar, Princess Nemenzo, Esperanza Cabral, Sylvia Estrada Claudio, Mary Racelis, Elizabeth Angsioco, and Jean Enriquez, and organizations like Likhaan and Women's Health playing a decisive role. And, of course, there was the simply sterling role of Rep Edcel Lagman, who had stayed the course for years and years. There were other important ingredients for success, like the support of President Benigno Aquino III and a split within the elite, between the ideologically reactionary and the less unenlightened ones, whose support for the bill was based on the calculation that state-supported birth control would defuse pressures for distribution from the poor. Thus, I found myself strategizing on the same side as Rep. Kimi Cojuangco, the wife of Mark Cojuangco, with whom I had engaged in a three-night-long gladiatorial contest on the reopening of the Bataan nuclear plant over three years earlier. Separated by class, wealth, and ideology, we had, unexpectedly, become friends.

Akbayan played a central role in passing the RH Bill, both in Congress, in the streets, and in the media. Other Left forces co-sponsored the bill, but it did not figure prominently in their legislative agenda, perhaps worried that the reproductive rights issue would overshadow their push for revolutionary change.

There were other memorable bills of which I was one of the principal sponsors that turned into law aside from the RH Bill in my six years in Congress. One was CARPER, which I have already discussed above. Another was the bill that provided monetary compensation for over 11,000 victims of human rights violations under the Marcos regime. But, as I wrote a few days after the RH vote, "I will look back with pride to the 15th Congress that passed the Responsible Parenthood and Reproductive Health Bill. Indeed, even if no other bill I am associated were to be passed in this Congress, the victory of this long overdue measure, which will enable our country to have greater capacity to confront the challenges of the 21st century, will be enough to bring me immense satisfaction."[142]

It was a battle over values, the kind that over the centuries spilled blood in other societies. Fortunately, in our country, the democratic rules prevailed. The RH victory in 2012 was historic. But it was not complete, and the hierarchy would continue to fight a rearguard battle, bringing the RH Act to the Supreme Court, instigating local executives to disobey it, and getting its allies in the Senate to gut the budget for its implementation. The biggest of these obstacles was removed when the Supreme Court declared the law constitutional in 2014.

Looking back 10 years after the passage of the bill, in December 2022, I wrote that while the RH Law was a milestone,

> [T]here remains much unfinished business when it comes to promoting women's rights and gender equality.
>
> There is a crying need for a divorce law; the Philippines is, along with the Vatican, the only country in the world with no divorce law, forcing thousands of women and men to remain trapped in loveless relationships.

Marriage equality, or same sex marriage, is another priority. Important in paving the way for it would be passage of the Sexual Orientation and Gender Identity Expression Bill . . . different versions of which have been filed over the last 22 years.

And then, there is the urgent need to decriminalize abortion. The statistics are sobering. 600,000 unsafe abortions are performed in the Philippines yearly. 100,000 women have to be hospitalized owing to complications. And about 1000 of them end up dead. The conditions specified in a law governing abortion should be debated, but decriminalizing it is the first step.

The RH law was the first step in a long march. It will not be the last.[143]

13. Fighting the New Slave Trade

MY MOST challenging—and frustrating—experience in my six years in Congress was heading up the Committee on Overseas Workers Affairs (COWA). What I found was a big racket where Filipino recruitment agencies connived with receiving country governments and employers to exploit millions of migrant laborers, with the Philippine government helplessly looking on, with some of its officials even participating in the exploitation. Yet the government and the Philippine elite bore a grave responsibility for this system of exploitation in a larger sense, in that labor export was a substitute—and a poor one—for promoting economic policies that could absorb the millions of Filipinos who saw no alternative but to work abroad. Neoliberal structural adjustment had created a surplus labor force that could only find decent employment outside the country.

Sexual Prey in the Saudi Jungle

Soon after I was appointed head of COWA by House Speaker Sonny Belmonte, I led a congressional mission to Saudi Arabia, the number 1 destination of Overseas Filipino Workers (OFWs), early in 2011. Along with me were Reps Emmeline Aglipay, Cresencio Paez, and Carmen Zamora Apsay. It was a chastening experience, the biggest takeaway for us being that we were practically sending our domestic workers to sexual hell where they were isolated in households where they had no rights and were subject to total control by domestic potentates. In our official report, titled *The Dark Kingdom: The Condition of Overseas Filipino Workers in Saudi Arabia*, we wrote that, "Rape is the ever-present specter that haunts Filipino domestic workers in Saudi Arabia."[144] After reviewing statistics for OFWs in distress and interviewing domestics in Philippine government shelters in Jeddah, Riyadh, and Al Khobar, we concluded that rape and sexual abuse were more frequent than the raw statistics revealed, probably coming to 15 to 20 percent of cases reported for domestics in distress. The reported cases were probably roughly representative of unreported cases of abuse of domestic workers throughout the kingdom, so that one could not but come to the conclusion that rape and sexual abuse of Filipinas throughout the kingdom were common. The victims of rape all recounted harrowing stories, but probably most harrowing was that of Lorena, which we detailed in the report:

> Lorena is in her mid-twenties, lithe, and pretty—qualities that marked her as prime sexual prey in the Saudi jungle. And indeed, her ordeal began when they arrived at her employer's residence from the airport. "He forced a kiss on me," she recalled. Fear seized her and she pushed him away.
>
> He was not deterred. "One week after I arrived," she recounted, "he raped me for the first time. He did it while his wife was away. He did it after he commanded me to massage him and I refused, saying that was not what I was hired for. Then in July he raped me two more times. I just had to bear it ["*Tiniis ko nalang*"] because I was so scared to run away. I didn't know anyone."
>
> While waiting for her employer and his wife in a shopping mall one day, Lorena came across some Filipino nurses, whom she begged for help. Upon hearing her story, they gave her a SIM card and pitched in to buy her a load [the length of time allowed for a purchase of data access and calls].
>
> But the domestic torture continued. She would be slapped for speaking Arabic since her employer's wife said she was hired to speak English. She was given just one piece of bread to eat at mealtime and she had to supplement this with scraps from the family's plates. She was loaned to the wife's mother's household to clean the place, and her reward for this was her being raped by the wife's brother; kinship apparently confers the right to rape the servants of relatives. Also during that month, October, she was raped—for the fourth time—by her employer.
>
> She not only had to contend with sexual aggression but with sheer cruelty. Once, while cleaning, she fell and cut herself. With blood gushing from the wound, she pleaded with the employer's wife to bring her to the hospital. She refused, and when Lorena asked her to allow her to call her mother in the Philippines, she again said no, telling her this was too expensive. The employer arrived at that point, but instead of bringing her to the hospital, he said, "You might as well die." Lorena had to stanch the wound with her own clothes and treat herself with pills she had brought with her from the Philippines.

Wildly desperate by now, Lorena finally managed to get in touch with personnel of the Philippine Overseas Labor Office (POLO) in Al Khobar. Arrangements were made to rescue her on December 30. That morning, the rescue team from POLO and the local police arrived at the residence. Lorena flagged them frantically from a second story window and told them she wanted to jump, but the team advised her not to because she could break her leg. That was a costly decision, since the employer raped her again—for the fifth time—even with the police right outside the residence. When she dragged herself to her employer's wife and begged her to keep her husband away from her, she beat her instead, calling her a liar. "I was screaming and screaming, and the police could hear me, but they did not do anything."

When the employer realized that he was about to be arrested, he begged Lorena not to tell the police anything because he would lose his job and offered to pay for her ticket home. "I said I would not tell on him and say that he was a good man, just so that he would just let me go [*'para lang makatakas ako'*]," Lorena said. When she was finally rescued moments later, Lorena recounted her ordeal to the POLO team and police, and the employer was arrested.

Released from captivity, Lorena was determined to obtain justice. However, arduous bureaucratic procedures delayed a medical examination to obtain traces of semen right after her rescue. When it was finally conducted, she was given an emergency contraceptive pill—an indication, said the [Philippine labor] officer who led the rescue, that seminal traces had been found in and on her. Also, the examination revealed contusions all over her body and bite marks on her lips.[145]

Lorena's case was not untypical, Filipino labor officials admitted, but they said they could not do anything about it since there was a massive flow of domestics to the kingdom, triggered both on the demand and supply side, mediated by unscrupulous labor recruiters combing Muslim Mindanao and other parts of the Philippines for fresh flesh to funnel to the Saudi jungle.

The main recommendation of our report was to "decertify Saudi Arabia as a country fit to receive domestic workers."[146] But even as we penned this conclusion, we were doubtful that it would even receive a hearing. The traffic in workers and sexual slaves was much too profitable and entrenched.

The Global Labor Trafficking System

Several visits to the Middle East in my role as COWA chair in the next few years enabled me to deconstruct the entrenched structure and dynamics of the institution that I called the "new slave trade."[147]

The freer flow of commodities and capital has been one of the features of the contemporary process of globalization. Unlike in the earlier phase of globalization in the 19th century, however, the freer flow of commodities and capital has not been accompanied by a freer movement of labor globally. The dynamic centers of the global economy, after all, have imposed ever tighter restrictions on migration from the poorer countries. Yet the demand for cheap labor in the richer parts of the world continues to grow, even as more and more people in developing countries seek to escape conditions of economic stagnation, poverty, and climate catastrophe that are often the result of the same dynamics of the system of global capitalism that has created prosperity in the developed world.

The number of migrants worldwide grew from 36 million in 1991 to 191 million in 2005 to 280.6 million global migrants in 2020—representing close to 4 percent of the world's 7.8 billion people. The aggregate numbers do not, however, begin to tell the critical role that migrant labor plays in the prosperous economies. For instance, the booming economies in the Persian Gulf and Saudi peninsula are relatively lightly populated in terms of their local Arab population, but they host a substantial number of foreign migrant workers, many of whom come from South Asia and Southeast Asia. Indeed, foreign migrant workers are a disproportionate part of the populations of the Persian Gulf states—ranging from 25 percent in Saudi Arabia to 66 percent in Kuwait, to over 90 percent in the United Arab Emirates and Qatar.

This gap between increasing demand and restricted supply has created an explosive situation, one that has been filled by a global system of trafficking in human beings that can in many respects be compared to the slave trade of the 16th century.

The dynamics of the current system of trade in repressed labor is illustrated in the case of the Philippines. This country is one of the great labor exporters of the world. Some 10 percent of its total population and 22 percent its working age population are now migrant workers in other countries. With remittances totaling some $38 billion a year, the Philippines places fourth as a recipient of remittances—after India, China, and Mexico.

The role of the Philippines as a labor exporter cannot be divorced from the dynamics of neoliberal capitalism and structural adjustment that I detailed in Chapter 11. The labor export program began in the mid-1970s as a temporary program under the Marcos dictatorship, with a relatively small number of workers involved—about 50,000. The ballooning of the program to encompass 9 million workers owes much to the devastation of the economy and jobs by the structural adjustment policies imposed by the World Bank and the International Monetary Fund beginning in 1980, trade liberalization under the World Trade Organization, and the prioritization of debt repayment by the post-Marcos governments in national economic policy since 1986.

Structural adjustment resulted in deindustrialization and the loss of so many manufacturing jobs; trade liberalization pushed so many peasants out of agriculture, with a great number shoved directly into overseas employment; and prioritization of debt repayments robbed the government of resources for capital expenditures that could act as an engine of economic growth, since 20–40 percent of the budget went every year to servicing the debt. In the role that structural adjustment and trade liberalization played in creating pressures for labor migration, the experience of the Philippines parallels that of Mexico, another key labor-exporting country.

For the governments of these two countries, massive labor export has also served another function: as a safety valve for the release of social pressures that would otherwise have been channeled into radical movements for political and social change internally. Those who migrate are often among the most intrepid, the most nimble, and the most acute people in the lower and middle classes—the kind of people who would make excellent cadres and members of progressive movements for change. Along with the crisis of the socialization of children owing to the absence of the mothers, this is one of the most damaging legacies of the massive labor migration in the Philippines—that it has allowed our elites to ignore overdue structural reforms because of its serving as a safety valve for social pressures.

Labor export is big business. It's spawned a host of parasitic institutions that now have a vested interest in maintaining and expanding the process. The transnational labor export network includes labor recruiters, government agencies and officials, labor smugglers, and big corporate service providers like the U.S. multinational service provider, Aramark. Labor trafficking is expanding to become just as big and profitable as sex trafficking and the drug trade. The spread of free wage labor has often been associated with the expansion of capitalism. But what is currently occurring is the expansion and institutionalization of a system of unfree labor under contemporary neoliberal capitalism, a process not unlike the expansion of slave labor and repressed labor in the early phase of global capitalist expansion in the 16th century elaborated in the work of sociologists like Immanuel Wallerstein.

This expansive system that creates, maintains, and expands unfree labor is best illustrated in the case of the Middle East. As Atiya Ahmad writes,

"With the booming of the Gulf states' petrodollar-driven economies from the early 1970s onwards, a vast and consolidated assemblage of government policies, social and political institutions, and public discourse developed to manage and police the region's foreign resident population. Anchored by the *kefala* or sponsorship and guarantorship system, this assemblage both constructs and disciplines foreign residents into becoming 'temporary labor migrants.'"[148] This elite-promoted construction of migrant identity promotes an internalization of the migrants' role as social subordinates and an emasculation of their status as political agents. They are expected to remain and so far have largely behaved as non-participants in the politics of their so-called host societies, even as these societies are swept by the winds of political change.

In 2021, over 50 percent of the more than 1.83 million Filipino workers that went abroad went to the Middle East. Most of these workers were women and the biggest occupational category was household service workers or maids.

Here is how the transnational labor trafficking system works. A recruiter from, say, an Arabian Gulf state contacts his man in the Philippines. The Filipino contact goes to the remote provinces to recruit a young woman promising a wage of $400 a month, which is the minimum amount set by the Philippine government. When she departs, the recruitment agency gives her another contract at the airport, one that is often written in Arabic, saying she will be paid only half or less than that amount. On arrival at the destination, she receives from the Gulf recruiter a temporary residence permit or *iqama*, but this is taken from her along with her passport by the recruiter or by her employer.

The migrant worker is then turned over to a family where she labors under slave-like conditions for 18 to 20 hours a day. She is isolated from other Filipino domestic workers, making her communication with the outside world dependent on her employer. She cannot leave the employer because her temporary residence certificate and passport are with him. If she runs away, however, and goes to the labor recruiter, she is "sold" to another family, sometimes at an even lower rate than that paid by the original employer.

Unable to leave the country since she has no documents, the runaway most often ends up being sold from one family to another by the labor recruiter. If she is lucky, she might find her way to the Philippine embassy, which operates a shelter for runaways, but it will take months if not years for the Philippine embassy to obtain the necessary permits to enable her to return home.

In its effort to curb this free market in virtual slavery or to prevent workers from going into countries where their physical security would be in great danger like Syria or Iraq, the Philippine government requires government-issued permits for workers to be able to leave or it has imposed deployment bans to some countries. However, labor recruiters, who are often in cahoots with Middle East employers, have found ways of getting around these regulations.

Clandestine networks have developed to smuggle workers from the southern Philippines to destinations in the Middle East. A number of women domestics I interviewed in Damascus during an investigating mission told of being smuggled out in the southern Philippine city of Zamboanga by small boat to the Malaysian state of Sabah. From there they were transported in the hold of a bigger boat going to Singapore, where they were then offloaded and brought by land transport to a site near Kuala Lumpur. In Kuala Lumpur they were forced to work for their subsistence for six weeks. Only after two months were they finally transported by plane from Kuala Lumpur to Dubai, then to Damascus—straight into a raging civil war.

Disposable Lives

These dangerous peregrinations of Filipina migrant labor typify the conditions of the vast majority of people in the Global South—that is, of human beings that lead what the Filipina social theorist Neferti Tadiar calls "disposable lives" in her remarkable book *Remaindered Lives*.[149] Taking off from Marx's identification of living labor as the source of the value of products or services under capitalism, Tadiar says that whereas those in the dominant capitalist centers that are integrated, either as exploiters or exploited, into the production of surplus value live "lives worth living," those who do not participate in this process in the Global South live "lives of waste and absolute expendability." Being a surplus population is the primordial condition of these masses, not in sheer demographic terms, but in the sense of being structurally excluded by capital as a direct source of value for its reproduction.

But even as they are marginalized from the process of directly creating value, they play a central role in the social reproduction of capital, in that they service the people who are engaged in the direct production of value or in its extraction. But while the latter live productive lives in the sense of yielding value and expanding it, the former live lives that are sucked of value, that is, the value of their lives "declines irreversibly over time."

Domestics and other providers of household work, migrant workers relegated to "'dirty jobs,' those in precarious occupations, migrant contract workers, and those deemed as having no value at all except when they are occasionally and temporarily called to service those who live lives worth living fall into this teeming mass of disposable lives. Their lives are marked by the "struggle to be human," to join those whose lives are worth living, but are barred by states that determine the conditions of "full citizenship" in a capitalist democracy and serve as border guards against those pressing to get in.

Those with disposable lives are forced into ever more marginal and unstable economic activities such as domestic work, providing security to the powerful, or itinerant farm work. Indeed, many are constrained to eke out a living in work where the legal is increasingly intertwined with the "illegal," where in order to cope with their precarious conditions of work, people resort to banned substances, like "shabu" or methamphetamine hydrochloride, providing the state, as in case of the Duterte regime in the Philippines—which is said to have taken some 27,000 lives via extra-judicial execution in its so-called war on drugs—with the rationale to cull them as a surplus population, as lives "worth expending."

Looking for OFW's in Homs

A solo mission I made to Syria at the height of the civil war there in 2012 underlined the consequences of uncontrolled trafficking of these disposable lives.[150]

I was awakened at dawn the day after I arrived in Damascus, my fourth visit to that ancient city, by what seemed to be an explosion. I promptly went back to sleep and forgot about it. When I went for my morning run, the streets were swarming with soldiers, who allowed me to jog, but only around the hotel. It was no fun doing that since the way I gotten used to knowing a foreign city was by running several kilometers downtown. That was how I had gotten to know Paris, London, Johannesburg, Beirut, Athens, Rio, Sao Paolo, Nairobi, and many other cities. So, after two rounds, I went back to the hotel and was informed by the front desk that a building just three blocks away had been bombed.

At the Philippine Embassy later that morning, I got a briefing. The civil war had come to Damascus, I was told. That was the message of the bomb that went off at dawn and brought down a whole building. I also learned from the Embassy staff that 90 percent of the 9,000 domestic workers in Syria were there illegally, that is, they had no valid exit papers from the Philippines. Among other things, this made locating them and contacting them very difficult after Manila issued orders to the embassy to evacuate all Filipino workers from Syria.

Ambassador Eric Endaya, one of the Department of Foreign Affairs (DFA) specialists in evacuation operations in the Middle East, informed me that his team was going to Homs to look for Filipinas that might have been trapped in that city, the site of one of the war's most ferocious battles. I said I wanted to go along with them. Endaya seemed reluctant, so I told him it was very important that I see what was happening on the ground so I could report this to my Committee in Congress, and I was willing to sign a document absolving them of any responsibility, should anything happen to me. I wrote the following account of that trip:

> . . . If any city has become emblematic of Syria's version of the "Arab Spring," it is Homs. This city, an opposition stronghold, was subjected to a 26-day siege by the Syrian Army in February. The estimates of how many people perished vary, with the city's Chief of Police admitting to some 3,000 dead and the western press reporting twice or more that number.
>
> The signs of war are fresh as we enter the city, which lies some 170 kilometers from Damascus. There is no one on the streets at high noon, and Baath University, where some of the most bitter fighting took place, is deserted. The streets are littered with trash, and block after block of apartment buildings we pass show no signs of life. The asphalted roads are rough, being imprinted with the tracks of tanks that were deployed to subdue the resistance. We pass the burned-out hulk of an armed personnel carrier.
>
> At a roundabout where a statue of the current president's father, Hafez Assad, casts a benign look at us a la Kim Il Sung, we encounter our first checkpoint. Soldiers armed with Kalashnikovs examine our papers as our driver, a Syrian named "Teddy" who speaks perfect English, explains in Arabic that we are trying to reach the police station to follow up the case of a Filipino OFW who was killed in an ambush during the fighting.
>
> We pass two more checkpoints manned by suspicious security men carrying the ubiquitous AK-47 before we reach the police station, the front of which sports a makeshift barricade of tires, wood, and stones.
>
> We are met by the chief investigator, a man named Tobias, and we tell him that we really need to know more about the death of Mer-an Montezor, a 23-year-old Filipina who was shot through the chest and killed while traveling at 11 o'clock at night with her employer and his eight-year old son on the main highway on

February 24, during the last phase of the siege of the city. We also want to locate her employer and collect her back wages so we could send them to her family in the Philippines.

Tobias tells us that he helped bring Mer-an to the hospital, but all he had was the cell phone number of the employer, and this was no longer functioning. There was no number for a landline and no address for the employer, and he tells us that, for all he knew, the man and his family might have already left the city. Tobias tries to project concern and friendliness, but he is obviously eager to get rid of us.

Before we leave, however, I asked if he knew if there might be more Filipino domestic workers who might have been hurt or died during the siege. Back in Damascus, Ambassador Eric Endaya had told me that there was a possibility that some OFWs apart from Mer-an could have died in Homs. Having myself heard stories of being trapped close to the fighting from Filipinas who fled Homs for the safety of the Embassy in Damascus, I could not but agree. But Tobias tells us he hasn't heard of any. Aside from him, we have no other contact in Homs for now, underlining the difficulties of finding out the fate of compatriots caught in a war zone when one does not get cooperation from the host government.

"This is very poor police work, for a guy who says he took personal charge of the girl's case," comments Teddy on Tobias' work on the Montezor case.

As we drive away from the police station, we see several clusters of people, but these soon disappear, and we pass by rows and rows of apartment buildings that are deserted. We see a child running here and there, and a few adolescents walking hurriedly, but that's it. When we come to a checkpoint we passed earlier, we are stopped again, and this time, the soldiers are more suspicious and ask more questions. They ask to see the papers of my Syrian companions and scan them for a long time, though for some reason they do not ask for my passport.

This is a city under occupation, I now realize fully. The soldiers regard the people as the enemy, and the people reciprocate. I do not see any prospect of reconciliation between the two sides. I suppress a wish to request Teddy to bring us to Bab Amr, the lower-class district that bore the brunt of the government siege. There are likely to be armed elements of the resistance there, and they might mistake our car as belonging to a government security agency.

When we finally get back to the highway after a good hour and a half in this shattered city, we all breathe a sigh of relief. One of us jokes that, with little knowledge about Southeast Asia, the soldiers probably thought I was Chinese and thus friendly to the Assad regime. Does that mean we say I am an Asian-American if we are stopped by rebel forces, I ask, and we all laugh. With Assad now isolated, with his allies for all practical purposes down to China, Russia, Iran, and Lebanon, most diplomats and foreign visitors are increasingly treated with suspicion.

An hour and a half later, we are in Tartus, off the shimmering Mediterranean Sea. People are in the streets, and even in the early afternoon, there are families taking leisurely walks in the cornice that is Tartus' most attractive feature. This place has been largely exempt from the unrest, the reason being that the majority of people here are Allawites, the president's people.

Tartus and Homs. Two different worlds. Two faces of the same country. . . .

Firefighter Extraordinaire

I had many frustrations in my role as COWA chairman. I led a congressional investigation of Filipino labor officials abroad trading offers like free trips back to the Philippines in return for sexual favors—the notorious "sex-for-flight" scandal—but was only able to get administrative sanctions, not criminal penalties, imposed on those involved, from a government labor bureaucracy that was reluctant to punish its employees.

I did a solo investigation of a scheme involving the U.S. firm Aramark, local labor recruiters, and accomplices within the U.S. Embassy who brought OFWs to the U.S. for professional jobs but actually channeled them to backbreaking hotel work in Mississippi. Lack of cooperation from other government agencies stymied the effort, however, though I was able to get the assistance of the FBI in Los Angeles.

Often, I was reduced to being a fireman, a court of last resort, for OFWs and their families who could not get the Department of Foreign Affairs (DFA) and Department of Labor and Employment (DOLE) to move on their requests. Often these involved people seeking the release of imprisoned relatives in foreign lands or assistance for daughters who had been raped. There were also requests to have the remains of relatives shipped back home from Saudi Arabia, which elicited the Kafkaesque response from the Saudis that the bodies in the morgue had to get an exit visa to leave the kingdom. Other members of Congress forwarded to my office requests from their constituents to assist relatives abroad since they knew we would take them seriously.

Much of my anger stemmed from the fact that the economic policies adopted by our government had been largely responsible for the plight of our OFWs. It bears repeating that neoliberal policies destroyed manufacturing and agriculture, resulting in the loss of millions of jobs. This has left going abroad to "take a chance of making it"—*"pakikipagsaparalan"*—as the only route to avoid ending up in low-wage dead-end jobs. Unless we reorient the economic direction of the country, our people will continue to rush out of the country like blood from an open wound, and all our measures to protect OFWs, like signing treaties with other governments to respect their rights and pay them just wages, will simply be unenforceable band-aid initiatives.

Yet my tenure at COWA was not all disheartening. There were exceptional individuals I met and worked with who inspired me. There were the DOLE and DFA personnel in Riyadh, Jeddah, and Al Khobar who rescued OFWs who were enslaved and imprisoned by their Saudi employers, who often found their already difficult task obstructed by Saudi authorities. There was Don Duero, a government welfare officer, who acted above and beyond the call of duty to expose the ring, referred to above, that brought OFWs to the U.S. supposedly for professional jobs but actually sent them to dead-end hotel work in Mississippi. There was Ambassador Grace Princesa, the same official who took care of our delegation to Baghdad a decade earlier, who brought a caring, human face to distressed OFWs in her various assignments.

Then there was Riahlee Manayan, alias Alma Guiao, who was one of 10 OFWs I accompanied back to the Philippines after my investigating mission to Syria in 2012. Alma operated as a one-person rescue mission, ferrying 25 trapped OFWs from Homs to Damascus via multiple roundtrips by taxi while the battle for Homs was raging. Asked what made her risk her life several times, she told me, "All I know is I had to take them out of danger." At my urging, the House of Representatives recognized her heroism and also gave her a cash gift in a ceremony during its plenary session, an unusual act for an institution that often only invited foreign VIPs and beauty queens to grace its proceedings.

"When the Assad regime finally fell on December 8, 2024, 12 years after that memorable mission to rescue OFWs in Syria, my thoughts returned to Riahlee. Did she return to Syria, like many repatriated workers, owing to lack of opportunities at home? A great many domestic workers were employed in middle class and elite households loyal to the deposed government. Would they find jobs in new households if their employers were stripped of their wealth or fled into exile? Of one thing I had no doubt: These women were survivors, and most would be able to roll through the latest hurricane and land on their feet.

From a sleepy committee that hardly ever met, the Committee on Overseas Workers Affairs became, under my tenure, probably the most active committee in the House, meeting every two or three weeks while the House was in session. The meeting room was always full, but perhaps "jampacked" was the most appropriate word when world boxing champion Manny Pacquiao, who had been named vice chair of COWA, attended a session in 2010. I helped him chair the meeting, for which he was grateful, and told him I would love for him to serve as chair whenever he felt like it. Unfortunately, that was the only session he attended during the years we both served in Congress, as he went on to compile one of the worst attendance records in the history of the House of Representatives.

14. Forays in Foreign Policy

THE MAIN initiative in foreign policy making is supposed to come from the Executive. Congress's role is mainly to weigh in on policies crafted by the president, and its powers to oppose or overturn them and stake out alternative policies are quite limited. There is, however, that fuzzy area called "influencing foreign policy-making," and my office explored this area on a matter of great import for the country: the conflict in the South China Sea.

Renaming the South China Sea

In 2009, Beijing presented to the United Nations its so-called Nine-Dash-Line Declaration claiming ownership of 90 percent of the South China Sea, thus denying the rights to an Exclusive Economic Zone of 200 miles to the five other countries, including the Philippines, that bordered on that body of water under the United Nations Convention on the Law of the Seas. China had valid strategic concerns. It was seeking to expand its defense perimeter to counter the threat of an attack on its southeastern and southern coasts, where its main industrial infrastructure lay, from the Seventh Fleet and the numerous U.S. bases on the offshore chain of islands in the Western Pacific. But instead of working with its neighbors in a multilateral effort to demilitarize the South China Sea, it was going about securing its objective in the wrong way, indeed in the worst possible way—through an outright sea and island grab. It had already occupied Mischief Reef, which was within the Philippines' 200-mile Exclusive Economic Zone, and the Paracel Islands, which Vietnam also claimed.

In this troubling context, where our rights were being brazenly violated, I felt that calling the South China Sea by that name was giving the psychological advantage to Beijing. So I proposed a resolution, House Resolution 1350, in July 2011, renaming the South China Sea as the West or Western Philippine Sea. People at the Department of Foreign Affairs called me to tell me that they were pleased with my resolution and told me it did not need to be approved by the plenary because they would urge the Executive to simply issue a presidential decree to rename the sea. And indeed, in a few days, the decree was issued, making it the legislative initiative associated with me that traveled fastest from conceptualization to execution!

Flying to Pag-asa

I followed up this success up with a plan to bring a congressional delegation to Pag-asa Island, the heart of the Philippine presence in the Spratly Islands. Like the bill renaming the South China Sea the West Philippine Sea, the aim of the trip was to emphasize the rights of the Philippines under UNCLOS. This would be a major logistical and financial operation. So, I

Walden on the beach of Pag-asa Island in the Spratlys, where he delivered a morale-boosting speech to Philippine contingent there in July 2011.

recruited Marylou Malig, who had a great experience in managing high profile events, to coordinate the project, with my very professional media liaison, Sabrina Gacad, assisting her. Word had gotten around the Manila media that we were going to Pag-asa and many wanted to come along, so another commercial plane had to be added, with the rental costs for the two planes coming to 1.5 million pesos. Fortunately, Loida Nicolas Lewis, a Filipina philanthropist based in New York, readily extended the sum.

The Chinese Embassy got wind of the plan and one of their diplomats, Ethan Sun, went to the Department of Foreign Affairs to file a protest. "It goes against the declaration of the parties in the South China Sea and serves no purpose but to undermine peace and stability in the region and sabotage Philippines-China relationship," Sun said.[151] The Chinese pressured Malacanang, the presidential palace, to call off the trip, but the palace, citing the separation of powers among the three branches of government, told them its hands were tied. President Aquino did convey to us that he hoped we would not cut off or take any of the floating buoys that the Chinese used to advertise their territorial claims to passing vessels, and we assured him we had no intention to do so.

Early in the morning of July 19, 2011, the two commercial planes bearing a congressional delegation composed of Reps Kaka Bag-ao, Teddy Baguilat, Ben Evardone, and myself, and some 20 members of the press left Manila, stopped briefly in Puerto Princesa in Palawan to pick up a few other passengers, then flew on to Pag-asa island. When we landed, we made history—on two counts. Our planes were the first commercial planes to land there, and we were the first congressional delegation to visit the island, which belongs to the province of Palawan. What happened next was recounted by Marites Vitug in her book *Rock Solid: How the Philippines Won Its Maritime Case against China:*

> Upon landing, Bello said, "We come in peace, we support a diplomatic solution, but let there be no doubt in any foreign power's mind that if they dare eject us from Pag-asa [and] out rightful territories, Filipinos will not take that sitting down."
>
> He brought two Philippine flags, one of which was hoisted in a flag ceremony. Videos of the visit showed the members of Congress singing the national anthem and reciting the pledge of allegiance with the soldiers and residents. They also unfurled a huge banner with WEST PHILIPPINE SEA emblazoned on it, posing with the residents for photographs.

"We were there for not more than four hours. We talked to Mayor Bito-onon, had a dialogue with the people, walked around and swam a bit in their white sandy beaches," Bello recalled.[152]

We were more relaxed on the way back to Palawan, and as I looked at the islands and coral reefs in the shimmering light green sea 10,000 feet below, I thought about how those maritime formations our governments were now fighting over had been there, uninhabited, one million years ago and how they would still be there one million years from now when our species, with its clashing drives for power and property, will have vanished.

The Murder of Jennifer Laude

President Aquino was probably secretly happy with our visit to the Spratlys. He was definitely not happy, however, with my other foreign policy initiatives. I co-authored two joint resolutions with Senator Miriam Santiago, probably the only nationalist in the Senate at the time, seeking the termination of the Visiting Forces Agreement (VFA), the treaty covering the roles and conduct of U.S. servicemen conducting joint exercises with the Philippine Armed Forces. The first, filed in 2012, was occasioned by the dumping in Philippine waters of toxic waste by a U.S. military contractor. The second, in 2014, was in response to the savage murder of Jennifer Laude, a transgender Filipina, by a U.S. Marine, Joseph Pemberton. Jennifer, a transgender woman, had been found dead in a hotel room in Olongapo City adjoining the Subic Bay Freeport Zone, her face showing a deep cut and her head immersed in a toilet bowl.

Vergie Suarez, the indefatigable progressive lawyer, was among the first to take up the Laude case and it was she who brought me into the effort to get the Philippine government to demand Pemberton's full transfer to the Philippine legal jurisdiction.

The Laude murder brought the country's attention back to the bad old days of Subic and Clark, the two former U.S. bases where Filipinos who were scavenging had been killed, sometimes for supposedly being mistaken for wild boars, and to the rape of a woman, "Nicole," by a U.S. marine in 2005. In all those cases, the soldiers who committed the crimes were shielded from Philippine justice and spirited out of the country by U.S. authorities who claimed extra-territorial rights over them. The Laude case also high-lighted an issue that was becoming a matter of public debate: the rights of transgender women and other members of the LGBTQ+ community. In an article I wrote about the case, I called attention to the explosive psychological mixture of participation in military maneuvers, training in the martial arts, and homophobic socialization among the marines, supposedly America's elite soldiers:

> With thousands of such walking weapons from the most homophobic of America's armed services prowling Olongapo's streets on R&R after testosterone-raising military exercises, the murder of Jennifer Laude was an event waiting to happen. The volatile mix of training in the lethal arts and aggressive homophobic socialization was likely to be among the factors that led Pemberton to cross the line from anger to murder that fateful night. And violence such as that meted out to Jennifer is likely to occur again and again, as the U.S. stations more and more troops in our country in pursuit of Washington's grand geopolitical design to contain China.[153]

The Laude murder, which created a national uproar, drew a muted response from the Aquino administration. A strong condemnation was entirely in order, even if the U.S. and the Philippines were allies. But the Palace did not fight to gain control of Pemberton, and he eventually was spirited away to the U.S. a few years later. Indeed, Malacanang spurned even gestures that recognized the value of a life that had been lost. Commissioner of Human Rights Etta Rosales and I were the only members of the national government present at Jennifer's funeral. The president did not bother to send an official representative, and this, coupled with his silence on the matter, sent Washington the message that the matter was a nuisance that should not be allowed to affect the relationship between the two governments.

Aquino did not want the murder of Jennifer Laude to detract from what his administration considered its crowning foreign policy achievement: the signing of the Enhanced Defense Cooperation Agreement (EDCA) with the government of U.S. President Obama in 2014, which gave the United States five military bases and more military privileges in the country. Neither did he appreciate my criticism, widely reported in the media, that the agreement bound us to a military alliance with one side in a struggle between two superpowers, and this made it impossible for our country to pursue an independent foreign policy. He sent a message via his subordinates that he considered me disloyal and "*mas oposisyon pa kaysa sa oposisyon,*" or "more in opposition than the opposition." I sent a message back, via Ronald Llamas, his political secretary, saying that being in a coalition did not mean keeping silent about differences with one's coalition partners. But that cut no ice with a president whose idea of governance was the code of a college fraternity, which put loyalty above everything else. Our very public split over EDCA, which was the focus of my televised interview by Karen Davila, one of the country's leading media personalities, was the beginning of the deterioration in our political relationship that ended with my resignation from the House of Representatives in 2015.[154]

A Plan for Peace in the South China Sea

The Aquino administration filed a case against China's claims in the West Philippine Sea with the Permanent Court of Arbitration (PCA) in the Hague in January 2013. I supported this move to resolve the dispute in the Spratlys through international law. China did not recognize the legitimacy of the court proceedings, thus rendering moot any move to effectively enforce a final judgment of the tribunal. But the Philippines nevertheless obtained in 2016 a moral victory that resonated globally when the PCA judged as without validity China's claim to waters and maritime formations included in its Nine-Dash-Line Declaration—a set of line segments on various maps that accompanied the claims of the People's Republic of China and Taiwan in the South China Sea—beyond those it was entitled to under the United Nations Convention of the Law of the Seas (UNCLOS).

I fully supported the PCA judgment but pointed out that it was robbed of much of its effectiveness by the Philippines' entering a military alliance with the United States directed at China. In an article for the *New York Times* in 2016, over a year after I left Congress, I wrote:

> The Hague decision rendering China's claim to some 90 percent of the West Philippine Sea null and void was the previous Aquino administration's biggest diplomatic victory. But its decision to enter into the Enhanced Defense Cooperation Agreement (E.D.C.A.) with Washington was its biggest blunder. It put us in the front lines of a superpower struggle for hegemony in the Asia-Pacific region, with all the liabilities and none of the benefits that come with being a junior partner in such an alliance. Washington's sole interest is to turn the main Philippine islands into a springboard for its strategy of containing China; it has no desire to resolve the Spratlys dispute in favor of the Philippines.
>
> Therefore, we must distance ourselves from Washington, cooperate with our neighbors in the Association of Southeast Asian Nations (ASEAN) and work with Beijing.[155]

I then outlined a gradualist strategy with five components:

First, since it is the fear of military encirclement by Washington that is driving China's behavior, the Philippines and China should engage in bilateral talks to reduce tensions between our countries. The aim of these talks should be military de-escalation, not to settle the territorial question. One possible proposal could be a freeze in China's base-building activities in exchange for a freeze in the implementation of E.D.C.A.

Second, with the Philippine-China bilateral talks, ASEAN and China can start the long postponed multilateral talks to govern the maritime behavior of all parties with claims to the South China Sea.

Third, should these two measures succeed, ASEAN and China should negotiate the demilitarization and denuclearization of the South China Sea, with the goal of signing a multilateral treaty that would be binding on all parties, including third parties like the U.S. Such an agreement would require the Philippines to abandon the E.D.C.A. and China to dismantle military structures in the South China Sea.

These measures, if successful, would pave the way for the fourth step: talks aimed at a final settlement of the territorial issue, with the Philippine position anchored on The Hague ruling.[156]

I concluded: "Filipinos and Chinese are both Asians, separated by colonialism, imperialism, the Cold War and the continuing external hegemonic forces on the region. It is time both sides commit to bridge that separation, no matter how difficult initially that process might be."[157]

But the proposal was too late for both me and President Aquino to act on. I had resigned from Congress in 2015 and he finished his term in July 2016. It was meant for Aquino's successor, President Rodrigo Duterte. But the latter had other ideas, and this was to execute a 180 degree turn and side with China.

An invitation for a Foreign Policy Dialogue from Vietnam's Madame Binh

If there was any government that listened to my views, it was that of Vietnam. I was frequently invited to Vietnam, particularly after my long introduction to the writings of Ho Chi Minh was published by Verso in 2007, apparently liked by many Vietnamese academics and officials who had read it.[158] At first, while I was at Focus on the Global South, I would be invited to provide advice on development policy, where I recommended a strategy focused on enlarging the domestic market by adopting more measures to reduce inequality and warned the Vietnamese against joining the WTO. When I joined Congress, however, Vietnam mainly sought my advice on how to deal with the explosive situation in the South China Sea.

In 2014, I was asked by Madame Nguyen Thi Binh, the legendary female member of the Vietnamese team during the Paris peace negotiations to end the Vietnam War, to make an official visit as a member of Congress to share my views on the worsening situation, where Vietnamese and Chinese ships were engaged in water-hosing fights. The visit began with a wonderful informal session with Madame Binh, where she reminisced about her experiences as a Vietnamese patriot fighting against the Americans. She easily assumed the role of a mother to my wife Ko, who was both very impressed and amused by the stories of this icon of the National Liberation Front. Nearing 90 then, she told Ko that "I am pleased to have the chance to meet friends of Vietnam like you before I go." (She has, thank god, not yet gone as of this writing.)

In the talks with government officials that followed, the Vietnamese told me that while they valued China's friendship, they would not allow violations of their sovereign rights and would respond strongly to these. But they were especially concerned about the absence of rules to govern conflict in the South China Sea. "Ships from different countries are playing dangerous games with each other, pretending to ram each other and swerving at the last minute," one official said. "What if they miscalculate? A mere ship collision could lead to something bigger." Asked about their position on the U.S., they said American warships, like those of other countries, were welcome to visit Cam Ranh Bay, the naval base the U.S. had built during the Vietnam War, but they would never allow any foreign government to establish bases in their country. They maintained a diplomatic silence, however, when I expressed extreme disappointment with the Aquino's government's giving the U.S. five bases under the EDCA agreement. After a day's exchange of views, they told me that their policy in the region was based on four noes: no military alliances with any country, no foreign military bases, no siding with one country against another, and no use of force or threatening the use of force in international relations.

I felt more at home at that meeting than I ever was either in Malacanang or the Department of Foreign Affairs, where allying with its former colonial ruler appeared to be the foundation and constant of the government's "Grand Strategy." Having fought the Japanese, French and the Americans for 35 years, the Vietnamese were not going to barter away their independence in foreign policymaking.

As in my previous visits, the Vietnamese were very hospitable, and they gave Ko and me the space to enjoy unhurried, graceful Hanoi, which both of us preferred to high-pressure Ho Chi Minh City. While Ko indulged in one her favorite pastimes of searching for and buying designer brands, which could be obtained in Hanoi at dirt cheap prices since Vietnam had the factories that turned out these brands, I made sure to take my daily 7 km run along the languid lakes that grace the center of the city. An aficionado of Vietnamese food, Ko brought me to a foodie tour that introduced me to *bun cha*, a dish of seasoned pork and marinated pork belly served in heavy broth, and other Vietnamese delicacies.

Hostage Country

To this day, my actions on the South China Sea issue have puzzled many, who have not been able to reconcile my strong assertions demanding respect for the economic rights of the Philippines from China and my opposing continuation of the military treaties with the United States. But there is a thread running through them, and that is support for the maintenance of an independent foreign policy and prioritizing diplomacy over force in the resolution of territorial disputes. What the Aquino III administration and the two succeeding regimes have done is to get the Philippines to side with either one of the superpowers, making our interests hostage to foreign designs, whether those of China or of the United States. With compliant heads of state and a timid foreign service, we have lost control of our defense and foreign policies.

15. Memorable and "Memorable" Moments at the House of Representatives

I HAD A NUMBER of personally memorable moments in Congress. Some were controversial. Some were on the light side. Some made history. But before I go into that, let me take the reader on a brief "tour" of the Philippines House of Representatives.

Unless things have changed significantly since I was there less than a decade ago, a typical day at the House of Representatives begins around 9 am, when the committees and subcommittees meet. Unlike the plenary, these meetings are relatively well attended by members, in particular when there are investigations—justified as being "in aid of legislation"—of juicy scandals or anomalies. In the committee, the chair is king or queen, with other members, whether allied with the administration or in opposition, being very careful to show the appropriate deferential demeanor, marked by very courteous and sometimes flowery language. Even outside committee proceedings and in the plenary hall, the chairs are often addressed by members of the committee, especially by its junior people, as "Chair."

Visiting members of the executive branch are expected to display in their behavior their inferior status as appointees compared to the status of the representatives as elected by the people. This is reinforced by their knowledge that their agencies' budgets are dependent on their exhibiting the appropriate language, including "body language." It's not quite bowing and scraping but it's close to it. A member of the cabinet who is seen as not communicating the correct language, oral or body, to the least of the congressional brethren risks being put in his place, and that can be very embarrassing. There can be no greater dissonance between those who really wield power, the agents of Malacanang, and those constitutionally vested with it, the members of Congress, than during a congressional hearing. Not surprisingly, it is during these hearings that some of the latter take their revenge on the president's men and women for their being ignored as nonentities for most of the year.

The plenary session begins at 4 pm, with the singing of the national anthem, but the roll is usually called at around 5:30 or 6, with members scurrying into the hall just in time to say "aye," "present," or "here," before disappearing again to their chambers or, in the case of not a few, taking off for the evening. Pilipino, an updated version of Tagalog, may be the national language but 99 percent of the proceedings in the plenary or the committees is conducted in English.

The plenary takes place Monday to Wednesday. Its main business, taking up bills on second or third reading, often proceeds with not more than a handful of members present in the plenary hall, except when word has gotten around that a really critical bill might be voted on. Compared to the plenary hall, there are often many more legislators in the adjoining members' lounge, a veritable country club where representatives smile at one another, exchange jokes and gossip, and deliver their opinions on everything but the country's problems. The congressional day rarely goes beyond 9 pm except when the budget is being considered, and marathon sessions like the debate on the Bataan Nuclear Plant that I had with Rep Mark Cojuangco in 2009 that I referred to earlier, which went till around 10 pm, are not common.

At least once a week there is a "privilege hour," where members can speak on any topic they fancy. The people who most frequently take advantage of giving speeches, whether during the privilege hour or the plenary proper, are those from progressive party lists who try to call attention to pressing national problems, undaunted by the fact that there may be only ten people or fewer in the hall. During my first three years in the House, I must have averaged one privilege speech every three weeks, delivered to a sparsely populated hall, though others, like Reps Teddy Casino and Neri Colmenares of the Makabayan Bloc, most likely took the mike more frequently. And then there are those—the vast majority—who never once deliver a speech, privilege or otherwise, or engage in debate during plenaries, because they're shy, don't have anything to say, or are simply serving as "benchwarmers"—that is, filling the district seats for their partners, usually husbands, who hit their term limits but will be eligible to come back to Congress after three years in mandatory exile.

There is a popular image of members of Congress as just sitting or jerking around and not paying attention to what they're supposed to do, that is, think up and pass legislation in the interest of their constituents. That might be true of 75 percent of the 316 members, but there's that 25 percent that really work hard and make up for the shenanigans of their colleagues. And, of course, there are the people who really make the institution function—the 3000 or so members of office staffs, committee secretariats, and the secretary general's staff. I have the greatest admiration for them since they toil unceasingly and without protest, even when given imperious orders by their bosses, and have to endure silly informal rules like to always underdress since one of the greatest sins one can commit is to be mistaken for your boss or any other member of the House.

Breaking Decorum

Now to some of the high points of my time in the House. Proper decorum is high on the values of the institution, much higher than in the Senate where sharp personal clashes often take place. I am not much into decorum, so it is not surprising that I sometimes got into trouble as a result. The most memorable occasion was when I frontally attacked the record of former President Gloria Macapagal Arroyo, also known by the acronym GMA, who had joined the 15th Congress as a representative from the province of Pampanga.

On August 2, 2010, in a privilege speech, I said that the nine-year reign of the former president had been characterized by "orgiastic compensation, brazen manipulation of government agencies and funds for political purposes, and massive waste of people's money." I also described her subordinates as behaving "like pigs" with her as a role model "on how to behave with impunity" and asserted that the former president must be hauled from "this august chamber to jail."[159]

Warned about what was coming, Arroyo had already left the hall before my speech. A few came to the defense of GMA after my speech, mainly on procedural or ethical grounds, but all hell broke loose in the next few days. Members crossed party lines to condemn my breach of elite decorum, according to one report:

> Lawmakers that included Davao del Sur Rep. Marc Douglas Cagas and Navotas City Rep. Tobias Tiangco called for the striking of the offending and unparliamentary remarks from the records immediately after Bello's privilege speech ... [Cagas] said allowing House members to use abusive language against fellow lawmakers could set a precedent that could result in the disregard for parliamentary procedures and courtesies in Congress ... Boxing champion and Sarangani Rep. Manny Pacquiao supported moves to have Bello investigated by the ethics committee. ... "If we talk like this, the image of the entire House would be affected. She is a former president and a congresswoman and served the

country so she deserves our respect," Pacquiao said . . . Siquijor Representative Orlando Fua said . . . "This is not a marketplace. We are all presumed to be gentlemen. We must also give due respect to seniority or those who have occupied a high position. No gentleman will openly hit his colleague. It is not as if the nation does not owe her anything. His language was vulgar and this should not go unpunished. We don't want him expelled because he has something to contribute to the nation but this must not go unpunished because what we do here reflects our character as a nation before the international community. . . . [160]

Three weeks after the speech, a case was filed against me before the Ethics Committee, citing my "disorderly behavior" and seeking my suspension from the House. I was summoned to two sessions of the committee, but the hearing on my case kept getting postponed until it was forgotten. I could only surmise that some deal had been made to shelve the complaint owing to fears among the powers that be that my defense would provide a platform to expose more misdeeds by the former president and her allies, most of whom had switched sides to the new administration in the time-honored Philippine tradition of "turncoatism."

Imelda in Hot Pursuit

Another memorable experience involved Imelda Marcos, who was also elected to the 15th Congress from the second district of Ilocos Norte.[161] I had been introduced to her briefly at the first meeting of ruling coalition convoked by President Aquino, of which she was, strangely enough, a part, but she did not seem to recognize me, thank god. But at one of the plenary sessions, Congressman Raul Daza, one of my colleagues in the anti-Marcos movement in the U.S., came up to me and warned me that Imelda, with her elephant-like memory, had placed me and I should not allow her under any circumstances to corral me into a discussion. He recounted how one fervent oppositionist in exile who came home post-EDSA Uprising and also served in the House had given Imelda a hearing out of politeness and ended up supporting some wacky proposals of hers. "I think she's out to convince key people who opposed them when they were in power that they were really not that bad," said Daza. "She's persuasive. So watch out, you're on her radar screen."

I certainly had no intention of giving Imelda an audience, but this was mainly out of concern that some mischievous media guy would snap a photo of us having a chat and this could go viral, giving the impression that we had buried the hatchet and all was forgiven and pfft, there went my reputation.

Daza was right—she seemed determined to sit down with people who had made life difficult for her and her husband. Avoiding her, however, was easier said than done. Several times I saw her making a beeline for me in the plenary session hall, forcing me to make a rude exit from whatever conversation I was having with colleagues. I had to be on high alert during plenaries at which she was present since she could sneak up at any time. And I had to avoid at all costs the members' lounge for that was a trap from which there was no easy exit.

But Imelda being Imelda, she would not be deterred. We were both members of the House Foreign Relations Committee, and at meetings where she was present, she would sometimes try ingratiating herself with me by saying something favorable about my initiatives. At one session, there was a proposal to close down the consulate in Barcelona, Spain. Being the head of the Committee on Overseas Workers Affairs, I objected, owing to my fear that this could deprive our OFWs in Spain of easy access to our government services. Suddenly, Imelda boomed out of the blue, "I support Congressman Bello's opposition to closing the consulate in Barcelona because Barcelona is the gateway to Africa."

The room fell silent, stunned, with many of us doubting for a moment what we had learned in our geography lessons in grade school: that Barcelona was in Europe. It took superhuman effort on my part not to burst out laughing, and a swift survey of the room showed other Committee members trying to contain themselves. Even the normally nonplussed chairman, Congressman Al Francis Bichara, was grinning.

Shortly before leaving Congress in 2015, I congratulated myself at having been able to avoid a handshake with Imelda for five long years, except for that perfunctory one I had been forced to extend at the first coalition meeting out of courtesy. Or so I thought. One of my favorite cousins turned 100 that year, and I was invited to a big party in her honor. As soon as I arrived with my wife, Ko, I headed straight for the table of honor to kiss my cousin. When we neared the table, I felt my wife's hand on my arm, trying to restrain me. I didn't give much thought to it, and continued rushing to kiss my cousin, and just when she embraced me, a hand emerged from beside her that I automatically shook. I looked up and there was Imelda, smiling triumphantly. She was there because my cousin's son had been one of her most dedicated subordinates when she and her husband were in power, and where else would she be seated but at the table of honor! Luckily, no cameras were there to record the historic event—at least, none that I was aware of. After the fiasco, my wife could not stop laughing at how, despite my best efforts to frustrate her hot pursuit, Imelda had gotten the better of me.

Still, I would say that on balance, I had gotten the better of Imelda, not only because she provided the material for my comic protests in the U.S., like the Kermit and Miss Piggy skit at the IMF mentioned in Chapter 7, but also because for years she had served as my "passport" to enter the United States. After 9/11, the new Department of Homeland Security consolidated arrest records from all localities in the U.S., so that an Immigration officer could simply press a button to see if someone entering the United States had a police record. So every time I entered the U.S., the list of my multiple arrests, detentions, and imprisonment in that country would pop up on the officer's screen, and this would subject me to what Immigration officials call "secondary screening," where I would be interviewed on why I had such a distinguished record. For a few years, saying those arrests resulted from acts of civil disobedience against the Marcos dictatorship was enough to get me past secondary screening. Even among hardened U.S. border control agents, Marcos was a bad name in those days.

After a while, however, referring to my opposition to the Marcos dictatorship would draw a blank in the faces of younger immigration officers. After all, Marcos was just one of the many dictators with unfamiliar foreign names that Washington had supported, and it was unreasonable to expect a frontline agent to memorize them all. At that point I had to devise a new stratagem to get past U.S. immigration, and this was to add after my story about opposing Marcos, "You know, Imelda and her shoes?" U.S. immigration officers may not have remembered Ferdinand, but how could they forget the story of Imelda's 3,000 pairs of shoes? It almost never failed. I would simply refer to Imelda's shoes, and the immigration officers would laugh and wave me out of secondary screening. Until very recently, that is, when it seems like the story of Imelda and her legendary shoes has not been passed down to the Gen Z border officers guarding America's frontlines against undesirable aliens like me.[162]

The Resignation

The third most memorable moment I had at the House was no laughing matter. Indeed, it was agonizing. It was my resignation, with over one year left in my third term.

During my six years in Congress, I did not hesitate to praise President Aquino when he deserved it, as when he defied the Catholic Church hierarchy and came out in full support of the RH Bill. But neither did I withhold criticism when it was justified. I was vocal in my objection to the Enhanced Defense Cooperation Agreement (EDCA) with the United States, which led him to characterize me as being "more opposition than the opposition." I was critical of the way he prized loyalty above all else and treated his cabinet like a "college fraternity." In my view, this was simply the way a progressive behaved—but being part of a coalition did not mean you gave up your right to be critical of the political behavior of your partners.

I felt, however, that disagreement on some issues, like EDCA, should not be a deal breaker. EDCA was not a dealbreaker since Akbayan had based its alliance with the Liberal Party on the anti-corruption platform and the LP's willingness to be open to discuss other issues of great concern to Akbayan, such as the deepening of agrarian reform, passage of the RH Bill, gender justice, and promotion of labor rights. Moreover, Akbayan had not anticipated the Enhanced Defense Cooperation Agreement when it made its alliance with the LP in 2010, and when Aquino and the U.S. did move on it, there was no consensus in the party on whether or not it was a deal breaker. This left it up to me and a few others to articulate our disagreement with the administration.

What would be a deal breaker in my view was if the administration went back on the foundation stone of the Akbayan-Liberal Party coalition, which was the fight against corruption, one that was inscribed in the slogan "*Kung walang korap, walang mahirap*," or "Where there is no corruption, there is no poverty." The Disbursement Acceleration Program (DAP), the 167 billion peso ($3.3 billion) secret fund that came to light in 2014 that was used to influence members of Congress was such a deal breaker.

Astounded by the discovery, I and Rep Barry Gutierrez, the other Akbayan representative in Congress, wrote a letter to the president, expressing Akbayan's view that such a fund, which was not appropriated by Congress and was used by the president with nothing to check him, was not compatible with good governance: "We remind the President that the DAP is one of the facets of such vast and unbridled fiscal powers of the executive—powers that have been gravely abused in the past and coveted by some of those who seek to replace him after his term." We said that it was "wrong to dismiss the DAP, more so the executive's fiscal powers, as non-issues in the overall reform process. Of all people, President Aquino knows too well the dire consequences of the unregulated fiscal powers of the executive, having filed the Budget Impoundment Control bill when he was still a senator during Gloria Arroyo's pillage of the people's fund."[163]

The DAP issue hit at the very center of the administration's good governance agenda. With the non-transparent, unaccountable, cavalier, and reckless manipulation of public funds, the administration was engaged in the same sort of behavior that it accused the previous administration of undertaking. What was even more worrisome was that some defenders of the administration, including some progressives, defended its actions by saying that manipulation of unallocated funds was a practice previous administrations had engaged in, the difference being that Budget Secretary Butch Abad was "stupid enough" to make the slush fund a formal program and give it a name.

For cooking up such a program that ripped to shreds the administration's *Daang Matuwid* ("the straight and narrow road") rhetoric, I asked the president in subsequent communications to fire Secretary Abad, who was doubly compromised by the fact that he was guilty of nepotism for brazenly allocating the sixth largest allocation from the DAP funds given to members of Congress to his wife, Rep. Henedina Abad, who represented Batanes, the smallest province and smallest congressional district in the Philippines.

I also asked him to get rid of cabinet members or members of his retinue who were exposed as corrupt or incompetent, including Secretary of Agrarian Reform Virgilio de los Reyes for his miserable performance in implementing agrarian reform, specifically for failing to meet the June 30, 2014, deadline for the completion of land redistribution under the CARPER. With over 550,000 hectares of the best land in the country undistributed, saving the reform program, I argued, demanded "a determined, resolute, and courageous secretary of agrarian reform, one who is not a timid technocrat but a bold political leader who will not be afraid to do battle with the landlords." As one of the principal authors of CARPER, I wrote that I felt "personally betrayed by Mr. de los Reyes' performance."[164] CARPER was in tatters, and all the effort we had put, six years earlier, into crafting a viable land reform law had gone down the drain, and there was now no way the powerful landlord bloc in the House was going to allow another extension of land acquisition despite the efforts of Rep Erin Tanada, Rep Teddy Baguilat, and myself to introduce such a measure. As readers remember, I had said in Chapter 15 that the CARPER struggle was a case of a good piece of legislation being preferred to an unattainable perfect law. I continued to believe this, blaming weak-kneed enforcement by the Executive for torpedoing a good, strong measure promoting agrarian justice.

My urgent pleas to the president resulted in a meeting between him and the Akbayan leadership, where I was able to articulate them in person. He made no commitments but jumped from one issue to another unrelated to the matter at hand as if he were on a pogo stick. I just wanted to put my hands on the guy's shoulders and scream, "PLEASE LISTEN, MAN!

When queried by the press on my demands, he answered that "he has a lot of complaints. If he thinks his visions are the right ones, he should try running in 2016. If he becomes president, he will be able to implement those visions."[165] On the question of Abad funneling huge amounts to the smallest congressional district in the country represented by his wife, the president told the media that size was not the only consideration in allocating the slush fund.

When the Supreme Court ruled the DAP as largely unconstitutional, I felt it was time for the party leadership to make a big push to get Abad out. However, most other members of the leadership did not agree with my initiative, though they respected my intentions. "While we maintain full confidence that Rep Bello's statements spring from an honest desire to promote the highest standards of accountability in government," the majority said in a statement to the press, "as we have made clear before, his proposals differ from the existing consensus within Akbayan." It added: "While this path has not been without its share of difficulties, we remain convinced in the sincerity of the President and are determined to exert all efforts in pushing the reform agenda with his administration in the few remaining months till the next Presidential election."[166] But, of course, I was disappointed. I had expected that the party had learned from previous experiences that a progressive party's stance towards coalition partners, including and especially with elite parties, was always to be critical when necessary. I did not want to entertain the thought that I was being left to my own devices because the party put a greater value on preserving the posts it had in the administration.

Over the Edge

Then an unsuspecting country woke up in late January 2015 to the devastating news that 44 members of Philippine National Police's Special Action Force, 18 Muslim insurgents, and several civilians had been slain in a mission to capture Zulkifli Abdhir, alias Marwan, a person tagged as a "terrorist" by the U.S. government, in Maguindanao Province. As the details of the bloody secret mission unfolded, the president, to my amazement, refused to accept responsibility for an initiative he had ordered, preferring to pin the blame on a subordinate on the ground.

The event in Mamasapano was an undiluted debacle, a dagger plunged in the heart of the administration's good governance agenda. It exemplified bad governance on three counts. First, the president refused to acknowledge command responsibility for an operation that he ordered that had gone awry, violating a basic tenet of presidential leadership. Second, he illegally placed in command of the operation a crony of his, General Alan Purisima, who had been suspended by the Ombudsman. Third, he ordered a mission that was a priority of the United States, not of the Philippines, and he did this knowing full well that a mishap in the mission, which involved an incursion into territory of the government's negotiating partner, the Moro Islamic Liberation (MILF), that was not cleared with the insurgent group, would endanger the passage of the Bangsa Moro Basic Law (BBL) that would serve as the corner-stone for a peace that had so far proven elusive in Muslim Mindanao.

The fingerprints of the U.S. were all over the place—the U.S. helicopter that showed up soon after the encounter, allegedly to evacuate the wounded; the disappearance of the alleged terrorist Marwan's index finger, which the operatives that killed him cut as proof he had been neutralized, which then showed up in the FBI lab in the U.S.; American operatives having the last say on the operational plan, that is, to have the seaborne unit carry out the neu-tralization unit of Marwan by itself instead of jointly with the quick reaction force as favored by the SAF commander; the training of the seaborne unit by U.S. Navy Seal personnel; and the order given by an American operative to a Filipino infantry general to provide artillery support for the embattled SAF personnel, which the Filipino general fortunately refused to carry out.

As the administration's crisis of authority mounted, I proposed to the party that we turn the debacle into an opportunity to push the envelope for reform. With the president in a weakened moral position, we should press him, I argued, not only to accept responsibility for Mamasapano but follow up his acceptance of the resignation of Purisima with the dismissal of Abad, de los Reyes, and other corrupt inept or corrupt officials.

This would, I contended, reinvigorate the tattered *Daang Matuwid*. The party leadership refused. Things moved inexorably to a climax in late February when Presidential Spokesperson Abigail Valte responded to my criticisms by saying, "Does Representative Bello consider himself an ally of this administration?"[167] When on March 9, the president used a meeting with selected members of the House to heap all the blame for Mamasapano on the ground commander, Col. Getulio Napenas, I decided that was the last straw. This was a mockery of good, responsible governance. I could no longer sup-port this man as president.

That meant I had to resign as Akbayan's representative in the House of Representatives. For even as I was fully convinced that the party leadership was wrong in not backing me by demanding that the president live up to the principles of good governance by ceasing to shelter allies who had brought discredit to the *Daang Matuwid*, I had also come to realize that being a repre-sentative of the party meant one could no longer stay in that role if one could not agree with a basic party position, such as continued support for the presi-dent. No one asked me personally to resign—indeed, party leaders urged me to stay—but the party's code of conduct requiring loyalty to a fundamental party line as a feature of a progressive party was clear: I had to go.

On the day I delivered my resignation speech, I was pleasantly surprised that a plenary session that had been empty when the session began was now two thirds filled, probably since word had gotten around that a very unusual event, a resignation on principle by a member of Congress, was about to take place. A newspaper report describes the occasion:

> Akbayan party-list Rep. Walden Bello toned down the stinging criticism he originally planned to give President Benigno Aquino III in his final privilege speech and instead appealed to the chief executive to accept responsibility for the Mamasapano tragedy.
>
> Speaking on the House floor for the last time on Monday, Bello said he would like to focus on "more pleasant things" during his six-year stint as congressional representative, such as the time he and Aquino were united in their defense of the Reproductive Health Law.
>
> Addressing the president, Bello said: "While our differences have predominated in recent days, I will not forget those times when we fought on the same side, like the epic struggle we waged for the Reproductive Health Law. That victory was the zenith of the administration, and it is one I will always remember."
>
> Bello was supposed to deliver a scathing criticism of Aquino on Feb. 11 after he announced his resignation as Akbayan's party-list representative but this was aborted due to lack of quorum.
>
> He said he could no longer be Akbayan party-list's representative to the House after he withdrew support for the president due to Aquino's insistence in having sacked Special Action Force (SAF) director Getulio Napeñas take responsibility for the Mamasapano incident.
>
> In his original speech, the lawmaker described Aquino's refusal to take responsibility for the botched police operation as "the latest development in the shrinking of a man I once admired from a credible president to a small-minded bureaucrat trying desperately to erase his fingerprints from a failed project to save his own skin."
>
> But in the session hall, Bello was apparently more careful with his advice to the president.
>
> "Mr. President, please accept responsibility for Mamasapano. The whole nation is waiting for this gesture. Do not disappoint the Filipino people who elected you to the highest office in the land. This act of courage may not bring closure to this national tragedy, but it will definitely bring us closer to it," he said.

Walden delivers his final privilege speech, announcing his resignation as Akbayan representative in the House of Representatives; it was the only resignation on principle in the history of the Congress of the Philippines.

Bello said he decided to resign from his post because Akbayan's code of conduct provides that its representative in Congress should promote the party's official views on fundamental policy issues.

"When he or she can no longer support the party's position on these issues, there remains only one way to resolve the impasse, and that is for him to resign," he said.

The lawmaker said he tried his best to remain Aquino's ally by supporting the president's priorities such as RH law, the increase [sic] funding for the Conditional Cash Transfer (CCT) program and the proposed Bangsamoro Basic Law.

However, he found it unfortunate that Malacañang changed its views about his allegiance to the President because he crossed swords with the administration on controversial issues such as the Disbursement Acceleration Program, the retention of "inept, reckless or corrupt officials" and the President's handling of the Mamasapano clash.

"It's unfortunate that Malacañang's expectations of its allies are different from mine. I feel that the best ally is one who tells the President not what he wants to hear but what he should hear, whether or not he wants to hear this," he said.

As a final request to his colleagues in the House, Bello appealed to them to ensure the passage of the pending bills on the BBL [Bangsa Moro Basic Law], Freedom of Information (FOI) Act and Comprehensive Agrarian Reform Program (CARP) extension. He also asked that the House's investigation into the Mamasapano clash be reopened.

Despite sometimes being at odds with his fellow lawmakers in the majority coalition due to his divergent views, Bello thanked his colleagues, the House leadership and staff, as well as the media for helping him grow as a legislator.

"I have formed friendships on both sides of the aisle, and I plan to keep and nurture these when I have left these august halls," he said.[168]

That was it. It was the first and only resignation on principled grounds in the history of the Congress of the Philippines.

As I shook hands with people who had supported me or who had clashed with me, I felt nostalgia for an institution that had housed me for six years, where some of my most memorable political victories had taken place, as well as some of my greatest disappointments. I was both sad and relieved to leave.

Reconciliation

I left knowing I had lived up to my personal political code of conduct. Being a progressive has several dimensions. It means having a vision about how society should be organized based on the values of equality, justice, solidarity, and sovereignty. It means having a political program to realize this vision. But it also means projecting an ethical, moral stance. And perhaps, at a time when people have become so cynical about visions and programs because words are cheap and because opportunism and corruption are so rife across the political spectrum, the distinguishing mark of a true progressive holding public office is her or his ethical behavior. For me, being a progressive in the corridors of power means, above all, being steadfast in holding on to one's principles and values, even if this means losing one's position, possessions, or life. The resignation, I hoped, would serve as an example, especially to young people, that a politics of principle was possible.

I was sad to have broken with my party in pursuit of this code. I loved Akbayan despite my deep disagreement with it on the question of remaining in the coalition with the president. I hoped that it would eventually understand why we had to part ways. Throughout the whole episode and afterwards, I tried to be very calibrated in my statements about my differences with the party. There were others who had harsher words for the party, like former party official Carmel Abao, who was interviewed by *Rappler:*

> Akbayan's founding secretary general Carmel Abao, who is no longer involved in party or electoral politics, lamented that the party leadership did not side with Bello in his criticism of the President. . . . "So, Bello's claims do not hold water? Defending a Liberal president whose claims are so indefensible—juvenile, even—while negating a party leader's justifiable claims is something that I never thought this Leftist party would do. But they just did, with this statement. Sad day for Leftist politics in the country," she said.[169]

Over eight years later, on July 16, 2023, at the event marking my being awarded the Most Distinguished Defender of Human Rights by Amnesty International Philippines, the words I most cherished were delivered by Senator Risa Hontiveros of Akbayan, for it was more than a speech but also a reconciliation.

> When we think of the most fearless voices today fighting for human rights, most, if not all of us, will arrive at Walden Bello's name. It is my privilege to honor him earlier as he received the award for Most Distinguished Rights Defender from Amnesty International. *Kasamang* [Comrade] Walden, this award is a thank you from all of us whose rights continue to be protected because you stood up first. Thank you for your integrity, your stamina, and most of all, for showing us the way. *Maraming, maraming salamat. Kasama mo kami sa laban mo para kay Inang Bayan.* Thank you so much. We are with you in your fight for the Motherland.[170]

16. Love, Death, and Love in Bangkok

I WAS MARRIED to three women, Madeline Kho, Marilen Abesamis, and Suranuch ("Ko") Thongsila—serially, that is. I treasured all three of my partners, though the first two relationships ended in divorce, for which I bore the burden of responsibility. The last one was ended by the Big C.

Women and Me

I have had relationships with other women, most of them in the long periods between my marriages. Chemistry is very strange. With some women, the attraction may be mainly "spiritual." With others, it may be intellectual. With still others, it may be mainly or only sensual. And, of course, there are those rare times when you hit the jackpot and the bells line up in a row on the intellectual, spiritual, and sensual columns.

A chemical reaction with someone is a powerful force, but it must nevertheless be tamed with rules to ensure it does no greater harm than a broken heart. I had my rules as to whom I could have a relationship with, which meant no minors, no students, no research assistants, no teaching assistants, no one that I had power over in a professional or organizational relationship. Married women? On this question, it is better to take the fifth, as the Americans say, though there were instances I was wrongly accused of breaking the ninth commandment, like the time an angry husband threatened to have a fellow congressman who was a friend of his file an ethics case against me, or when another irate fellow nearly beat me up in Singapore's Chianggi airport where I was only saved from sure hospitalization by the protection of his wife—which, of course, only confirmed his unwarranted suspicions. Jealous husbands are, indeed, worse than jealous wives, and the worst are jealous men who suspect that anyone who is on friendly terms with their wives is out to bed them.

But were there times when no rules stood in the way of acting on a chemical reaction but one declined to act on it? Yes, and maybe this may sound strange, but the reason was to save a great friendship, for that friendship was more valuable to me than an emotional relationship that stood a great chance of being evanescent. This was what made my relationship to Suranch ("Ko") Thongsila unique, for it was a great friendship that I had had no intention of turning into an emotional partnership, yet, owing to circumstances, it became one—indeed, the most memorable relationship I've ever had.

The Chosen One

I was with Ko for five years, from 2013 to 2018, when she was whisked away by the Big C. That was the only time in my life, where the political and everything else were subordinated to the personal. Nothing can better convey what this relationship was like than the essay I wrote while secluded at the residence of my friends Robin Broad and John Cavanagh in Maryland following her passing in March 2018. It is still my most memorable piece of writing.[171]

> ... Whenever she was in extreme pain, she would tell me that if this was going to be her life, then it was not worth living. But two weeks before she left forever, as her weakened legs made their way down the ramp, her right arm draped around her caregiver's shoulder, she gave me an imploring look. It said she wanted so much to live. It was then that I first really broke down in the four-and-a-half years that I had nursed her in her long-drawn-out battle with what we had named the "Big C", perhaps fearing bad luck should we call the Enemy by its name.
>
> A few days later, lying in bed, she asked me if stem cell treatment was still an option. "I know it won't reverse it, but probably it might delay things," she said. It took me some time to gather the strength to tell her that our doctor friend had told me that the treatment was only effective in reversing multiple myeloma or leukemia, not colon cancer.
>
> What I did not tell her was that our friend had also told me that he would look into immunotherapy, another treatment, but one that was still in an experimental stage and needed subjects. I did not want to raise false hopes, especially now that she was in a terminal state, but I desperately wished that she would still qualify for the treatment and that slight possibility buoyed me, almost becoming a reality in my imagination.
>
> The day our friend told me about the possibility of immunotherapy, I went around town looking for the best *tonkatsu,* a Japanese pork dish that she had fallen in love with when we stayed for a month in Tokyo last year. I brought her the best I could find

in Bangkok, and when she tasted it that night, she said, "It's not bad, but can you bring me some *sashimi* tomorrow night?"

Early next morning, our friend called me and said he was sorry to have disappointing news, but immunotherapy would only be licensed for experimental use in December. I was crestfallen, but I told myself that at least she could still look forward to having *sashimi* for dinner. But by the time I got to the hospice, I was told she hadn't woken up and had slipped into a deep coma at dawn.

No, she won't regain consciousness, the chief nurse told me, and about 30 hours later, at 4:34 pm, March 27, 2018, my wife, Suranuch "Ko" Thongsila passed away, with me, her relatives, and a few friends looking on numbly as the electrocardiogram flatlined.

The proposal

It was about 5 years ago, sometime in March 2013, while I was about to return to the Philippines from the United States, that I got a message from her that read, if I remember rightly, "My mother is dying. I need you." It was curious, but it was a message to which the only possible response was, "Yes, I'm coming right away."

Ko was a good friend, with whom I had kept in touch over the years, ever since she translated my book *A Siamese Tragedy* into Thai about 13 years earlier. We sometimes had dinner when I went to Bangkok while I was still on the staff of Focus on the Global South, a research institute I co-founded in 1995, but these were reunions where we caught up with each other's life, and a romantic love life was the last thing on our minds.

By 2013, Ko had moved into the center of humanitarian activity in Thailand. As the executive director of the Siam Cement Foundation, the corporate responsibility arm of one of Thailand's biggest corporations, she had played a key role in the rebuilding of Southern Thailand after the devastating tsunami that killed over 5,000 people in 2004 and in the government-civil society effort to stop the massive floods raging towards Bangkok in 2012.

In the process, she had built up an extensive network of friends and colleagues that included politicians, academics, and civil society activists. She was especially close to former Prime Minister Anand Panyarachun, who had become a father figure to her, and was on familiar terms with people from all parts of

Thailand's political spectrum, like former prime ministers Abhisit Vejjajiva and Chuan Leek Pai of the Democrat Party, and Chaturon Chaisang, a parliamentarian who was one of the leading personalities in the "Redshirt" government of Ying Luck Shinawatra.

Not surprisingly, being a very attractive and still unmarried career woman, she had many prominent males in hot pursuit of her, and over our dinners over the years, she sometimes talked about her liaisons and why she ended up turning down offers of marriage. The reasons were diverse, but the main reason, which she acknowledged in a joking fashion, was that she was a career woman in a hurry, who had no time for marriage.

I felt that the text she sent me in March 2013 was not an ordinary hey-good-friend-come-see-me message, and true enough, when I got to Bangkok, she told me that her mother had said she would be more at ease departing for the afterlife if she knew somebody would take care of Ko before she died.

Though not on easy terms with her mother, Ko took her request seriously, thought it over carefully, and came to the conclusion that the only person she thought would fit the bill as a lifetime partner was me. This jolted me, but I also knew that saying no to this extraordinary, beautiful woman that I had perhaps subliminally desired over the years was not an option. Still, I was curious why she chose me.

The one thing I was sure of was that she did not choose me because I was a member of Congress. If political or social prominence was a prime criterion, then there were certainly much more attractive personalities on the Thai social scene that she could have had for the asking.

It was an intriguing puzzle, but playing Sherlock Holmes as to her motives was the last thing on my mind at the time of her mother's funeral in Bangkok in May 2013, which also served as our formal coming out as a couple. To her close friends, like Maem Bhumiprabhas and Jiu Thabchumpon, it came as a total surprise.

"How come we never knew about you and this guy?" they would ask her, to which she would laugh and reply, "But I did not know about it myself." As for me, I was not exactly comfortable being sized up by some of her male friends, some of whom probably felt a national treasure was being snatched from them by a Filipino who came out of the blue.

Walden and Ko on their wedding day,
13 April 2015, in Honesdale, Pennsylvania.

Her mother's funeral also marked another development in Ko's life, and that was her exit from active participation in Thailand's social and political life. It was something that I only began to realize had occurred over time, but it eventually became as big a puzzle as why she decided to choose me as her partner.

The good life interrupted

Ko was eager to get on with what she regarded as her new life in the Philippines, and she happily adjusted to the role of being a congressional wife, one that was so different from her role as a decision-maker and activist in Thailand. When with friends, I kidded her that she might eventually regret having a partner 17 years older than her since she would end up taking care of me in my old age, to which she replied that adult diapers had greatly simplified that task.

We had a lovely five months, until she was diagnosed with fourth stage colon cancer during a routine visit to her gynecologist in Bangkok in August 2013. The first thing she did when she heard this was to sit me down and tell me, "You did not bargain for this. You are under no obligation to remain in this relationship. You are free to leave." I must have said something like, silly girl, did you think I would be that easy to shake off, and we hunkered down for the battle with the Big C.

Her first surgery took off a good chunk of her colon and some of her liver. Six cycles of chemotherapy followed, which left her drained of energy and numb in different parts of her body. A second surgery removed more of her liver, leaving her with just about a fourth of it, and this was followed by another debilitating bout with chemo, also 6 cycles long.

Two more surgeries followed, interspersed with chemotherapy and radiation therapy. The surgeries and treatments battered her body, with her complaining that what was causing her pain and discomfort was not the cancer but the different operations and treatments. Our lives begun to be built around early morning visits every two weeks to Chulalongkorn University Hospital for a daylong consultation with different specialists, inpatient and outpatient chemotherapy sessions, and when things really got rough, hospitalization for days or even weeks.

She tried everything, including undergoing alternative therapies like an all-vegetable diet, and she registered great frustration at how Western-trained doctors and alternative therapists would simply dismiss each other's prescriptions.

"I asked the doctor if I needed to avoid meat or cheese, as the nutritionists recommended, but he said I could eat anything and told me not listen to those people," she said, shaking her head at the feud between Western-trained cut-and-chemo doctors and the you-are-what-you-eat school of cancer nutritionists.

Gradually, my priorities shifted. These were tumultuous times for me politically, with me resigning from Congress owing to my differences with the policies of then president Benigno Aquino III and being drafted to run for the Senate in 2016. Ko was adamant that her condition must not interfere with my political agenda, and she insisted that I go home to the Philippines to campaign even as she underwent a particularly draining bout with chemotherapy in Bangkok.

But long before the 2016 campaign, I had already made a choice, and that was to place keeping her alive at the top of my agenda, with politics and writing relegated to a distant second. This meant long absences from Manila to be with her in Bangkok.

We lived through a number of false dawns, when the latest CT Scan or Pet Scan would show that the cancer indicator had drastically declined, pointing to the possibility that she was in remission.

It was on occasions like this, when the doctors would tell her she could afford to take a vacation from chemo, that her high school classmates, whom she christened the "Fatboys," would gather to celebrate at her house with food and drink. Happy reunions like these provided the opportunity for her friends and relatives to embrace me as one of their own, despite my very rudimentary Thai. It was then that an anti-corporation activist like me discovered that "Google Translate" not only facilitated communication but also created community.

Hopeful CT Scan readings also provided the opportunity for us to travel. With hope returned energy, and we took off for those countries she had longed to visit but somehow had never had the opportunity to do so, like Brazil, the Netherlands, Norway, Sweden, and Italy.

I applied for fellowships and teaching positions, which enabled us to live for months in New York, Wisconsin, and Japan. Looking back, I think she did not fully trust the cancer readings and wanted to absorb as much of life as possible in case these readings did not, in fact, portend the much-desired remission. These were happy times, when she could spend hours shopping at her favorite U.S. garments store, TJ Maxx, in Madison, Wisconsin, or when we would queue to get into the best *tonkatsu* hole-in-the-wall near the Kamata subway station in Tokyo.

She liked to cook, and would entertain guests in Manila with her home-cooked *tom yum kung* shrimp soup and *tom kha gai* chicken dish. She loved the Philippines, and one of her goals was to master Tagalog, though, like me when it came to Thai, she was endlessly frustrated by what she considered the complexity of Tagalog.

"You have all these crazy conjugations," she said. "We have only one tense in Thai." To which I replied, "Yes, but you have this crazy tonal language, where depending on the tone, the word *klai* could mean 'near' or 'far' or the word *suay* could mean 'beautiful' or 'ugly'."

Chemical warfare

But reality would always intrude, rudely. After a few months, the next CT Scan would register a rapid multiplication of cancer cells. The pattern became all too clear: the cancer would retreat before a new chemo formula bringing down the cancer reading, then it would regroup to find ways to get around the enemy, then having developed immunity to the formula, it would counterattack with a vengeance.

There was savage chemical warfare taking place inside my wife's body, and it was taking its toll. Yet the illusion persisted, perhaps in me more than her, that we could indefinitely stave off the final assault with more and more potent chemo formulas. Since her passing, I have been haunted by the question whether chemo delayed or accelerated her demise. I doubt if I will ever be able to find the answer.

In any case, the dream that chemo could prolong her life indefinitely was shattered in mid-January of this year [2018], when the cancer began attacking her brain, bringing about so much pain that we had to bring her to the emergency room where they pumped her full of morphine. A 10-day treatment with radiation therapy saw her regain both strength and spirit, so that at the end of it, she had become the lively center of activity at Chulalongkorn University Hospital's cancer ward. I kidded her that she would probably win if there were an election held for the ward's "patient representative."

The Big C's final offensive

We brought her home in mid-January, only to take her back less than two weeks later as the cancer resumed its attack on her brain. Again, a brief interlude of relative well-being after radiation therapy followed, after which she underwent another CT Scan. At that point, the doctors gave us the news that the cancer's offensive had broken through to different parts of her body and they were discontinuing chemo since it was no longer effective in containing the cancer's spread.

That was the handwriting on the wall, and she took it bravely. Lying together, she took my hand one evening and told me that despite all her tribulations during the last four-and-a-half years, this had been the happiest period of her life, much more personally fulfilling than when she had been professionally active.

"*Chan raak khun mak mak*," she whispered in Thai. "I love you very much." Then she asked, "What's going to happen to you? It's you I'm worried about. I told Jit to promise me that she'll take care of you," relating her conversation with her cousin.

On March 22, Ko marked her 55th birthday with a merit-making ritual officiated by a Buddhist monk, one that, in Buddhist belief, would help release her from the cycle of reincarnation and human suffering. The next day, an ambulance came to fetch her from her house for the last time to bring her to a Catholic-run hospice in downtown Bangkok. Four days later she passed away.

Unsolved puzzles

It was only during the five-day Buddhist departure ceremonies that I began to truly appreciate my wife's impact on people. Hundreds of people came upon learning of her passing, paying their respects to a person who had touched their life as a compassionate humanitarian worker, a political activist who sought to bring opposing parties to common ground, a person loyal to colleagues and friends and devoted to relatives.

But before the rituals ended, I wanted to take advantage of the presence of so many of her colleagues and friends to make sure I solved the two mysteries that still remained unanswered—queries that she used to gracefully sidestep with a kiss or a smile.

The first one was why Ko made such a drastic break from Thai public life 5 years earlier. One piece of the puzzle was provided by one of her closest friends who told me that part of her withdrawal was job-related. After 10 years as executive director of the Siam Cement Foundation, the mother company was doing a rotation and assigning her to a new post, and while she understood the rationale for the rotation, she felt that there was still so much more she wanted to do to improve humanitarian services in Thailand as head of the agency, so she resigned.

Another piece came from another friend, who speculated that the battle between "Yellowshirts" and "Redshirts" that had riven Thai politics during the Thaksin period had thoroughly disillusioned her, especially when her friends found themselves on opposite sides and close friendships were torn apart.

A third piece of the puzzle came from another confidant, who said that Ko told her that she had done everything else and the only thing remaining that she really wanted to do was to experience married life. But all this did not add up to explaining her sharp withdrawal from close friends like former Prime Minister Anand, who told me, "I tried to get through to her, but she just seemed to close all doors. I could not understand it at all."

Perhaps the mystery of my wife's break with Thai political and civil society will never be completely answered. Nor will the second mystery, which was why she chose me to be a partner in place of much more qualified candidates. But though I still was curious, the answer had become irrelevant. Though I think we started our relationship as good friends who were probably not yet in love with each other, by the time Ko departed, our battle against cancer had made our friendship evolve into deep, true love.

As he left the cremation rites at which he officiated, Prime Minister Anand, who had served as Ko's surrogate father, said to me, "Thanks so much for taking care of her." I choked and could hardly utter my response, "I would do it all over again if given the chance."

No surrender

The day after the cremation, under a soft sunlight in the Gulf of Thailand, I committed the remains of the person who had provided the meaning of my existence over the last 5 years to the sea.

The Big C had won, but having put up a good fight, Ko would have felt no dishonor at the outcome. She had not surrendered. I was reminded of the time 5 years ago, in May 2013, when she and I went out on a boat, probably to the same spot, where we lowered her mother's remains to the sea.

Did she have any inkling then, I asked myself, that nearly five years later, she would be joining her mother in the depths? She could not hold back her tears then, and I could not hold mine back now, as I thanked her for giving me the best years of my life. . . . "

The piece was probably the most widely read article I ever wrote, far outstripping my writings on politics, for a Chinese journalist translated it into Mandarin and released it on a Chinese internet site that had millions of subscribers. He assured me that it would reduce millions of Chinese housewives to tears. Well, why not, I said, thinking that that was probably the best way to say good-bye to my dear departed Thai wife.

Post Ko

Since her passing, I've had a chance to reflect more on our relationship, and how despite our love for each other, we were very different, in so many ways.

I am intensely political. She, in contrast, tried to avoid serious political discussion, except when it came to Donald Trump, whom she detested for his put-downs of Hilary Clinton, one of her heroes.

I am a radical and rather passionate when it comes to my politics and my feelings. She was a moderate on both counts, and my one regret was that she could have been much more expressive on the personal front.

She had a keen business sense and was successful as an investor in property and stocks, but she accepted my anti-capitalist views and did not let them come between us. She appeared in my dreams twice, suggesting buying bitcoin. Now, I don't believe in dreams nor in cryptocurrency, but as a nod to my fond memory of her and her curious belief that cryptocurrency would eventually eliminate the need for banks and Central Bank-backed currency, I said yup, why not, and arranged to have some of her legacy changed into bitcoin. It was her money after all.

I was 73 when Ko passed away in 2018, and I told myself that my relationship with her was the last one for me. But, again, fate had other plans, and Bangkok is a city that loves to spring surprises on the unsuspecting. Three years after Ko's departure, I was on one of the boats that service the Saen Saep Canal, and had reached the last stop, the Wat Sriboonreung, the Buddhist temple from where I would take a motorcycle to Ko's old residence. Agility is in great demand on these boats, and as my right foot landed on the pier, I lost my balance and could have fallen into the canal had not a hand reached out and grabbed my arm. I turned to say thank you, and saw a freckled face, with mischief in her eyes, that asked, "*Chan khunplai mu khun mai?* Should I let go?"

Unlike the bitcoin business, this was not some dream but an honest-to-goodness sign from Ko, and I was not about to ignore it.

17. Reign of Darkness...and Light

I THOUGHT I was done with parliamentary politics for good when Ed Tadem, a prominent public intellectual, published an op-ed in the *Philippine Daily Inquirer* urging the Philippine Left to run someone for president to offer an alternative to elite politics during the national elections of 2016, even if at this time, the chances of winning were nil:

> But why aim for the presidency? The main purpose is to challenge oligarchic and dynastic politics and offer a genuine alternative, which only the Left can do. It is also to offer hope to the toiling masses that not all its leaders are callous and insensitive to their plight. It is time for the Left to get serious and raise the highest bar for electoral participation. Anything less than the presidency, and the Left is hobbled from the start. Without discounting the value of fielding candidates for local governments and Congress, the fact is that in these contests, the Left's message is easily lost or muffled.[172]

Ed and others had me in mind, and after several meetings, I was drafted to run, not for president but for senator in the 2016 national elections. It was felt that, though it was a long shot, I stood a better chance to win running for senator than for president. Except for Akbayan, the non-CPP/NDF Left rallied behind my candidacy, including party formations such as Sanlakas, Kilusan, Partido Manggagawa, and Alab Katipunan; a host of NGOs, labor groups, and farmers' organizations; and independent personalities such as Francisco Nemenzo, Princess Nemenzo, and Tina Ebro.

The campaign showed the potential of the Left becoming a serious political force if only different groups could unite behind a candidate and a program. Though we were very short on campaign funds, and I spent half of the campaign season in Bangkok taking care of Ko, who was undergoing chemotherapy, I was able to gather more than one million votes.

A good part of those votes came, interestingly, from the bailiwicks of traditional politicians with whom I had worked during the fight for the

RH bill. I was, for instance, invited by Rep Kimi Cojuangco, an ally in that struggle, to campaign in her and husband Mark Cojuangco's district in Pangasinan. I could not believe my ears when Mark, whose initiative to revive the Bataan Nuclear Power Plant I had helped defeat during the 14th Congress, introduced me to his constituents as "a man of the highest integrity that I respect." Another ally from the RH days, Rep Imelda Dimaporo, invited me to Lanao del Norte, where she promised she could get me about 10,000 votes, and she delivered!

Cheered by the outcome, a number of the organizations backing me began a series of discussions that resulted a few months later in the formation of the coalition *Laban ng Masa*, People's Struggle.

Rodrigo Duterte won the presidency, with a tough-on-crime platform that had him promising to cut criminals, drug pushers, and drug users into small pieces and feeding them to the fish in Manila Bay. Duterte's message resonated at all levels of society, with many among the poor hoping that he would not limit his promise to doing away with common criminals but also ending corruption and bringing about economic betterment in their lives. Armed with a mandate of nearly 40 percent of the vote, he launched his campaign of extra-judicial execution of drug users and peddlers that eventually netted some 27,000 victims, according to some estimates.

Understanding Duterte

I related to Duterte in two contradictory ways. On the one hand, he was a political enemy of the worst kind, since he totally threw away due process and gave the police a blank check in doing away with people he considered undesirable. On the other hand, he fascinated me as an object of study, stimulating the interest in counterrevolutionary movements that had been with me since I was in Chile over 40 years earlier.

I dissected the Duterte phenomenon in a series of academically oriented articles. In my contribution to *the Duterte Reader*, edited by Nicole Curato, a leading expert on populism and a former student of mine, I called Duterte a "fascist original," justifying my use of the loaded term "fascist," to describe him if we saw,

> as central to the definition of a fascist leader (a) a charismatic individual with strong inclinations toward authoritarian rule who (b) derives his or her strength from a heated multiclass mass base, (c) in engaged in or supports the systematic violation of basic human, civil, and political rights, and (d) proposes a political

project that contradicts the fundamental values and aims of liberal democracy or social democracy.[173]

What accounted for Duterte's popularity? It was, I asserted, EDSA's failure to deliver.

What destroyed the EDSA project and paved the way for Duterte was the deadly combination of elite monopoly of the electoral system, the continuing concentration of wealth, and neoliberal economic policies and the priority placed on foreign debt repayment imposed by Washington. By 2016, there was a yawning gap between the EDSA Republic's promise of popular empowerment and wealth redistribution and the reality of massive corruption. . . . And the EDSA Republic's discourse on democracy, human rights, and rule of law had become a suffocating strait-jacket for the majority of Filipinos who simply could not relate to it owing to the overpowering reality of their powerlessness.[174]

But while being the central factor accounting for Duterte's appeal, EDSA's unravelling was not the only one. Duterte, I wrote in several articles, had charisma, not the traditional, inspirational kind, but one connected with his "discourse."[175] On this discourse, which was the very opposite of the EDSA discourse, I made three key points. First, from a progressive and liberal point of view, his discourse was politically incorrect, but that was its very strength. It came across as liberating to its middle class and lower-class audience. Duterte was seen as telling it as it was, as deliberately mocking the dominant discourse of human rights, democratic rights, and social justice that had been ritually invoked but was increasingly regarded as a cynical coverup for the very real lack of human rights, democracy, and genuine equality in post-EDSA Philippines and its pervasive corruption.

Second, Duterte's discourse involved a unique application of what Bourdieu calls the strategy of condescension. His coarse discourse, delivered conversationally and with frequent shifts from Tagalog to Bisaya to English, made people identify with him, eliciting laughter with his portrayal of himself as someone who bumbled along like the rest the crowd or had the same illicit desires, at the same time that it also reminded the audience that he was someone different from and above them, as someone with power. This was especially evident when he paused and uttered his signature, "*Papatayin kita*," or "I will kill you," as in "If you destroy the youth of my country by giving them drugs, I will kill you."

Third, Duterte's speechmaking did not follow a conceptual or rhetorical logic, and this was another reason he could connect with the masses. The formal conceptual message written by speechwriters was deliberately overridden by a series of long digressions where Duterte told tales where he was invariably at the center of things and knew would hold the audience's attention, even after they had heard it several times. Let me confess here that when I listened to Duterte's digressions, peppered as they were with outrageous comments, like telling an audience he would pardon policemen convicted of extra-judicial executions so they could go after the people who brought them to court, my mind had to restrain my body from joining the chorus of laughter at the sheer comic effrontery of his words. With Duterte, the digression was the message.

Duterte, I also pointed out, had also masterfully upended the psychological relationship of Filipinos to the United States:

> As many have observed, coexisting with admiration for the United States and U.S. institutions exhibited by ordinary Filipinos is a strong undercurrent of resentment at the colonial subjugation of the country by the United States, the unequal treaties that Washington has foisted on the country, and the overwhelming impact of the "American way of life" on local culture. One need not delve into the complex psychology of Hegel's master-servant dialectic to understand that the undercurrent of the U.S.-Philippine relationship has been the "struggle for recognition" by the dominated party. . . . Duterte has been able to tap into this emotional underside of Filipinos in a way that the Left has never been able to, with its anti-imperialist program.[176]

Duterte went on to court China in his first years in office and instilled expectations that there would be a fundamental change in U.S.-Philippine relations.

Opposing Duterte

As a political figure, the man from Davao evoked the warning to progressives that I had penned 15 years earlier in a commentary on the lower class uprising that was EDSA III, "Unless the Left looks at the recent crisis with humility, the fire next time might not only sweep away the elite but also decimate the progressive movement, rendering it . . . forever irrelevant."[177]

Thus, in contrast to my intellectual fascination with him as a sociological specimen, politically, I was on the warpath against Duterte from the very beginning. There was no honeymoon. A few days into his presidency, on July 11, 2016, my Facebook page carried this post: "There have always been crooked cops, but President Duterte and his Police Chief [Ronaldo] Bato de la Rosa have managed to convert the whole Philippine National Police into an uncontrolled collection of rogue cops that relish being able to kill, kill, kill with no constraints. 'There will be blood'—that's the presidential motto."[178]

This and succeeding posts earned angry responses from Duterte partisans. Other critics got the same treatment, or worse. It was war in cyberspace, leading some to say that Duterte had a vast army of paid trolls whose task was to take down the administration's opponents. I disagreed, deeply disdainful of conspiracy theories as I had been since I studied the middle-class-based counterrevolution in Chile. While there were paid pro-Duterte trolls, my analysis showed that 75 percent of the angry responses to my posts were not scripted but were spontaneous. Most of the attacks on me were coming from people who had a level of command of language, whether English or Tagalog, that betrayed a middle-class education or sensibility. I noted that while Duterte drew support from all classes, it was most aggressively displayed by both the aspiring and downwardly mobile middle classes. I also made the distinction, borrowing from the Italian thinker, Antonio Gramsci, that while the lower-class base of the president might be said to display "passive consensus," the middle class exhibited "active consensus," leading to their energetic domination of the internet, a medium that was especially suited to their skills. Aping their idol's penchant for the outrageous, pro-Duterte bloggers called for, among other things, the execution of two women journalists and the "brutal rape" of Duterte critic, Senator Risa Hontiveros.

Fighting for Leila

While I denounced the wave of extra-judicial killings of drug users, I was especially active in seeking the release of Senator Leila de Lima, who had been framed on charges of dealing in drugs or abetting the narcotics trade during the administration of Benigno Aquino III when she was secretary of justice. It was a clear frame-up that stemmed from her having dared to investigate cases of extra-judicial killing in Davao City when she was chairperson of the Human Rights Commission and Duterte was mayor of that city. There was simply no way Senator de Lima could be guilty of the absurd charges since I had worked with her on prosecuting officials who had sexually abused migrant workers when I was head of the House's Committee on Overseas Workers Affairs, and I had experienced her integrity firsthand.

I tried to understand why Duterte was so successful in isolating her, and my analysis highlighted the way he and his minions like Harry Roque were

Walden with former Senator Leila de Lima and brother Vicente de Lima, on the day Leila was granted bail and regained her freedom after nearly seven years of imprisonment on trumped-up charges.

able to tap into the always latent misogynistic and class biases of Filipino males by portraying her as a "fallen woman" for having had an affair with her driver.

I wrote articles on her case in both the local and international media, but perhaps the most effective portrayal of the injustice done to her was the speech I made at De La Salle University in a conference on the "weaponization of the law" on Feb 21, 2020—judging, that is, from the number of angry responses to it from Duterte partisans:

> I was wondering why at the beginning of Sen Leila's current odyssey there were not more people who stood up for her. I think I would attribute this to what I have termed elsewhere as Duterte's "blitzkrieg fascism."

While at the ground level, Duterte's panzers rolled over barangays indiscriminately killing people, at the national political level, Duterte and his minions, like the abominably ambitious or simply abominable Richard Gordon, focused their massive firepower on Senator Leila. Both at the ground level and national level, the aim of Duterte's panzers was to demonstrate the power of the administration to do anything it wanted and communicate that resistance was futile.

True, the persecution of Sen Leila was to Duterte partly a settling of personal scores, the guy's getting back at her for daring to investigate him for the Davao Death Squad killings. But, probably more important, it was a campaign undertaken for what social psychologists would call its "demonstration effect" on the citizenry.

Let me just share my thoughts on two of Duterte's blitzkrieg methods that proved so effective. One was the blatantly misogynistic line of attack, characterizing Sen Leila as "an immoral woman." This was, in a very real sense, a witch hunt, a drive to paint this particular woman who had the gall to stand up to the omnipotent patriarch as the source of all society's evils. One must admit that it was a stroke of evil genius to dredge up Jurassic age prejudices against women, the primordial Samson and Delilah complex about women leading men astray, that primeval fear that Freud called castration anxiety, and to link these subliminal male terrors to the legal accusations that Senator Leila was a high-level enabler of the drug trade.

Related to this misogynistic psycho-strategy was the sheer effrontery of the plan to paint a former Secretary of Justice as being at the center of the country's illegal drugs problem. This panzer punch was so bold that it stunned people and, among many of those who did not know Senator Leila, it made them question their initial common sense or instinctive reaction that the accusation was utterly false.

Now those of us who knew Senator de Lima and had worked with her and known first-hand her determination to combat injustice knew the accusations were nonsense. I had the opportunity to work with her briefly in pursuing cases against government officials abroad who were treating our OFWs as sexual prey while I was head of the House of Representatives' Committee on Overseas Workers Affairs, and I was thoroughly impressed with her commitment to rectifying injustice. But for those who had not had my chance to work with her, the panzer punch was so outrageously bold that it psychologically destabilized them and made them question their initial reaction to dismiss the charges against Senator Leila as absurd.

Those who did not know Senator Leila could perhaps be excused for being stunned by the lies of the President and his minions, and I am sure the good senator will not take this against them. But there were others who knew better but were so worried that the same public crucifixion would happen to them that they remained silent or did not come out to defend her as strongly as they should have. I mention this not to make anyone feel guilty but so we can understand why, despite their being fueled by falsehoods, Duterte's blitzkrieg tactics have been so effective in stunning people into inaction.[179]

My support for de Lima was not limited to taking up the cudgels for her. I appointed myself her supplier-in-chief when it came to books, providing her with some 1000 titles over a period of five years on topics ranging from law to economics to sociology to novels—from Thomas Piketty's *Capitalism and Ideology* to Arundhati Roy's *The Ministry of Utmost Happiness*.

Generous in her appreciation of my help as she was in that of others, she sent me this note when I received Amnesty International Philippines' Most Distinguished Human Rights Defender Award in 2023, "In your visits here at the detention center, it struck me that a man of your intellect could have undoubtedly achieved great personal success and recognition in various fields. However, you chose a different path—one of selfless dedication to the service of others. ... You are truly a source of inspiration for all who have the privilege of knowing you."[180]

Unfortunately, despite two of the three charges against her being dismissed and witnesses against her on the third charge recanting their testimonies, she remained in jail, with Ferdinand Marcos, Jr, afraid of his predecessor's wrath should he let her go. She declined an offer of house arrest, reasoning that this would be making an unprincipled concession and preferring to remain in jail unless the court granted her bail.

But the public pressure for her release could no longer be contained. On Nov 13, 2023, she was granted bail by Judge Gener Gito of Branch 206 of the Regional Trial Court in Muntinglupa, Rizal, after she posted a P300,000 bond, with only a weak objection from the prosecution. Her complete exoneration from the charges leveled against her by Duterte and his gang was only a matter of time. The three cases charging her with being engaged in drug trafficking had completely collapsed, with all key prosecution witnesses claiming they were forced by the government to bear false witness against her.

I was jubilant, and upon hearing the judge pronounce his decision in court, I rushed to embrace Leila, along with many who had stayed the course with her for six years, ten months, and 21 days. That evening, I issued a statement that concluded, "I join the whole country in celebrating the vindication of Senator Leila de Lima and demanding the legal and moral rectification of the outrage perpetrated against her by bringing Rodrigo Duterte, along with his minions, to justice for orchestrating a travesty of truth, morality, and due process. I also join the now universal clamor to send Duterte to the International Criminal Court in the Hague to stand trial for masterminding the extra-judicial execution of thousands of Filipinos."

We all knew that her complete exoneration from the charges leveled against her by Duterte and his gang was only a matter of time. And, indeed, on June 24, 2024, while I was in Brazil on a speaking engagement, the news reached me that the same judge that granted her bail less than a year earlier had cleared Leila of the third and last charge of conspiracy to commit drug trading. It was a bittersweet moment. Justice finally prevailed, but at the cost of nearly seven years taken from the life of an innocent woman.

No Redeeming Qualities

One development that puzzled many people was the National Democratic Front's flirting with Duterte. While one could write off Jose Maria Sison's comparing Duterte to Hugo Chavez as the words of someone seeking to begin a political relationship on the right foot, it was much more difficult to take the NDF's de facto alliance with Duterte, one that went to the point of providing him with cabinet secretaries during his first year in office. The NDF obviously thought that Duterte, with whom they had had positive relations in Davao while he was mayor there, would be open to a peace settlement that would be favorable to the New People's Army. But anyone who had followed the relations between the CPP/NPA and the NPA could have told them that the Armed Forces of the Philippines would have vetoed a peace deal. Still, the NDF kept its people in the cabinet for a rather long period after the massive killings of alleged drug users began in 2016. It was only in 2017 that they made a definitive break with Duterte when, at the prompting of the military that he was assiduously courting, he declared war on them. Their joining the opposition was welcomed but their credibility suffered from what many saw as their Machiavellian opportunism in having worked with a mass murderer and, to top it all, being outsmarted by him.

But did Duterte have any redeeming qualities? I thought he had, and this was his promise to terminate the Visiting Forces Agreement with the United States, which he made in January 2020. I wrote a piece for *Rappler* with the provocative title, "Duterte is a Mass Murderer, but I Support his Terminating the Visiting Forces Agreement," where I noted that Duterte had "rhetorically inveighed against the United States, but he has done absolutely nothing so far to interrupt the flow of U.S. troops and war materiel in the country. Washington is willing to put up with his curses. . . . So, yes, I support the president's expressed intention to withdraw from the VFA and would urge him to also include leaving EDCA and that useless relic of the Cold War, the Mutual Defense Treaty. The big question is: will he follow through, defying both his generals and their real boss—the Pentagon?"[181]

But the Pentagon had Duterte's number. It simply ignored his bark, and by the end of his term in June 2022, he was extolling the VFA; voicing approval of the AUKUS security pact joining Australia, the United Kingdom, and the U.S.; reestablishing the Philippines-U.S. Bilateral Strategic Dialogue; and launching expanded joint military exercises with the United States. While not repudiating his close relationship with China, Duterte ended his presidency in June 2022 on a warm note with Washington that contrasted sharply with the bitter row with Barack Obama that had launched his term in 2016.

Duterte left office with the country in ruins, having presided over one of the worst programs in the world to contain Covid 19, one that relied on the military and police to contain the pandemic while denigrating medical professionals; ending the quota on rice imports that had long been demanded by the World Trade Organization; instituting the most ambitious set of neo-liberal economic measures since the Ramos presidency in the late nineties; saddling the country with a massive foreign debt of $112 billion; and giving the military a free hand in a red-tagging campaign that resulted in the killing of a number of political activists. So much for the septuagenarian braggart that had called himself a socialist at the beginning of his term and who was feted by Jose Maria Sison as having the promise of becoming the "Hugo Chavez of the Philippines."

Yet, the braggadocio left office with a 75 percent approval rating.

By the end of Duterte's disastrous term, the government's Philippine News Agency (PNA) was calling me "one of the staunchest critics of the administration." That was meant to discredit me, but I wore it as a badge of honor.

The 2022 Elections

There was another attempt to draft me to run for president for the 2022 elections. One of my conditions, however, was that 30,000 signatures needed to be collected urging me to run. That figure was not reached. However, the prominent labor leader Leody de Guzman volunteered to run for president, and I found it impossible to refuse him when he asked me to be his running mate against Sara Duterte and Bongbong Marcos. As in 2016, we had little chance of winning and our main aim was to pose an alternative to elite politics.

In contrast to previous political campaigns, I was determined to enjoy the 2022 campaign. This began with a television interview with Christian Esguerra on ANC, where I asserted, "This is a family that has raped the country. It has not apologized to the country and it now wants to rape the country again. Fuck you, Marcos!"[182] Those were precisely the words that captured the sentiments of large numbers of people who were aghast that the dastardly family was making another bid to capture the presidency—and they resonated widely and globally, being adopted as the main "theme" of his program on the eve of the Philippine elections by the U.S.-based British comedian, John Oliver.[183]

I played bad cop to Leody's good cop image, calling Sara Duterte and Bongbong Marcos "cowards" for not appearing in the televised vice presidential and presidential debates. Atty Luke Espiritu, one of our senatorial bets, and I made a series of TikTok comedy acts, in one of which "Sara" tries to beat me up on the beach, then slips as I avoid her blows, calling the attention of viewers subliminally to Sara Duterte's televised beating of a municipal worker years earlier. In response to my exposing her poor record as mayor, I was accused by the Duterte camp of being a "narco-politician," declared persona non grata by the Davao City Council and slapped with a cyberlibel suit by Duterte's press information officer. My reply to all this was to enter the empty Davao City Council chamber, bang the gavel, and declare the whole Council persona non grata, an act that drew laughs nationwide.[184]

But there was a serious side to the campaign, which was run very professionally by Herbert Docena, Pang Delgra, Leomar Doctolero, Vim Santos, and Kat Leuch. Leody and I ran on a democratic socialist program, one that, at 25-single spaced pages that covered topics from agriculture to abortion, was probably the most detailed and comprehensive program ever presented to the Philippine electorate. We advocated the decriminalization of abortion, a taboo topic. We made the minimum wage an election issue that the others had to address. We exposed the impunity with which indigenous communities were being robbed of their lands, a point that was illustrated to a national audience when Leody accompanied the Manobos in Quezon, Bukidnon, to reclaim their land from a plantation and they were fired upon by the private army of the usurping corporation, resulting in injuries to a number of them.

The presidential and vice presidential debates were the climax of the campaign, and since Marcos, Jr, and Sara Duterte did not want to risk their lack of knowledge of the issues by participating in the debates, I sang Frank Sinatra's signature hit, "Where are you?," during the second vice presidential debate, the first time ever that someone sang in a nationally televised vice presidential or presidential electoral debate. Since the debates were supposed to assess candidates' fitness for the positions they were seeking, I brought the aggressive dissection of one's opponent's record typical of U.S. electoral debates to the confrontations. None of the other presidential or vice-presidential aspirants dared to do this, with most of them simply spouting motherhood statements and avoiding direct attacks on each other's records in office to avoid being attacked themselves.

My rivals, Senators Francis Pangilinan and Tito Sotto, did not take kindly to my efforts, with the latter, unused to being grilled, throwing me dagger looks for exposing his consistent pro-Duterte postures while he served as Senate President. "I don't think we should, *huwag nating patulan 'yung mga ganong style* (let's not engage this kind of style.)."[185] In the Philippines, losing one's cool, as Sotto did, is known as *pikon*, or poor sport, since one is expected to give as good as one gets in an exchange.

Washington's Man

The outcome of the elections, a massive victory for Marcos Jr and Sara Duterte, as predicted by the opinion polls, was a stinging slap in the face of the liberal establishment and the Left. In explaining the result to a shocked international audience and a not-so-shocked local audience, I said that while explanations highlighting the role of pro-Marcos and pro-Duterte trolls in the social media had some merit, there were two key factors behind the outcome. One, the vast majority of the voters had not yet been born during the martial law years or they were small children then, so they had no direct experience of the abuses of the Marcos period. But more important, I repeated what I said in accounting for the victory of Duterte in 2016, there was the disillusionment with the EDSA Revolution of 1986:

> [T]he Marcos vote can be interpreted as being largely a protest vote that first surfaced in a dramatic fashion in the 2016 elections that propelled Rodrigo Duterte to the presidency. Though probably inchoate and diffuse at the level of conscious motivation, the vote

for Duterte and the even larger vote for Marcos were propelled by widespread resentment at the persistence of gross inequality in a country where less than five percent of the population corners over 50 percent of the wealth. It was a protest against the extreme poverty that engulfs 25 percent of the people and the poverty, broadly defined, that has about 40 percent of them in its clutches.

Against the loss of decent jobs and livelihoods owing to the destruction of our manufacturing sector and our agriculture by the policies imposed on us by the World Bank, International Monetary Fund, World Trade Organization, and the United States. Against the despair and cynicism that engulf the youth of the working masses who grow up in a society where they learn that the only way to get a decent job that allows you to get ahead in life is to go abroad. Against the daily blows to one's dignity inflicted by a rotten public transport system in a country where 95 percent of the population doesn't own cars.

These are the conditions that most of the Class D and E Marcos voters [the lower classes] experienced directly, not the horrors of the Marcos period, and their subjective resentment of them, primed them for the seductive appeals of a return to a fictive "Golden Age."

In the presidential elections, the full force of this resentment against the EDSA status quo was directed at Marcos' main rival, Vice President Leni Robredo. Unfairly, since she is a woman of great personal integrity. The problem is that in the eyes of the marginalized and the poor that went for Marcos, she was not able to separate her image from its associations with the Liberal Party, the conservative neoliberal Makati Business Club, the family of the assassinated Benigno Aquino, Jr, the double standards on corruption that rendered Benigno Aquino III's "*kung walang korap walang mahirap*" ("where there is no corruption, there is no poverty") slogan as much an object of ridicule as the color yellow, and, above all, with the devastating failure of the 36-year-old EDSA Republic to deliver.

The rhetoric of "good governance" may have resonated with Robredo's middle class and elite base, but for the *masa* (masses) it smacked of the same old hypocrisy. Good governance or "*tapat na papamalakad*" sounded in their ears much like the Liberals' painting themselves as the "*gente decente*" or "decent people" that led to their rout in the 2016 elections and the ascendancy of Rodrigo Duterte.[186]

The full implications of what the country decided during the May 2022 elections did not become clear until February 2023, when Marcos Jr announced that he had decided to give the U.S. four more bases, in addition to the five that the Aquino III administration had given Washington nine years earlier. Both our defense and foreign policies were practically being outsourced to Washington, DC. In a piece I did for the *Nation*, I wrote that I was not surprised since what was involved was not ideology or realpolitik but cold, hard money, the most important motivator of Imelda and her brood:

> Marcos...cannot be unaware of how the U.S., with its global clout, has often been able to freeze the assets of people linked to regimes it considers undesirable, the most recent example being the holdings of Russian oligarchs connected to President Vladimir Putin in the wake of Russia's invasion of Ukraine. The Marcos family has *$5 billion to $10 billion* in landholdings and other assets distributed throughout the world, in places such as California, Washington, New York, Rome, Vienna, Australia, the Antilles, the Netherlands, Hong Kong, Switzerland, and Singapore. Being on the wrong side of the United States, especially in a dispute as central as the U.S.-China conflict, could have devastating financial consequences for the Marcos family. With this veritable sword of Damocles hanging over him, Marcos is not someone who would dare cross Washington. Indeed, when it comes to negotiating an independent path between two superpowers, he is the wrong person at the wrong place at the wrong time—which is another way of saying that from Washington's point of view, he's the right person at the right place at the right time.[187]

The Cyberlibel Drama

The Duterte camp, however, was not through with me. On August 8, 2022, police showed up at my residence and arrested me on the charges of libel and cyberlibel, or making false or defamatory claims about someone on the internet, that Sara Duterte's press relations officer had filed against me during the campaign. But it was the misfortune of the Duterte gang that August 8 and the next two days were slow-news days both locally and internationally. My arrest turned out to be one of the few newsworthy events happening, so the arrest of the electoral rival of the Philippine vice president was front page news everywhere. The arresting officers, worried about the impact of a photo of a 76-year-old former congressman in handcuffs, actually offered not to place handcuffs on me as per SOP, but I insisted, with my eye

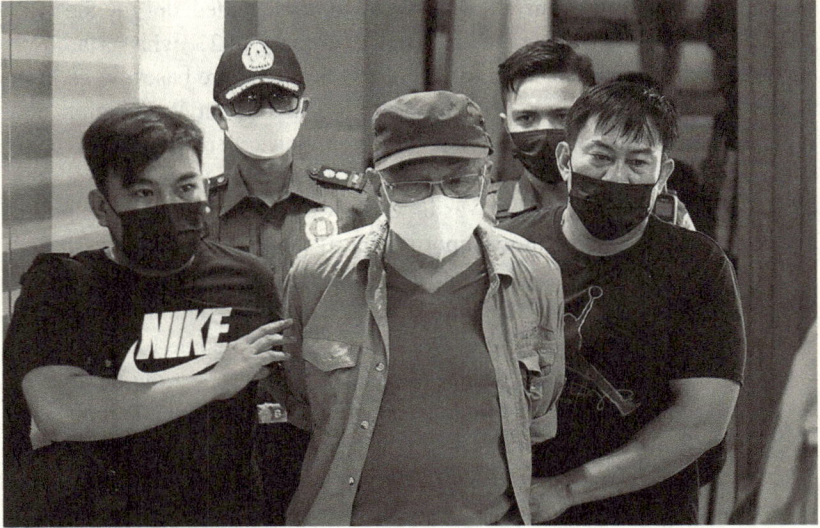

On 8 August 2022, police showed up at Walden's residence
and arrested him on charges of cyber libel.

COURTESY OF RUSSELL PALMA, *PHILIPPINE STAR*

on generating public sympathy, saying "I do not expect special treatment. Handcuff me since that's what the law says." It paid off.

I received emails from the most distant places—from Iceland, Nigeria, and Norway—expressing concern and solidarity. Among scores of organizations, the progressive bloc of the European Parliament and the ASEAN Parliamentarians for Human Rights denounced my arrest, and Amnesty International reported that the move was "widely regarded as aimed at silencing an opposition voice."[188] With all this negative publicity, the vice president publicly responded that she had nothing to do with my arrest and that I should quit "obsessing over" her.[189]

Over the next year and a half, I had to make periodic trips to Davao City, the Dutertes' bailiwick, for pre-trial proceedings and the trial itself, the first session of which took place on February 26, 2024. My legal team, composed of Attys Estrella ("Star") Elamparo, Danny Balucos, and Dexter Lopoz, had decided that rather than seek a change of venue, we would take our chances with the presiding judge of Regional Trial Court 10, Retrina Fuentes, who had a reputation of being a no-nonsense professional. We also decided to challenge the constitutionality of the cyberlibel law itself and filed a petition to the Supreme Court to decriminalize libel, citing its increasing use by political figures to silence dissent.[190]

Walden with Jeremy Corbyn in London in January 2024, as the former UK Labour Party leader demands the dropping of cyber libel charges against Walden.

Apparently acting on recently issued judicial guidelines, Judge Fuentes urged both parties to agree to a private settlement. The other side would not agree to a private apology, so we explored the possibility of a public apology. After months of exchanging drafts, we seemed to be on the verge of a mutually acceptable draft public apology that Atty Lopoz and the private prosecutor had crafted. I called my team for a final discussion. I did not expect the intensity of the exchange that followed. After the meeting, I decided to pull the plug on the negotiations. I laid out my reasons in the groupchat:

> I would like to apologize to Dexter for putting him in a quandary. It was at my urging that he went into negotiations with the other side for a public apology. I was definitely leaning towards a private settlement, but I wanted to make sure that the compromise statement was acceptable, and this was the reason I asked for a meeting with the whole team. I was confident the statement could be fixed, as Dexter assured us. It was the final discussion that made me move against accepting it.
>
> Three considerations were decisive. One was advanced by Star, which was that, however we worded the statement, most of the media will likely interpret it as an admission of guilt on my part. Second, related to this, I was convinced that Tupas and the

vice president's camp would spin the statement to reflect badly on me, and it would be naive not to expect them to do this. The third was, ironically, triggered by Dexter himself when he said that he had been shocked that I was open to making a public apology, given my past of consistent resistance to unjust acts for which he had admired me. That brought me to my senses. Was I really willing to make a move that, however legally justifiable, would nevertheless be widely seen as a deviation, indeed a reversal of my past political record? It would be seen as a surrender to forces I had been fighting all my life. My situation would be like that of a marathoner who gives up in the last few laps after leading the pack all the way. What is more, it will be this act that people will remember, not what I have done up to this point. Who remembers Raul Manglapus' record now? But people remember the horrible comment he made that "If you're going to get raped anyway, you might as well relax and enjoy it." I do not want to suffer the same fate. In other words, I have a responsibility to all those who have supported me and my brand of principled politics not to issue the proposed apology.

I am sure Dexter will understand my position, though it is unlikely the judge will; she will probably think I'm being pig headed or have an inflated sense of self-importance. (I would, however, love to be surprised.) So, Dexter, I apologize for asking you to embark on a course of action at a moment of clouded judgment on my part. I want to assure everyone in the team that I am now resolved to pursue the case all the way to the Supreme Court. Thanks for your continued confidence in me.

End of an Era

But fate is kind. It balances the bad with the good. In the midst of my legal imbroglio, while I was in Kyoto, Japan, on a research fellowship, I woke up to an email from Amnesty International Philippines that I had been named its "Most Distinguished Human Rights Defender" Awardee. In receiving the award in Manila a few weeks later, I joked, "What took you so long? Now I can die in peace." Well, it was not totally a joke since I considered the award the most prestigious of all I had been given. I then proceeded to give my acceptance speech, which urged that pivotal neoliberal thinkers and technocrats be arraigned before the International Criminal Court for their role in the destruction of the economies of the Global South:

Most of my life's work has been devoted to intellectually and politically demolishing the ideology and policies of neoliberalism that have wreaked so much havoc not only among our people but in countries throughout the world. The destruction of our manufacturing and the devastation of our agriculture has led to so much poverty and inequality and sheer misery, leaving so many of our youth with no other choice but to abandon our ruined country.

To borrow the distinction made by the philosopher Isaiah Berlin, there are negative rights, such as the right not to be tortured, and positive rights, or those that contribute to our full development as human beings. Human rights campaigns have traditionally focused on negative rights, that is, the protection of people from repression and persecution. I believe it is time we also campaign against individuals and institutions that violate the people's positive rights. Neoliberal policies such as those that have been imposed by the World Bank and International Monetary Fund, institutionalized in the Philippine political economy, and rationalized by a succession of economic managers and economists, have created massive poverty and inequality that have prevented millions of our fellow Filipinos over the last five decades from their full development as human beings, because they have destroyed, disarticulated, and disintegrated the country's base of physical survival, that is, the economy. That is a crime.

Neoliberal policies are now discredited. The Washington Consensus is in the junk heap. No self-respecting economic manager, except perhaps in the Philippines, any longer invokes the so-called "magic of the market" or the so-called benefits of free trade. Yet in so many countries, and not just in the Philippines, neoliberal policies continue to be the default mode, like the proverbial dead hand of the engineer on the throttle of a speeding train. They continue to inflict severe damage on the life chances of millions of Filipinos because they have been institutionalized.

Those who have been responsible for destroying economies cannot be allowed to just walk away from the wreckage, just as that monster Duterte cannot be allowed to just get away with spilling the blood of 27,000 Filipinos. The bureaucrats and technocrats of the IMF and World Bank, their local accomplices particularly in the Department of Finance and National Economic Development Authority, as well as the ideologues of neoliberalism that have spread the false gospel from their perches in such institutions as the University of Chicago and the UP School of Economics must also be brought before the International Criminal Court (ICC).

Duterte's hands are bloody, but so are the hands of these white-collar criminals very dirty. Like those bombing crews that drop their lethal payloads from 27,000 feet or the remote controller that directs a drone to destroy a wedding party in Pakistan from thousands of miles away in Nevada, USA, these people are not exempted from guilt owing to their distance from the sites of death, destruction, harrowing poverty, and misery.

It is high time we seek justice for economic crimes. It is high time we cease honoring such criminals with Nobel Prizes in Economics but bring them instead to the ICC. If the arraignment of such economic criminals cannot be immediately be done owing to the need to amend the Rome statute, then let us at least establish a "Hall of Infamy" where we can enshrine such dead and living stars of neoliberalism as the Nobel Prize laureate Milton Friedman, the ideological soulmate of the General Augusto Pinochet; Michel Camdessus and Christine Legarde, the best known faces of IMF-imposed austerity; former World Bank President Robert McNamara, who conspired with the dictator Marcos to make the Philippines one of the guinea pigs of structural adjustment; and Pascal Lamy and Mike Moore, who spearheaded the drive to imprison the global South in the iron cage of free trade, the World Trade Organization.

I would also push for the inclusion in such a Hall of Infamy local luminaries of technocratic neoliberalism, the people who worked with international technocrats to condemn us to permanent debt slavery, destroy our manufacturing, and bring our agriculture to a terminal state. Here I would include the economic managers and economists Jesus Estanislao, Gerry Sicat, Cesar Virata, Bernie Villegas, and Carlos Dominguez.

And, of course, one must not forget Cielito Habito, who as National Economic Development Authority chief almost single handedly wiped out Philippine manufacturing with his push to bring down average tariffs to 4–6% simply to prove that Filipinos could take economic pain better than Pinochet's Chicago Boys in Chile, who did not allow tariffs to go below 11%. Nor must we overlook the WTO-USAID mercenary Ramon Clarete, who famously sought to sugarcoat the impending murder of our agricultural sector by claiming that Philippines' joining the WTO's Agreement on Agriculture would result in 500,000 new jobs every year in the countryside!

But some people might object: Habito and Clarete are too mild-mannered individuals to deserve being tagged as economic criminals. So was the Nazi Adolf Eichmann, whom Hannah Arendt famously described as representing "the banality of evil." Others might say, well they were wrong, but were they not well-intentioned? This excuse does not even deserve an answer since Marcos Sr. and Duterte saw themselves as well-intentioned as they went about their grisly business. The road to hell, one must repeat again and again, is paved with good intentions.

Being tried at the ICC or honored with membership at the Hall of Infamy would be a lesson to all that bad ideas and bad policies have consequences, often devastating ones—that you cannot play academic and policy games with the lives of millions of people.

Let me end by demanding the release of my fellow Ignite awardee Senator Leila de Lima, packing off Duterte to the ICC jail in The Hague, an end to impunity, and the dismantling of all those neoliberal policies that have destroyed our economy and brought so much misery to our people. And, again, thank you Amnesty.[191]

With so many friends, comrades, and relatives in attendance who had accompanied me in many campaigns over the decades, it felt like that evening, July 16, 2023, marked the end of an era.

Unplugging People from the Matrix

Still, even as I gave the speech, troubling thoughts persisted. Was I preaching to the choir, to people in the room who already agreed with me? Outside that room, how many people would even understand what I was saying? Had neoliberalism become so normalized that people would not think of neoliberal policies as being the reason the economy had become a basket case. I felt like the Keanu Reeves' character, Neo, seeking desperately to unplug humans from the Matrix where they were fed a false dreamy reality that killed off their desire to rebel.

There were a number of reasons why neoliberalism appeared to be the "natural order" of things, as I tried to explain in Chapter 8, but the principal one was that people did not see it as a coherent system or paradigm, so that crisis in one front, like the destruction of manufacturing owing to the adoption of super-low tariffs, was seen as a discrete failure, not a systemic failure. The challenge was for our team to do a better job making our case that we were up against an ideological system, not random mistakes, if we were to succeed in unplugging people from the neoliberal matrix.

18. A Luta Continua

"POLYCRISES" are the distinguishing mark of our age, argues the prominent Columbia University historian Adam Tooze. My friend Alex Callinicos, one of today's leading Marxist thinkers, writes that we are on the brink of a new "age of catastrophe," much like the 1930s and 1940s. Both refer to the emergence of simultaneous crises that interact and amplify one another. Among these are the crises of global warming, global capitalism, the international liberal order underpinned by U.S. power, the return of fascism, and the geopolitical competition between the United States and China.

The signature and overarching crisis of our times is, of course, the climate crisis. Like so many, I am alarmed by the apocalyptic threat global warming poses to the planet. My engagement with it, however, has not been so much via active participation in global campaigns as in periodically writing about its dangers, the minuscule efforts of the big polluters to take action to reverse it, and the false solutions that global capital has offered, like geoengineering and carbon trading. When it comes to active campaigning, I am filled with admiration for the leading role played by fellow Filipinos like Lidy Nacpil, Tony Lavina, Yeb Sano, and Red Constantino, who have earned a good name for the country owing to their commitment and command of the key issues, especially their insistence that any solution to the climate crisis must involve "climate justice"—that is, place at the heart of negotiations the fact that it is those which have had the least greenhouse gas emissions—the countries of the Global South—that stand to suffer the most from the emissions of the big polluters in the Global North.

When it comes to global issues, my activist and analytical work in the last few years has focused on the deepening crisis of the United States, the ascent of China, and the threat of fascism globally.

Tracking Fascism Globally

As I've written earlier, I have had a long-time interest in movements of the far right ever since I studied the fascist movement that ousted Allende from power in 1973, an academic interest that has coexisted with a strong determination to keep the far right out of power.

But even if one did not have a special academic or political interest in the far right, you could not avoid dealing with them if you were jousting with neoliberalism and globalization and their consequences.

Why was fascism making a comeback? My first attempt to comprehensively deal with the phenomenon was my writing the book *Counterrevolution: The Global Rise of the Far Right,* which came out in 2019.[192] This book, which was a product of a project on agrarian transformations led by Jun Borras of the Institute of Social Studies in The Hague, provoked a great deal of interest, making me a kind of fixture in Zoom webinars, which took the place of physical mobilizations and face-to-face meetings during the Covid 19 pandemic. My commentaries on the electoral triumph of Donald Trump in the United States in 2016 and the January 6, 2021 attempt by his followers to take over the Capitol, apparently resonated with many Americans.[193] Important in helping me to keep my pulse on where America was headed were my courses at the State University of New York at Binghamton which I taught for six weeks every year, where students would share how they and their families and friends were reacting to Trump's tumultuous presidency. Also helpful were long discussions on trends in the political economy of the U.S. with colleagues Ravi Palat, Bill Martin, Denis O'Hearn, Leslie Gates, Marina Sitrin, and Josh Price.

A central point I made—one that was also made by others—was that while there were other factors explaining the rise of the far right in the U.S. and Europe, such as racism and anti-migrant sentiment, the neoliberal policies were a central cause. Adopted by center-right and center-left governments, these had led to stagnant incomes, unemployment and underemployment, a tremendous increase in inequality, and consequently the growing appeal of the far right for the bypassed masses. "By preaching that it would lead to the best of all possible worlds for America and everyone else if capital were free to search for the lowest priced labor around," I argued, "neoliberal theory provided the justification for shipping manufacturing capacity and jobs to China and elsewhere in the global South, leading to rapid deindustrialization, with manufacturing jobs falling from some 18 million in 1979 to 12 million in 2009."[194]

Trump smelled an opportunity here that a Democratic leadership tied to Wall Street ignored, and he made anti-globalization a centerpiece of his 2016 electoral platform. And, by tying anti-globalization to anti-migrant rhetoric and dog-whistle anti-black appeals, he was able to break through to the white working class that had already given signals it was ready to be racially swayed as early as the Reagan era in the 1980s.

The January 6 attempted coup dealt a body blow to

the once celebrated American way of succession in power via the ballot box, with a large sector of the electorate that has marched in lock step with their leader in refusing to accept the results of the presidential elections...Joe Biden will be seated this time around, but he may be regarded as illegitimate in the eyes of the 74 million Americans under the spell of Donald Trump. Future electoral contests for power may well end up being decided by a strong dose of street warfare, as the U.S. goes the way of Germany's ill-fated Weimar Republic. The violent storming of the Capitol by a Trumpian mob underlined the face of crises to come.[195]

I did not hesitate to baptize the far right in the Global North and the Global South with the "F" word. This apparently was the reason I was invited by the famous Cambridge Union for a debate on the topic "This House Believes That We Are Witnessing a Global Fascist Resurgence" on April 29, 2021, where I would speak for the affirmative. Of course, a great incentive for agreeing to participate was that one of my intellectual heroes, John Maynard Keynes, had been involved in a famous Cambridge Union debate. Joining me in the debate by Zoom that evening were New York University Professor Ruth Ben Ghiat, Russian journalist Masha Gessen, staff writer for the *New Yorker*, the prominent historian of the Second World War Sir Richard Evans, and Isabel Hernandez and Sam Rubinstein, two Cambridge University students. The Cambridge Independent carried the news the next day that "the motion was carried with 38 votes in favour, 28 against, and 2 abstentions."[196] Thank god, I didn't let Keynes down.

The Neoliberal Remaking of the American Economy

The crisis of the American economy has been the subject of much of my writing over the last few years, and at the center of my analysis was the crisis of profitability of American capitalism.

In the mid-1970s, the so-called *trente glorieuses* or 30 golden years of USA-led global capitalism came to an end, with the coincidence of stagnation and inflation that came to be known as stagflation. What the central cause of stagflation was continues to be debated, with the likely chain of events being more intense competition globally, leading to over-capacity, indicating an "over-accumulation of capital," and resulting in "cost-push" inflation, as Big

Capital and Big Labor engaged in a contest of strength, with one side deploying price increases to overcome the advantage of the other's wage gains via union power, to maintain or increase their respective shares of a decreasing rates of profit. What was indisputable was that there was a sharp decline in the rate of profit, from around 14% in 1963 to 6% in the early 1980s.

Economists who broke with the reigning Keynesian consensus saw the progressive, New Deal constraints on corporate profitability as the central cause of stagflation, and they developed a policy to counter it, matched by a counter-narrative, which became known as neoliberalism.

Neoliberal political economy in the U.S. had three key thrusts: reverse income distribution, financialization, and globalization.

The idea behind reverse income distribution was to reinvigorate capital by radically raising the rate of profit. This would be done by deregulation, halting real wage growth, cutting transfer payments from the rich to social security programmes for workers, and destroying the political power of labour. Reverse income redistribution also included lowering the marginal tax rate on the highest incomes from 91% in 1950–1963 to 39.6% in 1987–2002. One consequence of these policies was a decline in the share of wages in national income from close to 60% in 1977 to around 55% in 2011.

The second neoliberal response to the crisis of profitability was financialization, or channelling much investment to finance, where the return was much higher than in other sectors of the economy. Financialisation resulted in a situation where the financial sector (appropriately named "FIRE"—finance, insurance, and real estate) accounted for only 8% of U.S. gross domestic product but raked in 30% of total profits, with some analysts estimating as much as 50%.

The third thrust of neoliberalism was intensified globalization, a key factor of which was shifting manufacturing operations to places where capital could extract much greater value from workers who could be hired at much lower wages than in the U.S. Among these three principal ways of shoring up the rate of profit, the globalization of the productive process, or the marriage of capital with labor not located in the U.S. industrial heartland, appears to have been the most decisive, and here China became a central actor.

The neoliberal restructuring of the U.S. economy ended up as a disaster for American capitalism and a boon for China.

China and Me

I think my fascination with China began when, on a trip to Hong Kong in 1967 to work out a deal with Tuttle Publishing Company for the Institute of Philippine Culture, I went to the crown colony's border with Shenzen province and peered at the border guards through binoculars. China was then shrouded with mystery as news of a "Cultural Revolution" filtered to the outside world, with anti-communist propaganda chatter about bodies floating down the Pearl River to the South China Sea.

In the succeeding years, China was filtered to me through the prism of the Philippines' National Democratic Revolution, of which I was a partisan. The lessons of Mao's Long March and his strategy of surrounding the city from the countryside were fundamental, as were texts like Mao's "On Liberalism." So the main images one absorbed were that of China of the 1930s and 1940s, not that of Cultural Revolution-era China.

In the 1980s and 1990s, China's turn to capitalism held no attraction for me, and it was only in the 2000s that I was able to take a more detached view of the country, when Focus established its China program. China, I realized, was copying the Asian NICs' strategy of state-led capitalist development and telescoping into a few years developmental processes and crises that had taken centuries to unfold in the West. What was different from the NICs' experience was that China had a strong state that was beholden to no western power and thus had the confidence to invite foreign capital and impose conditions the latter had to follow, including the transfer of advanced technology, in return for offering foreign corporations super-cheap Chinese labor.

The trade-off of cheap labor for foreign capital and advanced technology was not without its costs. And they were considerable. A recent estimate shows that for the period 1960–2018, among developing countries, China suffered the greatest loss in terms of value transfer—or unequal exchange—the figure coming to some $19 trillion. But from the CCP's perspective, the cost in the short and medium term of allowing global capital to exploit China's labour in return for comprehensive development of its economy—and securing its own legitimacy in the process—was a devil's bargain that proved worth making. Moreover, by the end of the second decade of the twenty-first century, the relative power of China's foreign corporate enablers had been reduced by a decade-long stagnation in the U.S. economy followed by a COVID-19 recession, and by China's technological advances.

A number of visits to Beijing gave me the impression of dizzying change. In 2016, I began to seriously study China, coming out with my book, *Paper Dragons: China and the Next Crash*, in 2019.[197] Then followed a stream of articles and monographs that were meant to assist progressives in understanding what was going on and how to relate to China politically.

Not surprisingly, I noted, despite an accumulation of crises associated with capitalist growth, China was becoming a model for developing countries, its attraction being enhanced by its generous loan and assistance program, though this was not without its problems. Still, the World Bank's revelation of China's having reduced the poverty rate to two percent, coupled with such impressive appurtenances as developing the world's most advanced high-speed train network, was electric.

It also became clear that the obverse of the super-industrialization of China was the de-industrialization of the U.S. as American transnational corporations transferred their industrial corporations to the former, creating unemployment in the mid-West and key parts of the United States. Combined with the financialization of the U.S. economy, deindustrialization contributed to political crisis, leading to the termination of the de facto alliance between China and American TNCs in 2017, when Donald Trump ascended to the U.S. presidency and initiated a trade cum technology war with Beijing that was continued and intensified by his successor, Joseph Biden.

But with the Chinese economy accounting for 28 percent of all growth worldwide in the five years from 2013 to 2018—more than twice the share of the United States, according to the International Monetary Fund—China's ascent is virtually impossible to stop. Indeed, by some measures, like "purchasing power parity," it is now the world's largest economy.

In October 2021, on the occasion of the 100th anniversary of the founding of the Chinese Communist Party, I dared to offer some friendly though critical advice to the country's leadership:[198]

> One piece of advice has to do with the much-touted BRI. The BRI projects have to be designed to be more environmentally and climate-friendly, and more attuned to people's needs, instead of being what Arundhati Roy has called "gigantistic" top-down projects reminiscent of the mid-20th century.
>
> Also, China's commitments to reduce greenhouse gas emissions should be more radical in scope and speed, something that is demanded of the world's current champion in greenhouse gas emissions. Beijing should likewise end the practice of bringing in thousands of Chinese workers to work in projects it funds in Africa and elsewhere and hire and rapidly train many more local workers.
>
> Moreover, China should stop grabbing maritime formations such as Mischief Reef and Scarborough Shoal that belong to the Exclusive Economic Zone of the Philippines and making the outrageous claim that 90 percent of the South China Sea belongs to it. These moves are illegal and unjustifiable, even if they are understandable as strategic defensive moves to counter the very

real military threat posed by the U.S. 7th Fleet's domination of the South China Sea and West Philippine Sea. Instead, it should work with ASEAN for a treaty demilitarizing the Sea to eliminate the U.S. threat.

Finally, Beijing must end its forced cultural assimilation of the Uighurs in Xinjiang. And while Hong Kong and Taiwan are indisputably part of China—a fact not disputed by the international community, it must be stressed—it must be cognizant of the right of the peoples of these areas to have a say in the way they are governed, especially given the unavoidable issues of national identity created by their long separation from the rest of the country by colonialism.

But I ended by saying that while China has real problems, both domestic and in some of its relations with the global South, "[O]verall, Beijing's rise has been a large plus for most of the world. It has become a global economic force powering the economies of smaller countries, and it has achieved this with little, if any, of the force and violence that marked the rise to hegemony of the West. It has provided the countries of the global South alternative opportunities for aid and finance that have contributed to their becoming much less dependent on the U.S. and the rest of the West." I concluded:

But beyond these has been its inspiring lesson to so many countries: that with determination, grit, and organization, it is possible not only to break western domination but to use the West as a means of achieving national resurrection. In the long view, the rise of China is but the latest stage of the global South's 150-year-old struggle for decolonization to end the over 500-year-old yoke of western capitalist hegemony.

The U.S. Is Determined to Remain Number 1

The problem for China and the world is that the United States is not willing to be toppled from its position as the world's hegemon, even if China has disclaimed any ambition to displace it. And Washington has shown that it is increasingly willing to deploy military force to preserve its eroding status.

Similar to its push to incorporate Ukraine into NATO, the U.S. has increasingly taken a stance that appears to be aimed at provoking Beijing into some sort of military response. Biden has sent American warships through the narrow 130-kilometer-wide Taiwan Straits separating China and Taiwan.

276 | *Global Battlefields*

He has beefed up the U.S. military presence in the Philippines, adding four more bases there to the five the U.S. already has.

Taking their cue from the administration, U.S. military leaders have been even more confrontational in their rhetoric. Particularly alarming has been a recent leaked memo from General Mike Minihan, who leads the U.S. Air Mobility Command, declaring, "My gut tells me we will fight in 2025." Minihan, it bears noting, was not the first member of the U.S. command to predict conflict with China in the immediate future. Admiral Michael M. Gilday, Chief of Naval Operations, said in October 2022 that the U.S. should prepare to fight Beijing in 2022 or 2023. It may well be that Washington wishes to provoke a conflict with China before the latter can achieve military parity with the U.S., which Chinese President Xi Jin Ping estimates might be achieved in 2049.

Of course, China's case has not been helped by its actions in the South China Sea, of which it claims 90 percent. But as I made clear during internet debates and in Chapter 14, these moves have been defensive in intent—a desire to protect its exposed southeast and southern coasts from attacks from the scores of U.S. bases on the first island chain extending from Japan to Korea to Okinawa to Guam to the Philippines. Where Beijing has made a big mistake has been its decision to solve its strategic dilemma unilaterally, by violating the rights of the five other countries that border the South China Sea, instead of getting a multilateral agreement to demilitarize the area, which I proposed in the *New York Times* article mentioned in Chapter 16.[199]

Even without conscious intent, as I pointed out in article after article, relying on the balance of power to maintain the peace in the South China Sea, where there are no rules of the game, is dangerous, for without rules, an accidental ship collision between the aircraft and ships of China and the U.S. that play the game of "chicken," where ships or planes head for each other, only to swerve at the last minute, can escalate to higher level of conflict without prior intent of the parties involved, as was the case in Europe on the eve of the outbreak of hostilities during the First World War.

To the world at large, however, it was hard to avoid the reality that the U.S. was intentionally playing offense to China's defense, and that a desire to be top dog at all costs was driving Washington, leading to a dangerous situation since rational calculus was playing second fiddle to irrational passion.

America and Me

The geopolitical conflict swirling around my country triggered an assessment of my personal relationship to America.

Looking back at the 78 years since I was born in 1945, I realize that the arc of my life has paralleled that of the United States. I was born at the very beginning of the post-war period when the United States assumed the role of leader of the capitalist world as Europe and Asia lay in ruins. I am nearing sunset, just as is America, now in the midst of its decline as the global hegemon. All phases of my life have seen me engaged with the U.S. as an empire, capitalist power, and cultural force. That relationship has at times been benign, oftentimes antagonistic, always absorbing.

The two arcs may coincide timewise, but they do not do so in terms of substance. America's arc has been one of aggression but mine has been an arc of resistance.

As I negotiated my way through Philippine society and culture, I found that they were intimately twined with my country's former colonial overseer. My parents were lovers of American pop culture whose perfect command of English they passed on to their children. My education in an American Jesuit enclave brought me to an exposure to all things western in the realm of ideas, often at the expense of things native, and growing up in the fifties meant going to Hollywood movies and absorbing the music of Nat King Cole, Frank Sinatra, Elvis Presley, and the other American kings and queens of pop and rock.

Yet I was also aware of the perilous side to being in the American sphere of influence. I still remember how during the Cuban Missile Crisis, the whole family waited with bated breath as Soviet ships approached the U.S. warships that were determined to board them should they ignore Washington's unilaterally imposed quarantine. The two giant bases we hosted, Subic Naval Base and Clark Air Force Base, my brothers told me, made the Philippines a prime target for the "atomic bomb."

The height of the Vietnam War saw me in the U.S. as a graduate student. Vietnam was the beginning of my political education, the start of my disenchantment with America, which was no longer the country that "gave" the Philippines democracy according to popular mythology but rather the friend of a dictator, Ferdinand Marcos, Sr., whom I was dedicated to ousting from power as a member of the Communist Party of the Philippines. I also witnessed how the "thirty golden years" of post-war capitalism ended in the mire of stagflation in the mid-seventies. The sense of the end of the unending prosperity promised by American capitalism was brought home to me in Princeton as I queued for gas like everyone else following the eruption of the Arab-Israeli War in 1974.

The shame of defeat in Vietnam, the political disarray triggered by Watergate, and the mess of stagflation receded during Reagan era, while the collapse of the Soviet Bloc in 1989 along with the seeming restoration of economic health by the "light touch regulation" of Fed Chairman Alan Greenspan appeared to give the U.S. a second wind in the 1990s. But by this time, I had become a full-fledged activist against the American empire and the global capitalist system it guarded.

The dominance of finance capital in the U.S. was paralleled in the Global South by the IMF and World Bank's imposition of structural adjustment, pro-market policies. But all was not well with neoliberalism, and the first sign of this was the Asian financial crisis of 1997. The second, equally dramatic crisis was the collapse of Third Ministerial Meeting of the World Trade Organization in 1999, one brought about by resistance from civil society and developing country governments.

I was a participant in Seattle protest as well as other protests against globalization, the biggest being the Battle of Genoa in 2001. 9/11 was the beginning of the end of unchallenged U.S. hegemony though we did not realize it at the time, since the Bush Jr administration took Osama bin Laden's bait and drove the U.S. into unwinnable wars in Afghanistan and the Middle East. These years saw me constantly on the move internationally as both an anti-war and anti-globalization activist.

The 2008 global financial crisis exposed the hollowing out of the U.S. economy by neoliberal policies even as China, having become a favored site of U.S. transnational capital, leaped from strength to strength. From 2010 to 2017, the crisis of liberal democracy in the U.S. and Europe unfolded, fueled by the toxic brew of economic insecurity created neoliberal policies, racism, and nativism. I was never a believer in Fukuyama's thesis that liberal democracy was the end of history, but the rise to power of Donald Trump, Jair Bolsonaro in Brazil, and Rodrigo Duterte in the Philippines was nevertheless a cause for surprise.

My presence in the global frontlines as both an activist and academic wound down briefly as I joined the Philippine House of Representatives in 2009. But even as I focused on domestic issues, my jousting with the empire continued. I sought unsuccessfully to get the administration I was allied with to follow an independent foreign policy as China and the U.S. squared off in the South China Sea. The increasingly close alliance between Washington and Manila was one of the reasons I resigned in protest from the Philippine House of Representatives in 2015.

The ascendancy of Donald Trump and Rodrigo Duterte in the period 2010 to 2022 found me fighting fascism in the home front even as I tracked its rise in the U.S. and globally. I was also drawn to look more deeply at the roots, dynamics, and consequences of the geopolitical and geoeconomic competition between Washington and Beijing, not least because the Pentagon was converting my homeland into the forward base of its military containment of China. As Washington under Biden adopted an ever more hostile policy towards China, things have become increasingly dangerous since the U.S.'s "grand strategy" at present is grounded solely on preventing its decline as the global hegemon. Perhaps, nothing better expresses Washington's unvarnished, resentful imperial stance than those famous lines from Dylan Thomas:

> *Do not go gentle into that good night,*
> *Old age should burn and rave at close of day,*
> *Rage, rage against the dying of light.*

These were my thoughts as I saw Biden's televised address at the NATO Summit in Washington on July 12, 2024. He repeated former U.S. Secretary of State Madeleine Albright's description of America being the "indispensable country" whose role was to preserve the world for peace and democracy against authoritarian personalities like Vladimir Putin and Chinese President Xi Jin Ping. It was a desperate performance not only to save his candidacy for president but to legitimize the flailing, now anachronistic order that emerged at the end of the Second World War.

A few weeks later, after Biden passed the baton to Vice President Kamala Harris to serve as the standard bearer of the Democratic Party, I placed this post on Facebook:

> Does the Global South Have a Stake in the Outcome of the U.S. Elections?
> My problem with the U.S. elections is that is that the two forces in contention do not offer attractive alternatives for the Global South. Harris represents the old, anachronistic Cold War liberal international order that seeks to contain China militarily, pledges full military support for Israel, disdains negotiations for peace in Ukraine and indeed would drag our governments to the conflict there, and seeks continuation of the "multilateral economic order" that has kept the Global South down for the last 70 years. Trump and Vance offer a Fortress America agenda whose thrust is to disengage from what Trump has called "shithole countries," one that is focused on keeping the rest of the world out of the United States, and using unilateral military strikes like those employed by the Israelis to discipline those outside the Wall, meaning us. . . .

True, the Harris-Trump battle may have contrasting "visions" for the United States on domestic issues, but I ask, is it more of the same neoliberal pro-Wall Street/Silicon Valley policies cloaked with pious democratic rhetoric versus insurgent fascism that feeds on the failures of neoliberalism and liberal democracy? Fascism's best ally is a liberal democratic elite that presides over an economic order that has radically increased inequality while piously asserting it is the best defense against fascism.[200]

On November 5, 2024, Americans went to the polls and the majority decided to bring Trump back following a miserable four years under Biden and Harris. I was certain the next four years would be bad for the climate, for American democracy, for minorities, and for women. What the mercurial Trump had in store for the Global South was much less predictable.

Troubled Transition

The world, it is often said, is undergoing a hegemonic transition from the U.S. to China as the dominant global power. I am not so sure. With the U.S. in economic decline but determined to use its military power to preserve its position, and with China unwilling to step into the role of glonal hegemon, perhaps we should be thinking about another possibility. Perhaps we should be looking not so much at a hegemonic transition but at the emergence of a hegemonic vacuum akin to but not exactly the same as that which followed the First World War in the 20th Century, when the weakened Western European states had ceased to have the capacity to restore their pre-war global hegemony while the U.S. did not follow through on Woodrow Wilson's push for Washington to assert hegemonic political and ideological leadership.

Within such a vacuum or stalemate, the U.S.-China relationship would continue to be critical, but with neither actor being able to decisively address current trends: extreme weather events, growing protectionism, the decay of the multilateral system that the United States put in place during its apogee, the resurgence of progressive movements in Latin America, the rise of what the West deems "authoritarian" states and the likely emergence of an alliance among them to displace a faltering liberal international order, and increasingly uncontrolled tensions between radical Islamist regimes in the Middle East and Israel, due to its genocidal actions in Gaza, and its ongoing provocations seeking to resolve its dilemma by provoking U.S. support for a greater regional war.

Both conservative and liberal policymakers in the U.S. paint this scenario to underline why the world needs a hegemon, with the former advocating a unilateral Goliath who does not hesitate to use threat and force to enforce order and the latter preferring a liberal Goliath who, to slightly revise Teddy Roosevelt's famous saying, speaks sweetly but carries a big stick.

There are, however, those, and I am one of them, who view the current crisis of U.S. hegemony as offering not so much anarchy as opportunity. While there are risks and great dangers involved, a hegemonic stalemate or a hegemonic vacuum, opens up the path to a world where power could more decentralized, where there could be greater freedom of political and economic maneuver for smaller, traditionally less privileged actors from the Global South playing off the two superpowers against one another, where a truly multilateral order could be constructed through cooperation rather than being imposed through either unilateral or liberal hegemony.

Yes, the crisis of U.S. hegemony may lead to an even deeper crisis, but it may also lead to opportunity for us.

Having said that, I would not underestimate the dangers during the very fluid period we are in now. The Italian Marxist Antonio Gramsci wrote something about his era, the 1920s and 1930s: "The old world is dying, and the new world struggles to be born: now is the time of monsters." I think that is also an apt description or our era. Monsters will be encountered during the transition away from the liberal capitalist internationalist order.

Preventing a Pacific Apocalypse

There are multiple crises facing the planet, but I have decided to focus my activist intervention on preventing war in the Western Pacific, and most critical in this regard will be the role of citizens in the frontline states from which the U.S. deploys its offensive power towards the Asian mainland—Japan, Okinawa, South Korea, and the Philippines.

With this in mind, I took advantage of my sojourn at Kyoto University in the first half of 2023 to visit various places in Japan at the invitation of anti-war and social justice organizations. I was brought to a seaborne "tour" of the giant U.S. naval base at Yokosuka, where a U.S. patrol boat shadowed us to make sure we did not cross the invisible line on the water demarcating U.S. territory. I witnessed military aircraft taking off every five minutes at the Andersen Air Force Base in Okinawa. I gave anti-war speeches in Tokyo, Yokohama, Kyoto, and Hiroshima.

I had two lasting impressions from these events. First, that Japan continues to be a militarily occupied country—one that the Philippines may well become if the Marcos, Jr government continues to outsource its defense and foreign policies to Washington. Second, outside of Okinawa, which plays host to one fourth of the U.S. military presence in Japan, an effective citizens' movement against war still has to be built in that country.

When I raised this observation, people would ask, what happened to the U.S. bases in the Philippines that you drove out in the 1990s? Good question, to which I had no satisfactory answer, except that whatever it takes, we need to work together across borders to begin reconstructing that force for peace that is so necessary to keep the Pacific pacific.

19. A Reckoning

IT'S BEEN OVER fifty years since I leaped, with little regard for the likely consequences, into that opening in the chain of protesters confronting the police during the blockade of the Institute for Defense Analysis in Princeton University. That act transformed me from being simply a critical intellectual into an activist. Ever since then, searching for the truth and acting to change the world have coexisted and driven me. It has been this tension between the demands of truth and the demands of action that has defined my life.

Acting transformed me, changed the world around me, and turned factoids into facts—as in Seattle in 1999, where a historic mobilization I was part of made the truth "true" by disrupting the dominant narrative and showing that the emperor of triumphalist globalization really had no clothes in a way that no critical study ever could.

But a critical intellectual stance was just as central in my relationship to the world and became a hardheaded barrier to taking action based on orthodox, flimsy, easy, or seductive analysis. I saw and wrote about the ugly reality of a middle class mobilized for counterrevolution that the left found it convenient to ignore or slight when confronted by it in Chile in 1973 and even in interpreting the Chilean tragedy afterwards. I became even more hardheaded after the left's boycotting the 1986 elections in the Philippines, owing to its seemingly impeccable reasoning that Washington would never abandon Marcos, led to a political disaster from which it never recovered. When Marx asserted, in his 11th thesis on Feuerbach, which has been my north star, that "philosophers have hitherto only *interpreted* the world in various ways; the point is to *change* it," he meant to act following one's critical interpretation of the world.

But the tension between truth and action has not been the only engine of my politics. There has also been a third force, and that is good, old-fashioned ethics, a moral stand that is relatively independent of reason, but whose absence would lead to pure instrumentalism in the alliance between truth and action, between reason and politics. It is this absence of a strong moral compass or its underdevelopment that has led to the self-inflicted tragedies of the left, such as the Stalinism in the Soviet Union or the "Anti-DPA (deep penetration agent) Campaign" in the Philippine left that took 2000 lives in the mid-eighties. Indeed, it was this latter tragedy that firmed up my conviction that the worth of an individual cannot be reduced solely to her or his "class position."

But instrumentalism can be just as corrosive in day-to-day parliamentary politics. The demands of power often make ethical compromises seductive, especially in the pursuit of worthy goals, but making one unprincipled compromise is often the first step on the slippery slope to the discrediting of one's politics. Cabinet members that serve a tyrant may not have bloody hands but they lose credibility nevertheless for remaining silent and uncritical while their boss murders thousands. Tribunes of the people are judged not only by what they can deliver to the people but how they deliver it, by their moral stance. As I said in my explanation for my resignation from the Philippines House of Representatives in March 2015,

> Being a progressive has several dimensions. It means having a vision about how society should be organized based on the values of equality, justice, solidarity, and sovereignty. It means having a political program to realize this vision. But it also means projecting an ethical, moral stance. And perhaps, at a time that people have become so cynical about visions and programs because words are cheap and because opportunism and corruption are so rife across the political spectrum, the distinguishing mark of a true progressive holding public office is her ethical behavior. For me, being a progressive in the corridors of power means, above all, being steadfast in holding on to one's principles and values, even if this means losing one's position, possessions, or life.

Phases of My Political Engagement

The tension among reason, action, and ethics has been one driving force of my political trajectory. Related to it has been the tension between myself as a revolutionary subject and the broader movement. As I noted earlier, when I discussed my separation from the Communist Party in the late eighties, there have been four discernible phases to my life as an engaged intellectual. There was my existentialist phase during my college years, where existentialism became the vehicle of a secular revolt as an individual against religious mysticism. But what I was committed to was still an abstract state of affairs best described as a "progressive order."

Then came that period when I was at Princeton and in Chile, where I became a Marxist and activist in pursuit of a now less diffuse, less abstract end called socialism, but one that thought and worked independently. This was followed by those 15 years, 1974–89, when my subjectivity was totally submerged in the collectivity, the Communist Party of the Philippines, where I was, for the most part, unconditionally and uncritically obedient to central party decisions—in the stereotyped manner of the party member governed by democratic centralism, as I described it earlier.

My departure from the party in 1989–90, triggered by the boycott error and *Ahos* purge, marked the recovery of subjectivity or more explicitly, the emergence of a critical subjectivity in relation to the collective that was paralleled by a philosophical and political valuation of the rights of the individual vis-a-vis the bigger movement. It did not mean a relapse into the independence of those only intellectually engaged, but the adoption of a more critical stance towards the organization or the movement even as one recognized and prized the latter's indispensability. It has also been accompanied by the acceptance of contingency and uncertainty and the fact that there is no such thing as the historical inevitability of the triumph of justice and reason.

I am now in that phase of my engagement where I am periodically assailed by doubt as to whether my fundamental values and beliefs are correct—for instance my long-standing conviction in the superiority of socialism, understood in a broad sense as a cooperative, democratic society that is not subordinate either to the market or authoritarian rule. But whenever doubts of this kind emerge, I counter them by telling myself that right and wrong in these fundamental questions is not an issue that can be settled empirically but must be resolved by a kind of Kierkegaardian leap of faith.

It is in this fourth and most likely final phase that I am at today—part of a movement, part of progressive organizations at various times, but not an uncritical part of them.

Reflecting on my political trajectory, I've often wondered if there was an historical personality that I really admired and might have modeled my life after. If there was one that I might have subconsciously chosen to emulate, it would most likely have been my college-era hero, Albert Camus, of whom it was written that,

> In Nazi-occupied Paris, he took risks in support of the Resistance but was honest enough to admit later that the risks had not been very great. A fundamental honesty was his hallmark. It led him to question whether the horrors of Nazism in any way legitimized the horrors of Communism. His answer to that question . . . set him at odds with Sartre and the whole of the French left, although Camus, with good reason, went on calling himself a man of the left until the end.[201]

I have been called many things, bad and good, but if there is one indisputable fact about my life, it is that I have always been true to the ideals of the Left.

Boomer or Generation R

I belong to what has been called the "boomer" generation—people who were born in the roughly 15 years after the end of the second World War when population growth accelerated as reproductive restraints that had been imposed by the Depression and war loosened. This was the period called the "thirty glorious years" when capitalist economies bounced from wartime destruction to post-war reconstruction.

We grew up at the height of the Cold War, when Armageddon often seemed to be just around the corner, and cut our political teeth during the Vietnam War. We were Generation R, the "rebel generation." Anti-war protest in the Global North was paralleled by national liberation and decolonization movements in the Global South.

Prosperity, however, ended with stagflation in the Global North in the late seventies and, in the Global South with the Third World Debt Crisis that produced the infamous lost decade of development. Many in my generation had been greatly attracted to socialism as an alternative to capitalism, so the collapse of socialist regimes in Eastern Europe and the Soviet Union in 1989 and the early '90s and the turn towards capitalism in China were sources of profound disillusionment, leaving us ideologically adrift as the new ideology of neoliberalism that accompanied "globalization"—a revitalized capitalism that created a global structure of production and a global market that transcended national barriers—appeared to carry the day. Even those who adhered to the less radical, social democratic Keynesian economics that put an emphasis on income redistribution and a leading role of the state in development, though still within a capitalist system, felt beleaguered.

In the Philippines, the R in Generation R might be more appropriately translated into "revolutionary" rather than "rebel." We not only broke with the ideological constraints of the Cold War in the mid-sixties but many of us became the mass base and leadership of the National Democratic Revolution, which sought to end imperialism and semi-feudalism, and serve as the ante-chamber to socialism. We were the backbone of the resistance to the Marcos dictatorship in the 1970s and early 1980s, and our revolution was seemingly unstoppable because history was on our side. There was a saying in the 1980s that "The revolution is like a bus. Individuals get on and individuals get off. But the bus will never stop."

With the EDSA Uprising, the bus stopped, leaving the Left stranded on the sidelines of an electoral-cum-street uprising led by the anti-Marcos elite that mobilized the Manila middle classes with the support of Washington. There were efforts to restart the bus but attempts to reorient strategy to address the new conditions of struggle under a reinvigorated elite democracy were largely foiled by forces that preferred the seductive comforts of the old ideology instead of trying to grapple with the new conditions of struggle, with all its uncertainties.

Don't Mourn, Organize!

Still, even as many on the Left debated theoretically the reasons why we were stymied, there were those of us who placed the priority on acting to stop capital in its new guises and we reached across borders in that effort to understand and to bring our numbers to bear against neoliberalism and globalization. We acted ahead of theory, indeed often out of instinct, and we organized ourselves without the confines of the traditional progressive parties. We were part of a global movement that, for want of a better term, we called "civil society." Civil society left behind the doctrinal and academic debates about the nature and changing dynamics of capitalism and mobilized to challenge capital at its existing points of vulnerability, like the World Trade Organization.

Even as capitalism was being challenged by progressive movements and individuals inspired by critical secular ideologies like environmentalism and feminism, the U.S. empire was being drawn into a debilitating condition of overextension by fundamentalists employing terrorist methods, like Osama bin Laden. The anti-war movement did, however, make a vital contribution to delegitimizing the U.S. war in the Middle East that ended with the panicked American withdrawal from Afghanistan in 2021. I was fortunate to be part of that global movement for peace. While the methods of Osama, the Taliban, and other fundamentalists repelled most of us in the anti-war movement, it could not be denied that their actions did, objectively, contribute significantly to the weakening of the empire, especially in the Middle East. Unlike many others in the movement, I have been more than willing to give the devil his due, for it is often through ethically questionable or terrible events that, as in the case of Job, history unfolds in a progressive direction.

Assessing the Balance

I was part of the National Democratic Movement, and I also believed in socialism, so I shared in the sadness and frustrations triggered by the setbacks of these two movements. But I was also part of the sustained campaigns that stalemated the WTO, discredited neoliberalism and globalization, and stopped the U.S. in the Middle East. The millions of us in these movements did not come from one political or ideological stream. We came from a variety of beliefs and ideologies. But we were activists above all, pragmatic in method perhaps, and often acting spontaneously, but determined to do what was necessary to throw a monkey wrench into the destructive machinery of capital and empire. In Singapore in 1996, the global establishment invited us to give up our resistance and join the feast since globalization was the "wave of the future." We said *bullshit* and fought back, and now, thirty years later, the WTO is paralyzed as an engine of trade liberalization, and neoliberalism, while still institutionalized, has been intellectually discredited.

I will leave it up to others to calculate the balance of these wins and losses. Let me just say, as Gayle Forman puts it, that "You win some, you lose some. And sometimes you win and lose at the same time. Life's a bloody cockup."

A Few Lessons

So, what lessons have I learned in these nearly fifty-five years of political engagement? Well, first, that the struggle never stops. What you're fighting against may come back in a new form, in a new front. So, yes, the U.S. suffered a grievous setback in the Middle East, but it is now gearing up for an apocalyptic battle in the Western Pacific, determined to employ all its resources in the area, especially military force, to stay *numero uno*.

Then there is the question of one's perspective on the unfolding of time. Of course, one would wish the triumph of one's cause would take place within one's lifetime, but perhaps one should realistically adjust one's sights beyond, to a century if not more—to consider the possibility that while one may have been part of a generation that began a movement, it may be another generation that will enable its success or retrieve it from the dustbin of history. Stoic acceptance of the possibility of defeat in one's lifetime will make such an eventuality less devastating psychologically both if and when it does occur, for with it will come the sense that the present is not the end but just a phase in a longer struggle. There are no permanent defeats and no permanent victories. The important thing is that one has been engaged in the struggle for the future.

Then there is the paradox of victory and defeat. Yes, the Bolsheviks won in 1917, but the seeds of the collapse in 1989–1991 were probably already present then, just as the derailment of the National Democratic Revolution in the late 1980s made us aware of flaws that were hidden at the time of its ascent in the 1970s. As in medicine and the physical sciences, failure in the initial stages of social experimentation is the mother of ultimate success, and in the case of our struggle for a progressive future, one of the lessons we must internalize is how to ensure that the social revolution is carried out with the utmost respect for individual and democratic rights. 1989 does not mean that 1917 was not a step forward, but it does mean that progressives must learn from that 70-year-long experiment so that we can do things better next time. Yes, the Philippine Revolution was derailed in 1986, but the lessons from its defeat may serve as the guideposts for the triumph of a new and better version in the future—one that is both truly socialist and truly democratic and respectful of the rights of the individual.

Let me put it another way: the failure of both revolutions lay mainly in their sacrificing democratic participation and respect for individual rights in the pursuit of egalitarian social transformation. There are no short cuts like democratic centralism, for while seemingly efficient in the pursuit of revolutionary objectives, in the longer term they actually end up subverting them. My experience with the Communist Party of the Philippines was a tough learning experience on the consequences of the failure to institutional-ize these two principles, democratic participation and respect for individual rights. But I must also say that my post-CPP experience with organizations like Akbayan underlined the difficulties of making headway with a mass participatory democratic approach in an elite democratic system where the people's will is vulnerable to being subverted by the deployment of money politics in an impoverished electorate.

But let me go on. The challenge to these two related projects of social transformation, socialism and national democracy, is not just to learn from their failures but to incorporate the insights of other paradigms for change that share the same values and the same emancipatory goal.

The Necessity and Urgency of Vision

This leads to the question of vision. Programs for change and against empire and war will have limited traction unless they are attached to a larger vision that responds not only to "class interest" but to our fundamental values as human beings. Proverbs 29 had it right: "Without vision, the people perish." One cannot be simply anti-capitalist since such a stance eventually ends up in nihilism.

Old-style early 20th century socialism, with the overwhelming political and analytical priority it accords to the state, no longer inspires. Luckily, taking its failures into account, there are alternatives that have reflected seriously on the failures of traditional socialism, and these are not limited to the state-directed capitalism that China has on offer. These alternative paradigms reflect the spirit of equality and justice that motivated traditional socialism but leave behind its questionable or unworkable methods like central planning or democratic centralism. They emphasize the role of civil society and participatory engagement. Over the last two decades, we have witnessed the emergence of exciting paradigms like Food Sovereignty, Degrowth, Ecosocialism, Ecofeminism, Emancipatory Marxism, and "*Buen Vivir*," a perspective derived from the experience of indigenous people of the Andes. Deglobalization has been the modest contribution of Focus on the Global South to the dialogue and debate that is aimed at arriving at a common ground among them.

An overriding concern in this endeavor is not simply to move towards a post-capitalist order but also to reverse the more than 500 years of colonial and neocolonial subordination of the Global South, of which the Philippines is part, to the Global North. This would mean not only an objective, historical movement but a transformation of consciousness, from being acted on, to we in the Global South acting as a collective subject. Of we people of the South, it can truly be said that, to borrow James Joyce's line, history is a nightmare from which we are trying to awake.

But this question of vision cannot be settled in a leisurely fashion, it cannot be pursued in a vacuum, for we are now living in an era of intersecting extreme crises—climate change, capitalism's ever more destructive trajectory, accelerating the marginalization of the billions in the Global South; the worst inequality between and within states in the last 100 years; and the U.S.'s drive to war. The convergence of these crises is the "new normal."

Combat in Our Times

Other forces know this, and they are ahead of us in the race to win the mass allegiance of millions. The question is, can progressives and their allies mobilize across crises and across borders to come up with and promote an alternative to the precipice? Moreover, can we have a vision of a truly democratic future that not only makes sense in rational terms but sweeps people off their feet with approbation in these extreme times, for what we are up against are paranoid paradigms that do not appeal to reason or reality but seek to mobilize subliminal fears, like the Great Replacement Theory that claims that liberals and minorities are engaged in a conspiracy to replace white people as the majority in Europe and the United States or the "Love Jihad" allegedly directed at Hindu women by Muslims in order to demographically displace Hindus in India.

Related to this matter of ideological competition is the question of political combat in these extreme times. In such periods, politics becomes very fluid. It becomes, to use Gramsci's terms, a war of maneuver. But it seems to be the right that has absorbed this lesson, and whether on the Internet, in the street, or in institutional politics, it appears to be far ahead of the Left. The response of progressives and liberals, in contrast, still appears to be largely in the confines of the old liberal democracy, relying on institutions that have worked in the past rather than critiquing and repudiating them for the many crimes in which they have been complicit—of which the global public has become increasingly aware, though such awareness has yet to successfully counter the Western media's bullhorn.

Are we ready to move beyond the politics of the old normal, as we engage in combat with the far right on the net, in the streets, in institutional politics? This is, to borrow the title of Eric Hobsbawm's classic work, an "age of extremes," and unless we release ourselves from the politics of the old normal and engage in the Gramscian war of maneuver demanded by the new normal, we will lose.

The Challenge in the Philippines

That is the global challenge. In the particular circumstances of the Philippines, the problem faced by the Left is that the elite has been able to harness mass discontent in ways that strengthen the control of the political system by dynasties that compete and collaborate in a manner similar to what has been described as the unipolar party in the U.S. What should we progressives do when we're nearly completely marginalized, when competing elites dominate the system so completely that the masses are simply passive cannon fodder in the competition among them? Sloganeering and May Day marches simply won't do. One thing is certain: getting back on our feet will mean going beyond the doctrinal discussions that continue to replay the debate of parliamentary struggle versus the armed struggle or the vanguard party based on democratic centralism versus a more democratic mass party. Perhaps being placed at the nadir of our political fortunes is necessary for us to realize both the necessity of and achieve a total reformulation of strategy to make the Left relevant once more to the millions of our people that are now trapped in the cage of liberal democracy, Philippine-style. We need to break out—and quickly—from doctrinal navel-gazing.

But let me be provocative and suggest that only a new generation of the left, perhaps the one after Gen Z, will be able to thoroughly break with the ideological hang-ups that imprison us.

The Departed

So much for politics. I cannot end this book except on a deeply personal note. I have experienced losses not only in the political front but also, in addition to the departure of my wife Ko that I wrote about in Chapter 16, in the personal as well. My romantic father died in the most romantic way he could possibly have desired, in the arms of my equally romantic mother in the hilltop house on the island he loved in 1992, with just the two of them present to comfort each other. My mother followed him to eternity a year and a half later. Both of my brothers, Dennis and Melvyn, were laid low by a disease tied to their smoking, the first in 2012, the second in 2020. One of my closest friends, Dick Ng, died of still undetermined causes after playing basketball in 2014. Martin Khor and Jerry Mander, two of the greatest anti-globalization activists, departed in 2020 and 2023 respectively, to the great sorrow of a movement in which they were central actors. I had my differences—big ones—with Jose Maria Sison, but I mourned the passing of a giant who had a massive imprint on my political formation when he passed away in December 2022. Then I received word just a few days before I finished the final draft of this memoir that my best friend, Edgardo Rodriguez, the quiet patriot who provided so many of the confidential World Bank documents that allowed us to write *Development Debacle*, had died under sad circumstances. A few weeks later, Ricky Abad, my old pal of those wild days in Sulu, also succumbed, in his case to cancer.

At a recent gathering that took place while I was out of the country, it was revealed that more than 40 veterans of the revolutionary struggle of the 1970s and 1980s have passed away in the last three or four years. This has injected a sense of urgency to the task of coming out with this book, for it is

After visiting the Parque de la Memoria, where the names of some 30,000 victims of the Argentine military's "dirty war" are written in concrete, Walden addresses a rally of the Mothers of the Disappeared at the Plaza de Mayo in Buenos Aires in August 2024

an attempt to give a voice to a generation whose aspirations to change their society for the better must not be forgotten, despite their shortcomings and their being sidelined by history. Hopefully, there will be other efforts to do this, so that my generation can be rescued from that limbo to which history consigns "lost generations."

There is one more thing before I end. There have been many who have paid the ultimate price for their beliefs. I have been in many engagements with the other side, where danger was my constant partner, but never in a position of having to choose between my beliefs or my life. Sure, there were instances when I was in danger of losing my life, but these were not occasioned by my politics. My being relatively lucky in this regard was reinforced when I visited the Parque de Memoria in Buenos Aires, Argentina, in August 2024. Asked to speak at the weekly rally of the Madres de la Plaza de Mayo, the organization of the mothers of the disappeared, I said.

> I was at the Park of Memory two days ago, where the names of the 30,000 disappeared were written on the concrete slabs. I was rendered speechless, especially when I noticed that some of the names were those of young pregnant women, and some were the names of children as young as four. What barbarism could perpetrate such awful deeds? We will not be able to eliminate the problems of disappearances and extra-judicial execution until we abolish the armed forces. So long as this institution exists that

considers the people its enemy, disappearances and extrajudicial executions will recur.

I would, in conclusion, just like to repeat what I said on the occasion of expressing my appreciation of the accolade of outstanding public intellectual or activist scholar by the International Studies Association in San Francisco in 2008: "I do not think that I have been a better public scholar than others. Indeed, I think that in a world filled with contingency I have merely been more lucky, having been spared the really, really rough situations and really, really tough choices. To the less lucky but more deserving public intellectuals I dedicate this award." And this memoir.

I am part of the great Jamaican poet-singer Bob Marley's generation, and I think of no better way to end this memoir than reproducing a few stanzas of one of the immortal songs he left us, which sums up in an unforgettable seven minutes my generation's remembrance of shared comradeship in the trenches.

> *I remember when we used to sit*
> *In the government yard in Trenchtown*
> *Oba-observing the hypocrites*
> *As they mingle with the good people we meet*
> *Good friends we have had*
> *Oh, good friends we've lost*
> *Along the way*
> *In this great future, you can't forget your past*
> *So dry your tears, I say*
> *And no, woman, no cry*
> *No, woman, no cry*
> *Little darling, don't shed no tears*
> *No, woman, no cry*

Acknowledgements

An accounting of one's debt to society begins with one's family. Despite the few years we had together, my late wife, Suranuch (Ko)Thongsila, left a big imprint on me.

I am also profoundly grateful to my dear departed mother and father, Luz Flores and Jess Bello, and siblings Dennis and Melvyn. I am happy that my caring sister Gwethalyn and her husband Tom Edwards are still around to keep me company. Other close relatives whose companionship I have had the good fortune to enjoy over the years include Aldea Flores, Bernadette Bello Balundo, Armand Bello, Michelle Bello, Michael Bello, Jessica Joanne Bello Carreon, Cecile Navarrete Bello, Rudy Tamayo, Josette Tamayo, Lito Suarez, Ging Deocadiz, Alex Brillantes, Jr, and Mitos Bello Antazo.

I am deeply in debt to Madeline Kho and Marilen Abesamis for spending part of their lives with me, and to my stepdaughters Annette and Amy Ferrer for adopting me.

I regret that Edgardo Rodriguez, Benedict Ng, Boy Ramos, and Ricky Abad are no longer around to read this memoir. Fortunately, other friends from those wonderful years in school—among them, Eduardo ("Jun") Lopez, Vic Lim, Corrito Lim, Fred Sy, Nonie Zialcita, Freddie de Leon, Ramon Murillo, Ariel Abadilla, Louie Fernandez, Girlie Ng, Chay Rodriguez, Rely Rodriguez, Manny Tirona, Mandy Chavez, Rolly Villacorta, Dick Gordon, Manny Pangilinan, Joey Espejo, Titus Santiago, Luigi Francia, Leo Martinez, Lito Demonteverde, Ruben Gomez, Mon Paterno, Dean Velasco, Jolan Lumauig, and Grace Lumauig—will have the chance to do so.

So will Ed Fischer and Chester Cabel, longtime friends from my exciting year in Jolo, and Mary Racelis, Maria Clara Roldan, Pancho de Guzman, and Cherry Ferreros from my days at the Institute of Philippine Culture.

Comrades in arms in the US-based anti-Marcos movement to whom I owe much include Rene Cruz, Bruce Occena, Melinda Paras, Elaine Elinson, Cathy Tactaquin, Walter Yonn, Geline Avila, Cindy Domingo, Pacita Bunag, Elsie Castrence, Jon Melegrito, John Kelly, the late Totoy Castrence, Robin Broad, John Cavanagh, Edna Pugeda, Doug Cunningham, Becky Asedillo, Dante Simbulan, Chibu Lagman, John Gershman, Ike de la Cruz, Prosy de la

Cruz, the late Daniel Boone Schirmer, Romel Simon, Mars Estrada, Thelma King, Mila de Guzman, Lenny Marin, Dading Macaranas, Julio Macaranas, Rick Polintan, Edwin Batongbacal, Barbara Gaerlan, Boying Pimentel, Severina Rivera-Drew, Nancy Freeman, Emil de Guzman, Lester Ruiz, M.C. Canlas, and Richard Burcroff.

I was proud to serve in the international solidarity network in support of progressive change in the Philippines, along with Louis Jalandoni, Connie Ledesma, Marilen Abesamis, Tonette Garcia, Joel Rocamora, the late Geoffrey Flores Fabic, Jr, Judith Reyes, Rene Raya, Corrine Canlas, the late Rene Nachura, the late Sixto Carlos, Roland Simbulan, Cristine Ebro, Edicio de la Torre, Thea Fierens, Evert de Boer, Malu Padilla, Pierre Rousset, Sally Rousset, Thea Fierens, Brid Brennan, Nonoy Hacbang, the late Adonis Callanta, Miyoko Oshima, Nathan Quimpo, Sonny San Juan, Delia Aguilar, Edna Aquino, Alex Aquino, Al Senturias, Erlinda Senturias, Elmer Ordonez, Muriel Ordonez, Jess Agustin, and Hanneke Thieme.

I first met Anuradha Mittal at Food First, and I thank her for being such a steadfast friend over the years. It was also at Food First that I met and developed solid friendships with Peter Rosset, Marilyn Borchardt, Frances Moore Lappe, Stephanie Rosenfeld, Shea Cunningham, Martha Katigbak, and Rowena Garcia.

My fifteen years at the sociology department of the University of the Philippines exposed me to a vibrant intellectual circle that included Ging Gutierrez, Randy David, Rizza Kaye Cases, Cynthia Bautista, the late Laura Samson, Mara Baviera, and Sarah Raymundo.

Comrades that made Akbayan a great political experiment included Risa Hontiveros, Carmel Abao, Ronald Llamas, Joel Rocamora, Ric Reyes, Etta Rosales, Sabrina Gacad, Richard Heydarian, Onieng Policarpio, J.V. Villanueva, Barry Gutierrez, Arlene Santos, Eloisa Sagum, Percy Cendana, Jonas Bagas, Rafaela David, Anie Palana, Kit Melgar, Ellene Sana, Vimvim Santos, Ben Sumug-oy, Josua Mata, Marlon Quesada, Etta Rosales, Odette Magtibay, Jaye de la Cruz Bekema, Arnold Tarrobago, Raffy Albert, Mark Figueras, Elaine Teope, Blenda Rodriguez, Jesse Dimaisip, Raffy Albert, and Alvin Rull.

Focus on the Global South is what it is today, Southeast Asia's leading progressive research and analysis institute, because of the efforts of a great staff, board, and supporters over the last thirty years, among them Shalmali Guttal, Soontaree Nakaviroj, Chanida Bamford, Joy Chavez, Nicola Bullard, Kamal Malhotra, Marylou Malig, Aileen Kwa, Meena Menon, Herbert Docena, Jacques-Chai Chongthomdi, Marco Mezzera, Julie de los Reyes, Praphai Jundee, Shea Cunningham, Synth Wannaboworn, Alec Bamford,

Jayati Ghosh, Anisa Widyasari, Anusha Lall, Qiqo Simbol, Ros Sukunthy, Maryanne Manahan, Joseph Purugganan, Clark Militante, Pablo Solon, Minar Pimple, Dororthy Guerrero, Silvia Ribeiro, Alejandro Bendana, Nette Amora, Mansi Sharma, Nette Amora, Galil de Guzman Castillo, Bianca Martinez, Lynn de la Cruz, Boaventura Monjane, Benny Kuruvilla, Raphael Baladad, Gigi Francisco, Victor Karunan, Liling Briones, Junya Yimprasert, Suwattana Thadaniti, Mayuree Ruechakiattikul, Aya Fabros, Afsar Jafri, Seema Mustafa, Carmina Flores Obanil, Marissa de Guzman, Sajin Prachason, Ehito Kimura, Li Kheng Poh, Marco Mezzera, Afsar Jafri, Yasmin Ahammad, Varsha Rajan Berry, Mercia Andrews, Neary Peou Men, Ridan Sun, Sophea Chrek, Ranjini Basu, and Phun Phearun.

Members of the Chulalongkorn University Social Research Institute (CUSRI) and the Chulalongkorn University faculty who have provided a hospitable and stimulating intellectual atmosphere for Focus include Surichai Wan-geao, Suthy Unruan Leknoi, Prasartsert, Amara Pongsapich, Naruemon Thabchumpon, Nidiya Kiatying-Angsulee, Pakorn Lertsatienchai, Sayamol Charoenratana, Amara Pongsapich, Naruemon Thabchumpon, Nidiya Kiatying-Angsulee, Prapart Pintobtang, Suwattana Thadaniti, Naruemon Arunotai, and Angkarb Korsieporn.

Ko's good friends and relatives—Prida Tiasuwan, former Prime Minister Anand Panyarachun, Jaran Ditapichai, Subhatra Bhumiprabhas, Laddawan Tantivitayapitak, Surawut Pratoomraj, Punne Suangsatapananon, Naruemon Thabchumpon, Anicha Poolsawat, Chatchawan Chulamakorn, Samon Rangsirot, Nisarat Somkamnerd—adopted me as one of their own, and for this I am thankful. Thai is one of the most difficult languages in the world to master and what rudimentary capability I have developed I owe largely to my language instructors Sukanda Sodthisophon and her daughter Praewa.

While I was a public official, I had productive friendships with Erin Tanada, Teddy Baguilat, Kimi Cojuangco, Alex Padilla, the late Miriam Santiago, Bebot Bello, Leila de Lima, Imelda Dimaporo, Edcel Lagman, Loren Legarda, Satur Ocampo, the late Carlos Padilla, Al Francis Bichara, the late Leticia Shahani, Chris Lomibao, and Emmeline Aglipay Villar.

Since my retirement from the University of the Philippines, the Sociology Department of the State University of New York at Binghamton has provided an intellectual home for me, and for their wonderful, stimulating company, I am grateful to Ravi Palat, Bill Martin, Leslie Gates, Marina Sitrin, Ana Maria Candela, Michael West, Denis O'Hearn, Joshua Price, Celia Klin, Gladys Jimenez Munoz, Chungse Lee, Andrea Toth, Kenyon Cavender,

Anya Briy, Bronwyn Lee, Nancy Pineiro, Joseph Citriniti, Lorrie Hagerman, Denise Spadine, and Linda Zanrucha.

Playing a key role in my life as a public intellectual have been kindred spirits, among them Richard Falk, Carol Hau, Nicole Curato, Christophe Aguiton, Pierre Rousset, Naomi Klein, Peter Rosset, Pablo Solon, Grace Blakeley, Noam Chomsky, the late Renato Constantino, Red Constantino, Jayati Ghosh, Julie de los Reyes, C.P. Chandrasekhar, Eric Toussaint, Boaventura de Sousa Santos, the late Chalmers Johnson, Kevin Hewison, Max Lane, the late Franz Schurmann, Michael Burawoy, the late Erik Ohlin Wright, Peter Evans, Hilal Elver, Ed Tadem, Tessa Encarnacon Tadem, Peter Weiss, Cora Weiss, Robert Reyes, Isabel Ortiz, Jomo Sundaram, Jun Borras, Jenny Franco, Butch Montes, Men Santa Ana, Maitet Diokno, Alex Callinicos, Nicky Perlas, Prabir Purkayastha, Chayan Vaddhanaputi, Fiona Dove, Vijay Prashad, Charles Santiago, Lila Shahani, Vince Rafael, Mercy Barends, Eva Sundari, Raul Montenegro, Angkhana Neelapaijit, Shui-Meng Ng, Eva Sundari, Kasit Piromya, Lisa Dacanay, the late Saul Landau, Maude Barlow, Sara Larrain, Jerry Mander, Henry Veltmeyer, Susan George, Mario Ivan Lopez, Leloy Claudio, Tony Lavina, Richard Heydarian, Henry Veltmeyer, Yeb Sano, Natalie Sambhi, Raj Patel, Jojo Abinales, Wataru Kusaka, Nathan Quimpo, Takashi Shiraishi, Peter Hayes, Lyuba Zarsky, Roque Raymundo, Manny Lahoz, Angge Lahoz, Delle Tiongson-Browers, the late Temi Rivera, Muto Ichiyo, Jim Heddle, Marybeth Brangan, Setsu Shigemitsu, Christine Ahn, Paul Hutchcroft, Al McCoy, Mary McCoy, Ronnie Holmes, Ayame Suzuki, Varsha Gandikota-Nellutla, Maria Inez Cuervo, Beverly Keene, David Adler, and Dylan Rodriguez.

Since my high school days, I have done writing for the media. In the process I have made many friends who have generously allowed my opinion pieces to grace their publications, among them John Feffer and Peter Certo of Foreign Policy in Focus; Maria Ressa, Glenda Gloria, Chay Hofilena, and Margie de Leon of Rappler; the late Letty Magsanoc, the late Conrad de Quiros, and Juan Sarmiento of the Philippine Daily Inquirer; Sandy Close and the late Franz Schurmann of Pacific News Service; Roberto Savio of Interpress Service; Antonio Vergara Meersohn of MEER; Katrina vanden Heuvel and Don Guttenplan of The Nation; Gemma Nemenzo of Positively Filipino; Siddharta Mahanta, formerly of the New York Times and currently with Bloomberg News; Jamela Alindogan of Al Jazeera; Jim Gomez of Associated Press; and Inday Espina-Varona of ABS-CBN. Among those who have played a key role in bringing out my books are Sebastian Budgen and Tariq Ali of Verso; Karina Bolasco, formerly of Ateneo de Manila University Press and Anvil; Rica Remedios Santos and Julian de la Cerna of Ateneo de Manila University Press; Diana Collier of Clarity Press; Robert Molteno, formerly of Zed Press; and Roger Van Zwanenberg of Pluto Press.

My running for senator in 2016 and vice president of the Philippines in 2022 was an exciting political adventure, and those who made it memorable included Princess Nemenzo, Dodong Nemenzo, Leody de Guzman, Josua Mata, Jean Enriquez, Herbert Docena, Luke Espiritu, Sonny Melencio, Manjet Lopez, Lidy Nacpil, Reihana Mohideen, Pangging Santos, Bayang Barrios, Cookie Chua, Aida Santos, Lejun de la Cruz, Nilo de la Cruz, Gina de la Cruz, Ed Tadem, Rasti Delizo, General Du, Jose Cotada, Popoy Caision, Alex Arellano, Jenny Llaguno, the late Ka Rodel, Elijah San Fernando, Ia Maranon, Leomar Doctolero, Pang Delgra, Raquel Castillo, Dulce Natividad, Vimvim Santos, Cora Fabros, Vergie Suarez, Fidel Nemenzo, Marivic Raquiza, and Toinette Raquiza.

That campaign led to cyberlibel charges being filed by powerful people, against which I have been ably defended by my legal team composed of Star Elamparo, Danny Balucos, Kat Leuch, Dexter Lopoz, Leo Delgra, Nida Delgra, Leomar Doctolero, and Vimvim Santos.

I am especially grateful to family friends whose warm support has extended for years and years or who have provided invaluable assistance in business and personal matters, among them Tonette Garcia, Nic Jones, Salome Tibar, Elsie Castrence, Marybeth Brangan, John Cavanagh, Robin Broad, Qiqo Simbol, Sukanda Sodthisophon, Agapito Morillo, Jr, Bella Morillo, Jeff Morillo, Christine Morillo, Cathy Morillo, Van Eric Morillo, and Carmela Mogueis.

Writing this memoir has been a great cooperative process that has involved as readers Richard Falk, Nicole Curato, Ed Fischer, Elsie Castrence, Nicola Bullard, John Cavanagh, Julie de los Reyes, Robin Broad, Jessie Broad-Cavanagh, Nic Jones, Tonette Garcia, Gwethalyn Edwards, as well as the anonymous reviewers commissioned by the publishers. They definitely contributed to the improvements that have gone into the final copy, but I take sole responsibility for whatever lapses there might be in content, grammar, and form.

For their generously allowing free use of their photos, I am grateful to Associated Press, Russell Palma of the *Philippine Star*, Food First, and Pinky Colmenares, Executive Director of *Manila Bulletin*. I am also grateful to Shaid Quadir and *Third World Quarterly* for granting permission to use a long extract from a piece I authored.

Finally, a very warm thank you to Rica Remedios Santos, Julian de la Cerna, and Ace Vincent Molo of the Ateneo de Manila University Press and Diana Collier of Clarity Press for shepherding this memoir through the difficult process from submission to final publication.

Endnotes

1 Max Lane, *Indonesia Out of Exile* (Singapore: Penguin Southeast Asia, 2023), p. 192.

2 Alvin Gouldner, *The Coming Crisis in Western Sociology* (New York: Basic Books, 1970).

3 Perry Anderson, *Passages from Antiquity to Feudalism* (London: Verso, 1985) and *Lineages of the Absolutist State* (London: New Left Books, 1974).

4 Barrington Moore, *The Social Origins of Dictatorship and Democracy: Lord and Peasant in the Modern World* (Boston: Beacon, 1966).

5 Louis Althusser, *For Marx* (London: Verso, 2006).

6 Nicos Poulantzas, *Political Power and Social Classes* (London: Verso, 1975).

7 The full thesis, *The Roots and Dynamics of Revolution and Counterrevolution in Chile, 1970-73,* is available from University Microfilms, Ann Arbor, Michigan. My writings based on it include Walden Bello, "How Middle Class Chileans Contributed to the Overthrow of Salvador Allende," *The Nation*, Sept. 21, 2017, https://www.thenation.com/article/archive/how-middle-class-chileans-contributed-to-the-overthrow-of-salvador-allende/; and Walden Bello, *Counterrevolution: The Global Rise of the Far Right* (Halifax: Fernwood, 2019), pp. 34–48.

8 Walden Bello and Severina Rivera, eds., *The Logistics of Repression: The Role of US Assistance in Consolidating the Martial Law Regime in the Philippines* (Washington, DC: Friends of the Filipino People, 1977).

9 Daniel Boone Schirmer, *Republic or Empire: American Resistance to the Philippine War* (New York: Schenkman Books, 1972).

10 Carlos Bulosan, *America is in the Heart* (Seattle: University of Washington Press, 2014).

11 Rene Ciria Cruz, Cindy, Domingo, and Bruce Occena, eds., *A Time to Rise* (Seattle: University of Washington Press, 2017).

12 C. Wright Mills, *The Power Elite* (New York: Oxford University Press, 2000); Paul Baran and Paul Sweezy, *Monopoly Capital* (New York: Monthly Review Press, 1966).

13 https://th.mail.yahoo.com/d/search/keyword=aepf/messages/ACVS8Mt3cKyoY6YpcAvqyE7vkTI

14 https://th.mail.yahoo.com/d/search/name=Joseph%2520Scalice&emailAddresses=jscalice%2540berkeley.edu&listFilter=FROM&contactIds=6689.88dc/messages/APDFJ_YARBDYY6chvAczwNFljBI

15 See, for instance, *The Communist Party of the Philippines, 1983-93* (Quezon City: University of the Philippines Press, 2001); Joel Rocamora, *Breaking Through: The Struggle within the Communist Party of the Philippines* (Quezon City: Anvil Publishing, 1994); Francisco Nemenzo, "An irrepressible revolution: the decline

and resurgence of the Philippine communist movement," Manila, 1984, unpublished manuscript; Francisco Nemenzo, "Rectification process in the Philippine communist movement," in Joo-Jock Lim and S. Vani, eds., *Armed Communist Movements in Southeast Asia* (Aldershot, England: Gower, 1984), pp. 72–101; Joseph Scalise, *The Drama of Dictatorship: Martial Law and the Communist Parties of the Philippines* (Ithaca: Cornell University Press, 2023).

16 Walden Bello, "From the Ashes: The Rebirth of the Philippine Revolution," *Third World Quarterly*, Vol. 8, No. 1 (Jan. 1986), pp. 258–276, https://doi.org/10.1080/01436598608419897.

17 Amado Guerrero, *Philippine Society and Revolution* (Oakland, California: International Association of Filipino Patriots, 1979). (This volume also includes Guerrero's *Specific Characteristics of Our People's War*.)

18 Ibid.

19 US Senate Foreign Relations Committee Staff, *The Situation in the Philippines* (Washington, DC: US Government Printing Office, September 1984).

20 Paul Hume, "Four Protesters Arrested Kennedy Center," *Washington Post*, November 4, 1981, https://www.washingtonpost.com/archive/lifestyle/1981/11/04/4-protesters-arrested-at-kennedy-center/c5747f5e-d572-461f-844b-4e764a6bf886/

21 *San Francisco Chronicle*, April 14, 1978. https://sfchronicle.newsbank.com/search?date_from=April%201%2C%201978&date_to=Dec%201%2C%201978&text=Walden%20Bello&pub%5B0%5D=142051F45F422A02

22 *San Francisco Chronicle*, October 20, 1978. https://sfchronicle.newsbank.com/search?date_from=April%201%2C%201978&date_to=Dec%201%2C%201978&text=Walden%20Bello&pub%5B0%5D=142051F45F422A02

23 Daniel Boone Schirmer, Preface to *Logistics of Repression: The Role of US Assistance in Consolidating the Martial Law Regime in the Philippines*, edited by Walden Bello and Severina Rivera (Washington, DC: Friends of the Filipino People, 1977).

24 World Bank, "Political and Administrative Bases for Economic Policy in the Philippines," Memorandum from William Ascher to Larry Hinkle, Washington, DC, November 6, 1980.

25 World Bank, "Briefing for the Visit of Mrs Imelda Marcos: The Urban Sector in the Philippines," Memorandum from Gregory Votaw to Robert McNamara, Washington, DC, November 18, 1975, p. 4.

26 Walden Bello, David Kinley, and Elaine Elinson, eds., *Development Debacle: The World Bank in the Philippines* (San Francisco: Institute for Food and Development Policy, 1982).

27 Walden Bello, "Challenges and Dilemmas of the Public Intellectual," April 7, 2008. https://waldenbello.org/challenges-and-dilemmas-of-the-public-intellectual/

28 National Strategy Security Directive (NSSD), Washington, DC, Nov 1984.

29 NSSD.

30 Michael Armacost, Speech at Foreign Service Institute, Rosslyn, Virginia, April 23, 1986.

31 Ibid.

32 Nayan Chanda, "Dear Mr President...," *Far Eastern Economic Review*, October 31, 1985, p. 17.

33 Paul Wolfowitz, Answers to questions at hearings of the US Senate Foreign Relations Committee, Washington, DC, October 30, 1985.

34 US Embassy, Manila, Confidential cable to the Secretary of State, November 6, 1985. This cable was leaked by State Department sources to the author, who provided it to the press.

35 Ibid.

36 Ambassador Stephen Bosworth, "The Opposition: Uniting or Fragmenting," Cable to Secretary of State, US Department of State, February 1985.

37 Raymond Bonner, *Waltzing with a Dictator* (New York: New York Times Books, 1987), p. 408.

38 Armacost.

39 Richard Armitage, Statement to the US Senate Foreign Relations Committee, Washington, DC, December 18, 1985, p. 1.

40 Armacost.

41 William Sullivan, Remarks at a conference on the Philippines sponsored by the Washington Institute for Values in Public Policy, Washington, DC, April 30–May 1, 1986

42 John Monjo, "US Assistance to the Philippines," Statement to the House of Representatives Subcommittee on Asian and Pacific Affairs, Washington, DC, May 15, 1986.

43 Armacost.

44 "In US, Philippine-Americans Rejoice," *New York Times*, February 26, 1986. https://www.nytimes.com/1986/02/26/world/in-us-philippine-americans-rejoice.html

45 Walden Bello, "The Crisis of the Philippine Progressive Movement: A Preliminary Investigation," *Kasarinlan*, Vol. 8, No. 1 (Third Quarter, 1992), p. 149.

46 My article was not the only account published on the Ahos campaign. A gripping eyewitness account was Robert Francis Garcia's *To Suffer Thy Comrades: How the Revolution Decimated Its Own* (Mandaluyong: Anvil Publishing, 2017).

47 Bello, "The Crisis of the Philippine Progressive Movement," p. 150.

48 Armando Liwanag, "Reaffirm Our Basic Principles and Rectify Errors," *Kasarinlan*, Vol. 8, No. 1 (Third Quarter, 1992), p. 100.

49 Ibid.

50 Jeane Kirkpatrick, "Dictatorship and Double Standards," *Commentary*, November 1979. https://www.commentary.org/articles/jeane-kirkpatrick/dictatorships-double-standards/

51 Walden Bello, Peter Hayes, and Lyuba Zarsky, "500-Mile Island: The Philippine Nuclear Reactor Deal," *Pacific Research*, Vol. X, No. 1 (First Quarter, 1979).

52 Peter Hayes, Lyuba Zarsky, and Walden Bello, *American Lake: Nuclear Peril in the Pacific* (New York: Penguin Books, 1987).

53 Walden Bello, "The Racist Underpinnings of the American Way of War," *Foreign Policy in Focus,* July 1, 2020. https://fpif.org/the-racist-underpinnings-of-the-american-way-of-war/

54 *Food First News and Views*, Vol. 14, No. 47 (Summer 1992), p. 4.

55 "Food First and Robert McNamara Clash over World Bank at Notre Dame," *Food First News and Views*, Vol. 14, No. 47 (Summer 1992), pp. 1, 4.

56 Ibid.

57 Ibid.

58 Ibid.

59 Walden Bello, with Shea Cunningham and Bill Rau, *Dark Victory: The United States, Structural Adjustment, and Global Poverty* (London: Pluto Press, 1994), pp. 36–37.

60 Walden Bello, "Short-lived Legacy: Margaret Thatcher, Neoliberalism and the Global South," *Guardian*, April 16, 2013. https://www.theguardian.com/global-development/poverty-matters/2013/apr/16/legacy-margaret-thatcher-neoliberalism

61 Ibid.

62 Ibid.

63 Walden Bello and Stephanie Rosenfeld, *Dragons in Distress: Asia's Miracle Economies in Crisis* (Middlesex, UK: Penguin, 1991).

64 Robin Broad, John Cavanagh, and Walden Bello, "Development: The Market Is Not Enough," *Foreign Policy*, No. 81 (Winter 1990–1991), pp. 144–162.

65 Walden Bello, "Moscow Warms Up to the Asia-Pacific Region," *Philippine Resource Center Monitor*, Nos. 6–7 (August 1989), p. 3.

66 Florian Alburo et al., "Towards Recovery and Sustainable Growth," School of Economics, University of the Philippines, Sept 1985.

67 Quoted in Walden Bello et al., *The Anti-Development State: The Political Economy of Permanent Crisis in the Philippines* (Quezon City: University of the Philippines Press, 2004), pp. 25–26.

68 Conrad de Quiros, "World Class," *Philippine Daily Inquirer*, October 22, 2003. The "Brunei Beauties" were Filipina stars and starlets who were alleged to have gone to the Kingdom of Brunei to perform sexual services for the Brunei elite in exchange for monetary compensation.

69 Walden Bello, Herbert Docena, Marissa de Guzman, and Marylou Malig, *The Political Economy of Permanent Crisis in the Philippines* (Quezon City: University of the Philippines Press, 2004). Walden Bello, Kenneth Cardenas, Jerome Patrick Cruz, Alinaya Fabros, Mary Ann Manahan, Clarissa Militante, Joseph Purugganan, and Jenina Joy Chavez, *State of Fragmentation: The Philippines in Transition* (Quezon City: Focus on the Global South, 2014).

70 Quoted in Walden Bello, "Neoliberalism as Hegemonic Ideology in the Philippines: Rise, Apogee, and Crisis," *Philippine Sociological Review*, Vol. 57 (2009), pp. 9–19.

71 Sebastian Edwards, *The Chile Project: The Story of the Chicago Boys and the Downfall of Neoliberalism* (Princeton: Princeton University Press, 2023), p. 5.

72 These included Shalmali Guttal, Nicola Bullard, Chanida Bamford, Soontaree Nakaviroj, Joy Chavez, Praphai Jundee, Ehito Kimura, Marco Mezzera, Aileen Kwa, and Minar Pimple.

73 Walden Bello, "Asian Financial Crisis: The Movie," *Kasarinlan*, Vol. 13, No. 4 (1998), p. 17–18.

74 Associated Press, "IMF boss gets bye-byepie in face," *Associated Press*, February 13, 2000, https://archive.seattletimes.com/archive/?date=20000213&slug=4004732

75 Quoted in Walden Bello and Shalmali Guttal, "Honolulu Face-off: Civil society 1, Asian Development Bank 0, *Focus on the Global South*, May 10, 2001. https://focusweb.org/honolulu-face-off-civil-society-1-asian-development-bank-0/

76 Walden Bello, "Davos 2000: Has Asia Really Rebounded?," Institute for Agriculture and Trade Policy, February 24, 2000. https://www.iatp.org/documents/davos-2000-has-asia-really-rebounded

77 Walden Bello, "The Meaning of Seattle: Truth only Becomes True through Action," *Yes Magazine*, November 28, 2009. https://focusweb.org/the-meaning-of-seattle-truth-only-becomes-true-through-action/

78 Steven Pearlstein, "Tough Act for IMF, World Bank Leaders in Prague," *Washington Post*, September 24, 2000. https://www.washingtonpost.com/archive/politics/2000/09/24/tough-crowd-for-imf-world-bank-leaders-in-prague/8543d127-d036-4f78-afd5-57658811de3b/

79 Much of the following account is taken from a piece I did for the *Nation*, "The Battle of Genoa," *The Nation*, July 21, 2001. https://www.thenation.com/article/archive/battle-genoa/

80 Paolo Gerbaudo, "Twenty Years since the Genoa G8 protest, Globalization is Imploding, *Jacobin*, July 20, 2021. https://jacobin.com/2021/07/genoa-g8-summit-protest-anti-globalization-economy-national-capitalism

81 Aileen Kwa and Fatoumata Jawara, *Behind the Scenes at the WTO: The Real World of International Trade Negotiations* (London: Zed, 2004).

82 "Oxfam's response to Walden Bello's article on Make Trade Fair," *Internasjonale utviklingssporsmal*. http://www.rorg.no/Artikler/865.html

83 Quoted in Walden Bello, *Dilemmas of Domination* (New York: Henry Holt, 2005), p. 179.

84 Walden Bello, "Why Free Trade is Bad for You (or Most of You, at any Rate)," *Foreign Policy in Focus*, March 11, 2019. https://fpif.org/why-free-trade-is-bad-for-you-or-most-of-you-at-any-rate/

85 The following account is based principally on Walden Bello, "The Superrich at Davos are the Voice of the Past," *International Herald Tribune*, February 9, 2001. https://www.nytimes.com/2001/02/09/opinion/IHT-the-super-rich-at-davos-are-the-voice-of-the-past.html

86 Naomi Klein, Speech at World Social Forum, Porto Alegre, Brazil, February 1, 2002.

87 Quoted in "The Punch Card and the Hourglass," *New Left Review*, May–June 2001.

88 Quoted in Walden Bello, "The World Social Forum at the Crossroads," CADTM, May 20, 2007. https://www.cadtm.org/The-Forum-at-the-Crossroads

89 Ibid.

90 Naomi Klein, *No Logo* (London: Picador, 1999).

91 Walden Bello, "Book Review: No Logo," *Yes Magazine*, October 1, 2001. https://www.yesmagazine.org/issue/tech/2001/10/01/book-review-no-logo

92 Walden Bello, "A Very Capitalist Disaster: Naomi Klein's Take on the Neoliberal Saga." https://waldenbello.org/a-very-capitalist-disaster-naomi-kleins-take-on-the-neoliberal-saga/. Also, in *Review of International Political Economy*, Vol. 15, No. 5 (December 2008), pp. 881–91.

93 "A Message to the Filipino People on the 2022 Elections," *Aquarius Media*, https://www.reddit.com/r/Philippines/comments/uherrl/naomi_no_logo_klein_endorses_walden_bello_as_vp/

94 Walden Bello, "Revolution and Counterrevolution," *IDEAS*, August 4, 2002. https://www.networkideas.org/news-analysis/2002/08/revolution-and-counter-revolution/

95 Walden Bello, "I'll Miss Hugo," *Philippine Daily Inquirer*, March 7, 2013. https://opinion.inquirer.net/48265/ill-miss-hugo

96 "Turning Their Backs to the World," *Economist*, February 19, 2009. https://www.economist.com/international/2009/02/19/turning-their-backs-on-the-world

97 Karl Polanyi, *The Great Transformation* (Boston: Beacon Press, 2001).

98 Pierre Haski, "Is France on Course to Bid Adieu to Globalization?," *YaleGlobalOnline*, July 21, 2011. http://yaleglobal.yale.edu/content/france-bid-adieu-globalization

99 Walden Bello, "The Future in the Balance," Acceptance speech, Right Livelihood Award ceremony, Parliament of Sweden, December 8, 2003. https://rightlivelihood.org/speech/acceptance-speech-walden-bello/

100 Haski.

101 Haski.

102 Walden Bello, *Revisiting and Reclaiming Globalization* (Bangkok: Focus on the Global South, 2019), p. 9.

103 Walden Bello, "How to Lose a War," *Frontline*, November 10, 2001. https://frontline.thehindu.com/cover-story/article30252539.ece

104 Marco Mezzera, "Dark Clouds Amassing on Afghanistan's Political Horizon: A Brief Review of Post-Taliban Afghanistan," *Focus on the Global South*, July 27, 2002. https://focusweb.org/dark-clouds-amassing-on-afghanistans-political-horizon-a-brief-review-of-post-taliban-afghanistan/

105 Walden Bello, "International Peace Mission Visit to Basilan and Zamboanga," *Focus on the Global South*, April 28, 2002. https://focusweb.org/international-peace-mission-visit-to-basilan-and-zamboanga-preliminary-findings/

106 Aijaz Ahmad, quoted in "No Permanent Deployment of US Troops in RP, *Philippine Star*, March 21, 2002. https://www.philstar.com/headlines/2002/03/21/154613/145no-permanent-deployment-us-troops-rp146

107 Walden Bello, "Springtime in Baghdad," *Focus on the Global South*, March 17, 2003. https://focusweb.org/springtime-in-baghdad/

108 Walden Bello, "Pax Romana versus Pax Americana: Contrasting Strategies of Imperial Management," *Foreign Policy in Focus*, May 1, 2003. https://fpif.org/pax_romana_versus_pax_americana_contrasting_strategies_of_imperial_management/

109 Ibid.

110 Patrick Tyler, "Threats and Responses: News Analysis, A New Power in the Streets," *New York Times*, February 17, 2003. https://www.nytimes.com/2003/02/17/world/threats-and-responses-news-analysis-a-new-power-in-the-streets.html

111 While some of us, like myself, Chai Chongthomdi, Shalmali Guttal, Joy Chavez, Marylou Malig, Maryann Manahan, and Meena Menon, went on anti-war or anti-globalization missions, the mainstays that held the fort in Bangkok were Chanida Bamford, Nicola Bullard, Soontaree Nakaviroj, Julie de los Reyes, Praphai Jundee, and Qiqo Simbol. After I resigned as executive director to run for Congress in 2007, Chanida Bamford served as coordinator, followed by Pablo Solon, former Bolivian ambassador to the United Nations, and Shalmali Guttal as executive directors.

112 Richard Falk, "The World Speaks on Iraq: The Istanbul Session of the World Tribunal on Iraq," *Go Global*, Winter/Spring 2007, p. 7.

113 Walden Bello Speaking at the World Tribunal on Iraq, *Deep Dish TV*. https://vimeo.com/118819359

114 Arundhati Roy, quoted in Walden Bello, "The Perfect Storm," *Frontline*, July 25, 2005. https://frontline.thehindu.com/world-affairs/article30205553.ece

115 The following account is based on the author's notes and articles on the mission, including, "Bombing till the Last Minute: Report from Lebanon 2," *Focus on the Global South,* August 14, 2006; "A Bittersweet Day: Report from Lebanon," August 13, 2006.

116 Walden Bello and Marylou Malig, "I Prefer to Die by Assassination," *Frontline*, December 31, 2004. https://frontline.thehindu.com/world-affairs/article30225967.ece

117 Ben Hubbard and Maria Abi-Habib, "Behind Hamas's Bloody Gambit to Create a 'Permanent' State of War," *New York Times*, November 8, 2023. https://www.nytimes.com/2023/11/08/world/middleeast/hamas-israel-gaza-war.html

118 Ibid.

119 Walden Bello, "Imagine You're a Palestinian Youth…," *Foreign Policy in Focus*, October 23. 2023, https://fpif.org/imagine-youre-a-palestinian-youth/

120 Ibid.

121 Walden Bello, "How to Lose a War…"; Walden Bello, "Pax Romana versus Pax American…"

122 The bulk of this section is based on my article, "Why Biden Might not be Able to Extricate the US from its Middle East Quagmire," *Foreign Policy in Focus*, June 9, 2021. https://fpif.org/why-biden-might-not-be-able-to-extricate-the-us-from-its-middle-east-quagmire/

123 Osama bin Laden, quoted in Nelly Lahoud, *The Bin Laden Papers* (New Haven: Yale University Press, 2022), p. 27.

124 Ibid.

125 Spencer Ackerman, *Reign of Terror: How the 9/11 Era Destabilized America and Produced Trump* (New York: Penguin Books, 2022), p. 15.

126 Lahoud, p. 287.

127 "WSF Forum Had a Prophetic Voice," interview of Walden Bello by Al Jazeera's Gabriel Elizondo, February 25, 2009, reproduced in *Ritimo*. https://www.ritimo.org/WSF-had-a-prophetic-voice

128 Walden Bello, Herbert Docena, Marissa de Guzman, and Marylou Malig, *The Anti-Development State: The Political Economy of Permanent Crisis in the Philippines* (Quezon City: University of the Philippines Press, 2014).

129 Walden Bello, "Yellow and Black (With Apologies to Stendhal)," *Business World*, August 19, 1999.

130 Walden Bello, "The May 1st Riot: Birth of Peronism Philippine-Style?," *Focus on the Philippines*, Issue 20, May 7, 2001. http://focusweb.org/publications/Bulletins/Fop/2001/FOP20.htm

131 *Ibid.*

132 "Communist Party 'hit list' denounced, Akbayan leaders fear for their lives," *Philippine Daily Inquirer*, December 26, 2004. https://libcom.org/article/communist-party-hit-list-denounced-akbayan-leaders-fear-their-lives

133 Walden Bello, "Why We've Been Targeted,"ATC 115, March–April 2005. https://www.marxists.org/history/etol/newspape/atc/323.html

134 Jose Maria Sison, "Walden Bello Exposes Himself as a Pro-US Pseudo-Progressive," *INPS*, December 30, 2004. https://www.josemariasison.eu/inps/WaldenBelloExposesHimselfasaPro-USPseudo-Progressive.htm

135 Palparan is now serving a life sentence for the killing of those two students, Sherlyn Cadapan and Karen Empeno, one of the very few in the military that has been given his just deserts.

136 The initial recruits included Sabrina Gacad and Richard Heydarian, and the team eventually came to include Kit Melgar, Anie Palana, Eloisa Sagum, JV Villanueva, Alvin Rull, and Onieng Policarpio.

137 Leilani Chavez, "Push to Revive Bataan Nuclear Plant Timely?," *ABS-CBN News*, December 21, 2009. https://news.abs-cbn.com/special-report/12/21/09/push-revive-bataan-nuclear-plant-timely

138 Jess Diaz," Rethink Revival of Bataan Nuclear Plant," *Philippine Star*, March 13, 2011. https://www.philstar.com/headlines/2011/03/13/665409/rethink-revival-bataan-nuclear-plant

139 Walden Bello, "CARPER: Latest Chapter in the Struggle for Agri-reform Battle," *Focus on the Global South,* June 23, 2009. https://focusweb.org/afterthoughts-carper-latest-chapter-in-agri-reform-battle/

140 Marilen Danguilan, *The RH Bill Story* (Quezon City: Ateneo de Manila University Press, 2018), pp. 280–81.

141 Walden Bello, "Reproductive Health: Sidelined but irrepressible," *Philippine Daily Inquirer*, May 21, 2012. https://opinion.inquirer.net/29189/reproductive-health-sidelined-but-irrepressible

142 Walden Bello, "The Historic RH Vote: How a Democracy Manages its Conflict over Values," *Philippine Daily Inquirer,* December 15, 2012. https://opinion.inquirer.net/42783/the-historic-rh-vote-how-a-democracy-manages-conflict-over-values

143 Walden Bello, "The Reproductive Health Law: First Step but not the Last," *Rappler,* December 16, 2022. https://www.rappler.com/voices/thought-leaders/analysis-reproductive-health-law-ten-years-first-step-but-not-last/

144 House Committee on Overseas Workers Affairs, *The Dark Kingdom: The Condition of Overseas Filipino Workers in Saudi Arabia,* House of Representatives, January 9–13, 2011.

145 Ibid.

146 Ibid.

147 Much of the following account is based on Walden Bello, "Labor Trafficking: The New Slave Trade," *Foreign Policy in Focus*, May 11, 2012. https://fpif.org/labor_trafficking_modern-day_slave_trade/

148 Attiya Ahmad, "Beyond Labor: Foreign Residents in the Gulf States," *Migrant Labor in the Gulf: Summary Report* (Center for International and Regional Studies, Georgetown University School of Foreign Service in Qatar, 2011), p. 3. http://hdl.handle.net/10822/558543

149 Neferti Tadiar, *Remaindered Life* (Durham: Duke University Press, 2022).

150 Walden Bello, "Homs, Syria: Looking for OFWs in a Shattered City," *Philippine Daily Inquirer*, March 24, 2012. https://opinion.inquirer.net/25527/homs-syria-looking-for-ofws-in-a-shattered-city

151 Simone Orendain, "China Complains About Philippines Lawmakers' Visit to Disputed Islands," *Voice of America*, July 19, 2011. https://www.voanews.com/a/philippines-lawmakers-visit-disputed-islands-china-complains-125896538/142508.html

152 Marites Vitug, *Rock Solid: How the Philippines Won Its Maritime Case Against China* (Quezon City: Ateneo de Manila University Press, 2018), pp. 25–26.

153 Walden Bello, "Fatal Encounter: Jennifer Meets US Marine Corps," *Philippine Daily Inquirer,* October 20, 2014. https://opinion.inquirer.net/79430/fatal-encounter-jennifer-meets-us-marine-corps

154 https://news.abs-cbn.com/focus/05/20/14/edca-useless-wont-protect-ph-territory-bello (no longer available).

155 Walden Bello, "Duterte Is Right to End the U.S.-Philippine Military Exercises," *New York Times*, October 18, 2016. https://www.nytimes.com/roomfordebate/2016/10/18/can-the-us-philippine-alliance-survive-duterte/duterte-is-right-to-end-the-us-philippine-military-exercises

156 Ibid.

157 Ibid.

158 Walden Bello, Introduction to *Walden Bello Presents Ho Chi Minh: Down with Colonialism* (London: Verso, 2007).

159 See, among other accounts, Amita Legaspi, "Arroyo 'escapes' Bello tirade on her first session day," *GMA News Online*, August 2, 2010. https://www.gmanetwork.com/news/topstories/nation/197619/arroyo-escapes-bello-tirade-on-her-first-session-day/story/. Also, Paolo Romero, "Bello could face ethics probe over GMA tirade," *Philippine Star*, August 4, 2010. https://www.philstar.com/headlines/2010/08/04/599207/bello-could-face-ethics-probe-over-gma-tirade

160 Romero.

161 Much of the following account is based on Walden Bello, "Imelda and Me," *Rappler*, July 24, 2022. https://www.rappler.com/voices/thought-leaders/opinion-imelda-and-me/

162 The foregoing account is based on Walden Bello, "Imelda and Me," *Rappler*, July 24, 2022. https://www.rappler.com/voices/thought-leaders/opinion-imelda-and-me/

163 Walden Bello, "Why I Resigned as Akbayan's Representative in Congress," *ABS-CBN News*, June 12, 2015. https://news.abs-cbn.com/blogs/opinions/06/12/15/why-i-resigned-akbayans-rep-congress

164 Ibid.

165 Ibid.

166 Angela Casauay, "Akbayan: Support for Aquino continues; Bello's views personal," *Rappler*, November 3, 2014. https://www.rappler.com/nation/73918-walden-bello-aquino-reaction/

167 Quoted in Gil Cabacungan, "Walden Bello: I'm principled ally of the President," *Philippine Daily Inquirer*, March 2, 2015. https://newsinfo.inquirer.net/676185/walden-bello-im-principled-ally-of-the-president

168 Xianne Arcangel, "Akbayan's Bello urges PNoy to take responsibility for Mamasapano in farewell speech," *GMA News*, March 16, 2015. https://www.gmanetwork.com/news/topstories/nation/453461/akbayan-s-bello-urges-pnoy-to-take-responsibility-for-mamasapano-in-farewell-speech/story/

169 Casauay.

170 Senator Risa Hontiveros, Remarks at event marking Amnesty International Philippines' naming Walden Bello "Most Distinguished Defender of Human Rights." https://www.facebook.com/hontiverosrisa/posts/pfbid05DCQ8R9wHUDJ34LQZtShkc5e9vXncRSysinKTe6Z76LdKBSbTiah N3VMvZ3zBa6Rl

171 Walden Bello, "Part 1: My Thai Wife, the Big C, and Me," *Rappler*, April 18, 2018.https://www.rappler.com/voices/thought-leaders/200476-walden-bello-wife-colon-cancer-series-part-1/; "Conclusion: My Thai Wife, the Big C, and Me," *Rappler*, April 18, 2018. https://www.rappler.com/voices/thought-leaders/200480-walden-bello-wife-colon-cancer-series-conclusion/

172 Eduardo C. Tadem, "Why not a Presidential Candidate from the Left?," *Philippine Daily Inquirer,* August 7, 2015. https://opinion.inquirer.net/87387/why-not-a-presidential-candidate-from-the-left#ixzz8DczN55cm

173 Walden Bello, "Rodrigo Duterte: A Fascist Original," in Nicole Curato, *A Duterte Reader: Critical Essays on Rodrigo Duterte's Early Presidency* (Quezon City: Ateneo de Manila University Press, 2017), p. 78.

174 Ibid., pp. 79–80.

175 See, for instance, Walden Bello, "Democracy in the Era of Charismatic Politics in India and the Philippines," Talk delivered to audiences in Canberra, Perth, and Melbourne during a book promotion tour, November 26–December 10, 2019. Also, Walden Bello, "Democracy and Charisma: A Dangerous Liaison," *Open Democracy,* January 14, 2020. https://www.opendemocracy.net/en/oureconomy/democracy-and-charisma-dangerous-liaison/. See also Walden Bello, "A Dangerous Liaison? Harnessing Weber to Illuminate the Relationship of Democreacy and Charisma in the Philippines and India," *International Sociology,* Vol. 35, No. 6 (2020), https://doi.org/10.1177/0268580920942

176 Bello, "Rodrigo Duterte: A Fascist Original," p. 81.

177 Walden Bello, "The May 1st Riot: Birth of Peronism, Philippine-Style?," *Business World*, May 5, 2001.

178 https://www.facebook.com/walden.bello/posts/pfbid02Lua99sNAahiLGYhsRPpqMSkXeRi8W4t4wMWF9UVXKjgWPskijkuR4t7vngGSaPPpl

179 Walden Bello, "Lawfare and Warfare: The Blitz against Senator Leila de Lima," *Rappler*, February 24, 2020. https://www.rappler.com/voices/thought-leaders/252552-opinion-lawfare-warfare-blitz-leila-de-lima/

180 Senator Leila de Lima, personal message, July 16, 2023.

181 Walden Bello, "Duterte is a Mass Murderer, but I Support his Terminating the VFA," *Rappler*, January 27, 2020. https://www.rappler.com/voices/thought-leaders/250280-opinion-duterte-is-a-mass-murderer-but-i-support-his-terminating-the-vfa/

182 Jairo Bolledo, "Walden Bello Blasts Marcos with the F-Word during Live Interview," *Rappler,* October 22, 2021. https://www.rappler.com/nation/elections/walden-bello-blasts-bongbong-marcos-with-f-word-live-interview/

183 "Philippines Election: Last Week Tonight with John Oliver (HBO)," YouTube video [20:28], *LastWeek Tonight,* May 8, 2022. https://www.youtube.com/watch?v=FtdVglihDok

184 Ralph Lawrence G. Llemit, "Vice Mayor: Bello enters council session hall sans prior coordination," *Sunstar*, April 20, 2022. https://www.sunstar.com.ph/article/1926922/davao/local-news/vice-mayor-bello-enters-council-session-hall-sans-prior-coordination

185 Lian Buan, "Walden Bello is Disruptor of first VP Debate, Calls Sara Duterte a 'Coward,'"*Rappler,* February 26, 2022. https://www.rappler.com/nation/elections/walden-bello-disruptor-vp-debate-cnn-philippines-february-2022/

186 Walden Bello, "Why the son of a hated dictator won the Philippine elections," *MEER,* May 18, 2022. https://www.meer.com/en/69705-why-the-son-of-a-hated-dictator-won-the-philippine-elections

187 Walden Bello, "The American Repossession of the Philippines," *Nation*, March 4, 2023. https://www.thenation.com/article/world/us-philippines-military-deal/

188 Amnesty International, *Philippines 2022*. https://www.amnesty.org/en/location/asia-and-the-pacific/south-east-asia-and-the-pacific/philippines/report-philippines/

189 Raymund Antonio, "VP Sara to Walden Bello: 'Stop obsessing over me,'" *Manila Bulletin*, August 9, 2022. https://mb.com.ph/2022/8/9/vp-sara-to-walden-bello-stop-obsessing-over-me

190 Benjamin Pulta, "Bello asks SC to declare libel, cyberlibel laws void," *Philippine News Agency*, December 5, 2023. https://www.pna.gov.ph/articles/1214897

191 Walden Bello, "Time to seek Justice, not Hand Out the Nobel Prize, for Economic Crimes," *Progressive International,* June 13, 2023. https://progressive.international/wire/2023-06-13-walden-bello-time-to-seek-justice-not-hand-out-the-nobel-prize-for-economic-crimes/en

192 Walden Bello, *Counterrevolution: The Global Rise of the Far Right* (Halifax: Fernwood, 2019).

193 Walden Bello, "How Obama's Legacy Lost the Elections for Hilary," *Foreign Policy in Focus*, November 16, 2016. https://fpif.org/obamas-legacy-lost-elections-hillary/; Walden Bello, "America Has Entered the Weimar Era," *Foreign Policy in Focus,* January 7, 2021. https://fpif.org/america-has-entered-the-weimar-era/; "America Has Entered the Weimar Era: Walden Bello on How Neoliberalism Fueled Trump & Violent Right," *Democracy Now*, January 12, 2021. https://www.youtube.com/watch?v=feneGtQHSnU

194 Walden Bello, "America Has Entered the Weimar Era," *Foreign Policy in Focus,* January 7, 2021. https://fpif.org/america-has-entered-the-weimar-era/

195 Ibid.

196 Adrian Peel, "The Cambridge Union discusses whether we are witnessing a fascist resurgence," *Cambridge Independent*, April 30, 2021. https://www.cambridgeindependent.co.uk/education/the-cambridge-union-discusses-whether-we-are-witnessing-a-fa-9197525/

197 Walden Bello, *Paper Dragons: China and the Next Crash* (London: Bloomsbury, Zed, 2019).

198 Walden Bello, "In 100 Years, the Chinese Communist Party Goes through 3 Major Revolutions," *The Citizen*, July 10, 2021. https://www.thecitizen.in/index.php/en/NewsDetail/index/6/20605/In-100-Years-the-Chinese-Communist-Party-Goes-Through-3-Major-Revolutions

199 Walden Bello, "Duterte Is Right to End the U.S.-Philippine Military Exercises," *New York Times*, October 18, 2016. https://www.nytimes.com/roomfordebate/2016/10/18/can-the-us-philippine-alliance-survive-duterte/duterte-is-right-to-end-the-us-philippine-military-exercises

200 "Harris Will Be More of the Same," Facebook page, July 30, 2024. https://www.facebook.com/walden.bello/posts/pfbid02Tao636nJFusHtKXHC9eJrJxPR3pqDF4PVA7RzyYPCDMvAEesz3a6FyRstAxEPNFGl

201 James, p. 87.

Index

9/11 attacks (September 11, 2001), 151–52, 174, 180, 278

A

Abad, Butch, 230
Abesamis, Marilen, 11, 70, 84, 237, 295–96
abortion, 196, 200, 258
A.E. Havens Center, 2
Afghanistan, 151–53, 159, 174–80, 278, 288
Africa, 52, 87, 133, 134, 136, 227, 274
Ahos purge, 77, 78, 285
Akbayan, 184–95, 198–99, 228–36, 248, 289, 296
  coalition with Liberal Party, 228–36
Allende, Salvador, 21, 88, 269–70
Alliance for Philippine Concerns (APC), 59
Alternative Nobel Prize. *See* Right Livelihood Award
Althusser, Louis, 9, 11–12
Alvarez, Sonny, 67
"America First," 178, 181
America is in the Heart, 26
American Lake: The Nuclear Peril in the Pacific, 81–83
Amnesty International, 236, 262
Amnesty International Philippines, 236, 255, 264
Ang Bayan, 77
Angsioco, Elizabeth, 198
anti-globalization activism, 3, 101, 118–39, 142–43, 146–50, 182–83, 187
Anti-Imperialist League, 25

Anti-Deep Penetration Agent (Anti-DPA) Campaign. *See Ahos* purge
Anti-Martial Law Coalition (AMLC). *See* Coalition against the Marcos Dictatorship (CAMD)
Antwerp, 58
Anderson, Perry, 9, 11–12, 73, 300n
Aquino, Benigno, 32, 40, 55, 60–62, 66, 260–61
Aquino, Benigno III, 194, 198, 216–20, 222, 226, 228–29, 233. 242, 252
  Daang Matuwid ("the straight and narrow road"), 230, 232
Aquino, Corazon, 64–66, 69, 71, 76, 101–102, 184
Arab Spring, 142, 177, 209
Arbatov, Alexei, 93
Argentina, 15, 81, 87, 138, 293
Armacost, Michael, 62, 64, 65–66
Armed Forces of the Philippines (AFP), 36–38, 42–43, 64–65, 74
Arroyo, Gloria Macapagal, 102, 106, 153–54, 185–86, 189, 193–94, 225
Ateneo de Manila University, 8, 23, 99
Asedillo, Becky, 67, 295
Asian Development Bank (ADB), 114–15
Asian financial crisis of 1997–1998, 89, 105, 110–16
al-Assad, Bahar, 209
al-Assad, Hafez, 209
Assange, Julian, 58
Association of Democratic Youth (Samahan ng Demokratikong Kabataan, SDK), 23
AUKUS security pact, 257
Australia, 82, 109, 257, 261

B

Back to Bataan, 1, 8
Bamford, Chanida, 183, 305n
Bangkok, 1, 98, 100, 101, 109–113,
    151, 161, 181–83, 237–48, 305n
Barlow, Maude, 118
Bataan Nuclear Plant, 81, 190, 199, 224,
    249
Bautista, Cynthia, 98, 296
Baviera, Mara, 100, 296
Bayan coalition, 40
Bayan Muna, 188
Beirut, 160, 163–73, 176, 208
Belgium, 58
Bello, Buenaventura, 8
Bello, Dennis, 8
Bello (Edwards), Gwethalyn, 8
Bello, Jeese (Jess), 7–8, 56, 295
Bello, Luz Flores, 8, 56, 295
Bello, Melvyn, 8
Bello, Walden,
    co-founding Focus on the Global
        South, 98, 109
    debate at fall IMF/World Bank
        meeting in Prague (2001), 122–24
    debate with Robert Koopman at the
        Asia Trade Summit in Hong Kong
        (2019), 132–34
    family of,
        father (Jesse), 7–8, 56, 295
        mother (Luz), 8, 56, 295
        uncle (Buenaventura), 8
        wife (Madge). *See* Kho, Madeline
            (Madge)
        wife (Marilen Abesamis). *See*
            Abesamis, Marlien
        wife (Suranuch "Ko" Thongsila).
            See Thongsila, Suranuch ("Ko")
    involvement in the Communist Party
        of the Philippines, 22–32, 61,
        68–79, 89, 277, 285, 289
    branded a "counterrevolutionary"
        by, 77, 144, 186–87
    involvement in protests/direct action,
        9–10, 46–51, 67–68, 113–19, 128,
        131, 161–62, 181, 278,
            at the Kennedy Center, 46–47
            at IMF headquarters in 1982 (Miss
                Piggy Protest, 47–48
            at Marcos speech at the National
                Press Club, 48
            at WTO meeting in Seattle (1999),
                118–22
            at G8 meeting in Genoa (2000),
                125–28
            at WTO meeting in Doha (2001),
                128–29
        occupation of the Philippine
            Consulate in San Francisco,
            48–52
        theft of documents from the World
            Bank, 52–58
    member of the Philippines House
        of Representatives, 172, 182,
        188–236
    chairing the Committee on
        Overseas Workers Affairs, 195,
        201–13, 227, 252, 254
    resignation from, 232–36
    running mate of Leody de Guzman in
        2022 Presidential election, 258–60,
        299
Benjamin, Medea, 85, 119, 128
Berkeley, 28, 58, 85, 99
Bernabe, Riza, 103
Biden, Joseph Robinet (Joe), 136, 179,
    271, 274–76, 279
Bielski, Vincent, 54
Bikini, 83
Bin Laden, Osama, 152, 174–77,
    180–81
Black Bloc, 126–27
Blair, Tony, 129, 162–63
Bolshevik Revolution (1917), 4, 289
Brangan, Marybeth, 83, 97, 116, 298,
    299
Brando, Marlon, 13
Brazil, 81, 130, 134, 137–38, 143, 182,
    243, 256, 278
Bretton Woods Conference, 77, 117
British imperialism, 161

Broad, Robin, 54, 58, 85, 93, 148, 238, 295
"Brunei Beauties," 104, 303n
Buckley, Mary Anne, 68
Bullard, Nicola, 125, 153, 183, 296, 299, 303n, 305n
Bulosan, Carlos, 26
Bush, George W. (Jr.), 128, 145, 155–60, 162, 174–78, 278

C

Cabral, Esperanza, 198
Cadorna, Wilma, 49
Cambodia, 9
Camdessus, Michel, 113–14, 266
Camus, Albert, 6, 286
Cajiuat, Jocey, 103
Canada, 27, 103
Canlas, Corinne, 67, 296
Capital, 11
capital controls, 111, 115
capitalism, 3, 6, 9, 11–12, 80, 82, 84, 92, 94, 101, 106, 124, 139, 140, 142, 145, 147, 182, 204–205, 207, 269, 271–73, 277, 286–87, 290
Cardoso, Fernando Henrique, 56, 79
Castrence, Elsie, 67, 295
Castrence, Totoy, 67, 295
Carter, Jimmy, 45–46
Catholic Church, 6, 49, 64, 74, 96, 105, 184, 195–96, 198, 228, 245
Cavanagh, John, 58, 67, 80, 93, 118, 238, 295
Central Intelligence Agency (CIA), 12, 18–20, 31, 64–66, 78, 187
chaebol, 92, 111
Chavez, Cesar, 26
Chavez, Hugo, 141–45, 256–57
Chavez, Joy, 106, 183, 305n
Chicago, 29, 183–84
"Chicago Boys," 18, 266
Chongthomdi, Jacques Chai, 183, 296, 305n
Claudio, Sylvia Estrada, 198, 298
Chile, 13–21
    middle class in, 13–21

China, 3, 11, 32, 34, 130, 133–34, 136, 139, 160, 175, 178–79, 183, 204, 211, 214–22, 251, 257, 261, 269–70, 272–76, 278–80, 286, 290
    territorial claims in South China Sea, 214–22
Chino, Tadao, 114–15
Chulalongkorn University Hospital, 242–44
Chulalongkorn University Social Research Institute (CUSRI), 109, 297
civil society, 61, 114–20, 128–29, 131, 146, 161, 162, 180–81, 190, 195, 239, 246, 278, 287, 290
Church Coalition for Human Rights in the Philippines, 59, 67
Clinton, Bill, 120
Clinton, Hillary, 178, 247
Cultural Revolution in, 34, 273
China, Republic of. *See* Taiwan
Chinese Communist Party, 73, 92, 274
Chulalongkorn University Social Research Institute, 109
Church Coalition for Human Rights in the Philippines, 59, 67
Christian Democratic Party (Chile), 15–17, 19
Christian Democratic Party (The Philippines), 23
Cielito Lindo Island, 6
City College of San Francisco, 49
Clark Air Force Base, 6, 155, 277
Clark, Ramsey, 59
climate change, 3, 31, 182–83, 204, 269, 274, 290
Coalition against the Marcos Dictatorship (CAMD), 25, 59, 67
Cojuango, Danding, 190
Cojuangco, Kimi, 249, 297
Cojuangco, Mark, 190, 224, 249
Coming Crisis in Western Sociology, The, 9
Communist Manifesto, 11
Communist Party (Chile), 14, 16

Communist Party of the Philippines (CPP), 23, 25–26, 29–38, 41–43, 75, 77–79, 58–60, 70, 72–80, 89, 144, 186–88, 248, 256, 277, 285, 289
  purges ("Kampanyang Ahos," AKA Operation Garlic; *see also Ahos purge*), 73–76
Communist Party USA (CPUSA), 23, 26–27
Comprehensive Agrarian Reform Program (CARP), 191–92, 235
Comprehensive Agrarian Reform with Extension Bill (CARPER), 191–93, 199, 230
Congress Education Project, 23, 25
Cornell University, 11
Corpuz, Vicky, 118
Counterrevolution: The Global Rise of the Far Right, 270
COVID-19, 132, 257, 270
Cruz, Aimee, 23
Cruz, Rene, 23, 295
Cruz, Vera Phillip, 26
Cuba, 15
Cuban Missile Crisis, 277
Cunningham, Doug, 67, 295
Cunningham, Shea, 109, 112, 296
Custer, George Armstrong (General), 9

D
Damascus, 155–59, 163, 169, 207–212
Dark Victory: The United States, Structural Adjustment, and Global Poverty, 67, 144
Davao, 140, 251, 252, 254, 256, 258, 262
  City Council of, 258
  death squad killings in, 252, 254
David, Randy, 98, 296
Davos, 115–16, 137–38, 182
deglobalization, 110, 122, 145–50
Democratic Party (United States), 81, 177, 270, 279
Democratic Progressive Party (DPP), 91

Development Debacle, 54–58, 70, 85, 105, 144, 292
Disbursement Acceleration Program (DAP), 229–31
Domingo, Silme, 27
Dragons in Distress: Asia's Miracle Economies in Crisis, 93
Drew, James, 23
drugs, 28, 97, 194, 208, 250, 252, 254
Duterte, Rodrigo, 59, 208, 220, 249–57, 259–60, 265, 267, 278
  extra-judicial executions of drug users and dealers, 249, 256
Duterte, Sara, 258–59, 261

E
Ebro, Cristine, 296
Ebro, Tina, 248
Enhanced Defense Cooperation Agreement (EDCA), 218–19, 228–29, 257
Earth Summit. *See* United Nations Conference on Environment and Development (UNCED)
Eastern Europe, 3, 98, 106, 286
El Salvador, 81
"Elite Democracy and Authoritarian Rule," 80
Elinson, Elaine, 54, 295
Endaya, Eric, 209–10
Enriquez, Jean, 198, 299
Estrada, Joseph "Erap," 143, 184–86
  impeachment trial and ouster from the Presidency, 184–86
Evangelista, Crisanto, 31

F
Falk, Richard, 2, 59, 93, 162, 298, 299
Far Eastern Economic Review, 33–34
fascism, 40, 147, 253, 269–70, 278, 280
Federated States of Micronesia, 83
Financial crisis of 2007–2008, 116, 120–21, 142
financial liberalization, 112, 116, 120–21
Fischer, Ed, 9

Filipino-American community, 25–9, 48, 59, 66
"First Quarter Storm," 8, 10, 23, 29, 148
First World War, 276, 280
Fitzgerald, F. Scott, 6, 13, 138
Flores, Menchie, 103
Focus on the Global South, 100–101, 109–110, 112, 131, 134, 137, 139, 158, 161, 181, 182, 239, 264–65, 296, 303n, 305n, 307n
Food First, 70, 77, 84–87, 89, 93–94, 97–98, 109, 128, 130
Fort Santiago, 7–8
Friedman, Milton, 88, 266
Friedman, Thomas, 121
Friends of the Earth International, 123
Friends of the Filipino People (FFP), 25
From the Ashes: The Rebirth of the Philippine Left, 32–43

G
Gaza, 164, 168–73, 176, 179, 181
General Agreements on Tariffs and Trade (GATT), 134. *See also* Uruguay Round
Genoa Social Forum, 125–28
genocide, 82–83, 173, 179
George, Susan, 118, 125, 298
Gouldner, Alvin, 9
Global North, 3, 130, 269, 271
Global South, 2, 3, 12, 77, 80–81, 89, 98, 100–101, 107, 109–110, 112, 114, 117–18, 131, 134, 136, 137–39, 152, 158, 161, 179, 181–82, 207, 220, 239, 269, 271, 278–79, 281, 286, 290, 296
Gorbachev, Mikhail, 93
Globalization, 3, 4, 77, 98, 101, 110, 114, 116, 118–39, 142–43, 146–50, 162, 181–83, 187, 270, 288, 292
activism against. *See* anti-globalization activism
far-right rhetoric against, 149–50, 270
Gramsci, Antonio, 73, 252, 281
Great Replacement Theory, 291
greenhouse gas emissions, 269, 274

Greenpeace, 84
Greenspan, Alan, 116, 278
Guam, 82, 276
Guatemala, 81
Guerrero, Amado. *See* Jose Maria Sison
Guerrero, Dorothy, 183, 297
guerilla warfare, 31, 37–44, 164, 167, 174
Guevara, Ernesto "Che," 21, 151, 167–68, 174
Gulf War (1990–1991), 157, 175
Gutierrez, Barry, 229, 296
Gutierrez, Ging, 100, 296
Guttal, Shalmali, 183, 296, 303n, 305n
Guzman, Leody de, 258–59, 299
Guzman, Marissa de, 100, 105

H
Hague, The, 19, 219–20, 256, 270
Hamas, 164, 168–79
Oct 7, 2023 attack on Israel, 164, 172–73
Hamdan, Usamah, 168–73
Harris, Kamala, 279–80
Hau, Carol, 1–2, 4
Havel, Vaclav, 123–24
Hayes, Peter, 81, 298
Heddle, Jim, 83, 97, 298
Hernandez, Isabel, 271
Hernandez, Vee, 49
Hezbollah, 163–69, 176
Ho Chi Minh, 220
Ho Chi Minh City, 94, 222
Ho Chi Minh trail, 12
Hong Kong, 33, 89, 100, 110, 131–36, 272, 275
Honolulu, 25, 114
Hontiveros, Risa, 188–89, 191, 195, 198, 236, 252, 296
Hukbalahap (Huk) revolution, 31, 41
Hussein, Saddam, 156–59, 162–63, 175

I
individual rights, 74–77, 79, 195, 284, 289

India, 11, 52, 87, 130, 163, 165, 183,
204, 291
Indonesia, 2, 111, 123, 124, 155–56,
158, 197–98
Institute for Defense Analysis (IDA,
*currently known as Institute for
Defense Analyses*), 9–10
Institute for Food and Development
Policy. *See* Food First
Institute for Policy Studies, 80, 118
International Civil Society and
Parliamentary Mission, 163
International Criminal Court (ICC),
256, 264, 266
International Longshore and Warehouse
Union (ILWU Local 37), 27
International Forum on Globalization,
118, 121, 123
International Monetary Fund (IMF),
47–48, 87, 101, 106, 111–17,
122–23, 136, 205, 228, 260,
265–66, 275, 278
International Studies Association, 58,
294
Iran, 177, 178, 211
Iraq, 23, 141, 155–63, 168, 174–81, 207
Iraq War, 141, 159–63, 168, 174–78
Iraq Veterans Against the War, 162
Israel, 163–79, 279–80
2006 attack on Lebanon, 163–68
Apartheid practiced by, 163, 172,
174, 176
Itliong, Larry, 26

J

Japan, 1, 7–8, 11, 31, 33, 82, 83, 89, 93,
107, 110, 114, 118, 133, 161, 191,
221, 243, 264, 276, 281
Johnson, Chalmers, 56, 93, 298
Jolo, 8, 24, 295

K

Keynesianism, 56, 106–107
Kho, Madeline (Madge), 8, 10, 237, 295
Khor, Martin, 117, 118, 292
Kirkpatrick, Jeane, 80

Kirkpatrick Doctrine, 80
Kissinger, Henry, 9, 12, 22, 196
Kissinger Doctrine, 196
Klein, Naomi, 139, 142–43
Kuomintang (KMT), 91
Kuwait, 23, 159, 204
Kwa, Aileen, 128, 183, 296
Kyoto, 1

L

Laban ng Masa (People's Struggle),
30, 249
Lange, David, 84, 146
Laguna de Bay, 7
land reform,
in Chile, 14, 17
in the Philippines, 31, 33, 37, 188,
191, 230
in Taiwan, 91
Landsdale, Edward, 31, 68
Lane, Max, 2
Laos, 12
Lara, Francisco, 103
Lara, Pancho, 67
Larrain, Sara, 118, 298
Latin America, 10, 15, 56, 68, 79, 81,
83, 87–88, 134, 136, 138, 143, 280
League of Revolutionary Struggle, 27
Lebanese Communist Party, 167
Lebanon, 163–69, 173, 176, 211
Lenin, Vladimir, 9, 34
de Lima, Leila, 59, 252–53, 256, 267,
297
liberal democracy, 45, 67, 69–70,
278–81, 291
in the Philippines, 22, 70, 75–77,
80–81, 183, 250, 269, 292
Libya, 177
Line of March, 27–28
LGBTQ+ rights, 188, 194, 217
Llamas, Ronald, 72, 188, 195, 218
Logistics of Repression, The, 24
Los Angeles, 25, 27, 151, 211
Luzon, 31, 36–37, 42, 191

M

Maglaya, Becky, 11
Maglaya, Cynthia, 11
Magsaysay, Ramon, 31, 64
Makati Business Club, 106, 107, 184, 260
Malaysia, 86, 132, 207
Malhotra, Kamal, 109, 296
Malig, Marylou, 100, 105, 131, 168, 216, 296, 305n
Mamasapano raid, 231–35
Mander, Jerry, 118, 292, 298
Manila, 6–7, 36, 45, 52, 59–63, 66–69, 73, 89–90, 109, 116, 151, 182–83, 185, 189, 191, 194, 208, 216, 243, 264, 278, 287
Manila Bay, 249
Manila Bulletin, 6–7
Manila International Airport. 60
Manglapus, Raul, 23, 264
Mangaoang, Ernesto, 26
Mao Zedong, 26, 32, 34, 36, 91, 273
Maoism, 33, 78, 92
Marcos, "Bongbong" (Ferdinand Jr.), 255, 258–61
Marcos, Ferdinand, 22–25, 27–28, 32, 36, 38, 40, 42–43, 45–71, 78–80, 87, 90, 101–102, 105–106, 160–61, 188, 190, 194, 199, 204, 205, 226, 266, 267, 277, 281, 284, 287, 295
    martial law under, 22–23, 28, 35–39, 53
Marcos, Imelda, 46, 94, 226–28, 261
Marley, Bob, 294
Marshall Islands, 83
Marx, Karl, 9, 12, 283–84
Marxism, 10–12, 20–21, 25, 27–33, 72–73, 76, 79, 83, 89, 140, 182, 186–87, 269, 281, 285
Marxism-Leninism, 25, 27–29, 140
Mayer, Arno, 10
McCarthyism, 12, 35
McNamara, Robert, 54, 86–87, 266
Melgar, Junice Demeterio, 198
Melgar, Kit, 296, 306n
Menon, Meena, 182, 296, 305n
Mensalvas, Chris, 26

Mexico, 13–14, 130, 133, 134
Mexico City, 13, 160, 204, 205
Micronesia, 82–83
Middle East, 134, 159, 163, 174–81, 204–209, 278–80, 287–88
Mindanao, 37, 42, 73, 191, 203, 232
Mittal, Anuradha, 118, 128, 130, 131, 296
Mohammed, Mahathir, 86
model debtor policy, 102
Moore, Mike, 132, 260
Moro National Liberation Front (MNLF), 39, 58
Movement for a Free Philippines (MFP), 23
Mumbai, 139–40, 161

N
Naiman, Robert, 113–14
Nation, The, 261, 298
National Committee for the Restoration of Civil Liberties in the Philippines (NCRCLP), 23, 25
National Democratic Front (NDF), 23, 25, 36, 39–40, 58–59, 61, 64–67, 70, 72–73, 76, 78, 89, 187–88, 248, 256
    boycott of 1986 election, 65–66, 71, 75, 78, 285
Nasrallah, Hassan, 165, 167–68
National Democratic Revolution, 4, 28, 35, 43, 78, 273, 287, 289
"national democracy" (ideology), 11, 34
National Economic Development Authority (NEDA), 102
National Security Strategy Directive on the Philippines (NSSD), 61–63
Nautilus Institute, 81
Negros, 37, 38
Nemenzo, Ana Maria (Princess), 188, 198, 248
Nemenzo, Francisco, 31, 72, 100, 188, 248
neoliberalism, 4, 88, 98–109, 116, 121, 132, 135–36, 146–47, 181, 265–67, 270, 272, 278, 280, 286–88

New Delhi, 109
New Left, 27, 97
New People's Army, 35, 36, 78, 89, 186,
    256
New York City, 11, 23, 25, 27, 160, 161,
    172, 188, 216, 243, 261
New York Times, 67, 160, 177, 182, 219,
    276
"New York, New York," 95
New York University, 271
New Zealand, 84, 146
newly industrializing countries (NICs),
    56, 89–93, 98, 273
Nguyen Thi Binh, 220–21
Nicaragua, 70, 81
    Contras in, 81
    Sandinista revolution in, 70
Nixon, Richard, 9, 12, 22, 45
North Africa, 17
North Atlantic Treaty Organization
    (NATO), 177, 275, 279
North Korea, 94, 96, 104
Nuclear Free and Independent Pacific
    Network (NFIP), 84

O
Obama, Barack, 177–78, 218, 257
Ocampo, Satur, 89, 187, 297
Occena, Bruce, 27, 295
Occupy movement, 3, 142, 181
Oslo Agreement, 171
Overseas Filipino Workers (OFWs),),
    23, 201–213
Oxfam, 93–94, 129, 151
Oxfam America, 93–94, 151

P
Palestine, 2, 163, 168–74, 179, 306
Palestinian Authority, 171
Palparan, Jovito, 189–90, 306n
Panay, 37
*Paper Dragons: China and the Next
    Crash*, 274
Paras, Melinda, 27, 295
Paris Peace Accords
Parity Amendment, 33

Partido Komunista ng Pilipinas (PKP),
    31–32, 35, 41, 68
Pentagon, The, 9, 43, 63, 64, 257,
    279–80
People's Action Party, 90
People Power Revolution. *See* EDSA
    Revolution
Permanent People's Tribunal (PPT),
    58–59
Peru, 22, 32
Philippine Panorama, 6–7
Philippine Society and Revolution
    (PSR), 32–36, 78
Philippines, The, 3, 6, 7–8, 10–12,
    21–44, 52–55, 58–82, 84, 87, 89,
    91, 97, 98, 101–108, 133, 136,
    143, 153, 155, 163, 182–236, 239,
    241–43, 255–68, 273–78, 280–85,
    287, 289–92
and the East Asian financial crisis of
    1997–98, 110–11
EDSA uprising (1986) in, 3, 44,
    60–69, 71, 72, 76–78, 105, 184,
    226, 250, 259–60, 287
EDSA II mobilization in, 185, 194
EDSA III mobilization in, 185–86,
    251
Left wing politics in, 3, 21–44,
    45–46, 48, 60–79, 85, 185–86, 248,
    251, 259, 287, 289–92
Neo-liberal policies implemented in,
    101–108
overseas workers from. *See* Overseas
    Filipino Workers (OFWs)
territorial dispute with China in South
    China Sea, 214–21
U.S. military bases in, 6, 65, 155, 277
Philippines Congress, 155, 187, 189–36,
    240, 242, 248, 249
House of Representatives, 26, 153,
    172, 182, 188, 192, 212–13, 219,
    223–36, 278, 284
Committee on Overseas Workers
    Affairs, 195, 201–13, 227, 252,
    254

Senate, 103–104, 183, 184, 195, 199, 217, 225, 242, 259
Pilipino (*see also* Tagalog), 13n, 224
Pinochet, Augusto, 18–21, 88, 102, 266
Polanyi, Karl, 146–47
Porto Alegre, 137–48, 160
Poulantzas, Nicos, 9, 11–12, 73
Pramoedya Ananta Toer, 2
Pramoedya Problem, 2
Prasartsert, Suthy, 109, 297
Princeton University, 6–16, 22–23, 46, 59, 79, 93, 119, 133, 149, 277, 283, 285
protracted people's war, 35, 70, 72
Putin, Vladimir, 93, 179, 261, 279
Pyongyang, 94–96

Q
Quezon City, 98, 101
Quiros, Conrad de, 104, 298, 303n

R
Racelis, Mary, 198, 295
racism, 6, 26, 82–83, 139, 270, 278
Ramos, Fidel, 65, 71, 102–103, 184, 257
Raymundo, Sarah,100, 296
"Reaffirm Our Basic Principles and Rectify Errors," 76
Reagan, Ronald, 45, 46, 60, 63, 65–66, 80–81, 161, 271, 277
Regalado, Au, 103
Reproductive Rights (RH) bill, 195–200
Republic or Empire: American Resistance to the Philippine War, 25
Republican Party (United States), 81
Revolution of 1896 (Philippines), 33
Revolutionary Communist Party, 27
Reyes, Julie de los, 100, 298, 299, 305n
Reyes, Ricardo, 89, 186, 195, 296
Reyes, Virgilio de los, 230, 232
Right Livelihood Award, 84, 146, 148
Rivera-Drew, Severina, 23–25, 52, 296
Rocamora, Joel, 11, 58, 72, 188, 195, 296

Robredo, Leni, 260
Rosales, Etta, 155–56, 158, 186, 188, 190, 195, 218, 296
Roy, Arundhati, 161, 163, 274
Royandoyan, Omi, 103
Russia, 93, 125, 177, 211, 261, 271

S
Sachs, Jeffrey, 121
Sakuma, Tomoko, 118
San Francisco, 23, 25–28, 48–51, 58, 67, 70, 81, 84–85, 97, 294
San Francisco Chronicle, 49
Santiago, 13–14, 16, 21
Santiago, Miriam (Senator), 217
dos Santos, Theotonio, 56, 79
Saudi Arabia, 178–79, 201–204, 211–12
Schirmer, Daniel Boone, 25, 52
Seattle, 25, 26, 27, 117–22, 127, 131, 278, 283
    "Battle of," 118–22, 127, 131, 138–39, 278, 283
Singapore, 89–91, 93, 110, 117–18, 121, 207, 237, 261, 288
Sison, Joma, 29–39, 75–76, 187, 257, 292
Snowden, Edward, 58
socialism, 3–4, 13, 15–16, 27–29, 35, 59, 78, 93, 100, 106–107, 134, 146–47, 149, 188, 257–58, 285–90
Socialist International, 140
Seoul, 92, 95
Shiva, Vandana, 118
Soros, George, 121, 122, 124–25, 137–38
South Africa, 130
South China Sea, 179, 214–21, 273–76, 278
South Korea, 81–83, 89, 96–97, 107, 110–11, 161, 281
Southeast Asia, 83, 105, 109–110, 211
Southeast Asia Resource Center, 58
Southeast Asian financial crisis of 1997–1998. *See* Asian financial crisis of 1997–1998

Soviet Union, 3, 34, 93, 98, 106, 175, 277–78, 284, 286
Spain, 13, 33, 125
Stalin, Josef, 93
Stalinism, 16, 30, 78
State University of New York at Binghamton, 186, 270, 297
Stein, Stanley, 10
Stiglitz, Joseph, 121
Stockholm, 84, 146, 148, 161
structural adjustment programs, 54, 77, 87–89, 98, 102–103, 105, 116, 123, 201, 204–205, 266, 278
Subic Naval Base, 6, 155, 277
Suharto, 2, 123
Sulu, 8, 292
Summers, Larry, 86, 116, 124
Sunshine, Cathy, 68
Sweden, 146, 148, 243
Switzerland, 157, 261
Syria, 157, 158, 169, 178–80, 207–208, 212–13

T
Tadiar, Neferti, 207
Tagalog (*see also* Pilipino), 13n, 48, 188, 194, 243, 250, 252
Taipei, 91–92
Taiwan, 89, 91, 93, 107, 110, 179, 219, 275
Taliban, 153, 177–78, 288
Tanada, Erin, 40, 198, 230, 297
Tanada, Lorenzo, 40, 198
Tannenbaum, Martha, 68
Tet Offensive, 6
Thailand, 18, 98, 101, 109–114, 116, 196–98, 237–47
Third World Debt Crisis, 286
Third World Network, 117, 131
This Side of Paradise, 6, 13, 22
Thongsila, Suranuch ("Ko"), 2, 125, 221–22, 227, 239–48, 295
Thoreau, Henry David, 7
Tiananmen Square, 94

Trade Related Investment Measures (TRIMS), 132
Trade Related Intellectual Property Rights Agreement (TRIPS), 132
trade liberalization, 4, 88, 102, 127, 129, 131, 133, 205, 288
Trump, Donald, 134, 178–79, 247, 270–71, 274, 278–80

U
Ukraine, 179, 261, 275, 279
U.N. (United Nations), 2, 86, 121, 155, 162, 176
UN sanctions (Iraq), 162
UN Security Council, 155
Unidad Popular, 13–20
Union of Democratic Filipinos (*Katipunan ng mga Demokratikong Pilipino*, KDP), 25–29, 59, 66
United Farm Workers (UFW), 26
United Kingdom, 129, 163, 257
United Nations Conference on Environment and Development (UNCED), 86
United Nations Conference on Trade and Development (UNCTAD), 113
United Nations Convention of the Law of the Seas (UNCLOS), 215, 219
United States, 22–23, 31, 45, 61–65, 67–69, 78, 81, 83–84, 116, 152, 159–60, 163, 175, 179, 188, 218–20, 228, 250–51, 257, 261, 275–76, 278–81, 284, 287
   confrontation with China, 275–76
   imperialism, 33–35, 39–52, 80–84, 96, 151–83, 251, 277–81, 287–90
   role in the EDSA Revolution, 61–69
United States Congress, 59, 61, 63–64, 68, 71, 124
United States House of Representatives, 24
United States House of Representatives Subcommittee on Asia-Pacific Affairs, 43
United States Immigration Act (1965), 26

United States Senate, 24
  Foreign Relations Committee, 43
United States State Department, 57, 61,
  63–66, 187
United States Treasury, 57, 61, 116, 124

University of California at Berkeley,
  85, 99
University of Chicago, 88, 266
University of the Philippines, 98–102
University of Wisconsin, 2
Uruguay Round, 101,120, 129
Utrecht, 58, 76

V
Venezuela, 143–45, 186
Vera Cruz, Phillip, 26
Viernes, Gene, 27
Vietnam, 6, 9–12, 22, 27, 45, 59, 93–94,
  175, 181, 197–98, 214, 220–22,
  277, 286
territorial dispute with China in South
  China Sea, 221–22
Vietnam War, 10–12, 22, 27, 35–36, 45,
  59, 175, 181, 221, 277, 286
"Vietnam Syndrome," 42
Visiting Forces Agreement (VFA), 217,
  257

W
Wallach, Lori, 118
Walsh, Jeannie, 68
Wan-Geao, Surichai, 109, 297
"Washington Consensus," 89, 265
Washington, DC, 9, 10, 23, 25, 27–29,
  46–48, 60, 67, 70, 80, 83, 97,
  113–14
Washington Forum, 67
Washington Post, 46, 123
Wayne, John, 8
West Point, 9
Wheatley, Paul, 9
Wisconsin, 2
Wolfensohn, James, 122–25
Wolfowitz, Paul, 63
women's rights, 6, 188, 194, 199

Wong-kai, War, 100
Wonsan, 96
World Bank, 52–58, 67, 85–87, 101,
  106, 107, 114, 116, 117, 121–24,
  133–34, 136, 209, 286–66, 274,
  292
  aid to the Philippines under the
    Marcos regime, 52–56
World Bank/IMF meeting in Prague,
  122–25
World Economic Forum, 115, 137
World Social Forum (WSF), 137–45,
  148, 182
World Trade Organization (WTO), 4,
  101, 103–106, 116–18, 120–22,
  127–35, 135, 139, 141, 145, 183,
  205, 221, 257, 260, 266, 275,
  287–88
  Agreement on Agriculture (AOA),
    103–104, 133
  Third Ministerial Meeting in Seattle
    (1999), 117–22
  Fourth Ministerial Meeting in Doha
    (2001), 128–29
  Doha Development Round, 129
  Fifth Ministerial Meeting in Cancun
    (2003), 130–31
Wright, Erik Ohlin, 2

X
Xi Jin Ping, 276, 279

Y
Yemen, 178

Z
Zapata, Emiliano, 13
Zapatistas (EZLN), 140
Zarsky, Lyuba, 81

Praise for *Global Battlefields*

"When I was a young writer first trying to understand the huge changes to the global economy, Walden was one of the thinkers whose work I relied on most. He's a true visionary. He grasped the monumental shifts that were taking place in the way the modern economy worked, changes that were coming at a terrible cost to workers in the Philippines and the natural world. Again and again, Walden has been on the right side of history, siding with people against the power of multinational corporations."

Naomi Klein | Author of *The Shock Doctrine*

"Walden Bello, I've known him for many years, has compiled a stellar record in activism and scholarship, always on the frontlines of struggles for justice and freedom in the Philippines and worldwide. I've personally learned a great deal from his work, which has also been a constant source of inspiration for engagement and activism. It's my great privilege to have been able to join him in some of his efforts."

Noam Chomsky | Public Intellectual, endorsing Walden Bello's run for the Vice Presidency of the Philippines in 2022

"Walden Bello's extraordinary memoir engagingly recounts a remarkable life of global adventure and occasional misadventure. It combines an amazing array of uncompromising political commitments with the highest standards of progressive scholarship. Bello's childhood experience of artistically inclined parents in his native Philippines is told with a touch of comic bravado that serves as an unlikely prelude to a life of revolutionary political engagement.

"I have known of no one who succeeded so brilliantly in being both a revolutionary activist and an influential presence in academia, writing pathbreaking books as a political economist who puts people first, and for decades has been one of the most eloquent voices of the Global South. Bello's story is also an impressive compilation of lessons learned from a lifetime of activism animated by multiple challenges. This book offers readers a virtual tutorial for young progressives intent on dedicating their lives to a better future for all of humanity.

"And beneath the public narratives Bello reports on a personal life well-lived, with its inevitable ups and downs, integral to a life of love that Walden Bello so gracefully nurtured in all who experienced being his comrade, friend, and possibly even his adversary."

Richard Falk | Professor Emeritus of International Law and Practice at Princeton University and former United Nations Human Rights Rapporteur for the Occupied Territories

"I first met Walden Bello through Focus on the Global South in Mumbai. His work in trying to make the world understand fundamental inequality in the post-colonial world gives us so much inspiration, and so much hope. Walden has campaigned for justice in the Philippines, joined the anti Vietnam movement in the 1960s in the USA.

"He has exposed the role of the International Monetary Fund and the World Bank in the impoverishment of the people of the Philippines, and he joined the campaign for real justice and real democracy there when the Marcos dictatorship was in charge.

"Walden has amazing knowledge of radical movements the world over, and so we are all willing pupils of this expertise, as well as his determination."

Jeremy Corbyn | Member of Parliament, United Kingdom

"Walden Bello's life has been remarkable and inspiring in so many ways: as a scholar of sharp acuity and profundity, a public intellectual in the most organic sense, a streetfighter activist as well as a legislator, an internationalist who is deeply engaged in the political struggles of his own country. This candid, thoughtful and even racy memoir brings out much of what makes him so special and so cherished, and shows why he remains such a beacon for progressive forces everywhere."

Jayati Ghosh | Professor, University of Massachusetts Amherst, and
former Professor, Jawaharlal Nehru University New Delhi

"One can derive many satisfactions from reading Walden Bello's *Global Battlefields,* not least being his kaleidoscopic portraits of anti-military and anti-corporatist struggles in the Philippines and around the world. Indeed, I can think of few others besides Walden Bello who have witnessed and participated in so many of those struggles over the years. But the real benefit of this book resides in Bello's acute assessment of the setbacks and failures of these struggles—and what useful lessons can be drawn from this in our ongoing work."

Michael Klare | Professor Emeritus of Peace and World Security Studies,
Hampshire College, and author of *Resource Wars and The Race for What's Left:
The Global Scramble for the World's Last Resources*

"Walden Bello is one of the great activists and intellectuals of our time. His ability to move between the streets, the written word, and the corridors of power is truly remarkable—and we all have a huge amount to learn from his life. I am so excited to be able to endorse this immensely powerful and beautifully written memoir, and I urge anyone on the left to read it."

Grace Blakeley | Author of *Vulture Capitalism* and
Stolen: How to Save the World from Financialization

"Walden Bello has, for a generation at least, been one of the outstanding scholar-activists of the global radical left. Here he tells his story. And what a story it is —Jesuit schoolboy, researcher into the origins of counterrevolution in Chile, underground militant of the Communist Party of the Philippines, critical analyst and opponent of neoliberal globalisation and imperialist militarism, principled parliamentarian. Walden paints some wonderful vignettes, as he elopes in a Cessna, performs as Kermit the Frog outside the IMF in Washington, and bests its boss and that of the World Bank during the 1999 anti-globalization protests in Prague. History and his own life, with all its triumphs and disappointments, joys and bereavements, come alive in this fascinating book."

Alex Callinicos | Author of *The Age of Catastrophe* and
Emeritus Professor of European Studies, King's College London

"A rollicking adventure through time and space. Walden Bello has led an extraordinary life of international activism. In this page-turner of a book, he recalls stories of incredible heroism and courage from the dwellings of the marginalized to the halls of power. I have had the honour of working alongside Walden in our collective struggle against neoliberalism and economic globalization and can attest to his brilliant analysis and wicked debating style. Woe to the person arguing with that mind!!

"Walden has a great deal to teach young activists around the world. They couldn't find a better—or more interesting—teacher than this extraordinary man. I highly recommend Global Battlefields."

Maude Barlow | Founding Member of Council of Canadians and
Recipient of the Right Livelihood Award

"The name 'Walden Bello' is virtually synonymous with the struggle for global social justice and with clarion analysis of contemporary world politics and society. The story of Walden's life is the story of our world over the past half a century, as told from the perspective of the oppressed and from someone who has been on the frontlines of it all. Those of us who have had the privilege to get to know Walden on a personal as well as at a political level can attest that he is an exemplary human being— full of love and compassion for humanity, steeled in commitment to the downtrodden, exuding erudite clarity in his thoughts."

Bill Robinson | Author of *A Theory of Global Capitalism* and Distinguished Professor of Sociology and Global Studies, University of California at Santa Barbara

"Walden Bello's biography is a generous gift to everyone hoping to understand his unique fusion of unrelenting progressive political activism and piercing critical analysis. Equally, it is an invaluable lens for those trying to make sense of the world's tumultuous political evolution since the mid 20th century—essential for those who lived through these years and even more so for the generation that must face their aftermath."

Peter Evans | Professor Emeritus of Sociology, University of California at Berkeley, and author of *Embedded Autonomy: States and Industrial Transformation*

"Walden Bello is more than just a political activist or a progressive Filipino politician. He is, as his autobiography exhibits, a literary giant, capable of breathing life and painting colors to what otherwise could have been just another political memoir devoid of character and soul. In these pages, Walden creates in words a real world of people and events that could all but have been lost to history, if not for the brilliance of his recollection and the erudition of his writing."

Leila de Lima | Former Senator of the Republic of the Philippines and former political prisoner

"Amid many years of challenges, setbacks and triumphs, Walden Bello remains one of the most fearless and insightful voices fighting for democratic rights in the Philippines and beyond.

"This page-turning memoir of a respected figure of the broader Philippine left gives a blow-by-blow account of Walden's evolution as an activist and academic—his days as a leader of anti-war student protests at Princeton University, a cadre of the underground anti-dictatorship movement, and later a member of the House of Representatives for Akbayan, and an advocate against globalization and imperialist interests.

"His personal pilgrimage reflects the larger journey and sacrifices of a generation of Filipinos who struggled against the forces of dictatorship, capital, and empire."

Risa Hontiveros | Senator, Leader of the Opposition, Republic of the Philippines

"*Global Battlefields* vividly recounts personal trials and public triumphs in daring confrontations with political monsters. Relentless, fearless, and selfless, Walden Bello is an inspiration to all who want to join scholarship to radical politics."

Michael Burawoy | Professor of Sociology, University of California at Berkeley

"Walden Bello's memoirs are a mirror of his delightful personality—his commitment to social justice and his great sense of humour about the cruel absurdities of the capitalist world."

Vijay Prashad | Indian historian and journalist, and Executive Director of the Tricontinental: Institute for Social Research

"In this riveting memoir, Walden Bello transports the reader from street battles in Salvador Allende's Chile to the deepest recesses of the World Bank's document vaults, the din of Seattle's anti-globalization protests, and clandestine meetings with Hamas and Hezbollah in Beirut. At the center of this narrative is the author's candid recounting of his role in the long struggle against the Marcos dictatorship as a cadre of the Communist Party of the Philippines, his painful break with the organization, and his subsequent career as a democratic activist and crusading congressman. Bello's tumultuous political journey is emblematic of that global 'boomer' generation of activists that is still making an indelible imprint on world history."

Al McCoy | Professor of History, University of Wisconsin at Madison

"Here is the story of, first, an underground rebel and then a parliamentarian always fighting dictatorial rule in the Philippines; of a participant in a political robbery of World Bank documents to expose its neoliberal globalization policies; of a leading figure in international campaigns against the many instances of U.S. imperialism; and of a supporter of struggles for human rights everywhere, resulting in the deserved bestowal of international awards. In addition, he is a brilliant scholar whose volu-minous writings in the social sciences have won him global accolades. Yet Walden Bello sees himself as belonging to a 'Lost Generation,' namely those radicalized by the tumultuous events and upheavals worldwide of the 1960s and early '70s, and who believed that the momentum for a revolutionary socialist and deeply democratic transformation that had begun would, despite occasional retreats, only become wider and deeper over time. This was not to be. But through this memoir, he seeks to restore and promote the radical and militant spirit of those times that is necessary if we are to successfully overcome the great evils facing us today."

Achin Vanaik | Professor of International Relations and Global
Politics (ret.), University of Delhi

"How did one of the most talented public scholars from the Philippines become a highly effective actor on the global stage? How did he juggle intellectual integrity with the conflicting demands of activism and politics? Hang on for a riveting ride—from a small island, to chartering a plane for love, to the Philippine revolutionary movement, to protesting Imelda at the Kennedy Center, to the halls of the World Bank, to the streets and suites of the global justice protests, to the halls of Congress—and you'll find out."

John Cavanagh | Former Director of the Institute of Policy Studies
and co-author, with Robin Broad, of *The Water Defenders*

"This is one of the most important books I have read in recent years. I have been longing for someone to settle the accounts of a great generation that framed the pro-gressive politics after the Second World War on a global scale. No one could do it better than Walden Bello, and Walden Bello couldn't do it better than he did. This is a fascinating account of the struggles for social justice and liberation—struggles fought at local, national, and global level in the last half century."

Boaventura de Sousa Santos | Author of *The End of the Cognitive Empire* and
Professor, University of Coimbra, Portugal

"Walden Bello is the world's best guide to American exploitation of the global poor and defenseless." (2005)

Chalmers Johnson | Author of *The Sorrows of Empire*

"I know of very few activists, scholars or public intellectuals who match the breadth and depth of Walden Bello's commitment to the struggle for global social justice. His memoirs charts the long and winding road he took to battle the forces of oppression and greed, traveling many continents and linking with many other progressive groups, using tactics as creative as they were fierce. This memoir is not only a valuable record of the zeitgeist of his generation; it also provides lessons in the struggle that future generations stand to learn from."

Vicente Rafael | Professor of History and Southeast Asian Studies, University of Washington

"This is, by far, the best of the memoirs that have come out of the First Quarter Storm generation of radicals. Walden Bello takes us on a fascinating ride, from his years as the child of two artists, the renunciation of his Jesuit beginnings in favor of existentialism and, ultimately, Marxism, on to his struggles against the Marcos dictatorship, global capitalism, and garden variety tyrants. Bello is grounded in Philippine realities and is also a committed internationalist. A devoted cadre of the Communist Party of the Philippines for 15 years, he had no second thoughts of leaving the movement he so loved once its unrepentant dogmatism led to brutal consequences."

Patricio N. Abinales | Professor, University of Hawai'i-Manoa

"Not unlike Jose Rizal, the Philippine national hero executed by Spain at the end of the 19th century, Walden Bello's life has been both consequential and colorful to say the least. In his often-gripping memoirs, this Rizal of our times shares his often intimate and innovative encounters with power in Manila, Sulu, Princeton, Santiago de Chile, San Francisco, Amsterdam, Bangkok, Binghamton and various points in between."

Jomo Sundaram | Author and former Assistant Director-General at the Food and Agriculture Organization of the United Nations, 2012–2015

"Walden Bello's riveting memoir is not just a personal biography. It is also a legendary public intellectual's political adventure, a coming-of-age odyssey, and a lively tale of engagement with an international activist career. As a leader of the global struggle against neoliberalism and its key institutions, Bello brings the reader to the historic street battles of the 2000s—in Seattle, Prague, and Cancun. He offers reasons for his resignation from the Philippine House of Representatives in 2015—the only recorded resignation on a matter of principle in the history of the Congress of the Philippines. In these times of peril and possibility, Walden Bello's memoirs are deeply relevant for partisans of democracy, human rights, and the rule of law."

Katrina Vanden Heuvel | Publisher of *The Nation*